D1706547

SAGE was founded in 1965 by Sara Miller McCune to support the dissemination of usable knowledge by publishing innovative and high-quality research and teaching content. Today, we publish more than 750 journals, including those of more than 300 learned societies, more than 800 new books per year, and a growing range of library products including archives, data, case studies, reports, conference highlights, and video. SAGE remains majority-owned by our founder, and after Sara's lifetime will become owned by a charitable trust that secures our continued independence.

Los Angeles | London | Washington DC | New Delhi | Singapore | Boston

Advance Praise

'Any academic discipline, in order to move even a little away from its endur-ing static position, needs to have a critical look at the premises on which the discipline tends to lean perpetually. This book dares to produce that critical look at the way archaeological knowledge is created and passed on in Indian archaeology and should jolt its institutional leaders out of their seats of scientific complacency.'

—B.D. Chattopadhyaya
Former Professor of History, Jawaharlal Nehru University, New Delhi

'This book is a welcome and much needed addition to the existing literature dealing with the history of Indian archaeology. Diverging widely and radically from the storytelling and often eulogistic accounts of the rise and growth of archaeology in India, archaeological practices and archaeologists themselves, it seeks to place the growth of archaeological (and Indological) studies in the matrix of mutually interactive domains of the nineteenth-century intellectual trends in Europe and British colonial practices in India.'

—K. Paddayya
Emeritus Professor of Archaeology, Deccan College, Pune

'With this book, Sudeshna Guha fills in a wide gap in our knowledge of the history of antiquarianism and archaeology in India. Doing away with the inherited prejudices of colonial history, Dr Guha demonstrates the existence of a curiosity for the past, its monuments and objects across medieval and modern India—a curiosity that has been hitherto neglected by traditional historiography. To her fine tune knowledge of the history of archaeology in the Indian subcontinent, the author adds an evident familiarity with the history of antiquarianism in Britain. This book is one of the best examples of postcolonial historiography applied to archaeology and to the comparative history of civilisations. It also provides an important contribution to the epistemology of archaeology, considered as a full-fledged social science.'

—**Alain Schnapp**
Emeritus Professor of Archaeology,
Université de Paris I Panthéon-Sorbonne

Artefacts of HISTORY

Artefacts
of H I S T O R Y

Archaeology, Historiography and Indian Pasts

S U D E S H N A   G U H A

⑤SAGE www.sagepublications.com
Los Angeles • London • New Delhi • Singapore • Washington DC • Boston

First published in 2015 by

SAGE Publications India Pvt Ltd
B1/I-1 Mohan Cooperative Industrial Area
Mathura Road, New Delhi 110 044, India
www.sagepub.in

SAGE Publications Inc
2455 Teller Road
Thousand Oaks, California 91320, USA

SAGE Publications Ltd
1 Oliver's Yard, 55 City Road
London EC1Y 1SP, United Kingdom

SAGE Publications Asia-Pacific Pte Ltd
3 Church Street
#10-04 Samsung Hub
Singapore 049483

Published by Vivek Mehra for SAGE Publications India Pvt Ltd, typeset in 10/13 pts Adobe Garamond Pro by RECTO Graphics, Delhi, and printed at Chaman Enterprises, New Delhi.

Library of Congress Cataloging-in-Publication Data

Guha, Sudeshna.
Artefacts of history: archaeology, historiography and Indian pasts / Sudeshna Guha.
    pages cm
Includes bibliographical references and index.
    1. Archaeology—India. 2. Historiography—India. 3. India—Antiquities. 4. India—Historiography. I. Title.
    DS418.G84   954.0072—dc23   2015   2015006456

ISBN: 978-93-515-0164-0 (HB)

The SAGE Team: Supriya Das, Sanghamitra Patowary, Nand Kumar Jha and Vinitha Nair

For Eivind and Rohini

Contents

List of Illustrations

Acknowledgements

I may have never considered writing at length on aspects of the histories of archaeological practices and scholarship had I not spent a large part of my working life in Cambridge (UK) cataloguing 'archaeological' photographs, and thousands of them. The compulsions of data entry demanded the searches for names, dates, places, key words and other such sundries, which brought me, quite literally, to the histories of archaeologies. A Small Research Grant from the British Academy, which I received a decade back in 2005, allowed me to explore the recording practices of the archaeological scholarship, and this book is one of the products of the research.

The book conveys the importance of asking questions about the kinds of choices and omissions we make in recalling the past, regards the infinite ways in which we are able to historicise the practices of archaeology and explores the epistemic possibilities of the histories of archaeologies. If I have at all succeeded in the aims, it is largely because of the intellectual contributions of scholars, colleagues and friends who have shared with me their own historical researches, given directions to many research enquiries and, most importantly, interrogated some of my judgements.

Through his relentless pursuit of the fate of my 'manuscript' and its research, B.D. Chattopadhyaya has virtually seen to it that I have completed the task I had set out to undertake in 2009. I am greatly indebted to him and to Romila Thapar for the intellectual support, generosity of their scholarship and knowledge, and their inspiration. Additionally, I owe a massive debt of gratitude to Simon Schaffer and Tapti Roy, who have read a number of early and unformed drafts and exacted the logic of many arguments by imploring me to re-frame questions and bring coherence to hasty conclusions. Eivind Kahrs, Frederick Bohrer, Alain Schnapp, Kapil Raj, Tim Murray, K. Paddayya, Sheena Panja and Amrita Shodhan have read individual chapters. I am very grateful to them, and to the anonymous referee for the astute comments, and especially for spotting some of the glaring errors.

Alastair Gornall came up with a title for this book at a time when I had lost the ability of naming my own creation. I am thankful for his timely intervention. I also thank Emily Ray for taking the trouble to chase photographs on my behalf in Mumbai. I am very grateful for the impositions I have been allowed to make upon the kindness and generosity of many friends, and I specially thank Christine Adams, Sissell Bakken, Kjell Bjørgeengen, Peter De Bolla, Anita Herle, Timothy Mathews, Divia Patel, Jonathan Portes, Deborah Swallow and Patti White.

Many archivists, librarians and curators have helped me during my research. I take this opportunity to particularly thank Miki Jacobs and Catherine Sunderland (Faculty of Asian and Middle Eastern Studies, Cambridge), Kate Mole (British Academy), WlodekWitek (Nasjonalbiblioteket, Oslo), Amanda Wise (University College, London), Sally Crawford (Institute of Archaeology, Oxford), Mrinalini Pathak (CSMVS, Mumbai) and Jocelyne Dudding (Museum of Archaeology and Anthropology [MAA], Cambridge) for the time they have invested in locating references and helping with the reproductions. I thank SAGE for requesting me to publish with them, and I am particularly grateful to Elina Mazumdar for her enthusiasm and commitments to see the manuscript through the selection and publication processes, and for the hard work of Supriya Das, Shreya Chakraborti and Sanghamitra Patoway in shaping the final product.

Some aspects of Chapter 5 have appeared recently as articles in two books: C. Sandis (Ed.). 2014. *Cultural Heritage Ethics: Past Achievements and Present Duties* (Cambridge: Open Book Publishers) and D.N. Jha (Ed.). 2014. *The Complex Heritage of Early India: Essays in Memory of Ram Sharan Sharma* (Delhi: Manohar). I thank both the editors for allowing me the opportunity to formulate my views against the valorisation of civilisational ethos within the present-day academic scholarship of Indian archaeology, which shows increasing proclivity for contributing to myriad creations of heritage industry.

While writing this book, I have often thought of my father to whom I had promised that I would undertake the task. I have derived much inspiration from my memory of his enthusiasm towards all my ventures, and of his intellectual curiosity and vast knowledge. To Ma, I can only say many many thanks for your love, belief and support, and for instilling the regard for the academic discipline of history. I owe my sister, Suchi, massive thanks for the very precious gift of a brand new machine on which I have written most of this book, and I also thank her and my brother-in-law, Carsten, for their questions on aspects of historical enquiry; satiating the curiosity of two physicists in the family has often required a 'more' clear thinking on my part.

The two very special people in my life know who they are. They keep me going with their wry humour, intelligence, generosity and patience for which I dedicate this book to them.

Sudeshna Guha
20 October 2014

Histories, Historiography, Archaeology: An Introduction

My aim through this book is to create a regard of the importance of noting the manner in which we recall and historicise the archaeological scholarship. I hope to draw attention upon issues of methodology and historiography through which we configure and create archaeological knowledge, endow historicity upon objects and topographies, and reckon with the processes of historicising. The aim critiques the existing histories of South Asian archaeology, which often convey the understanding that the archaeological record exists in nature. The histories which I have selected and explored here are therefore quite specific, in that they provide a view of the transformations of ideological notions, including heritage and legacies, into tangible material evidence through the archaeological scholarship and practices. They also demonstrate the reasons for nurturing a trans-regional and transnational historical perspective while writing a regional history of archaeology, and convey the need for noting the epistemology of evidence.

The book follows the title quite literally in demonstrating that the practices and scholarship of archaeology, traditions of historiography and claims about the past are all artefacts of history. It is inspired by the intellectual shift within the academic scholarship of the history of archaeology that is taking place at present. Throughout much of the twentieth century, archaeology was historicised as a unified science. Its origins were located within the field enquiries of the European antiquaries of the eighteenth century, developments sought within the creations of 'field methods' during the latter half of the nineteenth century, and progress towards a disciplinary science was lodged within the specialist theoretical orientations from the 1950s, through which the explanatory potentials of the archaeological scholarship was enhanced. The evolutionary history of disciplinary progress, which has many regional variants, was established by archaeologists, who used it for contextualising their own research projects, and who ignored the omissions through which the narrative of developments was created. Since the close of the century, however, a distinctly new understanding of the practices of archaeology has emerged which opposes the earlier quests for seeking an edifying history of disciplinary formation. New historians of archaeology from within the profession have launched a sustained critique of the errors of the earlier historicising practices. Many among them now call for 'histories of archaeologies' that might tell us 'what archaeology is, and claims to be (or not to be) about, at different times and places, in different social, economic and political contexts, for different actors, protagonists, audiences and publics'.[1] The use of plural terms, namely histories and archaeologies, represents the confidence of a reflexive praxis that seeks to democratise the subject from the authoritarianism that attends the nurture of a disciplinary self-image. The new histories inevitably dismiss the positivist claims of scientific advances in challenging the 'meta-narrative' for archaeology. Their creators investigate whether archaeology can be at all historicised through an 'irreducible disciplinary core', and aim towards demonstrating 'great deal more variability of thought and practice in the field.'[2] The historians, therefore, endeavour to map the different claims and creations of the 'producers and consumers of archaeological knowledge', and question the logic of searching for a formal canon of archaeological historiography.[3] The book builds upon the expectations of the shifting perspectives and places emphasis upon the need to recognise, analyse and engage with the many different traditions of historiography that would allow an informed archaeological scholarship of the infinite diverseness of the past. In this, it also compels us to pursue the linkages of 'connected histories.'[4]

During the nineteenth century, the Indological scholarship was raised through the archaeological, philological, historical, ethnographical, curatorial and collecting practices, among others, and the modes of enquiry transgressed the constraints of existing disciplinary boundaries. The histories of this scholarship inevitably show us the errors of distancing the histories of the nineteenth- and early-twentieth-century archaeological scholarship of India and South Asia from those of the Orient. Besides, throughout the nineteenth

---

[1] Schlanger and Nordbladh (2008, p. 1).
[2] Evans and Murray (2008, p. 2).
[3] Ibid., p. 3.
[4] On the construct, see Subrahmanyam (1997).

century, the practices and principles of archaeology, antiquarianism, history, natural history, philology, ethnology and geology also developed in conjunction. Therefore, in exploring the histories of any of the aforementioned subjects, we are required to note the histories of the others, and attend to the manner in which ideas and influences across disciplines, practices and regions contribute to the methods of knowing the past. The discipline-seeking, region-specific existing histories of South Asian archaeology, which often appear as trait lists of field discoveries, pioneering archaeologists and advances in new methods and theories, add very little to the reasons of new histories of archaeology in the twenty-first century. Therefore, the aim here is to attend to the historical relationships between inferences, field practices, theoretical methods and subjects of enquiries, and create reasons for moving away from celebrations of discoveries, including of archives, for facilitating critical approaches towards a review of archaeology's pasts.

The historical enquiries that are initiated through the five chapters are premised upon the assumption that lineal narratives of disciplinary developments and progress not only overlook the different identities that sciences and practices acquire across geography, and often at the same time, but also that they remain inattentive to the changes in the kinds of information that are sought from the past over time. The histories that are recalled and mapped here show us why disciplinary boundaries and the past are both in the making rather than given, and thereby contribute to reasons for intellectually disengaging with the 'archaeology of origins' of various phenomena, including religions, population groups, and cultural practices, which is on the rise within South Asia. They also allow us to evaluate the constructs of archaeological evidence, analyse the notions and classifications of sources and schema of periodisation, and interrogate the manner in which archaeological cultures are often transposed as real societies. The ontological value of the histories of archaeology as objects of enquiry is, thus, the intellectual thrust of this book.

I begin the introduction with two caveats:

- I have chosen not to dwell upon the Indian explorations of Ancient India during the colonial period in any significant manner. The long traditions of post-colonial critique by now has shown us the powerful agency of the knowledge and expertise of the colonised subjects in resisting imperial politics, and also in resisting and contributing to the Western scholarship of Indology. By emulating some of the aims and methods of this critique, many historians of Indian archaeology now strive to explore the contributions of the Indians to the archaeology of India during British rule, and they have made valuable additions to the lists of local scholars, native 'knowledge workers' and their achievements.[5] The Indian historians and archaeological explorers of the nineteenth and early-twentieth centuries mastered the western traditions of historiography, and hence did not instigate any significant departure from the methods of the latter. They too saw the logic of emulating the views of a universal form for history, with clearly demarcated causes and events, although the pasts they searched for and sought to unearth were remarkably of the particular—of their own lands, communities and cultural traditions. Their scholarship appears within the chapters, as do some of the instances of the unequal intellectual transactions of the British and European Indologists against them. But their archaeological practices and field enquiries are not exclusively presented in meeting the aims of this book.

• I have not attended to the classification of practices into amateur and professional, and official and non-official while discussing the histories of Indian archaeology during the colonial period. The need for seeking such distinctions, as will be shown throughout, conveys the concerns of the academic discipline of archaeology of the mid-twentieth century and express presentism.[6]

In thinking about the methods for possible histories of archaeology we are made aware of the many contradictions, which we perpetuate by neglecting

[5] For example, articles in Sengupta and Gangopadhyay (2009), and Dutta (2009). My use of the term is from Heringman (2013).

[6] Even distinguishing the official from non-official scholarship of Indian history, well until the close of the nineteenth century, becomes a meaningless enterprise because a large number of colonial officers, and British and European officers in the services of the princely states undertook archaeological explorations and scholarship in their personal capacities. Two prominent examples are James Prinsep, the Assay Master of the mints at Banaras and Calcutta (1820–30 and 1830–38) who gained renown as an antiquary, and Charles Horne, a judge at Banaras, who along with the missionary Mathew Attmore Sherring, undertook pioneering excavations in the area surrounding Bakaria Kund in modern Banaras, in 1863–64.

the impositions of historiography. They are usually conceptual and easily bred; therefore, in introducing the chapters, I begin with an example in *L'Ecriture de l'histoire* (1975), the thought-provoking critique of the dominance of historiography by Michel de Certeau, the eminent French historian of early modern religion (1925–86). The example captures a common, if erroneous, understanding of the 'Indian culture' within the 'West' which, as will be discussed in Chapters 1 and 5, appear in many different guises within the archaeological literature of South Asia.

Certeau had reminded his readers that 'historiography had arisen from the European encounter with the unknown other', wherein the writing of history un-wrote the embodied traditions of the natives.[7] Critiquing the distinction between history and tradition that has enshrined the norms of the European historiography since the eighteenth century, he remarked that:

> a structure belonging to modern Western culture can doubtless be seen in this historiography: intelligibility is established through a relation with the other; it moves (or 'progress') by changing what it makes of its 'other'—the Indian, the past, the people, the mad, the child, the Third World.[8]

In order to disturb the embedded notions of progress within the traditions of this historiography, Certeau sought the anthropological study of caste in India by his peer Louis Dumont, for emphasising, and hoping to demonstrate, that 'resistance, survivals and delays discreetly perturb the pretty order of a line of progress'.[9] However, Dumont's ethnographic sketch was remarkably essentialist and echoed the orientalist and colonialist histories of a timeless and unchanging Indian Civilisation. Therefore, in selecting this study for interrogating the hegemony of the historiography he was familiar with, Certeau unwittingly showed little understanding of the unknown other and added to the phenomenon he challenged.[10] The example provides an opportune cue for framing contexts for the histories that are established within this book.

---

[7] Cf Conley (1988, p. vii).

[8] Certeau (1988 [1975], p. 3).

[9] Ibid., p. 4. Certeau quoted Dumont in declaring that 'new forms never drive the older ones away. Rather, there exists a stratified stockpiling [...] a process of coexistence and reabsorption is, on the contrary, the cardinal fact of Indian history' (ibid.).

[10] For an earlier critique of Certeau's essentialist profile of an Indian society, see Subrahmanyam (2005, p. 19).

Considering Historiography

The archaeological scholarship of the twenty-first century continues to provide many reasons for analysing the sourcing and uses of historiographical traditions. Thus, we note that although the new and growing archaeology of heritage practices seeks to incorporate the myriad ways in which different communities in the world historicise and engage with the past, it creates conceptual contradictions by only drawing upon the European historiographical traditions. For example, the pioneers of heritage archaeology in Britain emphasise that 'it is difficult to agree on the roots of heritage as a distinct practice and intellectual engagement'.[11] Yet, they locate the origins of a heritage-conscious society within the emergence of an educated public sphere within Europe during the seventeenth century that responded to the rising national consciousness with efforts to seek out and control the past through laws and objective field explorations.[12] This history, therefore, enshrines the many elements of Western Historiography, which contradicts the objectives of its authors to accommodate the othered.

The European histories of heritage practices create reasons for reviewing the hegemony of historiography within the twentieth-century histories of antiquarianism, in which a historical disjuncture was premised upon the faith that the pre-Renaissance Europe and the non-European worlds engaged with the past in terms of tradition, whereas Enlightened Europe sought rational histories. The historiography rooted the understanding that both modernity and rational enquiries were European quests. Thus, the foremost historian of the British antiquaries, Stuart Piggott (1910–96), historicised the intellectual valuation of antiquities from the sixteenth century within Europe, especially Italy, as 'the rediscovery of Greek and Latin literature from the newly found or the newly understood manuscripts [and] with recovering knowledge of antique past from inscriptions, coins, sculpture and architecture'.[13] Although Piggott had conceded that 'those concerned with *antiquitates* saw themselves, proudly and consciously, as the heirs of the ancients' curiosity about their own past', he emphasised that there was a clear distinction between the 'wider classical usage' of the term in the mid-first century BC and the new usage in

---

[11] Sørensen and Carman (2009, p. 13).
[12] Ibid., p. 14.
[13] Piggott (1989, p. 13).

the sixteenth century, which bespoke of the 'potential independence of the antiquarian discipline.'[14] Piggott's history of the 'rise' of antiquarianism was emulated by his contemporaries, and the premier historian of archaeology, Glyn Daniel (1914–86), added to his views and stated that:

> We may say then, that antiquarianism was born in England in the century and a half between 1533 when [John] Leland was appointed King's Antiquary and 1697 when [John] Aubrey died. It was a substitute for the study of classical antiquities. It may also be a reflection of the new national pride in England that existed from Tudor times. It may also be in part due to the Reformation, for the antiquaries saw the monasteries destroyed and libraries disposed […].[15]

The location of the 'origins' of heritage practices in the sixteenth- and seventeenth-century Europe by archaeologists of heritage today, therefore, comes perilously close to the histories of antiquarianism, which represented the traditions of historiography of the European Enlightenment.

However, all archaeologists of cultural heritage also relate intellectually to the aims of 'indigenous archaeologies' and regard the promise of this practice in de-colonising the archaeological scholarship from the biases of the 'western ways of categorising, knowing and interpreting the world'.[16] The aim of the indigenous and heritage archaeologies, therefore, demands methodological attention to the infinite expressions of historical consciousness within the world, and the ability to source the many diverse methods and processes of historicising the past. In contrast, the traditions of historiography that were established through the European Enlightenment overlooks the possibilities of enlightenments elsewhere, and upholds, as Certeau had explained, the 'value of a scientific model' of history which was built upon presumptions that facts lent themselves to visibility, and therefore interrogation, as opposed to myths and tradition with their esoteric and hidden truths.[17] The accommodation and exhibition of plurality in archaeology demands a conscious disengagement with the understanding of the forms of 'proper' history and

---

[14] Piggott (1989, p. 13).

[15] Daniel (1950, p. 20).

[16] Atalay (2006, p. 280). For a history and description of indigenous archaeologies, see Nicholas (2010), who has provided many examples of the ways in which this practice encourages the explorations of 'indigenous values, knowledge, practices, ethics and sensibilities' with respect to heritage claims (ibid., p. 11), and also Smith and Wobst (2005, pp. 11–13).

[17] Certeau (1988 [1975], p. 6).

European rationality. While interrogating the existing histories of antiquarianism within South Asia, Chapter 1 documents the importance of nurturing this disengagement within the archaeological searches for histories of historicity. The searches no doubt also represent the practices of heritage.

The Chapter creates a case for recognising the manifestations of antiquarian practices within the pre-colonial pasts of the Indian subcontinent and initiates a formal move away from the dictates of a historiography that was constitutive of the colonial period, but which is perpetuated even today through the histories of Indian or South Asian archaeology. It highlights the instances of presentism within the above histories, of which perhaps the most glaring is the manner in which the heuristic value of antiquarian practices is measured 'against anachronistic standards.'[18] It also introduces the critical stance of this book towards the archaeological searches for starting points of phenomena that are inherently non-measurable, such as civilisational legacies and cultural heritage. In this, it illustrates the reasons for emulating injunctions similar to those of the founding statute of La Société de Linguistique de Paris, which had ordained in 1866 that 'La Société n'admet aucune communication concernant soit l'origine du language, soit la création d'une langue universelle'.[19]

The Indian Archaeology of the British

The significant attempts that were made by the British during the latter half of the nineteenth century for establishing a history of their archaeological surveys of India contrast sharply with the lack of attempts in Britain during the same period for establishing any master narrative of the archaeological explorations and excavations within the country. Given that diverse nature of enquiries from diverse sciences fed into the archaeological practices, the formal credentials of archaeology as a unique science of historical enquiry

---

[18] The quote is from Pels and Salemink (1999, p. 1). Pels and Salemink, who are social anthropologists, have shown the manner in which the twentieth-century histories of social anthropology have established the teleology of a 'real' history of the subject from the time when 'theoretical and research expertise were fused together in the person of a professional fieldworker' (ibid.).

[19] Article 2, 8 March 1866. I am grateful to Eivind Kahrs for the information.

had appeared only during the close of the nineteenth century, when formal methods of undertaking archaeological excavations were designed and propagated. In this respect, the British histories of Indian archaeology, which were established in the 1870s, document the utility value of the teleological narratives in the make-up of the colonial historiography. For, the narratives were aimed at substantiating British achievements in exposing Ancient India's 'true history', and they fed the understanding that the British had brought to India the methods of historical enquiry and taught their colonised subjects the methods of sourcing the past. The histories were, therefore, specifically aimed at recording the British pioneering of Indian archaeology and for illustrating the British feats of bringing into India the scientific methods of archaeological enquiries.

The first conscious efforts towards documenting a history of Indian archaeology reflect the fledgling support of the colonial government towards the archaeological projects. The narratives date from the period of the two re-institutions, in 1871 and 1902 respectively, of the Archaeological Survey of India, and those written by the first three heads of the organisation, Alexander Cunningham (1861–65; 1871–85), James Burgess (1885–89) and John Marshall (1902–28) when read in succession provide a chronological summary of the British scholarship, field practices and administration of Indian archaeology during the nineteenth century.[20] The histories show us that the early British archaeology of the Indian subcontinent followed two different strands of enquiries, of which one involved the surveying and mapping of ancient sites, and the other the documentation of India's historical architecture. Cunningham (1814–93), who came to India in 1833 as a lieutenant in the Bengal Engineers, established his credentials as the pioneer of the first which he described as archaeological surveys. James Fergusson (1808–86), a contemporary, who left a declining indigo business at an opportune moment, established his pioneering status for the second strand.[21] Inevitably, the chronological and cultural classifications, which they both

---

[20] Cunningham (1871a), Burgess (1905) and Marshall (1904c). Two other significant histories were by two German Sanskrit scholars, namely Rudolph Hoernle who wrote the eighteenth- and nineteenth-century histories of antiquarian scholarship of South Asia for the centenary review of the Asiatic Society of Bengal (1885) and Georg Bühler, who summarised the activities and deficiencies of the nineteenth-century archaeological practices (1895). See references in bibliography.

[21] In describing his leave of the indigo business, Fergusson had mentioned a few details of his former life:

devised, often independently of each other and by assessing 'developments and debasements' within the iconographic and architectural styles of the monuments they visited, contradicted the local histories and local receptions of the ancient topographies.

Unlike Cunningham, who spent much of his working life in field explorations of 'Upper India', beginning with Sarnath (near Banaras) in 1834 and ending with a final tour of Central India in March 1885, Fergusson spent less than a decade, from 1836 until 1842, in the architectural surveys, mainly of western, southern and central India.[22] Unlike Cunningham, he was unable to engage with numismatic and epigraphic matters, as he lacked the will to learn the skills. The ensuing 'flaws' within his methods of dating architectural features, which Cunningham drew attention to, was mitigated to some extent by James Burgess (1832–1916) who succeeded Cunningham as head of the Archaeological Survey.[23] Burgess not only developed Fergusson's architectural histories, he also took cognisance of the related epigraphic and numismatic evidence, and rendered significant contributions to the scholarship of India's historical inscriptions by establishing the journals *The Indian Antiquary* (1872) and *Epigraphia Indica* (1888).

A mathematician by education, Burgess had joined the Indian Education Service in 1856, and from the early 1860s initiated the architectural surveys of the Bombay Presidency.[24] In recognition of the historical significance of

---

From school I passed to the counting-house; from that to an indigo-factory—of all places in the world, perhaps the some least suited for a cultivation of the fine arts; from this to become an acting and active partner in a large mercantile establishment [...] during this time this work has been in hand [...] I have [...] perhaps, also thought, more about the state of the money market, indigo, sugar, silk, and such-like articles, than I have regarding architecture, painting or sculpture. Fergusson (1849, p. xi)

Fergusson had made an enormous fortune in indigo trade in 10 years which allowed him to retire from the indigo business. As one obituarist had recorded 'a rise in favour of some Turhut indigo shares in his possession did him good service. Henceforth, his career became that of a devotee of art' (quoted in Pinney 2008, p. 70).

[22] For details, Fergusson (1846, pp. 30–92).

[23] Cunningham had stated: 'I freely admit the corroborative value of architectural evidence when it is founded on ascertained dates; but when it is unsupported by inscriptions, I look upon it, in the present state of our knowledge as always more or less uncertain, and therefore, weak' (1871a, p. xx).

[24] Burgess was inspired to undertake architectural studies when he arrived in Bombay as principal of Sir Jamshetji Jeejeebhoy Parsee Benevolent Institution in 1861. He visited the caves at Elephanta and Kanheri during school vacations that year, which inspired his maiden study of the *Temples of Satrunjaya* (1869). However, Burgess also kept up his scholarship in mathematics

his architectural explorations of western India, the Government of India deputed him to head the Archaeological Survey of Western India on its institution in 1873. Eventually, Burgess established the foundational histories of the architectural traditions of the Jainas, Buddhists and Hindus, and the 26 magnificent volumes, which he produced of his tours, between 1871 and 1889 and mainly within the Bombay and Madras presidencies, display his conscious attempts at creating the scholarship of, to use his own phrase, 'architectural archaeology'.[25]

Apart from the colonial officers and European and British officers in employ of the princely states, field explorations for ancient and medieval India in the nineteenth century were also undertaken by the missionaries and other European travellers who visited and lived in India and by the 'native informants' of all the western explorers. Additionally, from the latter half of the nineteenth century, officers of the Geological Survey of India also began to consciously search for the prehistoric landscapes of India, at a time when self-styled archaeologists, such as Cunningham, were undertaking archaeological explorations of the country. The latter noticeably neglected to mention the finds of his peers, and also the new revelations in prehistoric geology and advances in archaeological field methods that were being made in Britain by the 1860s. Thus, Cunningham's latest biographer has illustrated the probability of his ignorance of Charles Lyell's scholarship of the principals of geology.[26] Yet, such overlooks should occasion no surprise, as the British and other western explorers of India, who perceived their surveys to be archaeological in nature, concerned themselves with the history of the Indian Civilisation, which they firmly distinguished from the enquiries into prehistory. Hence, they would have seen no value in taking heed of the theories of Three Age System, archaeological discoveries of Prehistoric Lake Dwellings, and the growing knowledge of the geological principles of stratigraphy within contemporary Britain.[27] Cunningham's disregard of all the above simply illustrates the non-utility value of the new theories and

---

and was presented the Keith Medal of the Royal Society of Edinburgh in 1897 for his paper 'On the Error-Function Definite Integral' (cf. Fleet, 1917, pp. 1–4; Sewell, 1917, pp. 195–99).

[25] For a list of the volumes, see 'Archaeological Reports Published Under Official Authority' in Marshall (1915, pp. 199–226); for the phrase, see Roy (1961, p. 70).

[26] For example, Singh (2004, p. 339).

[27] By the mid-twentieth century, the three constituted 'the birth of archaeology' (cf. Daniel, 1950, pp. 57–121).

methods for his purposes, and we can substantiate the logic of the exemption through two specific examples.

In the first instance we note that Cunningham made no mention in any of his publications of the explorations of Robert Bruce Foote of the Geological Survey (1858–91), who had chanced upon the 'first genuine paleaolith' that was known in Modern India at the parade grounds of Pallavaram near Madras in 1863.[28] Foote, who was younger than Cunningham, began recording a vast number of palaeolithic and neolithic sites in south India from the 1870s, at the time when the latter was exploring north India for archaeological discoveries. Unlike Cunningham, he also showed a proclivity towards better excavation methods, and had possibly used the grid system during his excavations, with his son, at the Billa Surgam Caves (Kurnool Dist., Andhra Pradesh) in 1883–85.[29] We can assume that Cunningham's silence of Foote's discoveries reflects the nature of his publications from the 1870s, rather than his abject ignorance. They were mainly official reports of the Archaeological Survey of India, in which the finds of 'prehistoric' sites by officers in the Geological Survey had no relevance.

The second example involves the discrepancy in the knowledge of geology between Cunningham and his contemporary Philip Meadows Taylor (1808–76), who served the Nizam of Hyderabad and undertook archaeological explorations within the Nizam's dominion between the 1830s until the early 1850s. Unlike Cunningham, Taylor brought geological knowledge to his archaeological explorations. He, therefore, displayed knowledge of stratigraphy within his excavations in the Shorapur region (Andhra Pradesh), which he undertook between 1841 and 1853. Taylor referred to the megaliths he saw as 'cromlechs, cairns, dolmens and ancient scytho-druidical remains',[30] and as the terminologies suggest, he recalled the megalithic topography of Britain for describing the 'stone monuments.' He subsequently acknowledged in his autobiography that

[28] Foote explored the Madras area on joining the Geological Survey of India in September 1858, and found the first 'genuine chipped tool' in India in May 1863. He was inspired to look for traces of such 'early human art in South India' because of the finds of chipped flint tools that were made by Jacques Boucher de Perthes within the gravel beds of the river Somme (France). By the mid 1850s, they were confirmed as 'the earliest human artefacts' by John Prestwick, the British geologist, and, by 1858, also by John Evans and Hugh Falconer. Foote hoped to make similar finds in India. For the details of his finds, see Foote (1916, p. v).

[29] See Haslam et al. (2010, p. 6).

[30] Taylor (1851, 1853).

During my wanderings over the Shorapur district in this [1851] and former years I had discovered, in many places, cairns and dolmens, some of them of very large size corresponding in all respects to similar monuments in England, Brittany, and other places. I mistrusted my judgement in regard to them for a long time: but at length I drew up a paper on the subject, accompanied by sketches; and followed it up by another in regard to the contents of cairns which I had opened.[31]

Taylor's publications in the *Journal of the Bombay Branch of the Royal Asiatic Society (JBBRAS)* (for example, 1851 and 1853), and a subsequent note by him regarding the samples of limestone, which he presented to the collections of the Royal Asiatic Society of Bombay in 1854 illustrate his knowledge of the geological sciences, and the 'advances' that were made in the scholarship of geology in Britain during the 1850s.[32] Additionally, Taylor's detailed drawings of the archaeological soil strata and of the 'cairns' in their natural surroundings with their skeletal remains and other artefacts *in situ* were inspired by the geological illustrations in vogue within contemporary Britain. The illustrations were subsequently appraised by the last director general of the colonial Archaeological Survey, Mortimer Wheeler (1944–48), as an example of the 'true function of the excavator and recorder.'[33]

Cunningham's ignorance of the science-based methods within the archaeological explorations of the past, which were being established in the Britain of his times, has been explained as Indian archaeology's 'colonial phenomena.' His historians are of the opinion that the nineteenth-century civil and military officers, for whom 'archaeology was often an ancillary, part-time or postretirement activity' were careless in keeping with the latest developments, as they had not 'much in common, or significant degree of contacts, with European archaeologists'.[34] Such explanations convey presentism, in the erroneous understanding that a classifiable group of archaeologists existed in Europe in the nineteenth century. They also perpetuate the 'cocooning', to quote from one history,[35] of the nineteenth-century historical scholarship of Ancient India through archaeological and other field surveys from

---

[31] Taylor (1920 [1878], p. 261).

[32] For Taylor's donation of 'Argillaceous Limestone, dark, grey, and black, from the district of Shorapur' to the BBRAS Museum, and his geological description of the provenance of the objects, see section 'Official, Literary and Scientific', *JBBRAS*, January 1854, pp. 367 and 389–90.

[33] Wheeler (1956, p. 22).

[34] Singh (2004, p. 340).

[35] Ibid.

the influences of contemporary field explorations of the past elsewhere. But more strikingly, they overlook the relationships between subjects of enquiry and the adopted methods for research.

With reference to Cunningham's ignorance of the methods adopted by Taylor, we should note that Cunningham would not have been able to relate the Buddhist sites he chose to explore in India from the 1840s with the contemporary barrow-digging archaeology of Britain, which he knew of, and whose methods Taylor adopted. And with respect to Cunningham's overlook of Foote's discoveries, we may add that Cunningham might not have seen the uses of the geological principles that were being developed for the scholarship of prehistory in Britain in the 1860s in his by then quite specific archaeological explorations for the histories of Ancient India. However, it is also important to note that not every nineteenth-century antiquary in Britain accepted the new theories and ideas that were in circulation. Daniel had noted that James Fergusson's refusal to accept the idea of pre-Roman Bronze Age, which he had conveyed in his *Rude Stone Monuments* (1872), was in character with many of his contemporaries who were prominent British antiquaries, such as John Kemble and Thomas Wright. They all had looked upon the 'Three Age System as specious and attractive in appearance but without foundation in truth.'[36]

Contrary to the illustrations of 'the cocooning of Indian archaeology from Western influences' within the post-colonial histories of South Asian archaeology,[37] most nineteenth-century scholars and explorers of the Indian subcontinent had consciously aimed at communicating their archaeological discoveries rather widely. Thus, the journal *The Indian Antiquary* was quite specifically conceived for 'addressing the general reader with information on [the] Manners and Customs, Arts, Mythology, Feasts, Festivals and Rites, Antiquities and History' of India. It was designed 'to be a medium of communication between archaeologists in the East and the West' and 'by presenting its readers with abstracts of the most recent researches of savants in India, Europe and America, and by its translations from German, French and other European languages' it was also designed to 'make fully accessible to the many Native Scholars, unacquainted with these languages, the latest results arrived at by the greatest continental scholars'.[38]

---

[36] Daniel (1975, p. 83).
[37] Singh (2004, p. 340).
[38] Anon [Burgess, J] (1872, p. 1).

Considering that the existing histories of the nineteenth- and early-twentieth-centuries archaeological practices within the Indian subcontinent take very little note of the contemporary archaeological practices that were in vogue within Britain, Europe and the Orient, they convey little information of the histories of influences, consumptions and circulations through which new historical knowledge of India was created and nurtured. An example is the manner in which the spectacular discoveries of the Assyrian Civilisation during the 1840s and 'Homeric Troy' in the 1870s influenced interpretations and notions of aesthetics regarding the antiquities that were found and excavated within India. Thus, the pottery excavated and collected by Heinrich Schliemann at Hissarlik, 'the supposed old city of Troy', which was on display at the South Kensington Museum (London) in the mid-1870s, proved to be of immediate analogical value for describing the 'four-legged urns' and other 'earthenware' that were collected from the megaliths in Coorg (southern India). M.J. Walhouse, of the Madras Civil Service, who excavated some of the sites and collected the potsherds, noted similarities within the motif of the 'swastika' on the megalithic potsherds of India with 'the Greek archaic cross', and remembered, from his visits to the South Kensington Museum (London), that Schliemann had found the 'swastika painted both ways in the vessels in Troy.'[39] In noting his memory, we are reminded to reckon with the displays of collections and collecting practices within and outside India, of Indian and non-Indian antiquities, for exploring the ways in which archaeological knowledge of India was established and the unknown made known. Chapter 2 explores the histories of curation and neglect of the Assyrian antiquities within colonial Bombay, and draws our attention to the histories of collections and curation within the history making of Ancient India.

Economic Museums, Foreign Collections and Indian Histories

Historians of archaeology now increasingly engage with the collecting practices of the nineteenth century for exhibiting the 'ontologising of the archaeological discipline'.[40] They demonstrate the reasons for their study with

[39] Walhouse (1878, p. 176).
[40] Olsen *et al.* (2012, p. 37).

an obvious and important example, namely the collection of stone tools at the National Museum in Copenhagen, which had inspired Christian Jürgensen Thomsen and his colleagues to establish the Three Age System in ca. 1822. The collection created the possibilities of exploring an unknown history by inspiring a method for acquiring a temporal sequence that proved to be remarkably accurate. Within India, the collections of antiquities and their displays largely provided visibility and memory of the British undertaking of Indian archaeology. However, the public receptions of the museum exhibits illustrate the ambiguities and ambivalences that characterised the colonial pedagogic projects.[41]

The vast bulk of the antiquities, manuscripts and curiosities of Hindustan that were collected by the British and European antiquaries and travellers during the eighteenth century went home with them. Yet, a sizeable repertoire remained within India and entered the precincts of the Asiatic Society. As is rather well known, the Society was instituted in 1784 for the study of India at the behest of William Jones (1746–94), the stalwart scholar of Persian and Sanskrit, who served the East India Company as a Puisne Judge of the Supreme Court at Fort William (Calcutta) from 1783 until death.[42] A museum for the Society was formally mooted in 1796, but formally established only in 1814 for 'all articles that may tend to illustrate oriental manners and history, or to elucidate the peculiarities of art or nature in the East'.[43] This was the earliest British creation of museums within South Asia, and among the list of objects that were desired for its collections were 'inscriptions on stone or brass, ancient monuments, Muhammadan or Hindu', ancient coins and manuscripts, skeletons of animals particular to India, birds 'stuffed or preserved, native alloys, vessels used in religious ceremonies, instruments of war peculiar to the East' and 'instruments of music'.[44] The heterogeneous collections, which subsequently became the founding collection of the Indian Museum in Calcutta on its formal inauguration in 1878 within the present buildings, nurtured the scholarship of the members of the Asiatic Society well until the mid-twentieth century.[45]

[41] On this see Prakash (1999, pp. 47–48).

[42] For details of the foundation and the first hundred years of the Asiatic Society of Bengal, see Mitra (1885, pp. 31–47).

[43] Resolution adopted by the Asiatic Society in 1814, quoted in Mitra, ibid., p. 33.

[44] Ibid., pp. 33–34.

[45] The society's collection was transferred in 1865 to the newly founded Imperial Museum, which was renamed the Indian Museum in 1892.

The inscriptions and coins proved to be of immense value for the early archaeological scholarship of Ancient India, and were to a large extent deciphered single handed in the 1830s by James Prinsep, the most illustrious Secretary of the Asiatic Society (1832–38). Cunningham, as Chapter 1 will remind us, sourced Prinsep's intellectual genealogy strategically, for establishing a historical context for his own archaeological career.

The pioneering efforts that were made by the members of the Asiatic Society at the beginning of the nineteenth century towards the institution of a museum for housing its growing collections were followed by plans for museums that were quite different in nature.[46] Unlike this museum of a learned society, the others were conceived as 'economic' museums and were aimed at facilitating representative collections of India's natural and agricultural wealth. They were conceived, as Savithri Preetha Nair has aptly noted, 'as an agent of economic progress' although they aided the 'systematic exploitation of resources.'[47] The first of such museums was instituted in Calcutta in 1840, and thereafter they were established in Madras and Bombay, and even within the moffusil towns. As reference collections of India's 'tappable' resources, they were of immense value for British commerce, and in relating the histories of the displays of 'Nineveh in Bombay', Chapter 2 provides a history of the one at Bombay, which was planned in 1847 as the Central Museum of Natural History, Economy, Geology, Industry and the Arts.

The above was known as Bombay's Economic Museum, and throughout the 1850s and the 1860s, this was more of a virtual institution as it had no building of its own and functioned from the Town Hall. Although the Museum was planned for increasing 'native' knowledge of the Bombay Presidency, the collections were singularly useful for the non-Indian merchants of Bombay, as they represented the mineral, geological and agricultural resources of western India, whose knowledge could be used for enhancing commercial transactions. The institution was formally established with the creation of a building during the late 1860s, and came to be the Victoria Museum and Gardens—now Bhau Daji Lad—which was inaugurated in 1872.

---

[46] A proposal for a museum of the Madras Literary Society was mooted the same year, although the Madras Museum, as it came to be known, was instituted 40 years later in 1851 in a building on College Road, Nungambakkam. It was shifted to its present premises at Egmore in 1854.

[47] Nair (2007, p. 62).

The histories of museums in India were written nearer the end of the Raj, but they were strongly guided by the colonial historiography. Thus, the foremost publication, *The Museums of India* (1936), which was authored by Sydney Markham (1897–1975) and Harold Hargreaves (d. 1951) emphasised that the 'lamentably' few museums in India, in comparison to India's largest population in the world, lends to the enquiry 'whether this is due to its history or to racial, climate or other circumstances'.[48] Markham was honorary empire secretary of Museums Association in the UK (joined in 1928), and Hargreaves who retired from Archaeological Survey of India as director general (1928–31) had been in charge of many archaeological museums during his long career within the institution, which he had joined in 1911. Markham and Hargreaves had undertaken the surveys of museums in India between 1928 and 1935 as part of the Empire Surveys of Museums, and in inscribing their belief they not only overlooked the British policies of economic colonialism that had nurtured the British creations of 'local museums' within South Asia, but also the prominent financial support of the native population towards the establishments. Thus, we note that the Parsi and Marwari merchants and bankers of Bombay had provided the largest sum of money towards the building for the Economic Museum, and in making the donations in 1858, they followed the strong public appeal that was made by an Indian, the well-known medical practitioner of the city who was also a reputed scholar of Sanskrit, Dr Bhau Daji Lad (1822–74).

George Birdwood, who was the first curator of Bombay's Economic Museum, acknowledged the large sums that were donated by the Indians. In his efforts towards eliciting public support for a museum, he declared that 'when one reflects that science, the arts and literature were born of commerce, have grown with its growth, and spread with its diffusion, the contrast presented in Bombay, between the mercantile opulence and intellectual destitution, is as strange as debasing'.[49] Thus, in making a case for a museum which was to enhance British commercial ventures, Birdwood chose to emphasise the potentials of the collections as representations of local culture. Considering that arguments, such as his, continue to be aired in the twenty-first century for the upkeep and development of local and

---

[48] Markham and Hargreaves (1936, p. 4).

[49] 'The Annual Report of the Bombay Government Central Museum for the Year Ending 30 April 1859', *The Bombay Times and Journal of Commerce*, 25 June 1859, p. 406, quoted as 'Extract from Government Resolution—the thanks of Government should be conveyed to Dr Birdwood for his interesting Report'. On Birdwood, see Mathur (2007, pp. 30–33).

international museums, the economic museums of colonial India provide significant opportunities for enquiring into the transactions of commerce and culture more widely, and outside the histories of colonial politics.

The objects of Ancient Assyria reached the Indian shores between 1846 and 1848 through the routes of colonial politics and imperial commerce. The histories in Chapter 2 relate to their subsequent receptions in Bombay. They inform us of the various possible histories of archaeology which object-led enquiries allow, and implore us to look beyond the cultural geography of South Asia for understanding the ways in which specific aspects of the Indian Civilisation are often historicised.

Archaeology and Philology

The European field explorations for Biblical Nineveh from the 1830s document the powerful agency of the nascent philological scholarship in directing archaeological enquiries. Chapter 3 explores the connected histories of philology and archaeology that sustained the Indological scholarship of the nineteenth- and early-twentieth centuries, and creates reasons for adopting a nuanced view towards the 'consideration of [the] thingness' of archaeology, which is now emphasised by many theoretically minded archaeologists, as most 'relevant to [the subject's] epistemological debate as it is to understand social process'.[50]

In shaping a new trajectory for material culture studies in the twenty-first century, the above group of archaeologists also increasingly mine into the study of *Ancient History and the Antiquarian* by Arnaldo Momigliano (1950) for demonstrating that archaeology 'came into being when it became visible as a distinct ecology of practice'.[51] Momigliano, more than any other historian of the twentieth century, shaped the understanding of the evolution of Western historiography from the ancient to the modern world. Archaeologists, however, make uses of his study not for re-evaluating his views regarding the prominence of the antiquarian genre in the eighteenth century,[52] but quite

[50] Hodder (2012, p. 13).

[51] Olsen *et al.* (2012, pp. 38–39).

[52] For a careful examination of Momigliano's dialectic of the early modern historiography, and his explorations of other genres of history writing during the eighteenth century apart from 'antiquarian erudition', see Phillips (1996).

exclusively to emphasise that the 'new trust in the artefacts themselves and the material evidence from excavations' facilitated archaeology's emergence as 'something distinct and partly in a long-standing opposition to disciplines based on textual accounts'.[53] However, the problems of fetishising archaeology's 'material-thing world' can be demonstrated within the histories of Indian archaeology, which are explicitly written to celebrate the material pasts that the archaeological scholarship, ostensibly, finds. They exhibit archaeology as the most reliant interlocutor and representative of the past because of its engagements with visible and tangible remains.[54] Such histories, as will be shown throughout this book, prompt a recall of the European historiography of Enlightenment, in which distinctions between facts and myths were premised upon the realness of visual evidence.

Chapter 3 creates the space to interrogate the myth of a latent archaeological record, which continues to be perpetuated within the subject despite the understanding, perhaps, by all archaeologists, of the role of inference in evidence making. The Chapter draws upon the connected histories of archaeology and philology for illustrating some of the creations of knowledge-claims through the archaeological scholarship.

The 'decline' of the philological scholarship of India at the beginning of the twentieth century was brokered through the policies of the colonial government. But the regard of this scholarship by the contemporary archaeologists of India, both foreign and native, is one good reason for noting the distinctions between the administration of a subject and its intellectual valuations when considering the histories of sciences. In demonstrating the importance of regarding the overlaps in the archaeological and philological scholarship, and of the differences in their governance, the Chapter also demonstrates that the academic pursuit of Ancient India during the colonial period has entailed, if infrequently, transcending the habits of colonial prejudice.

Histories and Analogy

The 'Buddhist archaeology of India' that was initiated by the British in the nineteenth century drew inspiration as a political project. The surveys

---

[53] Olsen *et al.* (2012, pp. 38–39, 189).

[54] Ibid. For an example of the declaration that the archaeological scholarship is the best source for seeking the histories of India, see Chakrabarti (2009, pp. 1–3).

were conceptually directed towards attributing visuality and materiality to a physically absent religion for refuting local histories and memories of the continued uses of historical topographies by members of diverse religious groups.[55] It is possible to show that even Cunningham, the conscientious field observer, had aimed at demonstrating the superiority of the Christian faith through the 'application' of the 'archaeological study.'[56] However, the support of missionary activities by the British explorers and historians of India even in their personal capacities has left very little archival presence. Hence, the note by Burgess to the Bethel Association of Free Church Mission at Jalna (Maharashtra) is quoted below, as it is a rare example. Burgess instructed his Christian compatriots that:

> In country districts of India, I can conceive of nothing more calculated to spread the gospel than an apostolic 'two' going out together to 'preach and heal.' Each supplies the other's defects whether of language, knowledge of native character, personal idiosyncrasies, or other means of advantage. [...] I believe rural missions need to be developed far more than we have yet tried, I would deprecate another city mission at the expense of Bethel.[57]

The 'Buddhist archaeology' eroded the histories of plural worship of many religious sites and monuments, and fed the aims of the colonialist historiography. Yet the inferences of this archaeology, of a singularly Buddhist occupation of specific sites and monuments, perhaps also reveals British understanding of the dispositions of all religions and their practices through knowledge of their own. Noticeably, the Indian surveyors emulated the British histories, and in their uses of phrases, such as '*stupa*-like mound, which contains the grave of Laskari Bibi', they conveyed the strong imprints of the colonial pedagogy within the ways in which they had begun to see their own historical landscapes.[58]

Those who fashion the 'ontological turn' within the scholarship of archaeology today beckon us to disengage with notions of materiality and seek instead the agency of the material for exploring the 'cognitive life of things.'[59]

[55] For the 'Buddhist archaeology' of the British, see Guha (2012).

[56] Excerpted from the title of Cunningham's paper, written under the pseudonym 'Archaeologist' in 1848a.

[57] Letter from James Burgess, 22 Seton Place, Edinburgh, to Free Church Mission, Jalna, dated 27 January 1897. MSS 7830, National Library of Scotland, Edinburgh.

[58] Mukharji (1902).

[59] Malafouris and Renfrew (2010, p. 2); Hodder (2012, p. 10).

The view of the stupa-like grave of Laskari Bibi, however, is one example among many, which allows us to disagree with such absolute injunctions, as it reveals the mediating force of the materiality of vision within our acts of preliminary descriptions.

Colonial Governance, Archaeology and Heritage

Throughout the nineteenth century, the colonial government assured itself that the archaeology of India could be completed within a certain period of time. The pecuniary government periodically, but with persistence, brought up the issue of the costs of Indian archaeology to the imperial treasury, and allocated shelf lives for its investments to the archaeological explorations and conservation of India. The government disbanded the Archaeological Survey in 1889, and defended its policies to curtail expenditure on archaeological matters by highlighting the differential valuations of the archaeological and architectural surveys by Cunningham and Burgess, respectively.

Cunningham and Burgess had established the importance of their own surveys in a comparative manner, and in absolving its responsibilities towards the administration of archaeology in 1895, the colonial government conveniently built upon their rivalry. Thus, with respect to the 'architectural surveys', it declared:

> We have the most conflicting statements as to the work remaining to be done, mainly owing to the different ideas entertained as to the scope of the work. On the one hand we have General Cunningham in 1885 saying that next to nothing remains; on the other, Dr Burgess in 1889 sketching a programme for 50 years more. [...] Local governments can scarcely advise in a matter of this sort without knowing what the general limits of the work are to be [...].[60]

Therefore, the government declared that the above branch of work 'should be curtailed', and with it decided to 'practically close down on conservation.'

---

[60] 'Reorganization of the Archaeological Survey Department', File No. 40 of 1895, *Proceedings of The Department of Revenue and Agriculture, Archaeology and Epigraphy* (henceforth *A&E*), Part I, pp. 3–10, National Archives of India (NAI), New Delhi.

It envisaged that the 'future work should be in the main devoted to the scientific enquiries represented by excavation and epigraphy', and, therefore, it chose to abolish the 'arrangement of a central Director', and 'reduce the number of parties at work to one'.[61] Yet, the poverty of the administration of archaeology provoked the Viceroy George Nathaniel Curzon (1899–1905) to re-institute the Archaeological Survey in 1902, as the benefits of curating the archaeological undertakings for enhancing the visibility of the 'merits' of the colonial rule far outweighed the fears of draining the imperial treasury. The colonial government felt impelled to 'consider that the ultimate responsibility for the preservation of the great monuments of India necessarily rests with the Government of India' and 'to effectively discharge this responsibility'.[62] The new Archaeological Survey embarked upon the conservation of monuments as an archaeological policy and drafted the Ancient Monuments Preservation Act, which was passed in 1904. The Act gave the Survey remarkable authority to invade the temples and mosques for religious uses that were deemed as befitting the protection of the imperial government due to their unique historical importance. However, its chief architect, Curzon, also complained:

> At Bhubaneswar I climbed on to a roof, or platform, overlooking the temple wall, from which a fair view could be obtained of the interior. …I could form no opinion as to the restoration or the lintels of the doorways, because I could not see them from the wall. Neither could Mr Arnot, since he had not been admitted to the interior, and might for all that he knew, be humbugged or swindled at every turn by his native subordinates. It struck me as very absurd

[61] 'Reorganization of the Archaeological Survey Department', File No. 40 of 1895, *A & E*, Part I, pp. 4–7, NAI.

[62] Letter from Secretary of State George Hamilton 'To His Excellency the Right Honourable Governor General of India in Council', from India House, dated 29 November 1901, *A & E*, File 6, Serial No. 10, pp. 25–26, p. 25, NAI. The letter is part of the above official correspondence, which relates to the appointment of the director general of the Archaeological Survey of India, and Hamilton began with the declaration that:

> the present organisation of the Archaeological Department is defective in that, while providing a staff of archaeological surveyors whose services are placed at the disposal of Local Governments, it makes no provision for their control and guidance by a competent central authority, nor gives to your Excellency's Government any means of informing itself as to what measures are being taken for the proper preservation of ancient buildings, as to whether the Local Governments are sufficiently alive to the duties which, under the present constitution of the Archaeological Department devolve in this respect upon them. (ibid.)

that the Bengal Government should be willing to spend money upon the restoration of this group of temples, but that, owing to the supposed prejudices of the peasant population of this tiny place, which ought to be overjoyed to get any money spent upon it at all, the Engineer should not be permitted to inspect the work which it was proposed to undertake. This refusal to admit non-Hindus even to the Temple enclosure prevails, so far as I know, in no other part of India, where it is the shrine, and the shrine alone that must not be desecrated with alien feet (e.g. Benares, Brindabun, Muttra, Nasik, Madura, Tanjore, Srirangam- all of them very sacred Hindu sanctuaries), and ought not in my opinion, to be tolerated in the present case of Bhubaneswar. If the Government is prepared to expend money upon restoring the temples, the Government Engineer must be admitted to the enclosure, in order to see what should be done.[63]

The long quotation which highlights Curzon's ire provides a glimpse of the many confrontations that the Ancient Monuments Preservation Act facilitated with respect to the creations and uses of sacred spaces. Locals opposed the Act for the legitimacy it gave the government to trespass, and the oppositions increased over the years. They were largely directed at the men on the spot, who were often the Indian officers of the colonial survey, and usually at their efforts towards removing the 'valuable' minor antiquities from the excavated sites. Thus, Daya Ram Sahni, who as superintendent archaeologist of the Central Circle had excavated the 'Brahmanical sculptures' at Deogarh in 1922–23, complained a year later that the 'Hindus' had started worshipping the broken statues to obstruct the relocation of the excavated finds. Sahni felt obliged in recording that:

the sculptures with the exception of a few which were collected by me in the forest adjoining the village ... have been brought to light by excavations carried out at the expense of the government on monuments which belong to the government. The Varaha Temple in Deogarh Fort has always been regarded as government property ever since the Fort came into the possession of the British Government by the Treaty in 1844. The Gupta temple near the village of Deogarh also belongs to the Government.[64]

---

[63] 'Notes on the Bhubaneswar temple and the Pandua and Gaur Ruins by his Excellency the Viceroy', *Proceedings of the Dept. of Revenue and Agriculture, A & E*, 1903, No. 3, File 97, S. No. 1, pp. 819–20.

[64] D.O. letter to DGASI, by Daya Ram Sahni from Camp Harappa, 25 January 1925. *Protection of Monuments*, 1924–25, File No. 325, Survey Archives.

Sahni's invocation of the rights of the government to its property is particularly significant as he had also noted that 'the news that the sculptures in question have already begun to be worshipped comes to me as a surprise'.[65] By creating new histories of cultural patrimony and new artefacts of cultural heritage, the inhabitants of historical terrains resisted the advances of the Colonial State upon their lands. Similar instances of the spontaneous creations of heritage and inalienable cultural rights have followed the post-colonial legislations of Indian archaeology. The examples need reminders within the present scholarship of South Asia which often reckons cultural heritage as self-constituted, and demonstrates this to be 'out there' as monuments and ancient sites, without a regard of the shifting histories of the creations and uses of the phenomenon. Chapters 4 and 5, which engage with the archaeological histories of the Indus Civilisation, are therefore specifically aimed at addressing the manner in which ideational phenomena of culture, legacy, heritage and an 'ethos' of an Ancient Indian/South Asian Civilisation are often seamlessly transformed into visible artefacts through the archaeological scholarship. In the reviews of the transformations, mainly through acts of inferences, the chapters draw our attention to some of the most pernicious legacies of the traditions of the colonial historiography.

Gauging the Unknown

The *longue durée* of the archaeological scholarship of the Indus or Harappan Civilisation from the mid-1920s provides ample spaces for comprehensive analyses of the manner in which archaeology has been developed as a professional practice and an academic discipline within South Asia. The histories of the Indus Civilisation present a panoramic view of the shifting theoretical orientations and of the increasing sophistications in the technologies of

---

[65] D.O. letter to DGASI, by Daya Ram Sahni from Camp Harappa, 25 January 1925. *Protection of Monuments*, 1924–25, File No. 325, Survey Archives. Another example from this period is the removal of a broken Vishnu image found in the 'remote' jungles near Deopani, Guwahati by K.N. Dikshit. In this case, the local objections reached the Assam government, and John Marshall was forced to issue an official circular, dated 24 July 1924, to his staff, which instructed them to consult with the local governments before removing any 'cult objects', cf. 'List of Protected Ancient Monuments Maintained or Repaired by the Archaeology Dept', File No. 325, 1923–25, Survey Archives.

excavation, data analyses and recording. The various inferences regarding the composition of the societies, polities and economies of this Bronze Age phenomenon provide a sufficient set of data, which would allow us to critique the 'disciplinary history' of the archaeology of South Asia in the twentieth century. Yet, the scholarship of the Indus Civilisation remains largely non-self-reflexive in its neglect in interrogating the manner in which this has established truisms of disciplinary identities and innate civilisational heritage.

The Chapters explore two seemingly unrelated topics, namely: (a) the intellectual influences of the renowned prehistorian of the mid-twentieth century, Vere Gordon Childe (1892–1957) on the formative scholarship of the Indus Civilisation, and (b) the material creations of civilisational essence and cultural ethos through some of the theories that have been applied to the Civilisation's subsequent study from the 1960s. In recalling Childe, Chapter 4 develops a history of the ways in which the unknown is gauged and made known, and brings to fore the ethics of Childe's scholarship. Chapter 5 provides a view of the conflicts, competitions and nationalist contestations that have embedded the international scholarship of the Indus Civilisation. Both investigate the manner in which archaeological evidence is established, and highlight the conceptual slippage of representations between archaeological cultures and cultural identities in the real world. They also reveal the limitations of the archaeological scholarship in 'excavating' past perceptions of territorial boundaries and cultural identities, and cajole us into investigating the manner in which material descriptions and identities of 'foreign' and 'indigenous' are distinguished in relation to a vast geographical terrain, namely northern South Asia.

The ongoing scholarship of the Indus Civilisation in the twenty-first century conveys the hope that 'dynamic' theories would rectify the flaws of the culture–history approach. The approach prevails within the archaeology of South Asia and the young entrants to the field predict that robust alternatives would 'serve as empirical evidence for the construction, maintenance, contestation, and interaction of cultural categories with a contingent and conjunctional theory of history and culture'.[66] Yet, as the quote above clearly shows, they too often fail to address the fundamentalism of empiricism within the scholarship of the Indus Civilisation in their inferences of cultural

---

[66] Johansen (2003, p. 194).

categories.[67] The two chapters demonstrate the need for critical reflections upon the heuristic values of a dogmatic empiricism.

The Expectations from Archaeology

The growing demands for a nationalist archaeology of India in the twenty-first century and the increasing efforts to establish material realities of unique South Asian civilisational ethos through the scholarship of the Indus Civilisation sharply contrast with the trends towards the explorations for 'cosmopolitan archaeologies' within the Anglo-American world.[68] Bred through archaeological research on aspects of heritage, especially within South Africa, and among the Native Americans, Australian aboriginals and indigenous communities of the Pacific, this 'archaeology' shares the core tenets of the 'indigenous archaeologies', which has been mentioned in an earlier section.[69] The 'cosmopolitan archaeologies' appear inherently plural in the stated aims and methodological orientations, and is inspired by the philosophical scholarship of cosmopolitanism of Kwame Anthony Appiah, who has used his study as an ideological tool for negotiating the inequalities of the world.[70] In bringing Appiah's study to the practices of archaeology, the proponents affirm that 'archaeologists are not the primary stakeholders or arbiters of culture', and seek methods for mapping representations of multivocality.[71] As with the practices of indigenous archaeologies, this 'archaeology' too would pose significant challenges to the state-sponsored archaeology in South Asia,

---

[67] An example is the declaration: 'Looking to the physical characteristics of material remains can elicit information useful in reconstructing past practices, which in turn provides insight into aspects of culture and society' (Abraham *et al.*, 2013, p. 18). Chapter 5 specifically shows the 'problems' of such empiricism.

[68] For a nationalist archaeology, an example is Chakrabarti (2003, p. 279). The author, who has promoted the opinion in many different ways subsequently, has stated that 'the pursuit of a nationalist goal in archaeology is entirely justified as long as this does not bend archaeological data and is not used as an intellectual support for chauvinism' (ibid.); for the creation of an ethos of an Ancient South Asian civilization, see Elstov (2008). This has been referred to in Chapter 5. For the concept of Cosmopolitan Archaeologies, see Meskell (2009b).

[69] For examples of the new research, see articles in Meskell (2009a).

[70] Appiah (2006).

[71] Meskell (2009b, p. 7).

which invariably searches for a certain kind of past. The concluding chapter builds upon the promise of this archaeology for exploring the diverseness of the past and in contextualising the quest for methods examines the academic investments towards a nation-serving archaeology that were made within the newly independent India of the 1950s and the 1960s.

The young and hopeful Indian nation, which had emerged scarred from the violence of partition, consciously established the politics of secularism, which, in turn, was used for nurturing national archaeological projects. Thus, the leading Indian archaeologist of the time, H.D. Sankalia (1908–89) aimed at demonstrating that 'if archaeology and history teach us anything, it is the underlying cultural unity of India which our linguistic or religious frenzy tries to destroy'.[72] Through his scholarship, Sankalia had hoped to demonstrate that 'from a larger point of view, there is no fundamental difference between Andhra–Karnataka–Tamil Nadu culture and that of Maharashtra, Madhya Pradesh and the South U.P., Bihar and West Bengal chalcolithic cultures'.[73] The searches, such as his, for archaeological evidence of a cohesive cultural unity for India inevitably involved the dismissal of the 'aberrations' from the desired historical narrative of a secular nation.

A national archaeology, however well meaning, would always emulate the exclusive methods of an edifying history. In this respect, it is important to emphasise that all endeavours to represent a national history, which may hope to be inclusive and which may present the nation in its secular grandeur, create a resonance of the Whig historiography that was developed in England in the 1830s, which established the history of England as a 'triumph of victory.'[74] This is because a national history, by definition, entails demonstrating the 'triumph' of a nation. The efforts towards seeking an archaeological history of the Indian nation that might be capable of exposing the diversities and complexities of the Indian past will always remain a project of edifying an ethos of nationhood.

Considering that the nationalist historiography of India has been amply critiqued within the historical studies of Modern India, the increasing calls for a nationalist archaeology of India in the twenty-first century appear surprising. Such demands, no doubt, go against the contemporary aims of the scholarship of the histories of archaeologies. The concluding chapter

---

[72] Sankalia (1978, p. 123).
[73] Sankalia (1974, p. 541).
[74] See Louis (1999, p. 6).

critiques the calls by drawing upon the positivism that is inherent to all nationalist and colonialist histories. It reminds us that the historiography of a nation-serving archaeology for India and the British archaeology within colonial India share similarities in the methods. Both enshrine the innate authority of the archaeological field surveys for sourcing the realities of the past, and to meet this end both exhibit archaeological data as being out there. In contrast, the histories in this book add to the immense possibilities of the archaeological scholarship by disengaging with archaeology's 'feats.' They create expectations of being able to source through the archaeological scholarship the transformations over time of the understanding of *valid* evidence. And in this, they demonstrate one way in which we could bring reflexivity into our practices of archaeological research.

A Concluding Note with an Emphasis on Visual Histories

Throughout the book, I have made references to Indian archaeology, archaeology of India and Ancient India. This usage refers primarily to the archaeological scholarship and practices that were undertaken within British India. With respect to the post-colonial archaeological scholarship of the Indus Civilisation, I have noted the distinctions in the scholarship within India and Pakistan. The reference to Indian pasts in the title of this book is specific to the archaeological histories of India of the colonial and post-colonial times.

In establishing and analysing the histories of archaeology, I have drawn upon my previous research of visual histories. However, given that archaeological knowledge is anchored upon transcriptions of sight, visual histories inform us of the manner in which analogical frames of references are established during the archaeological fieldwork, especially through field drawings and field photography. Histories of archaeology draw our attention to this epistemic force of vision. In encouraging us to critically consider the acts of our knowledge creations, they also create reasons for reflecting upon the ways in which we see an absent past and shape its materiality in the present.

1

Antiquarianism and South Asia: Questioning Histories of Origins

Historians of South Asian archaeology often mine for 'facts' within the historiographies they discredit and consider error ridden. This chapter draws attention to the consequences of this mining and shows the contradictions this breeds within the narratives. It reviews the archaeological histories of antiquarianism within the Indian subcontinent and develops the argument that although the archaeological explorations of South Asia from the mid-nineteenth century emanated through the practices of the British and European antiquaries, this history does not lend to the inference that the scholarship in antiquities within the region was a 'western cognitive entity.'[1] It highlights the poverty of knowledge regarding the histories of antiquarian pursuits within the region and demonstrates the reasons for initiating critical research of the subject within pre-colonial India.

Between the sixteenth and eighteenth centuries, the nature of European enquiries into the cultural and economic geographies of Asia changed considerably, from viewing and collecting to surveillance and probing. The changes inform us of the changing relationships between once equal trading partners into those of the rulers and the ruled. By the close of the eighteenth century, the antiquary-minded British and Europeans under the employment of the East India Company were undertaking field surveys of the Indian subcontinent with a view to acquire deep knowledge of the region for commanding its resources and territories. Historians of archaeology select the western,

---

[1] Guha-Thakura (2004, p. 3).

mainly European, practices of searching for the past of Hindustan through antiquities and monuments for establishing the history of antiquarian pursuits within South Asia, which, they explain, led to the emergence of archaeology as a unique field science. In this, they follow the origin story for the history of Indian archaeology, which Alexander Cunningham had presented in the 'Introduction' of the official reports of his archaeological explorations between 1861 and 1865, as the archaeological surveyor of India.[2]

Cunningham had historicised the historical scholarship of India through the 'Introduction', whose opening sentence reads: 'The study of Indian antiquities received its first impulse from Sir William Jones, who in 1784 founded the Asiatic Society of Bengal.'[3] His selection of the scholarship of William Jones as the starting point for the 'proper' study of Indian history has been emulated by all subsequent historians of South Asian archaeology, perhaps with no exceptions.[4] The selection, however, illustrates the historiography of unequal encounters, as it was premised upon the understanding that antiquarian practices, which involved seeking histories through ancient things, were brought into the Indian subcontinent by the British and the Europeans. The Chapter historicises aspects of the British antiquarianism of India through histories of the antiquarian scholarship in Britain, and explores the imprints of the colonial historiography within the post-colonial histories of antiquarianism in South Asia.

---

[2] Cunningham (1871a).

[3] Ibid., p. i.

[4] Examples: Sankalia (1962–63, p. xvii); Chakrabarti (1981, p. 173; 1988, 2006, 2009); Singh (2004) and Ray (2004a, 2008).

Chakrabarti says quite specifically: The claim that some ideas of ancient Indian literature have been reflected in the Three Age archaeological system of the 19th century, and the fact that Firuz Shah Tughlak displayed an interest in the ancient remains by removing two Asokan pillars from their original contexts in Topra in Haryana and Meerut in western UP do not establish that archaeological curiosity developed in India before the European contact in the modern period (2006, p. 505).

The only archaeologist who has carefully mapped the 'indigenous epsitemological traditions' in his history of Indian archaeology is K. Paddayya, who undertook the task to emphasise that Indian archaeology has the potential for employing the above traditions to study its past. Paddayya illustrated the examples of the uses of antiquarian source in early India, although he stated that 'these instances, however, do not suffice at the moment to argue for the existence of an Indian tradition of archaeologial research. (see Paddayya, 2002, p. 126)

Cunningham's 'Introduction' and a History of Origin

The 'Introduction', which Cunningham wrote for his reports as the archaeo-logical surveyor of India (1861–65), provides an opportunity for reflecting upon the manner in which the British often established the pioneering value of their own contributions to the scholarship of Indian history. The report is one of the first formal documents of the history of Indian archaeology, and Cunningham who was aware of the precedence declared that a 'new era for Indian archaeology' began from 1834 through the logic that this was the year 'when James Prinsep gave to the world the first results of Masson's researches in the Kabul Valley and of Ventura's and Court's explorations in the Punjab, followed immediately by my own excavation of the stupa at Sarnath, Banaras'.[5]

The above 'era' also saw the commencement of Cunningham's professional career in India, in the army. Similar to most East Indiamen of his times, Cunningham had arrived in India in 1833 with no knowledge of the country or its languages, and by selecting the starting year of the era less than a year after his arrival, he created a chronological context for his own position as one among the harbingers of change.

In the decade of the 1830s, James Prinsep (1799–1840) had made substantive contributions to the scholarship of Ancient India through his epigraphic and numismatic discoveries of the chronologies and identities of kings, such as the Mauryan Emperor Asoka (r.c. 268–31 BCE). And in documenting the era as heralding a tangible change towards progress in the historical scholarship of India, Cunningham highlighted his tutelage under Prinsep. In this respect, it is worth noting that: (a) Cunningham concluded the 'Introduction' with the proverb *pygmaei gigantum humeros*, and thereby presented the value of his own archaeological field surveys, between 1835 and 1865, quite literally as the ability to see further afield than the past giants in the subject,[6] and (b) in recalling his maiden excavations at Sarnath (1834–35), Cunningham neglected to mention Prinsep's contributions to the plans and of previous excavations at the site, for example the one in 1815 that had been undertaken by Colin Mackenzie, a year before he became the

---

[5] Cunningham (1871a, p. xix).
[6] Ibid., p. xliii.

surveyor general of India (1816–21).[7] We are made aware of Mackenzie's excavations through the report of the excavations at Sarnath, which were undertaken in 1904–05 by Frederick Oertel (1883–1926) of the Public Works Department.[8]

One may explain Cunningham's omission of Mackenzie's excavations by drawing attention to retrospective judgements regarding their unplanned and desultory nature, and suggesting, thereby, that Cunningham may not have seen the merit in reporting them. Yet, we are reminded that Cunningham's own excavations, which he initiated at the Dhamek Stupa (at Sarnath) in January 1835, were also criticised retrospectively by scholars of Indology as desultory and representing the practices of a shaft-sinking, stupa-opening archaeology.[9] Similar to Mackenzie's practices of unplanned excavations, Cunningham too undertook excavations in a spontaneous manner, even though he planned his exploration routes. Therefore, Cunningham's overlook reminds us that histories of archaeology are replete with efforts to ignore and mask past practices of excavations and preservations, and condemn them as erroneous. Examples of such acts are rather well illustrated by David Karmon in his history of the archaeological preservations of Rome during the period of the Renaissance. They were, as Karmon has shown, committed for various aims, but they all perpetuated linear narratives of progress for demonstrating an incremental advance towards a technically, methodologically and theoretically developing practice.[10] Cunningham's fashioning of his own,

---

[7] Cunningham had vehemently denied James Fergusson's statement that the excavations were undertaken on Prinsep's initiatives (Cunningham 1871a, p. 107). However, Prinsep's own recollections demonstrate that Cunningham's retrospective denial did not present the entire truth. See 'Note on the image of the Buddha discovered by J. Stephenson' by James Prinsep (1835, pp. 131–33); Cunningham (1871b).

[8] Oertel (1908, p. 62).

[9] For example, James Burgess had written to Marshall hoping that Jean Phillipe Vogel would undertake better excavation procedures than the 'disastrous methods of Cole, Cunningham, Caddy and Beglar', and Vogel in turn had stated that 'the most effective way of preventing further destruction' of sites through looting by tourists and archaeologists alike 'is to secure for the museums the material, which is still under the ground. This can only be effected by systematic excavations being started, carried on scientific lines as are followed nowadays by European archaeologists in Egypt and Greece'. He emphasised that 'even a few months' excavations would yield more results to science than the many past years of desultory idol-digging. D.O. letter from Burgess to Marshall, dated 10 July 1902, and *Memorandum on the Preservation of Archaeological Material in the Peshawar Dist. (Antiquities of Gandhara)*, 1902, File No. 86 respectively. Survey Archives.

[10] Karmon (2011).

and the British, archaeological scholarship of India exemplifies the way in which such teleological narratives of developments are created.

Cunningham had historicised the scholarship of Ancient India as beginning with the 'Closet or Scholastic Archaeologists', who he stated had undertaken 'archaeological research [that was] chiefly literary', and who were succeeded by the 'Travelling Antiquarians' who were 'not Sanskrit scholars, and whose success [had] been achieved by actual measurements and laborious explorations in the field'.[11] Prinsep had coined the term 'travelling antiquarians', which in retrospect appears as an apt description of the practices of the late eighteenth- and early nineteenth-century Western antiquaries of India. Cunningham used the terms to periodise a shifting chronology in the methods of historical enquiry from a purely text-based research to the beginnings of field surveys. However, the ephemeral nature of the periodisation becomes rather apparent when we notice that the methods which the 'Closet Archaeologists', such as Charles Wilkins (1749–1836) and Horace Hayman Wilson (1786–1860) and other Sanskrit scholars of the late eighteenth and early nineteenth centuries adopted during the course of their historical enquiries of Ancient India drew upon the practices of the 'travelling antiquaries', which Cunningham dated from the 1830s, and among whom he listed himself, Fergusson, Markham Kittoe, Walter Elliot, Meadows Taylor, and Bhau Daji Lad.[12] Thus, on seeing an inscribed stone pillar near Badal at Dinajpur (Bangladesh) in November 1780, Wilkins not only transcribed the edict but also made a drawing of the monument and had it measured. He recorded the pillar as 12-feet high, and succeeded in translating and deciphering the inscription, which was subsequently dated more precisely as belonging to the Pala rule of Bengal in the ninth/tenth century CE. He also published his drawing to show the specimen of the inscription (Illustration 1.1).[13] Forty years later, in 1820, Wilson emulated contemporary practices of surveying the field, when he provided a visual and comprehensive account of the ancient sites he had encountered during a journey from Calcutta to Gaya.[14] In following Cunningham's periodisation, which was aimed at registering an apparent methodological shift from text-based to field-based historical enquiries, we misrepresent the powerful

[11] Cunningham (1871a, pp. xviii–ix).
[12] Ibid.
[13] For the translation and history of decipherment, see Kielhorn (1894).
[14] Wilson (1825).

agency of the text-based scholarship in directing the field-based explorations of Ancient India. This research method sums up the nineteenth-century Indological scholarship, including that of Cunningham's, which he also illustrated through the 'Introduction'. Yet, by devising the periodisation, he was able to create a historical context that permitted him to establish his own credentials as India's pioneering archaeological explorer.

Antiquarian Enquiries and Imperial Views: Elephanta

The historiography that Cunningham followed in characterising William Jones as the founder antiquary of India facilitated the British to historicise themselves as India's foremost historians. It was built upon acts of obliterations and bespoke of the historical connections between politics, power and authorship of knowledge. A field report of Elephanta from the early eighteenth century by the English East Indiaman Isaac Pyke (d. 1738) draws our attention to the 'colonialist' feature of the historiography, which masked all but the British attempts to know India. It draws upon the marginalisation of the Portuguese views, which is often forgotten within the critique of the colonial historiography of India, and through which the latter derived its truth claims.

Pyke had surveyed Elephanta (or Ghorpuri as it was called by the local population) near Bombay in 1712. His explorations accrued retrospective value as antiquarian surveys with the publication of his 'journal' in the *Archaeologia* (1785), notably at a time when the British East India Company was the ruler of Bengal and politically ascendant within Hindustan.[15] The journal was made known to the learned circles in Britain more than 40 years after Pyke's demise, when it was read before the Society of Antiquaries in London on 10 February 1870 by Alexander Dalrymple, who recalled Pyke as a 'journalist'. We may be right in conjecturing that Pyke received this retrospective attention because he subsequently rose to prominence as the Governor of St. Helena and held the post on two occasions, namely from 1714 until 1719, and from 1731 until his death in the island in 1738.

In his account, Pyke had highlighted the destruction caused to the 'cave temple' at Elephanta by the Portuguese Jesuits. He had recalled that his

---

[15] Pyke (1785).

informant, Ramajee Comje, a broker for the East India Company at Bombay, had informed him of 'several fine temples of this nature [...] but the Moors wherever they come from destroyed them because of the imagery, as do the Portuguese, on account of the idolatry these supposed to be practices: so that most of them now are fallen to decay'.[16]

He had also emphasised the ostensible lack of curiosity towards the ruins by the contemporary Portuguese community through the statement that 'they now fodder all their cattle' in the tank at the entrance to the 'Mahody's temple', and 'lately one of their Fidalgo's, to divert himself with the echo which is here most admirable, fired a great gun into it with several shot which has broken some of the pillars, but the fabric seems as durable as ever'.[17]

However, Pyke's careful overlook of the visits to Elephanta during the sixteenth century by Portuguese scholars who were not Jesuit priests fired by religious zeal, is quite striking. For example, the botanist Garcia da Orta had visited Elephanta in 1534 and had regarded it as 'the best of all'. The Renaissance humanist Joao Castro, who arrived in India four years after da Orta in 1538, had provided a more considered aesthetic judgement and had stated that 'indeed the proportions and symmetry with which each figure and everything is made [...] would be worth the while of any painter to study it even if he were Apelles'.[18] Their views were known within early eighteenth-century Europe and Britain because of the publication of a revised edition of Vincenzo Cartari's *The Images of the Gods*, which contained their descriptions, and which had been added to the book in 1615 by Lorenzo Pignoria. This revised edition was in circulation by the mid-seventeenth century and was thus quite well known among the European antiquaries more than 50 years before Pyke undertook his field surveys of Elephanta.[19]

We can, no doubt, suggest that Pyke's overlook of the views of da Orta and Castro reflected his ignorance. However, the suggestion would undermine Pyke's scholarship and curiosity as he comes across as an intellectually engaged man from the meagre references that are available of him. He corresponded with the Royal Societies, had publications within scholarly journals on many subjects, including 'The Method of Making the Best Mortar in Madras',

---

[16] Pyke (1785, p. 326). For a brief history of the Jesuit purging of the temples, see Mitter (1977, p. 34).

[17] Ibid., p. 329.

[18] Documented by Mitter (1977, pp. 36–37).

[19] For more information on this, see Mitter (1977, pp. 28, 37).

and similar to the contemporary antiquaries in Britain, undertook successful experiments for satiating his curiosity on disparate scientific topics, which included the 'hydrostatic method of calculating the composition of metals'.[20] He also emulated the historical methods of the well-known British antiquaries such as the Historiographer Royal Thomas Madox (1666–1727), who had studied the 'raw materials of state records and charters' and pioneered a methodology to which all antiquaries of the eighteenth century aspired. Madox, in fact, had appealed to creations of histories through 'testimonies' and 'account of things', and not through private opinions, and had established two criteria for the historical scholarship, namely 'the need to digest and to interpret antiquities rather than to amass and admire and the importance of providing the correct kind of scholarly apparatus'.[21] That Pyke followed the appeal and the second criterion can be assumed from the care with which he described the 'cave temple' at the site, which included taking measurements of the 'spacious room'. Although his expedition had only spanned a single day, he took with him a 15-member team, which specifically included Captain Baker as the draftsman (Illustration 1.2), and it was only upon reaching Elephanta that he realised that the visual recording 'would have taken up a month at least to have gone through the whole'.[22] Yet, considering the fact that systematic recording was clearly his agenda, Pyke's omission of the Portuguese views in his journal appears deliberate in retrospective.

Similar to Pyke, Dalrymple too failed to mention the visits of the Portuguese to Elephanta during the sixteenth century, when he communicated the former's journal to members of the Society of Antiquaries in London sixty-eight, 68 years after it was written. Dalrymple had annotated the journal to list the European and British visitors to Elephanta before and after Pyke. However, he began the list not with the Portuguese visitors to the site but with the visit by the Dutch merchant Jan Huyghen van Linschoten in 1579. Therefore, it is of relevance to note that Linschoten had emulated the views of da Orta in his understanding that the architects of the cave temple were 'the Chinos [which were verie ingenious workemen] … when they used to traffique in the countries of India'.[23] The selective recording by

---

[20] See *Philosophical Transactions*, 1731/32, pp. 231–35.
[21] Sweet (2004, pp. 15–17).
[22] Pyke (1785, p. 326).
[23] Dalrymple in Pyke (1785, p. 331); for quote, see Mitter (1977, p. 38).

Pyke and Dalrymple, of the European visitors to Elephanta, characterises the British colonial historiography of South Asia. And the memorialisation of the intolerant, destructive and indolent Portuguese by Pyke illustrates the cultural politics of British imperialism. Inevitably, by the close of the eighteenth century the British object of vilification shifted from their Portuguese predecessors in India to the Muslim rulers, whose territories they had started to successfully annex.

The Unhistorical Natives of the Colonial Historiography

We see the colonial historiography in the making quite clearly within the British accounts of the field surveys of the ruins and ancient sites in India 50 years after Pyke's survey of Elephanta. Thus, while narrating his explorations at Mahabalipuram, in 1772 and 1776, William Chambers, who was an interpreter for Persian in the Supreme Court of the East India Company at Calcutta (1776–92) and who was stationed in Madras between 1765 and 1790, had proclaimed that:

> among the Hindus 'their poets seem to have been their only historians, as well as divines, and whatever they relate, is wrapped up in this burlesque garb, set off, by the way of ornament, with circumstances hugely incredible and absurd, and all this without any date, and in no other order or method, than such as the poets' fancy suggested and sound most convenient. Nevertheless', Chambers conceded that 'by comparing names and grand events, recorded by them, with those interpreted in the histories of other nations, and by calling in the assistance of ancient monuments, coins and inscriptions as occasion shall offer, some probable conjectures at least, if not important discoveries, may, it is hoped, be made on this interesting subject'.[24]

Chambers wrote the above account retrospectively for publication in 1788. Thus, the account appeared 12 years after his last visit to Mahabalipuram, the once premier city of the Pallava kings (ca. 6–9 CE). Although he conveyed

---

[24] Chambers (1788, pp. 157–58). For a biography of William Chambers (c. 1748–93), see the discourse delivered by his brother, Robert Chambers, then President of Asiatic Society of Bengal. In Chambers (1789, pp. 3–4).

the recollections of the local population in the account, with respect to the number of temples, rathas and ruins that had once embellished the historic city's architectural topography, he also affirmed that:

> It is much to be regretted, that a blind zeal, attended with a total want of curiosity, in the Mahomedan governors of this country has been so hostile to the preservation of Hindu monuments and coins. But a spirit of enquiry among Europeans may yet perhaps be successful, and an instance which relates to the place above described, though in itself a subject of regret, leaves room to hope, that futurity may yet have in store some useful discoveries.[25]

The above statement allows us to anticipate the great historical service that the 'spirit of enquiry among the Europeans' would render the 'natives' of the Indian subcontinent during the nineteenth century. It also informs us of the various ways in which truisms about 'witnessing the field' were retrospectively created. During the surveys, Chambers had not measured the 'distances, nor size of the objects', and neither had he 'committed to writing at the time the observations he had made on them'.[26] But because he had aimed his account as a field report, he adopted the mode of careful description, which entailed providing blatant approximations of the measurements and dimensions, so that he could show his readers the things he remembered seeing. He reported that:

> On ascending the hill by its slope on the north, a very singular piece of sculpture presents itself to view. On a plain surface of the rock, which may once have served as the floor of some apartment, there is a platform of stone, about eight or nine feet long, by three or four feet wide, in situation rather elevated, with two or three steps leading up to it, perfectly resembling a couch or a bed, and a lion very well executed at the upper end of it by way of pillow, the whole of one piece, being part of the hill itself.[27]

For investigating the uses of the antiquarian scholarship in creations of the colonial historiography, it is important to recall the epistemic agency of visualisation within the knowledge claims that are made through field explorations. Because, although the dominant presence of vision within the traditions of the European historiography might be obvious, by taking cognisance of the uses of vision, we begin to see the ways in which notions

---

[25] Chambers (1788, pp. 157–58).
[26] Ibid., p. 145.
[27] Ibid., p. 149.

of true histories, correct observations and facts were employed by the British to create histories of the historically disengaged natives. The force of vision within the 'proper' modes of historical enquiries is well documented in the following declaration of a contemporary of Chambers, the English diplomat and antiquary John Strange (1732–99), who stated:

> If there is any faith in civil history it is surely in that part of it which is grounded on the real monuments of antiquity, which speak for themselves, *dum tacent, calamant*, and are neither offered to us through the medium of prejudice or party. A faithful register of such treasures is the most valuable literary acquisition that any county can make; we cannot therefore be too zealous or scrupulous in the research and preservation of them.[28]

The account of Mahabalipuram by Chambers and the above declaration by Strange of the source value of antiquities for history writing allow us to see the agency of vision within the historical linkages between antiquarian enquiries and colonial politics. Seeing facilitated the antiquaries 'to separate falsehood from truth and explode what rested only on the vanity of the native inventors and propagators',[29] and the colonial historiography nurtured the truth value of vision for its own ends.

Chambers and all subsequent British field explorers of South Asia in the colonial period followed the contemporary norms of antiquarian scholarship within Britain and western Europe, which disregarded the possibility of sourcing the past in an objective and rational manner through the sole study of texts and manuscripts. The European scholarship of antiquarianism, however, upheld the value of text-based field enquiries. The uniqueness of the colonial historiography, therefore, lies in the dismissal of the 'indigenous' literature of India in favour of the 'foreign' textual accounts, namely Chinese and Greek, and in promoting the superiority of the field observations of the 'Westerners' through tales of the 'imperfect' native eye that was, ostensibly, incapable of seeing correctly, and hence of producing accurate field records. An early example of the 'colonialist' judgements regarding native vision relates to the drawings that were made during the late-eighteenth century by the Indian painters and draftsmen who accompanied the British in their field surveys. For example, the drawings of Ellora (near Aurangabad), which

---

[28] Strange (1777, p. 26).
[29] Gough (1770, p. i).

were made in 1790–91 by Gungaram, the 'very ingenious native' who served Charles Malet, were dismissed by the latter, who subsequently commissioned the task to James Manley in 1793 and who also apologised for their quality to John Shore, the president of Asiatic Society. Yet, Gungaram's drawings were no more imprecise than the contemporary 'picturesque illustrations' of the caves, which were executed during the same period, namely 1791–92, by James Wales, whom Malet identified as an artist and whose drawings, he informed Shore, were of 'fine taste, masterly pencil and laudable industry'.[30] With the help of the landscape painters, Thomas and William Daniel, Malet published Wales's work posthumously after the latter's untimely death in 1795.

The Utility of Archaeology and Contradictions of Historiographical Intents

Chamber's judgement regarding the 'Hindus' provokes us to critically regard the displays of the utility value of archaeology within the twenty-first-century histories of South Asian archaeology. This is because we notice that in a manner quite akin to his methods—not aims—many historians of Indian archaeology today promote the importance of field surveys, field discoveries and the accompanying archaeological scholarship over the text-based philological scholarship of the past. Thus, an authoritative history, which is a standard textbook for students of Indian archaeology, highlights the inherent 'flaws' within the indigenous textual traditions of Ancient India and declares that 'except for the history of the Kings of Kashmir, written by Kalhana in the twelfth century, there is no proper historical chronicle dating from the ancient period of Indian history'.[31] The declaration echoes those of the nineteenth-century British historians of India, such as the administrative

---

[30] Malet (1799, p. 382); also Mitter (1977, p. 159); and specially Pinney (2008), who has explained the attack by James Fergusson upon Rajendralal Mitra, which is referred in Chapter 3, with reference to the British creations of the 'uneducated eye' of the natives. Fergusson accused Mitra, who was a competent photographer, of his inability to read photographs, use them as evidence and understand the nature of the indexical as 'being there', pp. 69–74.

[31] Chakrabarti (2009, p. 1). For a critique of the manner in which the *Rajatarangini* has been historicised since the nineteenth century, see articles in Cox (2013); also Kaul (2014).

scholar Vincent Aquila Smith, who held the view that 'the *Rajatarangini* (or "the history of the kings of Kashmir written by Kalhana") was the nearest approach to a work of regular history in extant Sanskrit literature'.[32]

The 'historical fact' that the *Rajatarangini* was the only indigenous text of Ancient India that contained a narrative of historical intent was formulated during the eighteenth century. Thus, William Jones, who had explicitly endowed the 'honour' of 'unveiling' the Sanskrit literature to the efforts of his fellow countrymen had declared that 'no *Hindu* nation, but the *Cashmirians*, have left us regular histories in their ancient language'. Yet, with the above statement, Jones had also presented a nuanced historical judgement of the 'Puranas, Itihasas, or poems mythological and heroic' as he saw in them 'fragments of history'.[33] No such qualifiers accompany the modern histories of Indian archaeology, which highlight the lack of historical contents within the ancient Sanskrit and Pali literary corpus and inscriptions, through another 'historical fact' that has also been shaped by the colonial historiography, namely that 'no Thucydides or Tacitus has left for posterity a genuine history in Ancient India'.[34]

The new histories of Indian archaeology today aim at serving the 'grass-roots history of the land'.[35] Yet the methods they adopt for presenting the field scholarship of archaeology as permitting better knowledge of the past, which entails exhibiting the 'contaminations' within the literary corpus of Ancient India and the absence of 'proper' historians within pre-colonial India, mirror those of the colonial historiography. The histories encourage us to rhetorically ask: What exactly is the distinction between the declarations of Pyke or Chambers, who had deliberately and explicitly marked the alleged ignorance and neglect of engagements with historical materials by their predecessors in the Indian subcontinent, whether European, Islamic or Hindu, and the historians of Indian archaeology today who cannot see any histories in the textual enterprises of the pre-colonial times?

[32] Smith (1924, pp. xviii, 10).

[33] Jones (1798, pp. vi–vii).

[34] Chakrabarti (2009, p. 1), quoting H.C. Raychaudhuri, *Political History of Ancient India*, who followed the British historiography of India, such as the history of Rapson, E.J., 1922, *The Cambridge History of India*, Vol. I, p. 57. For a history of why Thucydides and other Greeks, such as Herodotus, were celebrated historian exemplars of the ancient times during the eighteenth century, despite the 'fictions' in their narratives of histories, see Boer (1968).

[35] Chakrabarti (2009, p. 18).

The understanding that the ancient texts composed within the Indian subcontinent convey 'contaminated' histories and interpolations illustrates a disregard of history. It informs us that the contents of such texts are measured against modern notions of what the forms and contents of history should look like. We can exemplify the disregard by highlighting many assertions within the new histories of Indian archaeology of the twenty-first century, such as the statement that the archaeological scholarship provides a 'framework of a past acceptable to all segments of [India's] population', as it exposes the 'non-sectarian and multi-lineal image of the past of Ancient India'.[36] Expectantly, the ancient texts provide no such framework and allow no such revelations, as the characterisation mentioned above of the feats of archaeology is presentist. It informs us of the expectations of the author from the modern Indian nation.

Towards a Deep Antiquity of Antiquarianism

The 'rise' of archaeology from antiquarianism has established the histories of archaeology throughout much of the twentieth century, and as noted in the Introduction Chapter, this history has created truisms regarding the differential engagements with the past in the pre-modern and modern worlds. Thus, twentieth-century archaeologists have endeavoured to distinguish the antiquaries from the learned men of the ancient world who too collected artefacts of historical value, restored old monuments and classified and designed the schema of periodisation, such as the Babylonian king Nabonidus (r. 555 and 539 BCE) and the Greek scholar Hesoid (ca. 700 BCE). To exhibit the truism of their classification, they also defined the antiquaries quite specifically as 'Renaissance men—polymaths, scholars with deep curiosity and profound knowledge of a wide range of subjects'.[37] However, from the close of the twentieth century, there has been a growing intellectual thrust towards the possibilities of finding myriad forms of antiquarianism outside the European context and throughout the past. The new searches towards

---

[36] Chakrabarti (2009, p. 3).
[37] Renfrew and Bahn (1996, p. 18).

a deep antiquity of antiquarian activities are informed through the under-standing that all societies at all times have engaged with historical objects for acquiring historical knowledge. The searches compliment new enquiries into the histories of archaeologies, which, as will be shown here, prevail upon us to distinguish practices from histories of discipline-making.

The pioneering efforts to interrogate the Europe-oriented histories of anti-quarianism have been undertaken through reviews of the historiography of Ancient Greece. Inspired by the call for an intellectual history of archaeology that was made by Arnaldo Momigliano in 1950, the French archaeologist of the Ancient Greek Civilisation, Alain Schnapp, reviewed the genealogies of *historia* and *archaiologia* during the 1990s. Schnapp aimed at gauging the chronological depth and geographical spread of the activities, which the ancient Greeks had perceived as the 'discourse on ancient things' by men whom the ancient Romans had referred to as Antiquitates or Antiquarius,[38] and he has affirmed that:

> Alongside ruler and princes there have always been antiquarians who endeav-oured, with varying success, to collect, interpret, and indeed appropriate the past. Each society, poor, simple, or underdeveloped as it might be needs to secure its contacts with the past. Difficult as it is to recover traces of antiquarian activities in prehistoric times, there is no reason to deny these societies such notions and uses of past. Leroi-Gourhan, for one, directed attention to what he called a 'collection of curiosities'—unusual fossils, exotic or rare stones—deposited in the post-Mousterian layers of the Grotte du Renne at Arcy-sur-cure [...] Whatever the status of these particular objects, such 'collections', have been noted by other pre-historians in different contexts. This leads us to propose that some curiosity for the unusual, the distant, the remote, might be characteristic of human societies in general and also that this fascination lies at the heart of what we call the taste for the past [...] This reflection on the origins of collections leads us to another implication: the gathering of ancient objects or traces is, in all probability, anterior to the beginnings of recorded history, in so far as the existence of literacy is not necessary (although admit-tedly useful) to the antiquarian enterprise.[39]

In making his bid for the need to engage with the long chronology of antiquarianism, from prehistory, Schnapp established distinctions between the representative practices and a disciplinary history. With respect to the

---

[38] Schnapp (1996).
[39] Schnapp (2002, p. 136).

latter, he abided by the views of the twentieth-century historians, such as Stuart Piggott, who were of the opinion that the move towards the disciplining of antiquarianism as a form of scholarship occurred within Europe owing to the re-discovery of the Graeco-Roman antiquities in the post-Reformation era of the sixteenth century. However, Schnapp's was a more careful exploration, compared to that of Piggott and others, of the intellectual shifts during the sixteenth century towards a disciplinary practice, and he found that 'the Renaissance saw the social transformation of the antiquarian', in that the antiquary became part of 'a veritable community of like-minded savants [...]'.[40] In documenting Western antiquarianism as only 'one facet of the consciousness of the past', Schnapp has presented substantive reasons for envisaging a universal history of antiquarianism, which he now historicises as 'the art of memory'.[41] His formative research of the classical antiquity of antiquarianism is of particular value in documenting the errors of receiving the phenomenon, to quote the introspective historian of archaeology Tim Murray, as 'a wrong turning on the pathway to archaeological enlightenment'.[42]

Yet, despite the rapid marches in the scholarship of antiquarianism and its myriad regional and chronological histories that are being made at present, the histories of antiquarian practices within South Asia remain tied to the European historiography.[43] The curious neglect of the pre-colonial antiquarian practices within the region cajoles a recall of Theoretical Archaeology which was raised as a subject in the 1970s by British and North American archaeologists for emphasising developments towards the academic maturity of academic archaeology. This is because the aforementioned archaeology, which was meant to represent the 'loss of disciplinary innocence',[44] remained fixedly Eurocentric in its historiographical orientations even while engaging with non-European pasts. Considering that archaeologists now strive at recording the 'richness of expression and variation of the human mind *through* the material world',[45] their overlook of the histories of historical enquiries within pre-colonial South Asia illustrates the penchant, which we

---

[40] Schnapp (2002, pp. 135–36).

[41] Schnapp (2013, p. 14).

[42] Murray (2007, p. 14) (DOI: http://dx.doi.org/10.5334/bha.17203); also Momigliano (1950).

[43] For histories of antiquarian practices in Ancient Egypt, China and Mesopotamia, see in particular Schnapp (2002, 2013).

[44] Clarke (1973, p. 6).

[45] Malafouris and Renfrew (2010, p. 2).

notice within Theoretical Archaeology, for disengaging with the unfamiliar and difficult traditions of historiography.

Sourcing Antiquarianism in India Before the British

The methodologies that prevailed within the 'ancient' period of South Asia for eliciting information from the physical remains of the past are not well understood. But we do know from commentarial and exegetical traditions in Sanskrit and Pali, and through the instances of copying and re-copying of old manuscripts that critical engagements with historical traditions had rather well-established conventions during the first millennium. More than three decades ago, Romila Thapar demonstrated the historicity of the changing nature of historical traditions and their changing uses and had stated:

> If [the] changing forms in the expression of historical consciousness symbolise historical change, and if changes in the political forms of society are reflected in the nature of historical expression, then the *itihasa-purana* tradition would point to three phases in the unfolding of early Indian history.[46]

In her most recent magnum opus, *The Past Before Us* (2013), Thapar has provided a detailed sketch of the changing forms of historical consciousness and history writing between 1000 BCE and 1300 CE, and the concomitant changes they have entailed in the subsequent translations, re-copying and discourses of particular texts for different audiences. She has aptly remarked that although 'few pre-modern "histories"' would meet contemporary requirements, 'that should not stop us from investigating how authors of that world understood their past, and more importantly, why they understood it the way they did'.[47] By historicising the historiographical traditions of more than a thousand years through various genres of texts that emerged at different points of time, such as the *dana stuti* hymns in the *Rig Veda*, the epics, *Mahabharata* and *Ramayana*, plays such as the *Mudraraksasa*, chronicles such as the *vamshavalis*, *Kavya* and *carita* literature, and the inscriptional

---

[46] Thapar (1986, p. 366).
[47] Thapar (2013, p. 683).

prasastis (royal eulogy), Thapar has shown the changing forms of historical enquiries in northern India over a millennium and has magnificently
summed up the 'past looking at its own past'.[48] We can add to her thesis by
noting the growing examples of inter-textuality within the genealogies of the
authoritative *carita* and *tarikh* literature in the subsequent second millennium,
which illustrate the increasing traditions of historiography within the Indian
subcontinent. Additionally, the Muslim rulers of India, as the noted historian
Muzaffar Alam has shown through texts such as the *Rauzat al-Tahirin*, also
contributed to the enrichment of the Islamic historiographical traditions
by appropriating the 'Hindu' traditions as part of human history.[49] Thus,
Abu'l Fazl, the author of *Ain-i-Akbari* and *Akbarnamah*, wished objective
translations of the *Mahabharata* in Persian as 'he wanted Muslims in general,
who believed that the world is only 7,000 years old, to know how old was
the history of the world and its people. He wanted kings who loved to listen
to histories to learn from experiences of the past'.[50] Considering the growing populist literature of the intolerance of the Muslim rulers towards their
Hindu subjects within India today, it is indeed worth noting that unlike their
Muslim predecessors the British failed to find any valuable traditions of the
'Hindu' historiography.

Irrespective of the British proclamations of gifting Hindustan with the
methods of historical enquiry, we note that in crafting his methods for the
study of comparative philology, William Jones had drawn upon the etymo-
logical methods, which he had found existing within Hindustan, and which
had been developed by Persian lexicographers and grammarians.[51] Among
them, the noted poet of Delhi, Siraj al-Din Ali Khan Arzu (1689–1756)
demonstrated affinities between the Persian, Arabic and Sanskrit languages,
and he was well aware of the novelty of his discovery. In searching for
the 'forgotten texts', such as of Arzu's, historian Mohammad Tavakoli-
Targhi has documented 'the traces of creativity and agency' of their works
upon the works of the pioneering orientalists for demonstrating that 'the
archives of unpublished Persian texts commissioned by the eighteenth- and

---

[48] Thapar (2013, p. 683).

[49] For examples of inter-textuality, see Chatterjee (2009); Alam (2004, p. 67). For noting
different traditions within the Persian treatises, see the discussion by Alam on the distinctions
between the *adab* and *akhlaqi* literature (ibid., pp. 12–13).

[50] Alam (2004, p. 67).

[51] For references of connections among the Indo-European languages, and with Sanskrit,
which had been observed before Jones, see Campbell (2006, p. 246).

nineteenth-century British orientalists reveal the underside of Orientalism', wherein the latter had produced books that closely resembled the Persian works they had collected.[52] Tavakoli-Targhi's research prompts us to ask a similar question that has been asked in the context of 'colonial philology', namely how did the field explorers 'encounter the highly developed literary cultures of South Asia?'[53] The answer demands a search for the imprints of the methods of historical enquiry that existed in the Indian subcontinent within the field methods that were adopted and developed by the British and European explorers from the late eighteenth century during their searches for the histories of India. Philip Wagoner's research of the nascent Madras school of epigraphy provides a few promising clues.[54]

Wagoner has demonstrated that the Niyogi Brahmins, who aided Colin Mackenzie in his statistical surveys of the Mysore State in 1800, had developed 'the graphological ability to identify the author of a given document simply on the basis of its handwriting'.[55] Mackenzie had launched his career as a surveyor following the British defeat of the ruler of Mysore, Tipu Sultan (1750–99), and had explored the latter's annexed territories between 1800 and 1810 for 'providing statistical account that could contribute directly to the successful administration of the new provinces'.[56] To meet his aims, he had recruited members from the community of Niyogi Brahmins who had worked for the former Arcot bureaucracy. The Brahmins, as Wagoner has documented, were aware 'of the chronological implications of recurrent stylistic formulae and other distinctive lexical usages'. They could, thereby, 'actively contribute to the production of new epigraphic knowledge and, more fundamentally, even to the definition of epigraphy itself as a method of historical enquiry'.[57] Hence, Mackenzie had valued their distinctive knowledge and skills, and distinguished his Niyogi assistants as munshis (writers), mutasaddis (accountants) and gumashtas (administrative assistants).

Yet Mackenzie too, like all company men, created the rationality of his own theories by dismissing the views of the 'natives' and their methods of

---

[52] Tavakoli-Targhi (2004, pp. 141–42). On Arzu see also Alam (2003).

[53] Mantena (2005, p. 518). In her subsequent monograph, Mantena has documented some of the ways in which the creations of colonial archives establised the 'Indian practices of history and created the conditions for the ascendance of the positivist historiography of nineteenth-century India' (2012, p. 2).

[54] Wagoner (2003).

[55] Ibid., p. 800

[56] Ibid., p. 789.

[57] Ibid., pp. 802 and 810.

enquiries. On asking the resident Brahmins the meaning of the carvings on the external facade of the 'Pagoda at Perwuttum'—a temple dedicated to Mallikarjuna on the river Krishna, which he saw in 1799 and inside whose main shrine he was not allowed—he was told that 'it was to show how the Gods lived above', and to which he had quipped, 'but indeed, they seem to have lost all traces of any knowledge they may have formerly possessed and have sunk into the profoundest state of ignorance'.[58]

The reply of the Brahmins and the dismissal by Mackenzie illustrate the histories of unequal encounters, which fashioned the measure of 'valid' evidence. Mackenzie's enquiry regarding the age of the temple was governed by his belief that the building was older than the multi-armed sculptures he could see upon the exterior, as they held no matchlock amongst the vast array of weaponry in their innumerable hands.[59] For him, the value of the temple lay in its agency as a historical source, which clearly held no sympathy with the Brahmins for whom the temple constituted the present, alive with the presence of their god. The differential cognition of the natives and the British regarding the constitution of historical objects and topographies informed the colonial historiography in which the British saw and the natives were always shown as 'seeing things', that is, prone to fanciful imaginings.[60] The above example reiterates the linkages between the British practices of visualisation and their rationale for field knowledge of India's past.

Histories Through Things in India's Pre-Colonial Pasts

Antiquarian pursuits entailed the collection, sourcing and scholarship of objects, including manuscripts, for configuring and memorialising the past.[61]

---

[58] Mackenzie (1799, p. 314).

[59] Mackenzie had reported: 'I could get no information on this head; but I suspect the building to be of higher antiquity than the knowledge, or, at least, than the use of gunpowder among these people because among so great a variety of arms as are sculptured among the walls, swords, bows, pikes, arrows, and shields of a round figure, the matchlock is not to be found, though a weapon so much in use among the poligars' (ibid.).

[60] Term borrowed from Schaffer (2010).

[61] For details, see Schnapp (2013).

Therefore, we can suggest that the uses of historical objects and topographies within pre-colonial India for creating histories and recalling and using a specific aspect of the past can also be understood as examples of antiquarian pursuits. They were no doubt different methods, and bespoke of different kinds of historical transactions from those that were established subsequently within the parameters of the scholarship of antiquarianism.

The best-known historical objects that were variously consumed throughout the first and second millennia for invoking aspects of the past are the Rock and Pillar Edicts of the Mauryan Emperor Asoka. Through her study of the Mauryan Empire, Romila Thapar had formally drawn attention to their valuation as creators of historical memories within Ancient India, and had asserted that they 'came to be treated as a kind of historical palimpsest'.[62] In following Thapar's note, we take notice of the earliest known instance of the consumption of such objects for recalling histories—and, thus, of a possible expression of the antiquarian practice—in the re-uses of the Rock Edict at Girnar near Junagadh (Gujarat).

Apart from carrying the edict of Asoka, the Girnar rock bears the *prasasti* of Mahakshatrapa Rudradaman, which dates from ca. 150 CE, and an inscription of the Gupta King Skandagupta (r.c. 455 CE).[63] The inscriptions of Rudradaman and Skandagupta mention the dam that was built across the nearby lake Sudarsana by Pushyagupta, a provincial governor of the first Mauryan ruler Chandragupta (r.c. 340–298 BCE), who was Asoka's grandfather. The lake was important for agriculture throughout history, and the *Skanda Purana* alludes to the sacrality of the surrounding Girnar hills for the Brahmins and Jains. The location of the Asokan inscription certainly indicates the economic importance of this region in the Mauryan period, and we note that Harry Falk, who has undertaken an extensive field survey of all 'Asokan' artefacts, has visualised that 'as long as the Sudarsana lake was there, the way to the Girnar mountain had to bypass the rock edict'.[64] The shape of the rock, which is similar to the back of an elephant, would have facilitated the ease of inscribing upon it, and its location, no doubt, created its potential value as a public artefact. Rudradaman's commemorative *prasasti*

---

[62] Thapar (1973, p. 281).

[63] For details, see Hultzch (1925, pp. ix–x); Kielhorn (1905–06, pp. 36–49); Fleet (1888, pp. 56–65).

[64] Falk (2006, p. 120); for the historical topography of Girnar and Sudarsana, see Thapar (1961, pp. 230–31).

is also unique as there are no other inscriptions of the king. Its inscription on the 'Asokan rock' proves that the latter commanded considerable historical memory during the first century for the Mahakshatrapa to have selected it as the only material for documenting his resplendence as a powerful ruler. In inscribing upon this rock, Rudradaman would have tried to secure the historical value of his rule through a memorial object. Additionally, the models of Asokan pillars that were created during the Gupta period (ca. 3rd–5th CE) at Sanchi, Bhitari and Latiya for serving as *Kirti stambha* and *Dhvaja stambha* add to the above example of the use of memorial objects for history-making projects. They inform us of the 'recognition of the form as an imperial symbol', and in this, as the art historian Joanna Williams had emphasised, they merit 'exceptional discussion'.[65]

By the thirteenth century the Asokan pillars came to be known as, to use the adjective of Finbarr Flood, 'trans-cultural objects'.[66] The one at Allahabad may have been carted from Kausambi during the reign of the Mughal Emperor Akbar (1556–1605) when a fort was built near the present city, although the histories of the travels of this pillar are not clear.[67] The pillar bears upon the surface the following inscriptions: Pillar Edicts I to VI, Schism Edict and Queen's Edict, the *prasasti* of the Gupta Emperor Samudragupta (r. 335–75 CE), graffiti dating from the reign of the Tughlaq ruler Firoz Shah (r. 1351–88), an inscription recording a visit to Akbarabad (the name of the fort) by Raja Birbal, one of Akbar's trusted ministers, and an inscription by Jahangir, Akbar's son and successor, recording his genealogy. Jahangir (1569–1627) resided in the city from 1600 after his revolt against his father and until the latter's death in 1605, when at his accession to the Mughal throne (r. 1569–1627), he may have caused the 'Allahabad Pillar' to be re-erected with the inscription that records his lineage. Of this pillar Thapar had suggested that:

> There must have been some perception of the pillar incorporating the past that it comes to be treated as an agency of legitimizing the present. If this legitimation had arisen out of its being regarded solely as an axis mundi or a

---

[65] Williams (1982, pp. 96–97).

[66] Flood (2003).

[67] For more information on the history of transcription and travels of the pillar, see Bhandarkar (1981, p. 204).

lingam then it would have been venerated but would not have carried further inscriptions on its body.[68]

Precisely at what period the Asokan pillars also acquired the memory of Alexander, the Macedonian king, who had ventured into the Punjab during 324 BCE, is not known. However, on seeing the object during his travels within India between 1608 and 1611 the English traveller William Finch had stated that 'the Indians seem to think that this was placed by Alexander or some other great conqueror unable to cross the Ganges'.[69]

In noting the re-uses of the Asokan pillars during the second millennium, historians have suggested that Firoz Shah Tughluq had specifically used two, from Topra and Meerut, as markers of the boundary of his new capital Firozabad for obtaining 'dual-edged legitimacy' from Asoka and Alexander, 'which he needed to cover for his lack of expansionist policy' as a ruler.[70] A few Brahmins in Firoz Shah's realm then proclaimed their inability of reading the inscription. The script, in Brahmi, was successfully deciphered during the 1830s by Prinsep, and the instance of the decipherment remains the historical moment when the 'Asokan objects' came to represent British triumph at their successful retrieval from obscurity, a seminal Emperor of Ancient India.

The life histories of the Asokan artefacts within pre-colonial India inform of creations of historical memories and encourage us to delve into the histories of seeing. And in this, they inevitably draw our attention to the rich histories of visualisation that dominated the cultural realms of the Mughal Empire and enlighten us of the histories of cultural connections within the Eurasian world at the height of the Mughal power in India during the seventeenth century.[71] In recalling the Mughal rule, we also bear in mind that the amassing of old manuscripts, paintings, curiosities and objects of art by the Emperors and their nobility was contemporary in time to similar practices of the antiquaries in the West, and they all bespoke of the scholarly value of connoisseurship within the politics of imperial self-fashioning. Additionally,

[68] Thapar (1973, p. 281).

[69] Falk (2006, p. 161).

[70] Asher and Talbot (2006, p. 44).

[71] For a comprehensive summary of the connected histories of Mughal and European artistic traditions, see Koch, (2004, pp. 152–67).

despite the different intellectual genealogies of viewing, collecting, copying and connoisseurship within the Mughal realm and the contemporary worlds of Britain and Europe, the descriptions of monuments and artefacts in the former effectively matched the nature of descriptions that were considered mandatory by the antiquaries in the West for documenting the incorruptibility of material sources. An example is Emperor Jahangir's description of the Jami Masjid in Ahmedabad, which he saw on his eleventh regnal year, on 6 January 1617, and which he recorded in his *Jahangirnama* as:

> This mosque is a monument left by Sultan Ahmad, the founder of the city of Ahmedabad. It has three gates, and on every side a market. Opposite the gate facing the east is Sultan Ahmad's tomb. Under the dome lie Sultan Ahmad, his son Muhammad, and his grandson Qutbuddin. The length of the mosque courtyard exclusive of the *maqsura* is 103 cubits; the width is 89 cubits. Around the perimeter of the courtyard is an arcade with arches four and three-quarters cubits wide. The courtyard is paved in cut brick, and the pillars of the arcade are of red stone. The maqsura contains 354 columns, and above the column is a dome. The length of the maqsura is 75 cubits, and the width is 37 cubits. The maqsura paving, the mihrab, and the pulpit are of marble.[72]

The above description would illustrate Schnapp's contention that 'in widely differing circumstances, and given similar assemblages, antiquaries may produce similar statements'.[73] But the note of Jahangir has an added significance for evaluating the origin stories of antiquarianism within South Asia. For, it undermines statements, such as by Cunningham's latest biographer that 'the earliest notices and descriptions of Indian monuments, architecture and sculpture are to be found in the writings of the sixteenth- and seventeenth-century European travellers'.[74] It provokes us to reconsider the following two premises, which are inherent within all histories of South Asian archaeology, namely (a) that the European viewing of India led to the

---

[72] Thackston (1999, pp. 244–45).

[73] Schnapp (1996, p. 319).

[74] Singh (2004, p. 6). She has premised the history of antiquarianism in India as heralded by 'western' views of the land, and through the understanding that 'it is quite wrong to assume that indigenous, pre-colonial understandings of the ancient Indian past did not exist, or that Indians had developed a complete and collective amnesia about their history. At the same time there is no doubt that colonialism introduced a new Western conceptual and analytical apparatus to the investigation of India's past' (ibid., p. xviii).

recording of the historical topographies within the region, and (b) that this viewing initiated the historical enquiries into the antiquities of the land.

Jahangir's engagements with antiquities would, in 'Western terms', establish his status an antiquary. Those who were his contemporaries in Britain were influenced by the practices of the English philosopher, and antiquary, Francis Bacon (1561–1626), who was of the opinion that:

> antiquities, or remnants of history, are when industrious persons, by an exact and scrupulous diligence and observations, out of monuments, names, words, proverbs, traditions, private records and evidences, fragments of stories, passages of books, that concern not story, and the like, preserve and recover somewhat from the deluge of time.[75]

We can trace the kinds of methodologies of observation, classification and experimentation, which Bacon adopted, within Mughal India from periods prior to Jehangir. However, we can also be certain that within the traditions of the European historiography of antiquarianism in which Bacon presides, Jahangir would expectantly fail to make an appearance.

In thinking through the above omission, it is worth recalling the scholarship of the Arab philosophers and historians, such as Ibn Khaldun (1332–1406) and especially his *Muqaddimah*, which is a fourteenth-century treatise on the science of history, historical logic and notions of rationality. This text sought to distinguish between existence and essences and between laws of causes and effect and emphasised the rules and patterns of history.[76] Ibn Khaldun's scholarship and his historical methods, which are well-researched, bespoke of the non-European histories of sciences during the fourteenth century, that too built upon observation and notions of objectivity and rationality, and which included historical, ethnographical and antiquarian enquiries. Such histories inform us of the different representations of 'renaissances' within the non-European worlds.[77] So, although it would be an anomaly to locate within pre-colonial India the kinds of rationality and objectivity that brokered the methods of antiquarian pursuits within post-renaissance Europe, to overlook within this vast domain the various ways in which artefacts and topographies of the past were historicised with historical values and committed to historical memory would be to miss the historical realities.

---

[75] F. Bacon, *De Augmentia Scientiae*, II c. 6, quoted in Sweet (2004, p. 8).

[76] For a view of Ibn Khaldun's scholarship, see Fromherz (2010, pp. 115–22).

[77] For more information on the the possibilities of many renaissances, see Goody (2009).

Antiquarian Practices Following the Enlightenment of Britain

Within Europe, attempts were quite specifically made from the eighteenth century to formalise the scholarship of antiquities and historical topographies into distinct practices. In Britain, the antiquaries and dilettanti aimed at distinguishing their scholarship by establishing exclusive learned societies. Thus, the Society of Antiquaries in London was re-formulated in December 1707,[78] and this was followed by the creation of the Society of Dilettanti in London in 1732. The distinction in practices, which the two societies attempted at demonstrating, bore upon differential evaluations of universal and local histories.[79] The antiquaries perceived themselves foremost as historians of local terrains, and although they did not exclude the study of Egyptian, Greek and Roman antiquities from the remit of their enquiries, they disengaged themselves rather consciously from the dilettante quests for *virtú*, or connoisseurship.[80] Therefore, in his *Itinerarium Curiosum* (published in 1724), the Anglican clergyman William Stukeley (1687–1785), who was nominated the first Secretary of the Society of Antiquaries in 1717, presented himself as 'adept', or expert, in local history, as he knew that the description would be an anathema to his contemporary dilettante. In defending the subject of his study, namely to 'oblige the curious in the antiquities of Britain' which he undertook through 18 *Iters*, Stukeley scathingly remarked:

> We export yearly our own treasures into foreign parts, by the genteel and fashionable *tours* of France and Italy, and import shiploads of books relating to their antiquities and history (it is well if we bring back nothing worse) whilst our own country lies like a neglected province [...] It was ever my opinion that a more intimate knowledge of Britain more becomes us, is more useful and as worthy a part of education of our young nobility and gentry as the view of any transmarine part.[81]

Stukeley's remark makes it amply clear that we cannot expect the self-reference as an antiquary from men who worked for the East India Company during

---

[78] The original Society of Antiquaries was dissolved by James I (r. 1603–1625), and the new Society received its royal charter in 1751.

[79] For more information on aspects of distinction, see Hill (2010, pp. 26–27).

[80] Sweet (2004, p. 93).

[81] Stukeley (1776, pp. 1–3).

the early eighteenth century, such as Pyke, who surveyed and studied the historical topographies of the foreign lands they came to work in. However, his remark also shows us that the British antiquaries fostered the politics and intellectualisation of nationalism through their scholarship of local histories. Therefore, with respect to studies of historiographies, the significance of 'the antiquarian cast of mind' of men, such as Pyke, and other East Indiamen who worked and explored in the Orient,[82] lies in the uses of their scholarship and discoveries within eighteenth- and nineteenth-century Britain for enhancing pride in the achievements of the British nation, and the merits of the British Empire. By the close of the eighteenth century British antiquaries had formalised the dissemination of their research through the specialist journal *Archaeologia*, which was founded in 1770. The excerpt below of the 'opening' of a 'barrow' on Sanford Moor by William Preston, which was published within the journal, provides an example of the emphasis that they had begun to place upon systematic excavations as a mark of their unique practice. Preston had excavated the barrow in 1766 and had recorded:

> The labourers began by driving a level [...] At length one of them digging on the top of the barrow downwards, turned up, within half a yard from the surface, a piece of an urn [...] On one side of it, but somewhat lower, lay a broad two-edged sword, broken in two, the whole blade measuring in length better than two feet, and two inches and a half broad; the head curiously wrought. On the other side lay the head of a spear [...] About a yard below these the workmen came to an orbicular pile of stones [...] On removing this pile, they came to a fine black mould, about three inches deep, covering a square of about two yards, AND LYING AS NEAR AS THEY could guess under the place where the sword etc. were deposited. Here they found only some burnt bones. Under the whole lay a bed of gravel.[83]

The above quotation reveals the regard for recording different soil strata and artefacts *in situ*. It is a noticeable example of the measures that were adopted by the antiquaries towards exactitude in recording practices before Charles Lyell formulated the laws of superposition, in his three-volume *Principles of Geology*, which appeared between 1831 and 1833. Preston's account of his excavation thus refutes the assumptions that are conveyed within the

---

[82] The terminology is from Sweet (2004, p. 349), who has used the phrase for situating the practices of the British antiquaries of the eighteenth century within the contemporary political, social and intellectual milieu of Britain.

[83] Preston (1775).

histories of South Asian archaeology—that the method of minding the undertaking of excavations relate to the 'discovery' of stratigraphy by Lyell and contemporary geologists and palaeontologists, and that the foremost systematic excavations were undertaken in 1784 by Thomas Jefferson, future president of the United States (1801–09), in his property at Virginia, when he excavated a native Indian burial mound.[84] Preston's account is one among other examples in this book, which demonstrates why the fixations with histories of starting points obfuscate, instead of illuminating, histories of formation processes.[85]

By the early nineteenth century, the antiquarian scholarship within Britain had developed strong intellectual roots, and the valuations of the antiquaries regarding the scope and remit of their unique practices can be gauged from an incidence during the first meeting of the British Archaeological Association that was held at Canterbury in September 1844. A reporter from *Athenaeum* who was present at the occasion had ostensibly 'shown his utter want of perceptions of the objects of the Association', and had unfortunately expressed the view that the antiquaries were mainly concerned with the study of architectural details. Expectantly, he was reprimanded by one of the secretaries of the Association, Charles Roach Smith, who had retorted that the journalist's view bespoke of a situation 'like studying the drapery and dress and forgetting the man; or minutely criticising the form and the character of the masonry and buildings, and neglecting the people those buildings were erected to shelter'. In chastising the journalist, Smith also quoted the remarks of another antiquary, Alfred John Dunkin (1812–79), from the latter's report of the proceedings in the *Transactions* that 'the true antiquary does not confine his researches to one single branch of archaeology but in a comprehensive view surveys every fact and aims to bring in every object to serve the great end and purpose of a knowledge of man and his habits and customs in past ages'.[86]

In dismissing the views of the reporter for *Athenaeum*, Charles Smith had illustrated a self-assured scholarship that was aware of the strengths of

---

[84] Singh (2004, p. 339); Ray (2008, p. 5).

[85] Drawing attention to the careful stratigraphical excavations of Olof Rudbeck of a tumulus at Uppsala (Sweden) during the latter half of the seventeenth century, Schnapp has suggested that the idea was not invented by the Scandinavian antiquaries but can be also found among the contemporary Roman antiquaries; see Schnapp (1996, p. 201).

[86] Smith (1883, p. 12). See also Dunkins (1844).

its methods and its significant contributions towards the cultural histories of Britain. However, the incident also illustrates the ambivalence regarding the intellectual depth of the scholarship of many antiquaries, which persisted throughout the nineteenth century in Britain.

From the seventeenth century well until the Victorian Age, antiquaries were often caricatured by those who styled themselves as historians as parochial pedants obsessed with trivia and the minutiae of local history. Their scholarship and methodologies were contrasted unfavourably with the 'gentlemanly learning' of those who sought to study not coins and medals, but objects of artistic merit and aesthetic beauty and who wrote grand histories of statesmen and nations.[87] The caricature, which to a large extent bespoke of contemporary class hierarchies in Britain, imbues the representations of the antiquaries and their scholarship within the post-colonial histories of South Asian archaeology. In noting the manner in which the antiquaries are unfavourably compared with the archaeologists, and their scholarship marginalised within the histories of Indian archaeology, we see the rootedness of the nineteenth-century British historical scholarship within today's archaeological scholarship of South Asia.

Historians of South Asian archaeology historicise, or perhaps one should say dismiss, antiquarian scholarship as an amateur expression of the technologically and intellectually superior scientific archaeological pursuit. They deem the antiquaries as undiscerning eclectic and recall Cunningham as the 'first full time archaeologist of India' standing 'at the end of an important phase, to a period when archaeology in India ceased to be the exclusive and part-time preserve of surveyors, antiquarians, dilletantes [sic] and treasure hunters'.[88] The above characterisation of Cunningham, which aims at rescuing him from the classification of an antiquary, is built upon the understanding that he was the 'father of Indian archaeology'.[89] However, such acts of rescue fail to place Cunningham within the milieu of Victorian Britain to which he belonged, where even as late as 1899 archaeologists and antiquaries were grouped as a class, and to which the new 'Egyptologists' were then being added.[90]

During the first half of the nineteenth century, which spans Cunningham's formative military and archaeological careers in north India, the antiquaries

---

[87] Sweet (2004, p. 8). See also Piggott (1989, pp. 14–20).
[88] Singh (2004, p. 22).
[89] Roy (1953, p. 17).
[90] For example, in the 'who's who of Victorian Britain', in Plarr (1899, p. 1231).

in Britain formed a large and visible group. They had an enormous range of interests and absorbed many kinds of 'fringe' groups who studied the past. Additionally, the intent of the antiquarian scholarship coalesced institutionally and individually with that of archaeology. In fact, more than three decades back, Philippa Levine had shown that the failure to distinguish 'between antiquarianism and archaeology' even during the late nineteenth century 'neither aided the community's sense of unity nor made clear the significance of the break between textual and material analysis'.[91] Following Levine's study, cultural historians of antiquarianism now insist that the intellectual phenomenon 'should be never equated with fieldwork and development of archaeology', as this obfuscates insights into 'what the antiquaries hoped to discover or how their excavations related to other branches of inquiry'.[92] We also note that the archaeological approach which the antiquarian scholarship comprised was aptly summarised by Charles Newton, Yates Professor of Classical Archaeology at University College London (1880–88) in an essay he had written in 1851 'On the Study of Archaeology'. Newton had published the article when he worked at the British Museum, and his statements illustrate the importance of attending to Levine's views. He had remarked that:

> he who would master the manifold subject-matter of Archaeology, and appreciate its whole range and compass, must possess a mind in which the reflective and perceptive faculties are duly balanced; he must combine with the aesthetic culture of the Artist, and the trained judgement of the Historian, not a little learning of the Philologer; the plodding drudgery which gathers together his materials must not blunt the critical acuteness required for their classification and interpretation.[93]

It is unlikely that Cunningham knew of Newton, who was his contemporary. Yet, his pursuits, which included transcriptions and interpretations of coin legends and inscriptions, draftsmanship, and field explorations and excavations, substantiate Newton's views regarding the nature of archaeological practices. Significantly, Newton's remark conformed to the methods and enquiries of his contemporary, Charles Smith. Therefore, the characterisation of Cunningham and his 'era' as epitomising progress from antiquarianism to

---

[91] Levine (1986, pp. 88 and 93).
[92] Sweet (2004, p. 346).
[93] Newton (1851, pp. 25–26); also quoted in Levine (1986, p. 87).

archaeology, which his historians commit to, establishes an epistemological disjuncture that is historically non-existent.[94]

Back to Cunningham's 'Introduction': Querying the Pioneer

In undertaking archaeological explorations of northern India by following the trails of the Buddha and Alexander, Cunningham no doubt was a pioneer. However, among the enterprises that are also historicised as representing his pioneering contributions is the 'idea of a government-sponsored archaeology', which is located by his historians in his proposal to the Government of India in 1861, to commit to the undertaking of archaeological duties.[95] Yet, the history of Cunningham's historic proposal reveals the self-serving nature of his archaeological scholarship, which detracts from the merits of a pioneering leadership.

We can trace Cunningham's conceptions of the aformentioned proposal in a letter he had written in 1845 to Horace Wilson, then Boden Professor of Sanskrit at Oxford (1832–60). He had explicitly stated his hopes within the letter 'to be employed in making a general [archaeological] survey like that which [Francis] Buchanan [had] made of the Bahar districts'. The timing of Cunningham's letter to Wilson is instructive, as the latter had been elected to the 'Central Committee of the Archaeological Institute' that year, and Cunningham, who had been openly critical of Wilson's translation of the *Vishnu Purana* (1840), now hoped at eliciting his support. The following paragraph from the letter creates a view of Cunningham's ambition. He had stated that:

> I have been very much disappointed with the manner in which the Indian government has followed up the Court's instructions about the preservation and publication of the ancient monuments of India. I expected that a small party of well-qualified officers would have been selected for that duty—and they would have been chosen partly for their artistical abilities, and partly for Oriental knowledge and taste for antiquity. [...] Instead of this, the local govt.

[94] For example, see Singh (2004, p. 22).
[95] Ibid., p. 59; see Cunningham (1871, pp. iii–viii).

have contended themselves with calling upon all officers to furnish drawings and measurements of caves and cave temples at their own expense—a few may be thus obtained from officers who are fond of antiquarian pursuits, and at the same time possess the power of faithfully delineating architectural antiquity. I am making a very fair collection of materials towards a paper upon Gwalior; antiquarian and historical but with other duties to perform the progress is but slow, in fact after very long interruption I find that I am obliged to reread newly the whole of the authorities over again. I should like myself to be employed in making a general survey like that which Buchanan made of the Bahar districts—and I should not mind adding a topographical survey to my labours also, so as to make my work complete.[96]

Despite Cunningham's efforts, the Government of India appointed Markham Kittoe as Archaeological Enquirer of Northwest India (1847–53). However, Cunningham persisted in his aims and submitted a proposal for the archaeological explorations of the Buddhist sites in northern India to the Company directors in 1848, the year after Kittoe's appointment.[97] He was successful in his cause only after the establishment of the Raj and the death of his opponent Wilson (in 1860), when at his behest in 1861, the Governor General, Lord Canning, unambiguously 'entrusted' the archaeological investigations of India to him.[98] Yet, unlike retrospective perceptions of this act as representing Cunningham's initiatives in ascertaining that archaeological practices could be 'tamed, controlled and bureaucratised',[99] Canning had emphasised that the office of the surveyor was sanctioned upon the 'understanding that it continue during the present and following cold season, by which time a fair judgement of its utility and interest may be formed'.[100] The government created an official position for Cunningham as archaeological surveyor, and the latter demonstrated the importance of his own yearly archaeological explorations between 1862 and 1864, which were published in the *Journal of the Royal Asiatic Society of Bengal* between 1863 and 1865. The breadth of his explorations of Upper India, and the richness of his finds, established Cunningham's credentials in archaeological work, and when the government

---

[96] Letter from Cunningham to Wilson, dated 6 December 1845, MSS EUR/E 301/9, Wilson Papers.

[97] Cunningham (1848b).

[98] 'Minute by the Right Hon'ble the Governor General of India in Council on the Antiquities of Upper India—dated 22 January 1862', in Cunningham (1871a, p. ii).

[99] Singh (2004, 22); see also Ray (2004, p. 14).

[100] Canning in Cunningham (1871a, p. iii).

instituted the Archaeological Survey of India in 1871, at his and others' behest, he was appointed the director-general (1871–85). However, the personal nature of Cunningham's archaeological scholarship is apparent in his request to the Government of India to disband the institution of the Survey on his departure from India in 1885. After fulfilling his own archaeological feats, Cunningham, clearly, saw no purpose in retaining the Survey.

In reflecting upon the manner in which Cunningham established his pioneering status within the archaeological scholarship of India, we are drawn towards the shifting understanding of the histories of archaeologies in the twenty-first century. Possibly, following Schnapp's distinction between the myriad forms of antiquarian practices and the antiquarianism that developed within western Europe from the seventeenth century, archaeologists now make efforts at distinguishing the possibilities of myriad forms of archaeo-logical practices from the formal scholarship of archaeology that emerged during the late nineteenth century. Thus, they consider the excavations that were undertaken by the monks at the cemetery of the Glastonbury Cathedral (England) in ca. 1194 CE, 'between [the] two stone pyramids', as one of the earliest examples of archaeological work in Britain. It is to be noted that the excavations were aimed at finding the burial place of the legendary King Arthur.[101] This new understanding that excavations for myths and legends in the 'pre-modern' world can be considered constitutive of archaeological practices tempts a search for the traces of archaeological excavations within pre-colonial South Asia. However, the growing jingoistic nationalism within the region, which shows an increasing tendency to historicise all kinds of sciences as indigenous, also creates reasons for maintaining a careful academic distance from rooting the origin stories of the archaeology of India in such searches.

Yet, the possibilities of tracing practices that are akin to archaeology before the latter was even defined add to reasons for interrogating the histories of origins that facilitate the creations of pioneering statuses. In this respect, we are reminded of the remark with which the members of the Delhi Municipal Committee feted a departing viceroy of India, Curzon. They had stated:

> It would not be too much to say that your Excellency has bridged over the 500 years since the time of the Emperor Feroz Shah Tughlak, who was what would be called in modern parlance as Delhi's first great archaeologist.

---

[101] Briggs (2011, p. 12).

Curzon remains the principal architect of the archaeological restorations of historical India which, as has been mentioned in the Introduction Chapter, he facilitated through the restitution of the Archaeological Survey of India in 1902. The remark, however, provides a glimpse of the manner in which new practices are often endowed with an ancestry so that they can be placed within a historical context. It adds to reason for new enquiries into the antiquity of archaeological practices.

Indian Histories within World Archaeology

The close of the twentieth century saw many grand narratives of world archaeology, which document an assured archaeological scholarship confident of its academic and pedagogical value. The historians of such histories have usually mined into the histories of South Asian archaeology that have echoed Cunningham's narrative of the historical scholarship of India. Thus, even the second edition of *A History of Archaeological Thought* (2006), which is a well-researched textbook, perpetuates the colonial historiography in the understanding that:

> Systematic antiquarianism did not develop in India prior to the colonial period. Despite impressive intellectual achievements in other fields, Indian scholarship did not devote much attention to political history, perhaps because the Hindu religion and division of socio-regulatory forces between high priests and warriors directed efforts to understanding the meaning of life and of historical events more towards cosmology.[102]

The book was authored by Bruce Trigger, one of the leading historians of archaeology in the twentieth century (1937–2006), and his cultural histories of West Asia also echo the above essentialisms. Thus, Trigger attributed the 'failure of antiquarianism to develop' in the Near East to the Arab World's 'rejection of pagan pre-Islamic civilisations and their works, to a tendency to view many features of Islamic history as cyclical, and to a religiously based disdain for works or art'.[103] In using as references histories that promoted the

---

[102] Trigger (2006, p. 77). Trigger's sources were Chakrabarti (1988) and Pande (1985).
[103] Trigger, ibid.

understanding that the ancient societies of Asia were intellectually negligent of their pasts, Trigger exhibited his own negligence of sourcing informed and critical histories of the region that were also then being written. The example draws our attention quite specifically to the growing intellectual distance during the late twentieth century between the academic study of archaeology and history.

The first edition of Trigger's book dates from the time when astute historians of Ancient India were questioning histories of civilisational essences and also the erroneous notion that early India knew only cyclical time.[104] Yet the cultural fact that Trigger sought to highlight was that 'India and the Arab world indicate highly particularistic factors that must be taken into account in explaining the origins of archaeological research, or its failure to develop, in any specific culture'.[105] Trigger's overlook of the new historiographical orientations within the scholarship of Ancient India illuminates the reticence of many archaeologists to marshall bibliographic references outside the specialist archaeological literature. Additionally, the choice highlights the disinclination to explore issues of historiography of an unfamiliar domain. Thus, we are led to notice that as a student and specialist of North American archaeology, Trigger was deeply critical of Systems Theory, which he complained had wrested the 'culture [of the indigenous North Americans] out of its historical context and employed it in the interests of the Western Academe in order to make general statements'.[106] He had therefore demolished the Processualist approach towards the study of the Native American people in a very coherent and precise manner. Yet, in the case of the early histories of South Asia, he ignored the fundamentalism of positivism within the histories he selected as references. The selections illustrate his remarkable penchant for ignoring the histories of Ancient India, which might have looked unfamiliar to him as an archaeologist. Unwittingly, perhaps, he narrated an archaeological history of India for the 'Western academe in order to make general statements'.

Such overlooks of alien historiographical traditions within the archaeological literature simply document a known fact, namely that 'knowledge production is one of the major sites in which imperialism operates and

---

[104] For example, Thapar (1996).
[105] Trigger (2006, p. 77).
[106] Hodder (2003, p. 139); see also Trigger (1984).

exercises its power'.[107] The unequal representations of authorial voices can be sourced even within today's politically correct scholarship of intellectual histories. An example is the persistence of the European scholars to dwell upon the influences of Aristotle in the writings of Ibn Khaldun. Mohammad Salama has drawn attention to this fact, and in presenting the reasons has made the apt, if uncompromising, remark that:

> the main theoretical difficulty inherent in historicising intellectual history is the delimitation of borderlines that circumscribe the so-called European field of historiography by setting it apart from the different and familiar. [...] a close examination of European treatment of these Arab-Muslim texts evidences an unwillingness to understand the relevant texts in a way that would result in their acknowledged inclusion in (European) intellectual history. We should treat the aforementioned shortcoming [...] as symptoms of a deeper epistemic essentialism instead of dismissing them as isolated cases of biased intellectualization.[108]

The grand histories of world archaeology, such as of Trigger's perpetuate, to borrow a sentence of the historian B.D. Chattopadhyaya, 'congealed stereotypes', wherein cultural characteristics are drawn from 'essentially one source, namely, the colonial premise and their adaptations'.[109] Such histories inevitably echo the imperialist European representations of the Asiatic civilisations, in which the 'Hindus', supposedly immersed in spirituality, cosmology and myths, were historicised as careless and ignorant of the scientific scholarship of history that thrived within the ostensibly modern, rational and enlightened Europe. Additionally, such histories encourage a critique of the methodologies of classifications, which the archaeological scholarship builds upon. Since archaeological cultures are identified through particularistic traits of disparate material assemblages, we can perhaps suggest that this method prevents archaeologists from seeing their creations of essentialisms when they map cultural characteristics in the real world.

In following Schnapp and exploring the deep antiquity of antiquarian activities across the globe, we will invariably seek vernacular expressions of antiquarian pursuits. The challenge in presenting the regional histories of antiquarian pursuits would then be to ward off representations of

---

[107] Chen (2010, p. 211).
[108] Salama (2011, p. 99).
[109] Chattopadhyaya (2003, p. 272).

cultural essentialisms, such as those that prevail within the world histories of archaeology; although as this chapter has endeavoured to show, we can control the invasions of trait lists and conflicting historiographies within our historical methods if we attend to the issues of historiography. The vernacular expressions of antiquarian practices will not only accost us with the myriad methods of enquiries that were initiated through 'old objects' and historical landscapes in the past but also the myriad intents within the undertaking. In this respect, the move towards negotiating the universal history of antiquarianism holds a specific significance for the intellectual histories of Ancient India. Because it is only by intellectually committing to the understanding that historical engagements with objects is a universal phenomenon can we finally succeed in erasing the abiding resonance of the colonial historiography that continues to manifest itself within the tales of the 'coming of antiquarianism' into South Asia.

2

Nineveh in Bombay: The Curation of Foreign Antiquities and Histories of India*

Between 1846 and 1848, Bombay received many antiquities of Ancient Assyria. Most transited through the port as shipments on their way to London, although a few were gifted to the city. By presenting a history of the curation of the 'foreign' collections, this chapter prevails upon us to consider and evaluate the historical connections between the seemingly disparate but contemporary archaeological excavations and explorations, and creates a consciousness of the many different histories of the nineteenth-century South Asian archaeology outside the practices of explorations, excavations, decipherment of inscriptions and occasional conservation. In recalling the presence of 'Nineveh' in Bombay, it reminds us of the contributions of the archaeological scholarship to the politics of imperialism, and the losses and profits within the European archaeology of the Orient. The history of the archaeological unearthing of 'Nineveh' has been extensively studied.[1] But more importantly, the intellectual, cultural and political milieu within which the Assyrian antiquities circulated in the West, and the various expectations from them of the excavators, collectors, scholars and viewers have also been explored in depth in recent years.[2] Drawing inspiration from this scholarship of collections and consumption, this chapter attends to the reception of

---

* *Note:* In light of the destruction of the archaeological site of Nimrud in March 2015, the Chapter acquires heuristic value in informing of the history of the first display of the excavated artefacts.

[1] For an archaeological history of Nimrud, see Oates and Oates (2001); for the heroic history of Mesopotamian archaeology, see Fagan (2007).

[2] Bohrer (2003).

Ancient Assyria within the Bombay of the 1840s and the 1850s with the aim of establishing a local history of collections, exhibitions and museums, which adds to the histories of Indian archaeology during the nineteenth century.

The early excavations, classifications and exhibitions of Ancient Assyria draw our attention quite specifically to the ways in which the antiquities are made to 'work' in establishing archaeological knowledge. The histories of relating to the unknown and foreign objects also inform us of the influences of the archaeological scholarship of the Orient within the racial histories that were created for Ancient India. The histories, therefore, allow a critique of the histories of South Asian archaeology that highlight the racist Western philological scholarship of India as the only intellectual plank of the colonialist historiography.[3] Besides, the reception of the Assyrian antiquities in colonial Bombay inform us of the many meanings that historical objects accrue at a specific time and throughout their material lives, and demonstrates the need for future research of the ways in which different communities within a society often relate to the same object in different ways. It also prompts us to explore the kinds of historical knowledge about the ancient worlds that the British imparted to the Indians during the nineteenth century and take cognisance of the force of analogy within the field-based scholarship of the past.

The histories of 'Nineveh in Bombay' inevitably prompt us to remember the injunctions of William Jones who in conceptualising the Asiatic Society of Bengal had hoped that his peers would see the connected histories in their explorations of Hindustan. Jones had declared that:

> Since Egypt had unquestionably an old connexion with this country, if not with China, since the language and literature of the Abyssinians bear a manifest affinity to those of Asia, since the Arabian arms prevailed along the African coast of the continent of Europe you may not be displeased occasionally to follow the streams of Asiatick learning a little beyond its natural boundary.[4]

The creation of the Asiatic Society of Bengal by Jones, on 15 January 1784, is regularly invoked by historians of South Asian archaeology as the foundational event, which supposedly marked the beginning of the historical scholarship of India. However, the abject neglect of incorporating the 'view beyond' which Jones had advocated with such clarity remains a striking

---

[3] For example, Chakrabarti (1997).

[4] Jones (1788a, p. xii).

feature of their histories of Indian archaeology. Jones had hoped that the 'useful researches' of the 'Asiatick' could be 'inclosed' through that which we qualify today as a trans-regional view, and the curation of Nineveh in Bombay demonstrates the epistemic promise of Jones's vision for historicising the practices of archaeology.[5]

Archaeological Investments in the Biblical Land: An Early History

Following the success of the French invasion of Egypt (1799), the Biblical geography of Mesopotamia (north Iraq) acquired added geographical value during the early nineteenth century as the strategic place on the route to India from Europe. The excavations of Ancient Assyria represent the agencies of the East India Company and the competitive nationalistic politics of imperialism, especially of the British and French who wished to acquire a political foothold in Mesopotamia. The British were the first among the European countries to establish their presence officially within the region by creating a resident at Baghdad. The post was held by Claudius James Rich from 1808 until his untimely death in 1821, and the history of 'Near Eastern archaeology' began with the extensive field surveys, which he undertook during his tenure.[6]

Rich had applied for a military cadetship in the British East India Company at the age of 17. However, on his visit to the India House (London) to submit his application, he was introduced to Charles Wilkins who, impressed by his diligence in languages, including in Arabic and Turkish, recommended to the Company directors that he be given a civil office instead. He was sent to Constantinople in 1804, from where he travelled to Anatolia, Cairo, Damascus, Mecca, Aleppo, Mosul and Baghdad, and eventually he came to Bombay to work in the diplomatic sector of the East India Company in 1807. A year later he went back to Baghdad as a resident at the court of the Pasha. By then he had married the daughter of James Mackintosh (1765–1832), a jurist and recorder of the court at Bombay,

---

[5] Jones (1788a, p. xii).
[6] Near Eastern is a reference in relation to distance from Europe, and is therefore in inverted commas here.

who was instrumental in establishing the Bombay Literary Society (1804).[7] Mackintosh had hoped that the society would be different from the antiquarian intent of the Asiatic Society of Bengal. However, in 1828 the Literary Society was transformed into the Bombay Branch of the Asiatic Society, and subsequently many of the members made significant contributions to the antiquarian scholarship of Ancient Assyria.

In the Biblical account, Mesopotamia was the land where the descendants of Noah had settled and multiplied, and Babylon on the Euphrates was the site from where the tribes of Noah's descendants had dispersed. For Europeans and all Christians, therefore, the ruins of Nimrud represented the tower of Nimrod, the first king among men, who was the great grandson of Noah and founder of Babylon. Rich surveyed Babylon in 1811, when he also visited and surveyed Birs Nimrod (the ancient city of Borsippa built by the Akkadian king Hammurabi, 1792–1750 BCE). In 1820, he explored Kurdistan for four months and visited the site of Nimrud near Mosul. The site was subsequently identified incorrectly as the Biblical Nineveh in 1845 and then as the Biblical Calah in 1850. The latter historical association remains. Rich wrote three accounts of his journeys and explorations, and they all ran into several editions, with the last appearing in 1839, eighteen years after his death. His discrete collection of over 50 antiquities of oriental manuscripts, fine collections of Characene coins and Assyrian sculptures was acquired by the British Museum from his widow at the sum of £7,000, and until 1847 this was the sole collection of objects of Ancient Assyria within Europe.

Following the British creation of a Resident at Baghdad, the French created the post of a Consul at Mosul in 1841, and appointed Paul Émile Botta (1802–70). Through his archaeological survey, Rich had revealed the possibilities of discovering the cities of the Bible, and his publications inspired Botta to undertake excavations at the site of Kouyunjik (which is now regarded as Nineveh) near Mosul, in the knowledge that Rich had seen the archaeological potentials of the site. Botta began excavating in 1843. However, he soon judged the site not promising, and shifted his operations to Khorsabad, where he unknowingly unearthed the palace of Sargon II (r. 721–705 BCE).[8] His excavations, undertaken during 1843–44, inspired the British diplomat and explorer Austen Henry Layard (1817–94) to

---

[7] For details of the early life and career of Claudius Rich, see Errington, E. and Curtis, V.S. (2007, pp. 4–5).

[8] Layard subsequently excavated at Kouyunjik in 1850 to notable success.

excavate at Nimrud, in 1845 and 1846–47, in the firm belief that this site was Nineveh. Through his excavations, and without knowing at the time, Layard brought to light the palaces of Ashurnasirpal II (883–859 BCE), Tiglath-Pileser III (744–727 BCE) and Esarhaddon (680–669 BCE) (Illustration 2.1).[9] The two consignments of bas-reliefs, obelisks and massive sculptural pieces, which Layard shipped to the British Museum during the year 1846–47 were inevitably routed via Bombay, and the search in this chapter for the pieces of 'Nineveh' in Bombay is largely directed by the second shipment that supposedly got 'vandalised' when it came to the city in February 1848.

History and Colonial Pedagogy

In exploring the histories of the Assyrian artefacts in the nineteenth-century Bombay, the question that immediately comes to mind is what did the Indian residents of the city know of Ancient Assyria during the late 1840s when they first saw the objects. The search for an answer prompts an enquiry into the education in History, which the British imparted to the Indians as part of their colonial pedagogical mission to 'reform' the native mind through an education in the western sciences and in English medium, so that the administration of India could be made cheaper through recruitment of the Indians. The mission was fashioned in the 1830s through the Minutes of Education (1835), which was drafted by Thomas Babington Macaulay, wherein he had infamously declared that 'all the historical information which has been collected from all the books written in the Sanscrit language is less valuable than what may be found in the most paltry abridgments used at preparatory schools in England'.[10] By then, the British antiquaries of India had established the historical fact that the natives had no historical texts and were ignorant of the 'useful science' of History, the subject of which, they deemed, was the 'description of things as they are, or have been, with a regular account of their principal facts and circumstances'.[11] Within the next decade,

---

[9] For a critical history of the politics of finding Ancient Assyria, Layard's excavations and British reception of the objects, see Russell (1997).

[10] Minute by the Hon'ble T.B. Macaulay, dated 2 February 1835.

[11] Allbut (1835, p. 81). The other 'useful sciences', which had been mapped by then apart from History, were Natural Philosophy, Botany, Geology, Chronology, Grammar and Arithmetic.

i.e. the 1840s, we find that the British and Indians were jointly undertaking historical investigations, for example, through the Archaeological Society of Delhi (1847–54), which reveals the existence of an Indian intellectual milieu that was able to negotiate historical enquiries on the parameters of the western understanding of History.[12] This milieu made its presence at the same time as the Assyrian antiquities began to arrive in Bombay, which add to the reasons for searching the curricula in History that was devised by the British for consumption in India.

An early example of the contents of the History syllabus may be sourced from Bengal in the form of a bilingual textbook titled in English, *An Epitome of Ancient History Containing a Concise Account of the Egyptians, Assyrians, Persians, Grecians and Romans*, and in Bengali *Prachin Itihasa Samuchhai*.[13] Published in 1830, the text was compiled by James Prinsep 'from the works of [Louis-Pierre] Anquetil du Perron, [Charles] Rollin and others', and the selections were translated into Bengali by students of Hindu College at Calcutta, and John David Pearson of the London Missionary Society at Chinsurah.[14] In five chapters, the book provided an account of all the ancient civilisations that were known to the early nineteenth-century European world, namely Egyptian, Assyrian and Babylonian, Mede and Persian, Greek and Roman, and the text was aimed for the 'Native Schools'.[15] The bilingual nature of the text facilitated the targeting of the intended audience, and soon after, the book was edited by Horace Hayman Wilson who added 'more detailed notices […] of the leading occurrences of Asiatic history, and particularly of the history of India'. Wilson included the history of the Indian Civilisation, and the 'addition' was 'recommended by the locality of publication'. The new edition, which he titled *A Manual of Universal History and Chronology*, was published in 1835. It was specifically aimed for informing 'the Junior Classes of the Schools of Calcutta, and of the Hindu College', the 'important social and political relations, which connect[ed] Great Britain with the East'. The publication was also used in teaching in Britain, since it was considered 'serviceable to English youth'.[16]

[12] For details of the Delhi Archaeological Society, see Gupta (2000, p. 59).

[13] Anquetil *et al.* (1830).

[14] A page in English is followed by a page in Bengali; of the 623 pages, 20 pages were translated by Hindu College students and the rest by Pearson, see 'Advertisement' that precedes the contents page.

[15] 'Advertisement', ibid.

[16] Wilson (1835, p. ix).

Noticeably, the publication in Bengal dates from a period that in retrospect we also know was poised to launch the archaeological explorations for Ancient India through epigraphic and numismatic researches and field surveys of ancient sites, ruins and monuments. By then, the stupa at Manikyala had been prised open (1827), and the decade of the 1830s saw the epic feats by Prinsep in decoding the Brahmi and Kharoshthi scripts, which inspired Cunningham to undertake an archaeological excavation at Sarnath (1834–35). The decade also saw the launch of the field explorations for the architectural history of India through Fergusson's surveys of the 'rock cut cave temples' in western India (1836–37). The epigraphical and field researches contributed to the formulations of historical methods for 'discovering' Ancient India, and initiated the searches for the dynastic chronologies of the 'Buddhist' and 'Hindu' India, which the British ordained had been lost and ignored by the natives through their inept epistemic traditions.

The *Epitome* offers an insight into the moral values of historical knowledge, which the contemporary western world upheld, and which the British imparted to the Indians. Regarding the intellectual and moral relevance of the discipline of history, Indian students were told that:

> various advantages are to be derived from the study of history; amongst others, we are thereby led to amend our own lives. [...] Observing the actions which are there recorded, it is our duty to reject what is evil, and to adopt that which is good.[17]

Every chapter in the text concluded with a section on 'reflections', which was aptly translated into Bengali as 'advice', since they illustrated the lessons that could be learnt from the histories which the chapters contained. The book began with the history of the Ancient Egyptian Civilisation then considered to be the earliest of all, whose moral value was summed up as exhibiting the 'fatal tendency [...] to generate pride in the heart of men'. Students were asked to remember that although Egypt was once 'most powerful' it 'is now one of the least of the nations of the Earth', and were instructed to see this historical fact within 'the [architectural] vestiges which still remain [and which] serve only to point out to us its former greatness'.[18] The uses of the ruins and historical landscape for creating the visibility of the moral

---

[17] Anquetil *et al.* (1830, p. 64).
[18] Ibid., p. 72.

lessons of history allow us, readers of the text today, to anticipate the manner in which the British used their archaeological scholarship of Ancient India for substantiating their brand of the colonial historiography.

Within the western historiography of the 1830s, the Ancient Assyrian and Babylonian empires conveyed the Fall of Man. Thus, the *Epitome* claimed that the ruins of Nineveh and Babylon, 'once the proudest cities in the world' demonstrated that 'in proportion to the pains, which men take to display their power, so in the end, is their weakness made evident'. Excerpts from Rich's publications were used for presenting the history of the Assyrian and Babylonian empires, and the archaeological terrain he had explored was drawn upon in the 'reflections' for emphasising the historical fact that even 'the walls, and gates and bars of Babylon proved of no avail, when the period appointed for its destruction had arrived'.[19] The 'catalogue of crime' that had led to the 'fall' of the great Assyrian and Babylonian kings informed the students that whereas 'the beast of the forest preys not upon his own species [...] myriads of the human race' have been 'slaughtered by the hands of their fellow men'. Thus, Indian students learnt that the history of Mesopotamia 'teaches us to form a very humble opinion of, and at the same time exceedingly to mistrust our own hearts'.[20] The potential propaganda value of the 'advice' of the above history can hardly be missed. For, the advice could be used to plant seeds of suspicion between and among the communities in India.

The *Epitome* was created as a textbook for schools in Bengal and led to the publication of similar kinds of bilingual texts in the other two presidencies. We can conjecture that the knowledge of the discoveries of Botta and Layard may have been followed by some of the educated members of the Parsi community of Bombay, as the interest in West Asian matters of this community stemmed from its historical connections with Iran. The Parsis also became a visible presence within the community of the European and British antiquaries of Bombay, who reluctantly admitted Maneckjee Cursetjee to the Bombay Branch of the Asiatic Society in 1840, as the first Indian member.[21] With respect to knowledge of Ancient Assyria among the educated inhabitants of Bombay during the late 1840s, it is perhaps also worth noting that the antiquaries in Bombay paid special attention to the

[19] Anquetil *et al.* (1830, p. 118).

[20] Ibid., p. 120.

[21] See *JBBRAS*, 'list of members...' (1857, p. 707). From 1847, we find an incremental increase of Parsis as *ordinary* members.

historical connections between India and its neighbours in the West. The geography-specific scholarly orientations can be documented through the contents of the *JBBRAS*. The journal was established in 1841, and by the 1850s it had built up a formidable reputation in conveying and encouraging research of the history, geology, languages and tribes of Arabia, Egypt and Persia, and of the cultural exchanges between the civilisations of Ancient India and Ancient Near East. Thus, we note that it was the *JBBRAS*, and not the *Journal of the Royal Asiatic Society of Bengal*, which provided the first notices of all new archaeological discoveries in the above areas, and the new section on 'Literary and Scientific Notices', which was created in October 1844, contained an excerpt from *Athenaeum* (No. 895) of the excavations by Botta at Khorsabad, and 'letters from Baghdad' that informed that 'Mr Layard, a gentleman sent down by Sir Stratford Canning, has cut into the great Mound at Nimrod'.[22] The French excavations had inspired Layard to approach Canning, then British Ambassador at Constantinople, for supporting the cause of British excavations at Nimrud.

Retelling a Story of Loss

The sensational receptions of the archaeological discoveries of Botta and Layard within France and Britain, respectively, were to a considerable extent due to the massiveness of the finds, whose representative samples were first displayed in the Louvre in May 1847. The 'advantages' for the British, in comparison to the 'French' site of Khorsabad, lay in the location of Nimrud, which was nearer the Tigris. Thus, George Percy Badger, who had undertaken an excavation at Nimrud in 1844, a year before Layard's excavations, had written to Canning of the 'drawback' he anticipated for the French with respect to the removal of the 'massive relics'.[23] Yet, the French, not the stringent British, made concerted efforts towards supporting the transportation

---

[22] *JBBRAS*, 'M. Botta's discoveries in the ruins of Nineveh' (1844–1847, 1845; pp. 214–17); *JBBRAS*, 'Magnificent Sculptures found on Opening the Mound of Nimrod, near Nineveh' (1845, p. 322).

[23] Badger (1847). Badger had excavated at the site when he served the East India Company from Malta. He became a Chaplain in Bombay in 1845, and his note in *The Bombay Times* is retrospective. He published his letter to Canning, which is dated 26 October 1844, on seeing several notices of Layard's excavations in the *Times*. In his letter, he reported that:

ventures of Botta in the pursuit of the logic that was aptly expressed by the latter's patron and oriental scholar Julius Mohl, that 'until the Louvre shall be embellished by a hall of Assyrian sculptures, Europe cannot profit by the discovery of Khorsabad'.[24] The travails of the shipments of antiquities, however, call for a nuanced view of the profits that were made within the archaeology of the Orient by the participating European nations.

In his *Nineveh and Its Remains*, which became the nineteenth-century bestseller upon publication (1849), Layard had provided a poignant description of the rafts laden with Assyrian relics drift away from the shores of Basra. He had remarked that:

> I could not forbear musing upon the strange destiny of their burdens; which after adorning the palaces of the Assyrian kings [...] were now to visit India, to cross the most distant seas of the southern hemisphere, and to be finally placed in a British Museum. Who can venture to foretell how their strange career will end?[25]

The objects of Layard's attention were two colossal winged bulls, which reached the British Museum. However, his apprehension regarding their destiny creates a reason for enquiring into the fate of the objects that failed to reach their intended destination.

The first shipment that Layard sent to the British Museum left Basra in October 1846, reached Bombay in December 1846 and reached London in June 1847. A subsequent consignment he sent from Basra reached Bombay in February 1848, and ostensibly remained within the dockland area for more than six weeks despite the injunctions of the Governor of Bombay, George Clerk, who was away from the city during the period of the transit, to 'set [it] out for exhibition' at the Town Hall, where 'each stone [was] to be accompanied by a description of the character and history of the sculptures

---

another great advantage is the vicinity of the Mound of Nimrood to the Tigris where any remains might be embarked on rafts and floated to Basra, from whence they might be shipped at once for England. Khorsabad is at least ten miles from the river, and there being no means of land conveyance for such massive relics as have been dug up there, the French will find this a great drawback whenever they begin to remove them, which I understand is their intention.

[24] Note by Julius Mohl in Botta's letter to him from Mosul on 31 October 1843, Letter V, in Mohl (1850, pp. 59–74); also quoted in Bohrer (2003, p. 72).

[25] Layard (1849a, p. 105).

it contained'.[26] This cargo left Bombay on the 'H.M. Jumna' in April 1848. The ship ran into a hurricane and the captain anticipated that the alabaster pieces would be defaced due to the rolling.[27] On checking the consignment in London in October 1848, Layard lamented bitterly that:

> the cases containing the small objects recently opened in the British Museum were not only opened without authority at Bombay, but their contents exhibited, without proper precautions, to the public. It is remarkable that several of the most valuable (indeed, the most valuable) specimens are missing; and the whole collection was so carelessly packed that it has sustained injury.[28]

The losses that Layard complained of, proved to be remarkably insignificant in comparison to the sheer magnitude of the subsequent French loss in 1855, when local Arabs capsized one of the rafts carrying more than 120 cases destined for the Louvre. The destruction was an act of retaliation against the failure of the French excavator Victor Place to pay an expected bribe. The cargo not only contained objects found and excavated by Botta and Place, but also a large collection of objects excavated by Layard at Nimrud, which Place had been allowed to select for the Louvre. Yet, Layard's emphasis of the vandalism of his cargo as representing the loss of 'the valuable ruins of a great city and of a great nation' is indeed worth noticing as this set the trend for all future recollections of the fate of his shipments via Bombay.[29] Subsequent historians have conveyed the vandalism as the only act upon the only shipment of Assyrian objects that came to London via Bombay through remarks such as 'the cases were opened, some of the antiquities stolen, and even lectures given on the remains', and that the contents had been rifled out of curiosity.[30] Such remarks obliterate the fact that of all the shipments of Assyrian objects that were sent from Basra to London via Bombay, only one might have been handled with undue care.

---

[26] *The Bombay Times and Journal of Commerce*, 14 March 1849, Editorial Article No. 8, p. 172.

[27] Ibid.

[28] Layard (1849b, p. xii).

[29] Ibid., p. xiii.

[30] Daniel (1975, p. 72); Fagan (2007, p.130), who has reported that the cargo 'sat on the quays in Bombay's harbour for some time […] the British residents in Bombay had opened the precious cases out of curiosity. Some pieces had even been stolen, but the British Museum did not care'.

As the scandal of the loss of Layard's cargo in Bombay became prominent news in Britain, the Bombay government was compelled to make a spirited defence. Thus, *The Bombay Times and Journal of Commerce* (henceforth *The Bombay Times*) pointedly asked:

> But what shall we say of the intense narrow mindedness of the Trustees of the [British] Museum when we find that permitting the specimens to be seen at all, or suffering copies to be made of them, has formed ground of blame to the Bombay Government. The only specimen which have suffered are those which were packed at the place where they were excavated, and which were not when here interfered at all. The lesser relics complained of as having been lost, were when here exhibited loose in a basket; they too had broken loose from their original packings—how they were re-packed, we know not. This however, we do know—that the only fault that seemed capable of being found with the acting store-keeper, Captain Robinson was that of an over anxiety to take care of the relics. There was neither invoice nor description nor any means whatever of knowing what had been sent, what were present, or what absent.[31]

The editorial clearly blamed the management of the packing of the objects at the port of departure, namely at Basra. However, embedded within the expression of injustice is also the important information that some of the artefacts, which were 'loose in a basket', had been exhibited at Bombay, of which contemporary news journals, including *The Bombay Times* provided no details. In this respect, an excerpt of a letter, possibly from April 1848 written by the captain of 'H.M. Jumna' which was printed with the editorial, provides additional information. The captain had stated that:

> The Jumna it will be remembered, carried with her, for the trustees of the British Museum, some sixty pieces of sculptured alabaster or marble obtained from Nimrud; these had arrived from the Persian Gulf by the sloop *Elphinstone* in February [1848] and it was the most anxious wish of the late Governor— and we believe of every member of Council—that they should be exhibited to the public and casts in plaster made of them. After some six weeks delay a single obelisk with some fragments were shown: the rest were at once sent on board as soon as they could be secured—the public saw nothing of them whatsoever.

---

[31] *The Bombay Times and Journal of Commerce*, 14 March 1849, Editorial Article No. 8, p. 179.

The letter was published as an excerpt without any information of the addressee and with the title, 'amongst the most intemperately expressed official documents ever penned'.[32] As the captain's statement clearly shows, Layard had a cause for criticising the handling of the contents of his shipment in Bombay, which were probably displayed, 'without proper precautions'. However, Layard's undue emphasis of vandalism has obliterated the histories of the previous exhibitions of Assyrian antiquities in Bombay, in 1846–47. The instances of the exhibitions inform us of acts of curation of the archaeological objects from Mesopotamia in Bombay, which are contrary to the stories of negligence and vandalism, which Layard, and following him the Trustees of the British Museum, propagated.

Displaying Ancient Assyria in Bombay

The very first shipment of Assyrian antiquities that came into Bombay was not of Layard's, although this too arrived in 1846 and was a collection of artefacts that had been picked up at Baghdad by a British merchant, Mr Hector, of whom no information appears with the notice which states that he had collected them 'from a heap thrown aside as useless by Botta', had sold the collection to the British Museum via an intermediary for the sum of £400, and that the objects were transported to London by the firm Messrs, Dirom, Hunter and Company.[33] The collection, or parts of it, was displayed in the 'Grant Road Buildings in 1846', and was the first exhibition of Ancient Assyria in Bombay.[34] There are no reports of precisely when the exhibition was held and what exhibits were on view. A subsequent report in *The Bombay Times* provided information of the venue. Written at the time of the Great Exhibition at the Crystal Palace (London) in 1851, it recalled the 'Grant Road Building' as a 'swamp theatre, with surrounding marshes and burial grounds', in which 'half a lakh' of public money was 'thrown away unwisely'. The report emphasised that although the building was 'called a

---

[32] *The Bombay Times and Journal of Commerce*, 14 March 1849, Editorial Article No. 8, p. 179.

[33] *The Bombay Times and Journal of Commerce*, 15 December 1847, Editorial Article 15, p. 989.

[34] *The Bombay Times and Journal of Commerce*, 14 March 1849, Editorial Article 8, p. 179.

place of public amusement [...] no one ever went there to be amused'.[35] It informs of the searches for a suitable property for housing the Central Museum of Natural History, Economy, Geology, Industry and Arts', or the Economic Museum whose establishment, as mentioned in the Introduction Chapter, was planned in 1847. The unflattering characterisation of 'the Grant Road Buildings' spoke of their outright elimination.

Layard's first shipment to the British Museum was the next to reach Bombay. Specimens from this consignment were exhibited within the library of the Asiatic Society (Colaba) between December 1846 and February 1847. The *Athenaeum* of 6 February 1847 informed readers in London that 'a collection of sculpture figures and cuneiform inscriptions from the mound of Nimrud on its way to England—latterly excavated by Mr Layard—has been on view in Bombay, by direction of the Asiatic Society'.[36] The news was substantiated by *The Bombay Times* (within the issues of December 1846 and January 1847), which added significant details. The newspaper reported that plans to host an exhibition was decided at a meeting of the Bombay Branch of the Royal Asiatic Society on 10 December 1846, when a member informed the Society of the arrival of Layard's shipment in the port. The Society approved the display of the 'hoar antiquity [...] to the community of Bombay' and 'made [arrangements] with a view to the opening of the sculptures to public inspection in the beginning of the ensuing week'. The report concluded with the statement that 'it is not too much to say that the exhibition will be one of the most interesting and attractive that has ever taken place on the Island'.[37] By 19 December, the exhibits were on public view and 29 objects were described in detail in *The Bombay Times* of the day.

In recalling the exhibition we recall that Layard, and Botta, had no knowledge of precisely what they had excavated, apart from the strong belief that their discoveries were related to Biblical tales, and that they were from Ancient Assyria. The objects they shipped to Europe acquired semantic values upon their arrival in London and Paris, and in the sensational reception of their displays within the British Museum and the Louvre, respectively. The many meanings that the displayed objects accrued in Europe throughout the nineteenth century, including the historical identity as remnants of the

[35] *The Bombay Times and Journal of Commerce*, 9 July 1851, Editorial Article 13, p. 449.
[36] *Athenaeum*, February 1847, p. 154.
[37] *The Bombay Times and Journal of Commerce*, 12 December 1846, Article 2, p. 874.

palaces of the Assyrian kings, were therefore endowed outside the context of their find spots, without the knowledge of the script the objects carried upon their surfaces, and through varying and often conflicting responses of their historical value by the European public and members of the establishment. The 'status' of the artefacts within the Western world remained contentious as the objects resisted and eluded consensual aesthetic valuations.[38] The Biblical associations, which attended all meaning-making ventures challenged interpretations of the imagery, and hence the winged bulls, massive lions and human heads, obelisks, alabaster vessels, fragments of incised and carved tablets and bricks, and other big and small finds came to be, to quote Mirjam Brusius who has traced an aspect of the cultural histories of their reception, the 'misfit objects' of the British Museum.[39] For much of the nineteenth century the collections were stored, displayed and seen within this institution, and others, as material with historical potentials but with no actual histories. In recalling their exhibition in Bombay, we are therefore informed of a history of their reception that preceded the vexation of the European world with their exoticism.

Of the pieces from Layard's cargo that were selected for public display in Bombay, many were small human figures and heads, horse heads and 'pieces of stone with writing specimen'.[40] Their viewing was directed through contemporary historiographical dictates regarding the ancient Christian World. Thus, the reporter who reviewed the exhibition for *The Bombay Times*, and who signed his name as J.B.Z.Z., mentioned that two male figures were holding a 'rosary in the hand' and created the understanding of the importance of the Assyrian Empire for his readers through the historical fact that it was the 'first recorded [empire] after the flood'. He also deemed the exhibits as 'intensely interesting to all whose minds are not debilitated from the exercise of power pursuits'.[41] In the valuation of the objects, he therefore echoed the 'reflections' in the *Epitome* with respect to the Assyrian Empire. However, he also saw many Indian features within the exhibits. Thus, he noticed that 'on the arm of a male [...] an armlet corresponding exactly with those now in use with the lower classes of male Hindoos', saw that the finely executed 'heads of horses with trappings' were 'a better representation of the horse

---

[38] Bohrer (2003).
[39] Brusius (2012).
[40] *The Bombay Times and Journal of Commerce*, 19 December 1846, Article 2, p. 894.
[41] Ibid.

dressing of the Rajahs and Sirdars of the Dekhun [...]', and drew attention to the sword among the 'three warriors' instruments' as it was a 'true likeness of that now in use with the Mahomedans and Mahrattas, being straight, double-edged and short-handled'.[42] Such descriptions of the embellishments of the human statues may have contributed to the selective description of some as 'king', 'prime minister' and 'prime ministers' servant'.[43] The descriptions were unique, and are noticeable examples of the analogical methods, which we instinctively use in making sense of unknown entities. Equally noteworthy is the high aesthetic value that was placed upon the sculptures. The items were considered 'not inferior to many of the Egyptian and Grecian efforts of doubtless a much later date', despite the style of 'perspective representation', which contributed to the judgement that 'now a days' the carvings would 'be considered as mere infantile performances'.[44]

The high aesthetic value that Layard's objects commanded in Bombay in 1846 abided by the estimations of the excavator. A year later, in December 1847, a unique gift of 'ten beautiful slabs' from Nimrud was given to the city by the British resident at Baghdad, Henry Creswicke Rawlinson (1810–95),[45] who was appointed in 1843 to the post as the successor of Rich. The gift arrived two months before the cargo of Layard that was ostensibly vandalised, and with its receipt, the Bombay government initiated plans for casting operations. The operations were reported in many issues of *The Bombay Times*, and the edition of 12 January 1848 emphasised that 'it is not unworthy to notice that the first of this sort of work executed at Bombay has been so by the Abyssinian boys taken from the slavers by the [ship] *Mahi*'.[46] Members of the Asiatic Society, who drew up the proposal based their request also on the abundant presence of the raw material, namely gypsum, in the neighbourhood of Bombay, and emphasised that 'casts of the whole collection might be stowed away in the space a single block would apply'.[47] In the light of the charges of vandalism, which Layard subsequently made,

---

[42] J.B.Z.Z., 1847, 'The Nineveh Antiquities', *The Bombay Times and Journal of Commerce*, 23 January, p. 59.

[43] *The Bombay Times and Journal of Commerce*, 19 December 1846, Editorial Article 2, p. 894.

[44] J.B.Z.Z. (1847, p. 59).

[45] *The Bombay Times and Journal of Commerce*, 15 December 1847, Editorial Article 15, p. 989.

[46] *The Bombay Times and Journal of Commerce*, 12 January 1848, Editorial Article 8, p. 32.

[47] *The Bombay Times and Journal of Commerce*, 14 March 1849, Editorial Article 8, p. 172.

it is important to note that the Asiatic Society had made a formal plea to the Bombay government for making plaster casts of a selection of objects in the cargo on the grounds that 'the whole collection was public property intended for the information of the people of England, and paid for, in part at least, from the purses of Her Majesty's subjects in India—it was considered expedient that casts should be taken of it for preservation in Bombay'.[48] The information certainly adds to the international career of Layard's shipments. The black obelisk of Shalmeneser, which came to Bombay in February 1848 as Layard's cargo, was replicated into plaster cast (Illustration 2.2), and in retrospect it was noted that 'had the other specimen now complained of as being broken or destroyed, been similarly treated, they might readily have been restored'.[49] The obelisk was mentioned by the Captain of the H.M. Jumna in his 'intemperate' letter as 'understood to be unique as a specimen of Assyrian art, and incapable of being restored at any price if lost or injured in its progress home'.[50] With reference to its plaster cast, the members of the Asiatic Society had pointed out that 'few of us are ever likely to see it in the British Museum'.[51] The plea for securing replicas therefore touched upon issues of preservation and documentation, attended to the logic of meeting the hopes of the Indians who funded the British government's expenditure of moving the Assyrian artefacts from *in situ*, and was fully conceived upon procuring examples of the exotic objects for the city of Bombay.

Bombay Receives a Gift

Since Rawlinson had started his spectacular career in the East India Company in Bombay in 1827 as a cadet, and had risen in the ranks in the city while serving the Company his gift to Bombay was not extraordinary. Yet the nature of the gift was novel. It was the foremost donation of a 'foreign'

---

[48] *The Bombay Times and Journal of Commerce*, 14 March 1849, Editorial Article 8, p. 172.

[49] Ibid.

[50] Ibid.; for a description of the obelisk, see Bohrer (2003, pp. 144–45). It was illustrated by George Scharf Jr., on Layard's instructions, and Bohrer has noted that the drawing did not resemble the manner in which it was found, or its exact provenance.

[51] *The Bombay Times and Journal of Commerce*, 14 March 1849, Editorial Article 8, p. 172.

collection towards the cause of a 'local' museum, and contemporary reports had emphasised that 'we may have but one Rawlinson amongst us, but we have many of the same school, who have hitherto succeeded in kindred avocations, and who perhaps only require to have the opportunity of exerting themselves [...]'.[52]

By the latter half of the 1830s, Rawlinson had acquired considerable reputation as a philologist and textual scholar through his stay in Iran, where he was sent from Bombay by the East India Company to re-organise the Shah's army.[53] After his appointment as British resident at Baghdad, he came close to deciphering the Assyrian cuneiform in 1844, and participated in Layard's excavations at Nimrud in 1846. He made the compelling argument, which he subsequently revoked as erroneous, that the site of Layard's excavations was the Biblical Nineveh.[54] Yet, unlike Layard, he did not consider the Assyrian objects as being of high aesthetic value, because in his estimation they did not measure up to the classicism of the arts of the ancient Graeco-Roman world. The antiquities he declared were to be appreciated for their inscriptional contents. In differing with Layard he posed the rhetorical question, namely 'Can a mere admirer of the beautiful view them with pleasure? Certainly not, and in this respect they are in the same category with the paintings and sculptures of Egypt and India'.[55]

In refusing to endow the status of fine art to the Assyrian objects, Rawlinson echoed the misgivings of many intellectuals and artists of the British establishment. However, his gift to Bombay in 1847 was locally received as 'beautiful specimens of ancient Assyrian art'.[56] The objects were housed in the Town Hall as the Economic Museum's infant collection along

[52] *The Bombay Times and Journal of Commerce*, March 14, 1849, Editorial Article 8, p. 172.

[53] Rawlinson was sent to Tabriz in 1833 to reorganise the Shah's army. For a comprehensive summary of his successive meteoric career as a diplomat, military man and orientalist scholar, see Errington and Curtis (2007, pp. 5–7).

[54] He subsequently changed his judgement and assigned the identity to Kouyunjik, when Layard's publication, *Nineveh and Its Remains* was in the press. Rawlinson was also a brilliant diplomat and military man. After Layard's permanent departure from Mosul in 1851, he successfully undertook charge of the British excavations at Mesopotamia, for which he sought support of the Assyrian Excavation Fund. The Crimean War of 1855 put a stop to all archaeological work in the Near East.

[55] Letter from Rawlinson to Layard, 5 August 1846, in Bohrer (2003, p. 104).

[56] *The Bombay Times and Journal of Commerce*, 15 December 1847, Editorial Article 15, p. 989.

with artefacts representing Indian arts and manufacture.[57] They were publicly exhibited in 1850, and the viewers of Bombay bestowed upon them similar values of high art, which they had bestowed upon the exhibits from Nineveh in 1846–47. Unlike the fate of the exhibitions of the Assyrian antiquities in London and Paris, the exhibits in Bombay retained their high aesthetic valuations throughout the 1850s. The information regarding the manner in which the different communities of the city responded to the antiquities is not known to us as of now. However, we may anticipate that future enquiries into this realm will allow us to establish critical histories of the different receptions of the foreign antiquities by the different communities of Bombay, because the histories would be informative of the local viewing of the curation of archaeological objects.

A Museum Collection of Assyrian Objects

The conceptualisation of an Economic Museum for Bombay is an exemplar of the commercial museums that were planned by the British for the cities of India from 1840. The Museum was aimed as a repository of the local agricultural, mineral, technological, artistic and handicrafts wealth of western India, and by 1845 similar museums had been conceived even for cantonment towns, such as Agra and Bolarum (near Hyderabad), and their pedagogical mandate was built upon the stipulation that

> It may be laid down that the more we know of India, the more valuable it will become; and there is nothing that we can see more likely to conduce to this desirable acquaintance with this country and its resources than the general establishment of Museum.[58]

---

[57] 'Indian Arts and Manufacturers', *The Bombay Times and Journal of Commerce*, 18 December 1852, p. 813. The report mentioned:

> A sort of transient vitality was conferred upon [the collections] in January 1850 when the exhibition in the Town Hall of the models meant for Baroda had its attractiveness enhanced, that splendid but useless apartment being for once filled with objects of art and specimens of manufacture—after which it once more returned to a state of repose.

[58] *The Bombay Times and Journal of Commerce*, July 16 1845, Editorial Article. 3, p. 466.

Although Rawlinson's gift to the Economic Museum does not qualify as a suitable sample of the local wealth for which the institution was established, the 'foreign' objects played a significant role in the political economy of Bombay. The presence of the objects may have also inspired a section of the educated residents of Bombay to keep abreast of news regarding the archaeological explorations of Nineveh, and we notice that many related to the contemporary archaeological work in terms of their own contemporary requirements. Thus, the magnificent maps of the 'topography of Nineveh' that were made during the survey of 1851, which was sponsored by the British Museum, were recalled by the residents of Bombay in 1855 in their demands for civic amenities, and they had declared that:

> we desire no less for Nineveh, but should like to see the streets and alleys of the metropolis of Western India, surveyed and laid down with something like the fullness and precision with which the capital of Assyria has been represented.[59]

The quotation reveals the different referential fields of the archaeological mapping of Ancient Assyria, and we can perhaps build upon the above demand of the citizens of Bombay for exploring whether there was an oppositional aesthetic within the 'Indian approach' to the antiquities from Nineveh. The aesthetic has been historicised very coherently by one artist of North America through the ideas of art which the African slaves had brought into the United States, to show that it expressed the belief that 'beauty, especially that created in a collective context should be integrated aspect of everyday life, enhancing the survival and development of community'.[60] This aesthetic has been consciously bred by African Americans from the mid-twentieth century. It grew in opposition to the intellectualisation of art within the 'West', which has historically denied artistic judgement to the marginalised, subjugated and othered, and it allows expressions of the purposes and functions of beauty and artistry in everyday life, especially of the poor people. The aesthetic, therefore, conveys resistance and protest.

[59] *The Bombay Times and Journal of Commerce*, 2 April 1856, Editorial Article 3, p. 210; see also Jones (1855).

[60] Hooks (1995, p. 66). I am grateful to Frederick Bohrer for prompting me to consider the oppositonal aesthetic after reading a draft of the chapter. Bohrer has carefully documented the oppositional elements in the reception of Assyrian art in Britain during the 1850s by the populace and establishment. These, he has shown, subverted the prevalent notions of aesthetics and high art and their progress (see Bohrer, 2003).

In searching for the different viewing of the foreign Assyrian objects within the different communities in Bombay, we might be able to establish another history of this aesthetic as an expression of local resistance to the dictates of the British regarding the corrupt and decadent art of Hindu India.

By the mid-nineteenth century, Bombay was no doubt the commercially ascendant cosmopolitan city of the British Empire. It was by then one of the important port cities of the Empire, and we note that the Assyrian antiquities were sought by the administrators to enhance the city's commercial value. They were often invoked for emphasising the requirements of the European visitors, and an example can be gauged in the statements of the Curator of the Economic Museum, George Birdwood in seeking financial support towards a building for the institution. In asking for support from the Indian businesses in 1859, he emphasised that 'a read and shrewd traveller recalling the story of Babylon, Nineveh, Tyre, Jerusalem [...] would naturally anticipate the highest manifestations of intellect within the gates of such an active a mart as Bombay'. But, declared Birdwood, such a visitor would 'search in vain' for stately streets, theatres, markets, temples, public offices, museums, fountains, monuments and art galleries.[61] As the above statement might guide us to consider, Birdwood incorporated the extraordinary foreign antiquities into the civic need for a museum that would serve the cosmopolitan ambience of the growing port of international commerce.

Although Birdwood did not create any visitor records of the displays in the town hall for his building-less museum as he felt that 'it would be of little value in the temporary settings',[62] reports within contemporary news journals provide a glimpse of some of the ways in which the exhibits caught the imagination of the citizens. For example, they inspired unique public lectures, of which one was given by Mr Beddows in January 1855 to the accompaniment of a harmonium. The musically scored lecture—no doubt Christian in content—was aimed at securing the 'fleeting grandeurs of the world', and was reported in *The Bombay Times* as the 'highest intellectual treat of the highest order', which not only placed 'Nineveh and its antiquities' before a large audience, but also 'enabled to place before the institution [...] a sum of money which will aid in helping it forward in its infant career of usefulness'.[63] The agency of the foreign objects for the cause of a museum

---

[61] Birdwood (1859, p. 406).
[62] Ibid.
[63] *The Bombay Times and Journal of Commerce*, 17 January 1855, p. 37.

displaying local wealth provides reasons for reflecting upon the transnational and culturally hybrid nature of all antiquities.[64]

In his annual report of 1859 for the Economic Museum, Birdwood listed the antiquities of Assyria as the only specimen of 'fine arts' in the holdings of the virtual institution.[65] The evaluation differs quite radically from contemporary judgements in Britain, where as early as 1853 the sculptor and designer of the pediment of the British Museum, Richard Westmacott (1775–1856), had warned of the futility of further procurement of such objects for the institution through the declaration that 'if we had one-tenth part of what we have of Nineveh art it would be quite enough as specimens of the arts of the Chaldeans, for it is very bad art'.[66] In Bombay the objects possibly lost their pre-eminence a decade later, during the 1860s, as they were not accommodated within the Victoria and Albert Museum and Gardens, which the Economic Museum was eventually fashioned into, and which opened to the public in 1872. Knowledge of their viewing therefore arouses our curiosity.

Following the plans of the Economic Museum, the Victoria and Albert Museum aimed at providing the residents of Bombay with the 'great practical uses of an economic and industrial museum'. However, the entire space, including the sprawling gardens in which it was located, was also conceived as an 'education appliance, as a means of awakening interest and as a source of pleasure'.[67] The Indians of the Museum Committee who supported the establishment were more vocal than their British peers that the 'high and low, rich and poor, could meet in the pursuit of common objects, in the environment of innocent and ennobling pleasures, producing a community of view' that 'is desirable for improvement of the mind'.[68] Rawlinson's gift would have found easy accommodation within the vast physical space of the museum and its lofty aims. Yet, despite shaping the imaginations of the city throughout the 1850s, lending to the curiosity of the citizens and visitors of Bombay, and fuelling antiquarian and speculative researches regarding the origins and nature of the Zoroastrian faith, the objects and their plaster casts were literally forgotten within the very offices that had made them prominent.

[64] On the transnational nature of objects, see Cuno (2008).

[65] Birdwood (1859, p. 37).

[66] In Bohrer (2003, p. 124).

[67] *The Bombay Times and Journal of Commerce*, 24 December 1859, Editorial Article 1, p. 818.

[68] Speech by Dr Bhau Daji in seconding the resolution for the 'Victoria Museum and Gardens', *The Bombay Times and Journal of Commerce*, 18 December 1858, p. 788.

Thus, it came to be that in 1891, Rustomji Pestonji Karkaria, a scholar of Parsi history and a member of the Asiatic Society of Bombay, noticed a few 'marble' pieces 'lying on the landing place of the Society's office reclining against the wall near the northern entrance into the Hall'. He identified them correctly as Assyrian in origin and reported that 'none of our members it seems knows anything about them', and only 'one gentleman, Mr [Henry] Cousens, an official of the Government Archaeological Survey was aware of the archaeological value of their inscriptional contents'. However, Karkaria stated that 'since Cousens was not a member of the Society he had not brought the matter before it'.[69]

Through his research Karkaria at first proclaimed his find to be the missing pieces of Layard's collection, but upon finding a reference of the Rawlinson gift within *The Bombay Times* of the year 1847, he changed his mind, and proclaimed them to be the 'Rawlinson slabs'.[70] Following his inference, which may have been verified by Cousens who subsequently headed the Western Circle of a newly instituted Archaeological Survey of India in 1902, the reliefs were selected for the archaeology gallery of a new museum that was planned for Bombay in 1904, namely the Prince of Wales. The donation history of the objects that Karkaria had found remained officially lost, although the objects might have been the Rawlinson–Clerk gift. They made their public appearance in 1922 when the Prince of Wales Museum was inaugurated. From valued specimen of fine art, which they had represented to the Bombay spectators half a century before, they came to represent an archaeological collection.

With respect to the fate of the 'missing marbles' in Layard's cargo that left Bombay for London in 1848, it would be amiss to neglect a singular instance of the display of the antiquities of Ancient Assyria within the Asiatic Society of Bombay in July 1855, by Rawlinson. He was then in charge of the British archaeological explorations of Mesopotamia, and had excavated a new site, at Warka in 1854. He was invited by the Society to present a lecture, and spoke on 'Researches and Discoveries in Assyria and Babylonia'. During the course of this lecture he exhibited a sample of objects for demonstrating his periodisation of the 'Chaldean', 'Assyrian' and 'Babylonian' chronologies of Ancient Mesopotamia to the Society members.[71] The objects which

[69] Karkaria (1894, pp. 99, 102).
[70] Ibid., p.102.
[71] Rawlinon (1856).

Rawlinson displayed were destined for the British Museum. Although the occasion of the display prompts a thought regarding whether any member recalled the exhibitions of Layard's cargo in reference to Rawlinson's lecture at the time.

Rawlinson's gift to Governor Clerk in 1847 had comprised 10 'fine slabs'. The present Assyrian collection of the Chhatrapati Shivaji Maharaj Vastu Sangrahalaya (the new name for the Prince of Wales Museum) comprises 12 alabaster reliefs from Nimrud. Of them eight are from the palace of Ashurnasirpal II, three from the 'central palace' of Tiglath-Pileser III, and one from the palace of Sargon II at Khorsabad (for example, Illustration 2.3).[72] We are tempted to ask whether the two extra objects came from Layard's cargo, or from Rawlinson's display to the Society members in 1855. We shall probably never know.

Ancient Assyria in Ancient India

Cunningham and Fergusson had both recalled Layard and his excavations, at Nimrud and Kouyunjik for presenting the values of their respective scholarship. Cunningham had mentioned Layard in the preface of *The Bhilsa Topes* (1853), his first monograph that was a lavish documentation of the excavations of the 'Great Stupa' at Bhilsa (near Sanchi) which he had undertaken during January and February in 1851. He had declared that 'in illustration of the ancient history of India, the bas-reliefs and inscriptions of the Bhilsa Topes are almost equal in importance to the more splendid discoveries made by the enterprising and energetic Layard in the mounds of Euphrates'.[73] Through the invocation Cunningham most certainly aspired for a European publicity for his own excavations if not the hope of achieving comparability with Layard's status of a pioneering British archaeologist, of India. Fergusson recalled Layard in a remarkably different manner from Cunningham. He used Layard's discoveries theoretically and at great depth, for creating his own pioneering status as a historian of art and architecture. He developed a history of the ancient art of Assyria through Layard's discoveries, and used

[72] Information from Assistant Curator of Archaeology, Mrinalini Pathak, August 2012. There are also two 'palace' reliefs from Egypt in this Collection.

[73] Cunningham (1854, p. viii).

this history for establishing a universal history of art and architecture, and for developing a racial history of India.

Unlike Cunningham, Fergusson, as we know from the Introduction Chapter, took very little notice of inscriptional evidence. In his very first publication, *On the Rock Cut Temples of India* (1846) he had clearly stated that 'inscriptions will not certainly by themselves answer' the 'age' of architecture.[74] Hence, he laid great emphasis upon field surveys, and upon seeing and observation. He created the understanding that the archaeological relics of Ancient Assyria provided the facts that substantiated his theories regarding the histories of ancient art. However, in reviewing his historicising processes, we are shown the virtual nature of his material evidence, because Fergusson established many of his theories without having seen the antiquities. His classifications of the antiquities and architectural remains within India and elsewhere, and his forays into the ethnology of a non-existing entity, namely race, allow us to establish a critical narrative of his emphasis on visualising the field. In this respect, Fergusson's uses of the Assyrian antiquities, which were excavated by Layard and Botta inform us of his evidence-making endeavours, and bring home to us the importance of analysing the analogical methods of field enquiries.

The increasing notices from the second half of the eighteenth century of the architectural similarities between the rock-cut monuments of Egypt and India prompted the theory that the builders of both were of the same racial stock. Thus, in celebrating the aesthetics of the sublime within the gloom, darkness and interiority of such monuments, the British landscape painter William Hodges (1744–94) had declared that 'the flat roof hundred pillared Egyptian temple, the Indian pagoda, and choultry [were] evident copies of the numerous caverns, cool grottos, and excavations in the rocky banks of the Nile in Upper Egypt, and in the island of Elephanta and Salsette in Bombay'.[75] Hodges emulated the views of William Jones who held the opinion that 'the remains of architecture and sculpture in India […] seem to prove an early connection between this country and Africa', and 'that Ethiopia and Hindustan were peopled or colonised by the same extraordinary race'.[76] Fergusson chose to demonstrate the errors of the above

---

[74] Fergusson (1846, pp. 30–31); see also Cunningham's criticism of this remark in Cunningham (1871a, pp. xix–xx).

[75] Hodges (1793, p. 76).

[76] Jones (1788b, p. 427).

postulations by drawing upon the importance of engaging with visible truths. He exhibited the authority of sight and asserted that:

> I have passed myself from India to Egypt and Egypt to India, and with my mind full of either style, and while its forms were still fresh on my memory, tried in vain to trace the slightest resemblance. [77]

Yet, despite his strong bid for field presence and seeing, Fergusson blatantly subverted his own dogma by deriving objective histories through *a priori* assumptions. The contradictions of his method are carefully illustrated by Tapati Guha-Thakurta in her study of his architectural 'proof of a preconceived historical cycle' of the decay and degeneration of the Indian Civilisation,[78] and we can add to the critique. Fergusson had gathered racial data from the surfaces of the monuments, which he had surveyed in India through the existing theory that the Indian subcontinent was inhabited by 'two distinct and separate races', one aboriginal and speaking the 'Tamul' languages who 'inhabited the whole of the Southern part of the peninsula' and the other, Sanskrit-speaking race, which 'came into the region at a very early period, but as conquerors across the Indus'. However, he differed from prevalent opinions, including those of Jones and Hodges, in his understanding that 'in speech, manners and religion' this latter race showed 'closer affinity to the Persians and nations on this side of the Indus'.[79] Although he dismissed the racial connections between the 'Sanskrit-speaking' races and Ancient Egyptians on the basis of the absence of architectural evidence, the absence of evidence did not deter him from postulating that 'if any connexion with any foreign style [with respect to their architecture] do exist', then it 'must be traced through the countries west of Indus, and into Persia and countries of Central Asia'.[80]

During his field apprenticeship among the rock-cut monuments of western India, Fergusson had devised a method of dating architecture through their stylistic features, which involved comparing the similarities

---

[77] Fergusson (1848, p. 11).

[78] Guha-Thakurta (2004, p. 18). See also Fergusson (1847); in the opening paragraph he had stated that although it 'may perhaps at first sight appear that some apology is due to the public' for writing about a city he had not seen, he feared that the 'subject itself demands more apology in which it is treated', and thus created the value of his 'correct' inferences (p. ix).

[79] Fergusson (1848, p. 3).

[80] Ibid., p. 11.

and differences for devising schemes of a linear evolutionary stylistic history. After this initial study of the architectural history of India, which he published as a lavish volume, *Picturesque Illustration of Hindoostan* (1848), he embarked upon a grand project of creating an architectural history of the ancient world through the method. He stated that such a project would serve British national interests, and aimed the resultant publication, *An Historical Inquiry into the True Principles of Beauty in Art* (1849), wherein he drew upon the monuments of Ancient Egypt, Western Asia (including Assyria, Babylonia, Persepolis, Syria and Asia Minor), Greece, Etruria and Rome, for serving the British 'public a better standard by which to judge the merits of art'.[81] Fergusson declared that the education in the arts and architecture of the world was mandatory for the British people, so that they 'could at least re-create as high and as vigorous a native art' as that which had existed within 'Protestant Christianity' and 'an art that will be worthy of our [British] nation, and worthy of engaging and employing the highest class of intellects that exist among us'.[82] He presented his endeavours towards the upliftment of the British mind through art as pioneering, and stated that:

> At present we have not an upper class capable of conceiving or creating, and consequently no lower class trained merely to execute; but art rests half way on a class combining both attributes, and who practice it only for its money-value as a trade, thinking and executing themselves. [...] A higher aim, and more means than these men can command, are requisite before much can be done.[83]

The above quotation demonstrates that the moral value which the European historiography of the eighteenth and nineteenth centuries attributed to historical enquiries, and which nurtured the pedagogical value of History as a useful science for the politics of nationalism and colonialism, permeated Fergusson's nationalistic history of art and architecture. He followed the historiography, and thereby also mapped the architectural history of the ancient world with origins in Ancient Egypt, followed by the arts of Ancient Assyria. He declared that both had inspired the classical arts of the Ancient Greeks. However, he classified the Assyrian art, devised a relative chronology for this entity, and made assumptions of its character without

---

[81] Fergusson (1849, p. xvi).
[82] Ibid., pp. 13–14.
[83] Ibid., pp. 9–10.

having seen the objects. As he himself recorded, he undertook to write the history of Assyrian art on the basis of a 'few plates' from Botta's excavations at Khorsabad, 'but without either texts, or plans, or references of any sort that could make them intelligible', and through the drawings, which had been made by Layard of his excavations at Nimrud, but with no 'materials' that could enable him 'to make up [his] mind definitely on any one point considering these wonderful discoveries'. Yet, despite the cursory reference material, Fergusson felt compelled not to 'pass over so interesting a chapter in the history of art' because, as he stated, much of what he wished to write regarding the value of engaging with architectural histories would 'remain forever unintelligible' if he were to exclude Assyria.[84]

From the drawings Ferguson concluded that 'notwithstanding its superior mode of phonetic utterance the Assyrian sculpture marks a lower grade of civilisation and of mind than the Egyptian'. Upon this understanding, he formed the opinion that Assyrian antiquities displayed a 'taint of vulgarity and childishness', of which he declared 'the other [i.e., of Egypt] is quite free'. To him, therefore, 'Assyria [was] like an unformed child, but in a right path of art; Egypt like a full-grown and fully developed man, but in a wrong path', and he deployed the judgement to ingeniously connect Ancient Assyria through its arts to Ancient Egypt and Ancient India.[85]

The novelty of Fergusson's universal history of art and architecture from other contemporary histories of the phenomenon in Europe lies in the two historical paths he sketched for recording progress and decay; one towards the supreme aesthetic achievements of the Ancient Greek Civilisation, which he stated came via the influences of the arts of Ancient Assyria, Asia Minor and the Etruscans, and the other to the architectural representations of the Hindus, and their 'monstrous many-limbed and many idols, and still more monstrous doctrines' via Mesopotamia and Persia.[86] In establishing the history of artistic progress from Asia into Europe, and of decay within Asia, Fergusson re-assured his readers that

when the specimens on their way home are once accessible to the public, and the complete drawings made by Mr [Eugéne] Flandin of the Khorsabad

[84] Fergusson (1849, pp. 267–68). Botta and Flandin subsequently produced the magisterial folio *Monument de Ninive* (1849–50), which had limited circulation, and Layard published the grand folio *The Monuments of Nineveh* (1849–52) with 100 drawings 'made on the spot'.

[85] Fergusson (1849, p. 274).

[86] Fergusson (1848, p. 8).

monument, and those of Mr Layard, are published, I feel convinced that they will throw a stronger and clearer light, not only on the ancient history of Greece and Italy, but also on that of India, than any other discovery that has yet been made; and even if we should not be able to decipher the inscription, the details of art will be suffice to point out the affiliation of almost all the primitive nations of Asia and Europe.[87]

For Fergusson, the cultural geography of the Assyrian Empire was the historical corridor that connected Asia and Europe, and which had conveyed the artistic impulses from Egypt into Asia, and he developed upon the theme of the historical geography of Ancient Assyria in *The Palaces of Nineveh and Persepolis Restored*, which was published in 1851.[88] By then, he had seen the massive Assyrian reliefs and other antiquities in London and had affirmed that they represented the 'germ', which subsequently 'ripened into greater perfection' that 'raised everything the Greeks touched, whether it was an earthen jar or a marble temple, to such a pitch of perfection and of beauty'.[89] He thus rooted the value of the arts of Assyria in what they allowed, namely the 'most instructive aspirations towards perfect style of architecture' and the arts of the Greeks.[90] In this valuation, he substantiated the views of Rawlinson, and Layard's first patron Stratford Canning, and probably added to the convictions of Westmacott and others to publicly deride the 'bad' Chaldean art. The publication of *The Palaces of Nineveh and Persepolis* prompted Layard to select Fergusson as the architect of the Nineveh Court at the Crystal Palace at Sydenham (London) in 1854. The Court was a spectacular creation. The lower storey was conceived as a representation of the palace at Khorsabad, and the lower outside wall with five bay entrances carried painted plaster reproductions of winged bulls on the façade, human headed lions and giants strangling lions. The upper portion of the wall was columnar roofed 'adding a further twenty feet exclusive of the battlements, and was modelled on Persepolis. The arcade consisted of columns with double bull capitals'. The main hall was modelled on the palace of Nimrud and contained four great columns modelled on those at Susa and Persepolis.[91]

---

[87] Fergusson (1849, p. 279).

[88] Fergusson (1851).

[89] Ibid., p. 358.

[90] Ibid.

[91] Piggott (2004, pp. 109–10); For details, also see Bohrer (2003, pp. 210–11 and 214–16); Malley (2012, pp. 150–52).

However, the architecture was criticised by the British press, for example *The Builder*, as representing an unhistorical combination of Nineveh and Persepolis.[92] Despite his involvements with the plans and the construction of the Nineveh Court, Fergusson's visualisation of the city of Nineveh was rather different from the creation. He viewed the non-existent city in a picturesque manner. This vision was informed through the plans and drawings of Layard's excavations at Kouyunjik in 1849, which he had seen in London, and which he illustrated as Plate One, which is the frontispiece of the folio of the 71 drawings and lithographs of Layard's second expedition to Assyria in 1848–49. The coloured drawing was created in 1851 under Fergusson's supervision, and it illustrates his belief that the Assyrian people may have displayed a 'love of polychromatic decoration', and their palaces may have been 'gorgeously coloured'. However, this use of colour, Fergusson added, was 'perhaps not always in the best taste' (Illustration 2.4).[93]

The histories of professional relationships between Fergusson and Layard, construction of the Nineveh Court and the impact of the architectural representations of Ancient Assyria upon the growing arts and crafts movements within nineteenth-century Britain are topical subjects of the cultural histories of the Victorian age. In contrast, Fergusson's empirical contributions to the racial histories of India through his assessment of the arts and architecture of Ancient Assyria remain conspicuously absent within the histories that relate specifically to the archaeological explorations of the Indian subcontinent during the nineteenth century. His contributions are therefore specifically recalled here for critiquing the logic of 'visible facts', which Fergusson so strongly perpetuated, since many archaeologists of South Asia continue to propagate his views.

The archaeological 'exposure' of Ancient Assyria allowed Fergusson to challenge the antiquity of the 'Sanskrit-speaking people'. Through *The Palaces of Nineveh and Persepolis*, he reminded his readers that because the 'language' of this group 'is the only one studied and the literature in consequence is the only one known in Europe, so that they are generally, but most erroneously, looked upon as the only people of India'. However, he insisted that 'so closely were they indeed allied to the Assyrians on their southern and western frontiers, that it is almost impossible but that some light must be

---

[92] Quoted in Piggott (2004, p. 110). Also see *The Builder*, XII, 10 June 1854, p. 298.
[93] Fergusson (1851, p. 267).

thrown on them by these discoveries'. He illuminated the heuristic value of the discoveries of Botta and Layard for the history of Ancient India in his statement that even if the Brahmins had passed into India at 'too early a date and by too direct a route, the Vaishnave religion was certainly closely allied to the Assyrian'. So too, he stated, were the Buddhists, who were 'closely allied to the Magian [and] came from this fertile source'. Fergusson concluded his historical sketch of people migrating into India through Mesopotamia in the ancient past with the emphasis that 'there is scarcely a point of history and religion in India that these discoveries will not illustrate'. For 'it is when the whole are compared and weighed one against the other, that we shall be able to solve the great problem of primaeval antiquity, where all has hitherto seemed so dark to the wise, and so wild to the more imaginative inquirer'.[94] Yet, in ascertaining that the 'Hindu races' of India did not have 'primaeval antiquity' he offered no visible proof for distinguishing his hypothesis from the 'wild imaginations', which he so sardonically dismissed.

In contrast to his transparently evidentless histories of races and migrations into India, Fergusson historicised the innate characteristics of the 'Eastern' people quite specifically through his study of the mode of lighting within their architecture. He began his enquiries into the way in which historical monuments had been designed to receive natural light during his explorations of the rock-cut architecture of India, and this enquiry remained an important aspect of all his subsequent architectural investigations. In conceptualising the manner in which the ruins of the palaces of Nineveh and Persepolis may have admitted light, he recalled the roofs and domes of the Muslim monuments in Gujarat and Bijapur, and of the Moghul mosques at Delhi and Agra. Through the recollection, he assumed stylistic similarities between the non-existing roofs of the 'Hall of Xerxes' and 'Principal Rooms at Khorsabad' (Illustrations 2.5a and 2.5b), and the roofs of the mosques, an example of which he sought from Ahmedabad, whose architecture he declared 'though wholly of stone, bears strongly the impress of wooden original, from which it is very slightly removed'. He stated that:

> the peculiarity, however, which makes it [i.e the mosque] valuable as an illus-
> tration here, is the mode in which the light is admitted, between two rows of

---

[94] Fergusson (1851, pp. 10–11).

dwarf columns, not placed on a solid wall, but on an open gallery, like that of the palace of Thothmes III. (Illustration 2.5c)[95]

Through the realities of his section drawings, he allowed the 'wood cuts to tell their own tale', for confirming his inference that the mode of lighting which he conceived for the palace at Khorsabad, was still in use in the East.[96] By establishing the above history of the unchanging mode of lighting through his vision of the architectural realities of non-existent buildings, Fergusson concluded that the 'Asiatic mind' was not capable of anything much higher than oscillating towards perfection, which it never reached. This mind, he asserted, which may seem 'ever changing to the superficial eye [...] remains the most unchangeable of all the inhabitants of this sublunar world'.[97] The methodological step through which Fergusson derived his evidently visible evidence was actually built upon his inferences, conjectures and recollections, and was based upon the stark absence of the physical remains of the architectural features, within the Assyrian and Persian palaces, which he drew attention to. This absence of 'hard facts', or evidence on the ground so to speak, does not fail to strike his readers today.

Considering that Fergusson dismissed the Egyptian and Indian racial connections, which Jones, and following him Hodges and others had built upon, on the grounds that they had not been made through field observations, the absence of tangible material data in his own theorising of the histories of art, race and architecture is therefore important to note. His histories home in on the fallacy of pitting the superiority of field-based enquiries of the past over text-based philological enquiries, including of inscriptions, as a more robust method of historical enquiry, and allow us to note that often such comparisons are derived from the unwillingness to master the more difficult philological scholarship. In documenting the importance of seeing the 'facts of history', Fergusson had quite skilfully woven his own, and existing, inferences into the truth values of vision. In this respect, the histories of Nineveh in Bombay and of Fergusson's both provide many examples of the manner in which ideational notions are seen and given physical forms. They implore us to take a critical note of the ways in which we consider the ontology of the non-present past.

[95] Fergusson (1851, p. 290).
[96] Ibid., p. 291.
[97] Ibid., p. 368.

3

The Connected Histories of Philology and Archaeology

The histories of Indology show us the imprints of the philological scholarship within directions of archaeological enquiries. They remind us that academic archaeology disengaged with philological enquiries during the twentieth century because of the fashioning of a theoretical profile for the subject through the scholarship of prehistory. Similar to all histories of disciplines, they create awareness of the importance of distinguishing between the intellectual nurture of a subject and its governance for non-academic purposes. In this, they also illustrate the constraints of focussing only upon issues that relate to the control of scholarship, which the post-colonial critique of the European oriental scholarship has remained mainly committed to. The histories illuminate the problems of polarising the historical scholarship of India into 'Western' and 'Native', and show the fallacy of approaching disused archives that have been created within the recent past as objects of our discoveries.

This chapter draws upon the connected histories of the archaeological and philological enquiries within the Indological scholarship of the nineteenth century. The histories of connections were built upon the corroborative method, which was adopted by the western antiquarian scholarship, and which entailed seeking equivalence between different kinds of information from different entities that were unproblematically classified as textual and archaeological. The method was premised upon the understanding that data could be simply extracted from sources. The errors of positivism, which this method has nurtured for over 200 years ought to encourage us to interrogate our expectations of historical sources and review the manner in which we select and classify them. Therefore, in attending to the connected histories, this chapter aims at creating an awareness of the need to focus upon issues of methodology within the writing of archaeology's histories.

In seeking the connected histories of the archaeological and philological scholarship, we are invariably brought to the scholarship of epigraphy. Apart from James Fergusson, all western field surveyors of India of the nineteenth century regarded inscriptions as inestimable historical sources. This regard may appear as flouting the dictates of the colonial historiography that the 'Hindus never had any historical writings'.[1] However, the valuation of inscriptional evidence conformed to the practices of European antiquarianism, although the efforts to note the errors within the inscriptional contents of the subject population may have been more focused within the colonial historiography. As is well known, the British and other Western antiquaries of India discarded the 'indigenous' literary corpus of the Indian subcontinent but mined into the 'foreign accounts'; predominantly of the Greeks who came with Alexander to the Punjab in 326 BCE, the Chinese Buddhist pilgrims Faxian and Xuanzang and Yijing who visited the Indian subcontinent in the fifth and the seventh centuries, respectively, and the Romans, such as Pliny and Strabo, who wrote about the travails of the 'Indo-Roman' trade (200 BCE–200 CE). The non-native texts, which bespoke of the Buddha's travels, invasion of Alexander, Greek embassies to the courts of the Mauryan rulers and the lucrative Indo-Roman trade became both a guide for directing archaeological enquiries and a source for corroborating the histories of dynasties, architecture and religions, which were gathered from the field surveys.

In 1836, the travelogue of Faxian, of his journey through the northern parts of the Indian subcontinent in the years between 399 and 414 CE, was translated into French. This translation spurred the archaeological explorations of India, and until the publication, the visible 'residues' of India's past had been aptly summed up by Horace Hayman Wilson through the remark that many inscriptions, including on 'Firuz Shah's lat' and within the 'cavern temples' could not be read, 'no buildings of undoubted antiquity' had been found, and the 'oldest [buildings] appear to be the remains of Buddha temples, which are found at Gaya, Bhilsa and in the Punjab'.[2] Wilson seized the opportunity of the 'great value' of the French translation of Faxian's text 'as offering living testimony of the geographical and political divisions

---

[1] Wilson (1835, p. 16). On the anomaly, see Ali (2000, pp. 167–68, 225–28).
[2] Wilson, ibid., p. 4.

of India at an early date'.[3] He conceptualised the novel method of seeking the historical geography of 'Buddhist India' by mapping the route that had been taken by Faxian in his descent from Kashmir into the Gangetic plains. Cunningham developed Wilson's method, and, as is well known, established his own archaeological career by physically trailing the possible routes of Faxian, Xuanzang and Alexander within north India.

Although Cunningham endeavoured to create distinctions between field-based and text-based enquiries of Ancient India, field archaeologists, including him, endowed high epistemic value to the historical scholarship of the philologists, and the latter inevitably documented the heuristic value of the field surveys of the archaeologists in their writings. Thus, while editing the *History of British India*, which had been written by James Mill (1817) for amending its many errors, Wilson, the 'textual' scholar, expressed his criticism towards Mill with respect to the latter's claim of having authored a dispassionate and objective account of India by not visiting the country. Championing the importance of field surveys for knowing the land, its people and its languages, Wilson declared:

> Personal knowledge of a country, and especially India, possesses one great recommendation, of which Mr Mill does not seem to have been aware. It secures one important historical requisite, of the want of which his pages present many striking examples. It enables the historian to judge the real value of that evidence to which he must have recourse for matters that are beyond the sphere of his own observation. [...] He will be in a situation to estimate with accuracy the opportunities which the author of an account of any part of India may have enjoyed, of gathering authentic information; he will be in the way of learning something of the narrator's pursuits, habits, occupation, and prepossessions, and will by daily experience be prepared for the many circumstances by which observation is biased, and opinions instilled. He will know what to credit, what to mistrust, what to believe. He will be qualified to select the pure from the dross, to separate the false from the true. [...] With very imperfect knowledge, with materials exceedingly defective, with an implicit faith in all testimony hostile to Hindu pretentions, he [Mr. Mill] has elaborated a portrait of the Hindus, which has no resemblance whatever to the original, and which almost outrages humanity.[4]

[3] Wilson (1839, p. 109).
[4] Wilson (1858, pp. ix–xii).

Wilson's injunctions for acquiring field knowledge summarises the practices of the antiquarian scholarship of Indology, which prevailed well until the mid-twentieth century. He also exhibited the heuristic value of field surveys for expressing a measured criticism of the 'harsh and illiberal spirit' of the British administration of India by the Utilitarian Whigs. Following the paternalistic mode of expression, which was typical of the colonial milieu in which he lived, he emphasised that field knowledge of India, by visits to the country, creates 'generous and benevolent feelings' towards the Indians.[5] The above emphasis of a British Sanskrit scholar for a liberal and kind British rule is worth a note as it disturbs the narratives of the inherently racist Western philological scholarship that permeate the post-colonial histories of Indian archaeology.[6]

Inscriptions of 'Native' Agency

The scholarship of Indology was built upon 'native' knowledge and local information although the repressive cultural politics of colonialism tried to thwart the agency of the natives. At the behest of James Fergusson, the Bombay government instituted the Cave Commission in 1848 with the aim of supporting field explorations of the rock-cut architecture of the Presidency.[7] The surveys were comprehensively presented in two 'Memoirs' (1850 and 1853), which were authored by John Wilson, the then President of the Bombay Asiatic Society. Both provide many examples of the contributions of the local inhabitants and 'natives' employed by the East India Company to British and European field discoveries, who brought to their masters'

---

[5] Wilson (1858, p. viii).

[6] For example, Chakrabarti (1997) for a polemical account of the colonialist Western scholarship of India. The author wonders whether the 'civilised value of Western academia have not left its Indology mostly untouched' and is of the opinion that 'Western Indology is an essential by-product of the process of the establishment of Western dominance in India. Racism—in this case a generic feeling of superiority in relation to the natives—was quite logically, one of the major theoretical underpinnings of this process. It is but natural that Western Indology should carry within it a lot of this feeling of superiority. We are not surprised by this (p. 1). The errors of the above generalisation should be apparent throughout the chapter.

[7] See Fergusson (1880, p. xiii).

attention the ancient ruins and inscriptions, and deciphered and transcribed the inscriptional contents.[8]

Thus, we note that Vishnu Sastri Bapat, who was 'Mahalkari of a district in Konkan' and who had previously 'assisted' the Collector of Thana, J.S. Law and also '[John] Wilson and others', was deputed in 1848 to explore the caves in Kuda and Kondana.[9] Unlike his British masters, Sastri knew the terrain he was asked to explore, which is evident in his report of the inscriptional findings within the ancient sites.[10] Besides, he also provided detailed information of many Buddhist *viharas* in the Konkan, within the neighbourhood of 'Chiplun, Dabhul, Sangameshwar, Gavhane-Belgaum, Wade-Padel, Cheul-Astagar and Chandansar near Agashi' of which the Europeans knew nothing.[11] Yet, although Sastri correctly copied, transcribed and translated many inscriptions within a vast geographical terrain in a single-handed manner, in appending an extract of his report in Marathi to the *Memoir*, Wilson felt compelled to add that Sastri's descriptions have been 'found to be correct'.[12] Sastri was Wilson's 'quondam pandit', and was lauded by Wilson for his palaeographic skills in taking copies of the Asokan inscription at the Girnar Rock, near Junagadh. However, Wilson felt compelled to emphasise that Sastri's skills 'commenced with Dr Babington's paper', which he had shown to him 'a few years ago; and they were matured under Mr Wathen'.[13] Thus, Wilson made it very clear that Sastri was able to develop his 'skills' because the British had shown the natives the methods of epigraphy and the historical value of their ancient inscriptions. He stated that he had chosen to mention the above 'facts' because of his 'desire to act according to the maxim, *suum cuique tribue*'.[14] In articulating an ostensibly fair appraisal of Sastri's endeavours, we note that Wilson stopped short of acknowledging the latter's invaluable local knowledge, the high quality of which contributed to the aims of the Cave Commission.

Within the nineteenth-century accounts of the archaeological explorations of India, the non-acknowledgement of local knowledge and 'native'

---

[8] Wilson (1850).

[9] Ibid., p. 44.

[10] Ibid., p. 46.

[11] Ibid., p. 47.

[12] Ibid.; the 'Memoir' is replete with information regarding notices of the caves brought by the natives.

[13] Ibid., p. 95.

[14] Ibid.

scholarly expertise appears as a persistent British effort to erase the agency of the Indians. Such efforts have many expressions, and we find one within the decision of the Cave Commission to award the successful explorers. The decision was taken 'with a view to encourage efforts being made' to bring the caves of western India to notice, and in 1853 Wilson reported that the:

> Bombay government had authorised the Cave Commission to offer rewards, varying from twenty-five to a hundred rupees, for the discovery of any series hitherto overlooked, according to its importance. By the promise of these rewards, European gentlemen interested in antiquarian research may possibly induce some of their native acquaintances to make minute inquiries in the different districts to which they find access.[15]

The presumption that the natives had to be induced with money to show the Europeans their archaeological heritage represented the British characterisations of the Indians as slothful and secretive. This sketch of the 'native nature' in the colonial historiography was a ploy to dismiss the immense and significant Indian contributions to the archaeological knowledge of India that the British recorded, and often presumed, were theirs.

The British developed many strategies of appropriating 'native' knowledge for knowing India. Thus, we note that in April 1856, Sastri was given official charge of the assignment that had been previously given to Lieutenant Brett, in 1851, by the Bombay government. The job involved copying and making facsimiles of the inscriptions within the rock-cut monuments of the Presidency, which Brett had failed to undertake satisfactorily. The reasons for transferring the responsibility to Sastri were clearly expressed by James Fergusson who had stated that 'having some knowledge of the ancient characters and of Sanskrit, it was [also] expected that he would be serviceable in preparing the translations'. By 1860, Sastri had translated 88 inscriptions into Marathi, although 'no results of his work were ever published' because he passed away in 1861, the year in which the Cave Commission also ceased to exist.[16]

The Cave Commission was instituted by the East India Company, and therefore it folded with the commencement of Crown rule. Many senior Company officers such as 'Sir Bartle Frere, Captain Meadows Taylor,

---

[15] Wilson (1853, p. 367).
[16] Fergusson (1880, p. xv).

Dr E. Impey, Dr Bradley, Sir W. Elliott and Mr West' had undertaken field surveys through the support of the Commission. Their field reports were archived and preserved as 'valuable additions' to the knowledge of the Bombay Presidency.[17] In contrast, the translations of inscriptions into the modern Indian languages, and transcriptions of the inscriptional finds which were made by native informants such as Sastri, for meeting the 'Great Objective' of the Company to list India's architectural histories, were carelessly lost.[18] The loss represents the colonial mentality of eroding the contributions of the Indians, and in trivialising the importance of the philological finds, histories of Indian archaeology perpetuate this carelessness of the colonial politics.

Disturbing the 'Colonialist' Historiography: German Sanskritists in India

Since the eighteenth century, the British and European Indologists complained quite expressively of the 'scarcity of authentic materials' for the study of Ancient India.[19] However, the understanding that the Indians had no regard for history was not ubiquitous to the western historiography. Thus, in his *Annals and Antiquities of Rajasthan* (1829), which is one of the classic texts of the ascendant colonial historiography, James Todd had noted that the 'axiom' that India had produced no 'national history' had been questioned by the French Orientalist Abel Remusat, who had rhetorically asked in his *Melanges Asiatiques* (1825) 'whence Abu-l Fazl obtained the materials for his outlines of ancient Hindu history?' Todd had quoted Remusat to 'oppose' the 'apposite' remark, and a search for views of Hindustan within the non-British literature of the eighteenth century may reveal the existence of many different western perspectives of the historical consciousness of the

---

[17] Fergusson (1880, p. xvi).

[18] For the resolution of the 'Great Objective', see Public Despatches to Bengal, No. 1 of 1847, 27 January, IOR/L/PJ/3/1021, Asia, Pacific Africa Collections, British Library, London.

[19] Quote from Thomas Colebrooke's *Essays II*, p. 213, on the frontispiece of *Corpus Inscriptionum Indicarum* whose first volume (1877) of collection of Asokan inscriptions was prepared by Alexander Cunningham. The full quotation: 'In the scarcity of authentic materials for the ancient and even for the modern history of India, importance is justly attached to all genuine monuments, and especially inscriptions on stone and metal'.

inhabitants.[20] The scholarship of the German Sanskritists who taught in India during the heydays of the raj between the 1860s and the 1880s adds to the reasons for the contention mentioned earlier, and demonstrates the importance of trying to maintain distinctions between the representations of scholarship and those of politics within the nineteenth- and early twentieth-century histories of Indology.

The German scholars of Sanskrit came to India during the latter part of the nineteenth century in search of careers within the new colleges of the new universities at Calcutta, Bombay and Madras.[21] Of them, Martin Haug (1827–76) was the first European professor of Sanskrit in India. He taught at Poona College (which was re-located and re-instituted as Deccan College in 1864) between 1859 and 1866. He was followed by Hofrath Johann Georg Bühler (1837–98) who arrived in Bombay in 1863 with recommendations from Friedrich Max Müller, whom he met during his short period of employment at the India Office (London) after completing his studies in Germany. Bühler found immediate employment as Professor of Oriental Languages at Elphinstone College (Bombay). In 1866 came Lorenz Franz Kielhorn (1840–1908), who had worked with Müller in Oxford after completing his studies in Germany. He took over the teaching of Sanskrit from Haug in the newly established Deccan College, and remains one of the youngest professors of the institution. Of the two other German Sanskritists who built their formative careers in India, Augustus Frederick Rudolph Hoernle (1841–1918) returned to the country of his birth, that is India, in 1865 for missionary service, after completing his studies in Sanskrit in London. However, he soon parted ways with his family vocation, and, in 1869, found employment at Jay Narayan College (Banaras) as a professor of Sanskrit. He subsequently served as the principal of Cathedral Mission College at Calcutta (1878) and joined the Indian Education Service in 1881. The last to arrive, in November 1886, was Eugen or Ernst, Julius Theodor Hultzsch (1857–1927), as epigraphist to the Government of India.[22]

---

[20] Todd (1920 [1829], p. lv).

[21] Over the last 30 years, and following the marginalisation of the German scholarship of the Orient in Edward Said's *Orientalism* (1978), cultural histories of the scholarship of Indology and Sanskrit studies in Germany, from the late-eighteenth to the first-half of the twentieth centuries, are being increasingly researched, of which two examples that are recent are Sengupta (2005) and McGetchin (2009).

[22] Of the period of the stays in India of the German Sanskritists mentioned here: Haug 1859–66, Bühler 1863–80, Kielhorn 1866–81, Hoernle 1865–99 and Hultzsch 1886–1903.

The German Sanskritists who taught and worked in India did not become public intellectuals like their fellow countrymen in England, Max Müller, who was Taylorian professor of Modern European languages and professor of Comparative Philology at Oxford (1854–68; 1868–75). Although they worked for the colonial government and their British employers held their scholarship in very high esteem, they could not aspire to influence British policies regarding the support of the study of Sanskrit. A notable aspect of this scholarship was its academic pre-eminence, which, as Suzanne Marchand has reminded her readers, played a crucial role in the 'unmaking' of Western identities.[23] Many, like Haug, also showed a willingness to 'unlearn much that [they] had learnt in Europe, and accept the fact that European scholarship must often stand corrected before Indian tradition'.[24] Their practices exemplify the errors of writing a history of the nineteenth-century western Indology with an avowed focus upon the uses of scholarship for political and other non-scholarly ends.

Of them all, Bühler's contributions to Indology and to the philological scholarship of Sanskrit were indeed outstanding. On the eve of his departure from India in 1880, the director of Public Instruction, Bombay Presidency, lauded him for laying 'the foundation of a sound and popular education in Gujarat', successfully exerting 'in the collection of some thousands of manuscripts in Central India, Rajputana, the Panjaub, Kashmir, etc., as in this Presidency', preparing 'standard works on Hindu law and literature' and adding considerably 'to the stock of philological and archaeological lore'.[25] Bühler was commemorated ubiquitously in the magnificent obituary, which his peers published for him in *The Indian Antiquary* (1898), for his intellectual commitment to know India. Thus, Emile Senart emphasised that:

> Bühler wanted to study India in itself, and for itself [...] With this object, he decided to seek in the familiar intercourse of the country in itself, in its scholastic traditions, in a methodical research for manuscripts and documents, the information that this great work required.[26]

To this, Mauritz Winternitz added 'that India has produced such scholars as Bhandarkar, Shankar Pandit Telang, Apte, and others [...] is to a very

[23] Marchand (2009, p. xxvii).

[24] Haug (1878, p. 44); quoted also in Marchand (2009, p. 191).

[25] Winternitz (1898, p. 339). For a short list of the collections which Bühler 'discovered' and collated, see Jacobi (1898).

[26] Senart (1898, p. 365).

great extent due to the beneficial influence of him and it must be said later on also of Kielhorn'.[27]

The recollections of Bühler by his peers present a noticeable feature of the scholarship of the nineteenth-century German Orientalists, namely that they did not 'other' and 'racialise' the Orient 'on either the English enlightened critique of backwardness or on German romantic traditions'.[28] In fact, all who contributed to the obituary highlighted the spirit of equality, which Bühler had nurtured in his scholarship and scholarly practices. The history of the collaborative ventures of Bühler with Pandit Bhagvanlal Indraji (1839–88) provides many examples. In recalling Indraji, who passed away at a comparatively young age of 49 years, and whom he had considered a personal friend, Bühler had noted:

> short as was the period during which it was permitted to him to stand forward as an independent scholar, his indefatigable zeal and rare ingenuity have contributed materially to the progress made of late years in the field of Indian epigraphy and history.

The above is an excerpt of the obituary of Indraji, or as Bühler phrased it 'a short notice of his life', which the latter wrote for *The Indian Antiquary* because he was 'able to do justice to [Indraji's] character, to his scientific attainments, and to the results which he achieved'. Bühler concluded the long obituary with the remark that 'I gladly acknowledge now, as I have done already on special occasions, that I have learnt a great deal from him'.[29]

By presenting the nineteenth-century western Indological scholarship through the Foucaultian prism of power and knowledge, we erase the personal histories of collaborations, be they between westerners and natives or within the two groups, which influenced the quality of the scholarship and the knowledge acquired. The intellectually reciprocal relationship that Bühler consciously nurtured with the pandits and shastris stemmed from his conviction that their 'services' to indological studies were to be 'by no means underrated'.[30] Thus, it becomes important to note that the intellectual

---

[27] Winternitz (1898, p. 338).

[28] Marchand (2009, p. 190).

[29] Bühler (1888, pp. 293, 295).

[30] Winternitz (1898, p. 338). Of Bühler Winternitz had recalled that:

he counted among his friends members of all classes of the native population, among learned Brahmans, as well as among the Jaina monks. He tells us [...] how much of his

hierarchy, which he felt he ought to record 'in the interest of truth' was 'that Pandit Bhagvanlal's name ought to have been mentioned by Bhau Daji in his article on cave numerals'.[31] The information of the non-divination of Indraji's authorship by Bhau Daji creates an awareness of the errors of pursuing the histories of the indological scholarship only through the examples of the unequal exchanges and confrontations between the Indian and western scholars. It also reminds us of the fraught professional relationships during the latter half of the nineteenth century between the shastris and pandits, who were trained in traditional ways, and the Indian professors of Sanskrit who were educated through the modern, western pedagogical methods.[32]

In comparison, perhaps, to all his peers, be they western or Indian, Bühler's practices appear the most democratic. Thus, we note that he carefully acknowledged the co-authorship of Indraji with scrupulousness in all publications after the latter's demise, such as those in the *Ephigraphia Indica* between 1892 and 1898–99.[33] He was also perhaps the only European scholar to address his letters to Indraji in Gujarati.[34] Of his efforts at disseminating Indraji's scholarship, Winternitz had remarked that had Bühler not translated Indraji's papers into English from Gujarati, the latter's contribution to 'Indian history, epigraphy and archaeology would have been lost to the European world of learning'.[35]

Bühler's reception of 'native' scholarship and expertise contrasts sharply with the sensational racist attack by James Fergusson of Rajendralal Mitra (1822/3–91), to which all historians of Indian archaeology make a point of

---

success in searching Jaina libraries he owed to his intimate friendship with the Sripuj Jinamuktisuri [...] he was devoted to Pandit Radhakrishan, who had brought him the first MSS. of his Kashmir collection [...]. (p. 344)

[31] Bühler (1888, p. 297).

[32] Deshpande (2001, specifically pp. 126–27).

[33] A prominent example is Bühler (1894), in which Bühler illustrated Indraji's contributions as well as his own for affirming that the 'ancient' arts of the Buddhists and the Jains were not that dissimilar (p. 322); on Bühler's disagreement with Indraji's interpretations, see Bühler (1892, p. 16).

[34] See Yajnik (1898, p. 23). Yajnik summed up Indraji as: 'He combined in himself the mildness and urbanity of a Hindu, with the steadiness, patience, and inquisitive spirit of a German, the ceaseless activity and energy of an Englishman, and the sereneness and contemplative turn of mind of a Jain Tirthankar' (ibid., p. 41).

[35] Winternitz (1898, p. 345).

referring.[36] Fergusson had judiciously timed his attack of Mitra to coincide with the proceedings of the Ilbert Bill which was passed in 1883.[37] The viciousness of his denunciation of Mitra's credibility as a scholar provides a reason for enquiring into the history of communication between Indian and western Indologists during this politically fraught year of the colonial rule of India, and in this respect, a note by Hoernle in the correspondence section of *The Indian Antiquary*, which dates from 1883 catches the eye. The note represents Hoernle's response to the criticism by Ramakrishna Gopal Bhandarkar, who was then professor of Sanskrit at Deccan College (Poona, 1882–93), of his translation of an inscription that had been found at Nasik. He concluded his response with the statement that

> I have read Professor Bhandarkar's review of my paper on the Nasik inscription with great interest, and I will add, with much pleasure; for it *is* a pleasure to have to deal with an antagonist so able and so courteous. [...] Literary warfare would be something different from what it often is, if it were always carried on in the spirit of Professor Bhandarkar's review.[38]

The above statement is noticeable because similar to Fergusson, Hoernle too was criticised by an Indian scholar who was a beneficiary of the supposedly 'enlightened' western education system.[39] Bhandarkar (1837–1925) had received his higher education in Sanskrit at Elphinstone and Deccan colleges, which were both established in 1860. He received his M.A. from the latter in 1863, and was subsequently conferred a doctorate from the University of Göttingen (in 1885). As Madhav Deshpande has emphasised, he was the 'first fully modern professor' of Sanskrit, 'who did not come from a Pandit background', and 'in some ways went much further than his mentor, Professor Kielhorn in modernizing the teaching of Sanskrit for the newly emerging schools and colleges'. Thus, for instance

---

[36] For example, see Dharamsey (2004); Guha-Thakurta (2004, pp. 108–11); Dutta (2009), Chakrabarti (1997).

[37] Fergusson (1884, pp. 4–19). See Pinney (2008, p. 70), for noting the antagonism of Fergusson towards Mitra for the latter's strong denunciation of the cruelties perpetuated by the British in their indigo plantations. Fergusson, as is well known, had made a fortune in the indigo trade by the mid-1830s that allowed him to pursue his vocation in the arts.

[38] Hoernle (1883, p. 206).

[39] See also Hoernle's review (1904, pp. 639–61, specifically p. 643) of Bhandarkar's thesis on the Gurjaras (in *JBBRAS*, 1903).

Bhandarkar produced the first successful book of the modern methods of teaching Sanskrit grammar in India.[40]

Hoernle's reply to Bhandarkar affirms that by the late nineteenth century many western scholars complied with the protocols of scholarship, and many treated their Indian colleagues as their peers. We can also add to the histories of the collegiate relationship between the Indian and western Indologists through histories of the reception of Mitra's scholarship.

Mitra was invited to present a lecture at the Asiatic Society of Bombay in April 1879, a year and a half before he was denounced by Fergusson. The occasion was the endowment of the honorary membership of the Society to him in recognition of his 'successful investigations into the history of the archaeology and history' of India. By then, one of his two volumes of the *Antiquities of Orissa* had been published (1875), and also his seminal research of the history of Bodh Gaya, which was published as *Buddha Gaya, the Hermitage of Sakya Muni* (1878). In introducing him to the Society, Justice Kashinath Telang had declared that:

> For upwards of a quarter of a century his name has been quite familiar to all who have any connection with the pursuits in which he is so successful an enquirer—the pursuits of Oriental literature and antiquity. His performances in these departments of study have already familiarised his name all over the learned societies of Europe and America, and he has been elected honorary member, and has received honours from various societies throughout Europe and America.[41]

Telang's recall of Mitra's scholarly engagements, illustrates the latter's growing international standing among the world of Indology, and, in 1885, he became the first 'native' president of the Asiatic Society of Bengal. Although Telang's appreciation may have reflected the Indian view of Mitra's scholarship, this was aired amidst many non-Indian members of the Asiatic Society of Bombay who held high offices. In noting Mitra's growing reputation in the scholarship of Indology, we also note that the German Sanskritists often demonstrated the errors and flaws in his Sanskrit translations.[42] Yet, neither

[40] Deshpande (2001, pp. 134–35).

[41] Telang (1880, p. xxxix).

[42] For example, in response to Mitra's criticism of his alleged mistranslation of a legend of Krishna, Albrecht Weber had complained to the editor of *The Indian Antiquary*: 'We European scholars are not bound to swear by the authority of his scriptures and go our way without

they, nor did any other 'Western' scholar of Indology apart from Fergusson spar with him in such a vicious manner. We could suggest, with a reasonable degree of certainty, that the reason why contemporary western Indologists ignored Fergusson's remark was because he had so blatantly flouted even the semblance of maintaining the protocols of academic courtesy. Thus, it behoves to examine the simple classifications of scholarship and its critique into representations of native or western mindsets.

In a lecture to the Asiatic Society of Bombay after his return from the Oriental conference at Vienna, which was held in 1886, Bhandarkar had presented the contributions of the German Sanskritists to the historical scholarship of India. He perceived them to be the 'Brahmans of Europe', perhaps because he was a beneficiary of their teaching. But he was also critical in his estimation of their research, as he believed that, like all European Sanskritists, they too presented 'instances of comprehensive conclusions based upon slender judgements'. However, he made the point of emphasising that

> the great excellence of German scholarship consists in the spirit of criticism and comparison that is brought to bear on the facts that come under observation, and in the endeavour made to trace the gradual development of thought and language and to determine the chronological relations to events.[43]

Bhandarkar highlighted as unique the links which the German Indologists had sought to establish between India and Europe for furthering the scholarship of Sanskrit. To illustrate his statement, he drew attention to Bühler's efforts as the professor of Sanskrit at Vienna University for creating an assistant professorship in the subject, with the stipulation that the post was to be held by an Indian candidate with a Master's degree in Sanskrit from Bombay University.[44]

In their scholarship of Sanskrit, the German Indologists showed the need for greater sensitivity towards the reading of the textual sources. The note by Hoernle in *The Indian Antiquary* which is quoted above also provides an example of the methodological focus, which he, possibly unwittingly, created towards perceptions of 'valid' historical evidence. He cautioned

---

being fettered by so curious a specimen of human credulity as the Bhagavata appears to us'. See Weber (1880, p. 227). Also, see Fleet (1888, p. 50), who criticised Mitra's reading of the Indore grant of Skandagupta.

[43] Bhandarkar (1889, pp. 85–86).

[44] Ibid., p. 87.

against the seeing of 'errors' within inscriptions when the readings did not match expectations of the contents, and in explaining the translation that Bhandarkar had faulted, he declared that:

> we ought not, I think, to attribute errors to ancient records, unless when absolutely compelled to do so. I have shown, I think, that this particular Nasik record may be explained without importing into it any errors at all. If we once allow ourselves to correct and revise ancient records, according to what we fancy the author ought to have written or intended to write, we open a way for a dangerous licence of criticism.[45]

Such examples of wariness towards the frequent notices of 'errors' within the contents of inscriptions are representative of the growing awareness among the European Indologists of the sheer diversity of India's literary corpus. To a considerable extent, the awareness bespoke of the efforts of Bühler in bringing to light vast amounts of previously 'unknown' manuscripts during his stay in India. Indeed, Bühler was retrospectively recalled by Ernst Leumann as one who:

> not only equals Rask, Hodgson, Chambers, Colebrooke, Wilson and Wright as a collector of manuscripts, but far surpasses them all. And therefore, had he done nothing else for Sanskrit Philology, he would be one of its greatest promoters—one of those whose activity most decidedly and most happily determine the progress of Indian Research.[46]

The following summary of the government-sponsored 'search for manuscripts', which Bühler initiated is specifically presented for illustrating the errors of the judgement, which has been expressed by one historian of Indian archaeology, that 'after 1871, although occasional support was given to the publication of ancient texts, it was the archaeological track of inquiry that was given firm organisational basis and sustained financial support by the colonial state'.[47] For, not only were the field surveys for manuscripts and archaeological surveys of India contemporary activities throughout the latter half of the nineteenth century, the colonial government also supported both in its characteristically intermittent and pecuniary manner.

---

[45] Hoernle (1883, p. 205–6).
[46] Leumann (1898, p. 369).
[47] Singh (2004, p. 353).

The 'Search for Manuscripts' Project (1868–98): A Short Note

Just as the government in 1861, impressed by Cunningham's explorations and at his behest, had sanctioned a one-man led Archaeological Survey, similarly five years later in 1866, impressed by Bühler's explorations for manuscripts within the Bombay Presidency between 1863 and 1866, and at his behest, it supported his one-man enterprise of field explorations for manuscripts. The explorations were undertaken within the southern Maratha and northern Kanara countries during the cold seasons of 1866–69, and led to significant discoveries through which Bühler was able to persuade the Bombay Presidency to initiate an official project for the 'Search for Manuscripts'. The project was sanctioned in 1868 with an annual budget of ₹25,000, and Bühler was designated officer in charge. He was also appointed Education Inspector of Gujarat at the same time (that is, 20 December 1868), which allowed him to meet his plans of surveying Rajputana, between December 1873 and March 1874. He exposed vast collections of Jain manuscripts within many *Saraswatis* or libraries—many within temples—and in the following year between July 1875 and April 1876, he extended his surveys to Kashmir and central India.

By initiating the official project, Bühler enhanced the scope for studying the 'Hindu period' through textual sources. He single-handedly rescued 'two whole branches of literature from oblivion, namely Kashmiri branch [that comprised] Vedic and Sanskrit texts and the extensive Prakrit and Sanskrit literature of the Svetambara Jains', and his discoveries proved to be of immense benefit for the libraries of Elphinstone College and Deccan College. The latter, for example, acquired over 2,363 manuscripts within a decade of its formal establishment. As a manuscript collector, Bühler far surpassed the efforts that had been undertaken previously by individual scholars and was feted for the discoveries of 'all branches of Indian literature' many 'altogether unknown'.[48] He also encouraged European libraries to buy the copies that had representations within the collections, which he secured for the Government of India.[49] The University of Berlin, which had only eight

---

[48] Winternitz (1898, p. 368).

[49] Leumann (1898, p. 368). Leumann had recorded that Bühler gave 300 manuscripts to the India Office Library (London) between 1883 and 1866, and 200 to Elphinstone College,

Sanskrit manuscripts around the time of Franz Bopp in 1827, had over 2,000 by 1886, of which 500 came from him.[50] In noting the increasing collections of Indian manuscript in Europe throughout the nineteenth century, Marchand deemed that although the collecting ventures were underwritten by 'deeper imperialist penetration into India, the bringing home to Europe of more and more Sanskrit texts ... meant that [European] scholars [from mid-century onwards] were able to depend less on conventional, classical, and biblical sources'.[51] Thus, the collecting and editing ventures of the German Orientalists allowed many to forsake trust in their own ancient (that is, Biblical) authorities, and seek new ways of writing the history of the ancient East. The textual scholarship and philological exegesis also allowed them to push for more exact and 'culturally authentic' readings and make attempts at understanding 'the Sanskrit texts from within'.[52] Hoernle's scepticism towards the sighting of errors within the inscriptions, which has been mentioned earlier, is one example of the historical phenomenon, which Marchand has described.

The Antiquarian Scholarship of Indology

After Bühler's departure from India, the field explorations for manuscripts continued until 1898 through the efforts of Kielhorn and by Peter Peterson and Bhandarkar.[53] As Peterson reported after his first survey between August 1882 and March 1883:

> The operations in search of Sanskrit manuscripts in Bombay Circle have been under the joint chare of Professor Bhandarkar and myself since August 1882, when Professor Bhandarkar, who on Dr. Kielhorn's departure, had been put by the Director of Public Instruction in sole charge, was invited by that office [...] to make over part of the work to me. It was then agreed between us that

---

between 1866 and 1868. Among the European libraries, Berlin acquired 500 manuscripts from his collections between 1873 and 1880. Leumann (ibid., p. 369).

[50] On numbers and history of increase, see Sengupta (2005, pp. 121–35); also quoted in Marchand (2009, p. 135).

[51] Marchand (2009, p. 134).

[52] Ibid.

[53] See Bhandarkar (1887); Peterson (1899).

we should divide equally the amount that remained (Rs. 4,952) of the grant for the year, and that while the Bombay Professor [Peterson in this instance] should be generally in charge of the Northern, and the Poona Professor in charge of the Southern Division, it should be open to either of us at any time, after mutual consultation, to push the objects of the search in any part of the Circle that might be deemed expedient.[54]

The 'Bombay Sanskrit and Prakrit Series', which was initiated in 1880, the year of Bühler's leaving, provides an example of the wealth of the philological scholarship, which the government support of their field explorations contributed to.[55] Therefore, it is curious that Bühler's field surveys remain largely unnoticed within the modern histories of Indian archaeology, because they included archaeological explorations.

As the laudation of the director of the Public Instruction of Bombay Presidency, which has been mentioned earlier in this chapter, informs us, Bühler's scholarship was noted during his time for its significant contributions to Indian archaeology. The director spoke of Bühler's additions to the 'archaeological lore'. Like all field surveyors of India during the nineteenth and early twentieth centuries, Bühler also recorded the ancient settlements he passed through, and meticulously gathered ethnographic information of the local terrains. His success in locating many ancient sites through the system of place names, which was famously perfected by Cunningham, was also due to the inventories of the manuscripts which he undertook at the time of their discoveries, often in the field. A pertinent example is his survey of the town of Khunmoh (Kashmir) in August 1875. He recorded the possible traces of the ancient Khonamukha within the modern town after noting the description in the *Vikramankacharita*, a text of the eleventh century from Kashmir, which was composed by Bilhana, whose copy he had found in a library at Jaisalmer during the exploratory season.[56]

Additionally, Bühler's 'notes on past and future archaeological explorations in India' (1895) are the most inclusive report of the archaeological

<hr />

[54] Peterson (1883, p. 1).

[55] Examples of publications in the Bombay Sanskrit Prakrit Series: Kielhorn's critical edition of *The Vyakarana-Mahabhasya of Patanjali* (1880), *Vakpati's Gaudavaho*, edited by Shankar Pandurang Pandit (1887), *The Mahanarayana-Upanishad of the Atharva Veda, with the Dipika of Narayana* (1888), edited by A. Jacob, and the *Kavyaprakasha* of Mammata, with *Balabodhini* of Vamanacarya Jhalkikar (1900).

[56] Bühler (1877, pp. 4–7). The town of Khunamusha in the *Rajatarangini* was identified as Khunmoh by Cunningham.

explorations of the Indian subcontinent during the latter half of the nine-teenth century. He took care to include the archaeological activities that were initiated outside the British domains, within the princely states of Mysore, Baroda, Bhavanagar, Jaipur and Udaipur, expressed his criticism of the stupa-opening excavations that had been undertaken throughout the century, including by Cunningham, and implored upon the urgency of undertaking scientific excavations through the comment that 'the costliness of extensive excavations made it advisable either to merely prospect or to attempt a full exploration only in such places where success was an absolute certainty'.[57] The remark presents Bühler's informed views of the destruction that excava-tions entail, and the possible preventative measures that could be taken. He also accurately gauged the potentials of many archaeological sites during his explorations for manuscripts. Thus, in 1900, on seeing the ruins at Taxila, his former student, Marc Aurel Stein, who subsequently acquired formidable reputation as an archaeologist, announced that 'the scanty remains [...] below [the ground] are fortunately safe and may yet someday prove that Prof. Bühler was right in looking upon Taxila as one of the most promising places for systematic excavations'.[58] Stein had been taught by Bühler in Leipzig after the latter returned to Germany. Hence, his recall of his teacher's views at some length is not surprising. However, the excavations at Taxila between 1913 and 1934 by John Marshall, and his officers of the Archaeological Survey, subsequently demonstrated the accuracy of Bühler's judgements.

Bühler's Indology bespoke of the inclusiveness and breadth of the anti-quarian scholarship at the close of the nineteenth century, when the colonial government began to create the utility value of archaeology for building a visible profile of its civilisational mission to document and preserve India's past. In comparison, the government found little reason for promoting the knowledge and scholarship of Sanskrit and Persian within Britain or India, since the languages no longer held any use-value in the administra-tion of the colony. By exhibiting the merits of archaeological enquiries over the philological scholarship of Ancient India, archaeologists of India in the twenty-first century embrace the utilitarian measure that had governed the colonial administration of Indology.

---

[57] Bühler (1895, p. 656).
[58] Stein (1900b, p. 145). Stein was regarded as one of the 'great explorers of the moment' among nine others in *The Illustrated London News* of 30 January 1909.

Scholarship and Its Governance

The re-institution of the Archaeological Survey in 1902 provided contemporary Indologists the occasion to see the differential valuations of archaeology and philology by the colonial government. The new Survey was specifically aimed at facilitating large-scale projects of archaeological restorations and excavations, which publicly displayed the ostensible benefits of the raj in nurturing India's monumental and civilisational heritage. Since philological scholarship could not emulate the visible transparency of the merits of archaeological work, its utility value as a useful science was further compromised.

At Cunningham's initiatives, the government had established the post of Government Epigraphist, in 1883, within the Archaeological Survey that was created in 1871. The British Sanskritist John Faithfull Fleet (1847–1917), who worked with the revenue department of the Bombay Civil Service was seconded to the post for preparing a volume of the inscriptions of the early Gupta kings. Fleet filled the post until 1886, when Hultzsch succeeded him. With the dissolution of the Survey in 1889, the post was transferred to the Madras Government, and subsequently, under the re-organisation scheme of the Archaeological department in 1898, it was deemed supportable as long as Hultzsch held the job.[59] The 'rumour' that circulated at the time of the latter's resignation from the post and acceptance of a professorship in Sanskrit at Halle in 1902, was that he chose to return to Europe as he was frustrated by the government's lack of support for an institution similar to the Archaeological Survey for the study of epigraphy.[60]

The official noting of the 'rumour' makes it quite apparent that the re-institution of the Survey in 1902 occasioned the stock-taking of government support towards the scholarship of Oriental languages. Rightly judging the support to be on the decline, professors of Sanskrit and Arabic at Cambridge and Oxford raised the 'Question of The Appointment of European Sanskrit, Persian and Arabic scholars in the Archaeology Department'.[61] They proposed the creation of teaching fellowships at the cost of Indian revenues so that 'young orientalists' in Britain could find

---

[59] For details of Hultzsch's term of appointment, see Marshall (1904b, p. 235).

[60] 'Rumours regarding Dr Hultzsch's resignation and acceptance by him of Sanskrit Professorship at Halle', File No. 54 of 1902, Survey Archives.

[61] 'Question of Appointment of European Sanskrit, Persian and Arabic Scholars,' *Proceedings of the Home Department, A&E,* Nos. 13–14, December 1906, pp. 299–312.

employment in India, and declared that 'it cannot be too strongly emphasised that the possession of a high degree in Oriental languages without continued study or practical knowledge of the East is not as a rule sufficient'.[62] Although the proposal was forwarded to the Governor General by the Secretary of State for India John Morley as 'the study of Sanskrit as an Indian question', it was drawn up 'as an imperial question', and one of the signatories, the Boden professor, Arthur Macdonell presented a lecture at the Royal Asiatic Society (London) at the time of submission, in which he emphatically documented the utility value of philology for archaeological work.[63] He stated unequivocally that the knowledge of Sanskrit was an essential qualification for the superintending archaeologists, 'or else' he retorted:

> How are the inscriptions to be deciphered, ancient sites to be identified, antiquities to be interpreted, history to be extracted from archaeological finds, by men who have not learned Indian epigraphy, who have no first-hand knowledge of ancient mythology, and to whom the various clues afforded by a direct acquaintance with the ancient literature are inaccessible? Would the archaeology of Greece yield any valuable results if investigated by men who know no Greek?[64]

In 1906, when Macdonell and other professors of Sanskrit and Persian in Britain, including E.J. Rapson at Cambridge, presented their proposal to the Imperial Government, Sten Konow had been appointed by the Archaeological Survey of India as government epigraphist (1906–08). The appointment would have raised their hopes of the possibility that the government would accede to the nurture of the British scholarship of Sanskrit, Persian and Arabic through the Survey. In illustrating the reasons for placing support for the scholarship of Sanskrit as an 'imperial question', Macdonell noted that since the closure of the East India College at Haileybury in 1858, the study of Sanskrit from being a compulsory subject for probationers of the Indian Civil Service was made into an optional subject, which many continued to choose. However, with the regulations of 1892–93, which reduced the duration of the Civil Service course from two to one year, and with the withdrawal of prize money for attaining proficiency in Sanskrit, student numbers dropped

---

[62] 'Question of Appointment of European Sanskrit, Persian and Arabic Scholars,' *Proceedings of the Home Department, A&E*, Nos. 13–14, December 1906, p, 301.

[63] Ibid., p. 299; Macdonell (1906).

[64] Macdonell (ibid., p. 310).

to 'four or five'. In 1903, when the number of optional subjects a probationer was required to take was reduced from two to one, Sanskrit students reached 'almost vanishing point as owing to the highness of the standard no English candidate [found] it worth his while to offer the subject'. The 'net result', Macdonell pointed out, was that 'of the fifty-three or fifty-four young Britons who leave England every year as future rulers of India, two at the most now go out equipped with even an elementary knowledge of the classical language of that country'. Emphasising that Sanskrit was the key to all Indian vernaculars, Macdonell exposed the inadequacy of the linguistic incompetence of the British Civil Servants by asserting:

> Let us suppose, for the sake of argument, that Italy were a province of Germany and ruled by a staff of German Civil Servants educated for the purpose in their own country. Is it conceivable that these highly trained officials would be allowed to enter on their duties without knowing a word of Latin, the mother of Italian and the language in which the ancient literature and laws of Italy are written?[65]

Many colonial administrators would have supported Macdonell's vision; an example is a letter of reference that Richard Carnac Temple, the former administrator of Upper Burma (1886–94), wrote to the education department of Burma in 1900, in support of Taw Sein Ko's application for a junior post. Temple, then chief commissioner of the Andaman Islands (1894–1904), supported Ko's candidature in the hope that the post would allow the latter to be considered for the post of government archaeologist of Burma. He, thus, emphasised Ko's expertise in 'Burmese and Pali' and asserted:

> It is not to my mind a question of how many people are studying Talaing now a days or its value as a living tongue worth preserving as a vernacular.

[65] 'Question of Appointment of European Sanskrit, Persian and Arabic Scholars,' *Proceedings of the Home Department, A & E*, Nos. 13–14, December 1906, pp. 304–05. Macdonell had studied Sanskrit at Göttingen and hence, he also valued the German scholarship in the subject. He presented a retrospective account of his proposal and the British Government's response in his acceptance speech for The Campbell Memorial Gold Medal, which he received from the Royal Asiatic Society in London on 14 March 1914. In this, he maintained that although a few Indian scholars had benefitted from government scholarships for the study of Sanskrit in the UK, he was unsure whether the scheme 'will also result in the production of research work of a more general character and in the organisation of Sanskrit studies in India, without the aid of European scholars'. cf. 'The Campbell Memorial Gold Medal', *Journal of the Royal Asiatic Society of Great Britain and Ireland (JRAS)*, 1916, pp. 577–90, 588.

The real question is that half the history of the monuments of the country lie buried in that language and for the sake of recovering an understanding of the past, I say it is still well worth the expenditure necessary to maintain a chair of research into that valuable language hopelessly moribund though it be.[66]

Ironically, Temple's argument, in support of the colonial curation of the archaeology of Burma remains equally valid in today's world, and presents the fallacy of axing language-based teaching of South Asia's 'pre-modern' cultural histories from the university curricula internationally.

In addition to his argument of the utility of Sanskrit for the archaeological scholarship of India, Macdonell demonstrated the importance of the British scholarship of Sanskrit as 'the practical need of the Empire'. Like most of his British colleagues, he was wary of the quality of the Indian scholarship of Sanskrit apart from 'exceptions such as Bhandarkar', and was of the view that the presence of British Sanskritists in India would make 'the Indian people understand their own civilisation historically, and acquire that enlightenment, which will prove the surest means of delivering them from the bonds of superstition and caste'.[67] He chanced upon the possibilities of his government's recognition that similar to the archaeological undertakings, the British scholarship of Sanskrit could also be employed for meeting the colonial civilisation mission. However, the Government of India vetoed the proposal. Although it 'admitted that a knowledge of Sanskrit [was] of substantial value to the officers of the Archaeological Department', it maintained that since the:

> greater part of a Superintendent of circle, at present and for many years to come, will consist in the oversight and conservation of Indian monuments [...] an expert acquaintance with these languages is not so essential for the work of an archaeologist as it is for that of an epigraphist.[68]

In refusing to commit to the intake of western philologists in Sanskrit, Arabic and Persian within the Survey, the government reminded the signatories

---

[66] Demi-official letter from Richard Carnac Temple, C.I.E., Chief Commissioner, Andaman Islands, regarding Taw Sein Ko, Officiating Assistant Secretary to the Govt. of Burma, dated 2 August 1900, *Proceedings of the Home Department, Education*, June 1901, Nos. 8–9.

[67] Macdonell (1906, p. 310).

[68] Despatch No. 411 of 1906 from Finance Department, Letter to John Morley from J.B. Brunyate, deputy secretary to Government of India, dated 29 November 1906, *Proceedings of the Home Department, A&E*, No. 14, December, pp. 311–12.

that the organisation had superintendent officers, such as Theodore Bloch, Jean Philippe Vogel and Denison Ross, who were in fact expert scholars of the said languages.

The decision of the government to ignore the proposal bespoke of the inherently parsimonious colonial governance of India, which showed persistence in its reluctance to support all enterprises that had no perceptible political and economic benefits. In this respect, it should be emphasised that the move to recruit Indians within the new Archaeological Survey, which can be noticed from the beginning of the twentieth century, was a way of keeping costs down, although it no doubt met the strategies of the colonial government to display its benevolence. Thus, following Konow's resignation as government epigraphist in 1908, V. Venkayya Avargal, then assistant superintendent of epigraphy in the Survey's southern circle, was persuaded to take up the post at a third of Konow's pay. Of this appointment, Marshall, who was then director general of the Survey, had observed that 'had [this] been given to a man from home, we should have had to pay him hardly less than Rs. 1000/– the salary of Dr Konow'.[69] The observation demands a note, because many Indian historians of Indian archaeology applaud Curzon for preventing the 'western "oriental scholars"' from taking over the 'reins' of the new Archaeological Survey of the twentieth century, which he had envisioned and established. With Curzon, they, mistakenly, say, 'the racist dictates of colonial Indology did not apparently cut much ice'.[70] They overlook the stark reality that the 'western oriental scholars' were an unnecessary expense considering the availability of cheap native labour. The in-built racism in the government decision to recruit Indians for the purposes of epigraphic work is blatantly apparent, and does not merit the need for further exposure.

By foregoing the expensive European philologists, the Survey was able to employ British architects as superintendent officers for meeting the demands of Curzon's mastermind—of initiating large-scale archaeological projects to ostensibly restore a decaying civilisation. The recruitment of architects as superintendent archaeologists, such as James Page, Henry Longhurst,

---

[69] D.O. letter of John Marshall, in 'Retention of the Services of Dr. D.B. Spooner, Mr. A. H. Longhurst and Dr Sten Konow', 1908, File No 178, S. No. 1–28, Survey Archives. Konow was paid ₹1,000 a month, although the salary sanctioned for him was ₹850. Venkayya wanted his salary to be ₹800, but was given ₹650 instead.

[70] Chakrabarti (2009, p. 13), who has applauded the choice of John Marshall over Vincent Smith as the Survey's director general through the statement.

William Nicholls, Richard Froude Tucker and Gordon Sanderson, within the first decade of the new Survey was effectively built upon the logic that professional Indian architects were non-existent. Yet, the lacunae of British Sanskritists, which the proposal of 1906 informs us of, and which Macdonell had addressed, was carefully articulated by Jean Philippe Vogel in 1911 outside the 'imperial question' and through the statement that 'this fact does not remain unnoticed by the cultured and learned classes and it cannot but create the impression that in the matter of Sanskrit studies England does not take the lead of European nations as it ought to do'. Significantly, Vogel had added:

> It should be remembered that in few countries in the world, learning is held in as great an estimation as in India and that to the great majority of Indians true learning is unthinkable without a knowledge of the classical language in which the Shastras are written.[71]

The distinctions in the reception of the scholarship of the Indians by the European and British Sanskritists demand a note, and also critical histories.

The Archaeological Survey of India instituted two fellowships for Indian graduates in 1903, one each in Sanskrit and Persian, so that it could raise native epigraphists to fill in the services of the Western Indologists. However, the intake did not change the regard for the appointment of Western philologists as heads of the Epigraphy department. Marshall lucidly explained the need to recruit from this cadre in a letter to the Secretary of Education when the post of Government Epigraphist fell vacant after Venkayya's death in November 1912. He declared:

> The Government is aware I am an advocate of employing Indians in the Archaeological Department whenever it is possible to do so, but in this case it is essential that there should be someone at the head of Epigraphical staff, who can be relied upon to sustain in his own work and impart to other the scholarly traditions laid down by Hultzsch, Fleet, Bühler and others.

Showing his ambivalence of the candidature of Krishna Sastri as government epigraphist, he presented his understanding of a suitable candidate as:

---

[71] Letter by J.Ph. Vogel, then officiating director general ASI to Secretary, Education, dated 2 March 1912, with respect to memorandum, 'Staff of the Archaeological Section of the Indian Museum' (27 February 1912), *Proceedings of Education Department, A&E*, No. 422, pp. 109–110.

He must be a first rate Sanskritist and sufficiently familiar with all other languages used in Indian inscriptions, to be able to control the work done by his subordinates. He must be versed in modern critical methods and able to keep well abreast of the progress made in the study of Indian History and Philology throughout the world. He must have reasonable acquaintance with all that has already been done in the epigraphic field, and be prepared to initiate and plan new schemes of research. He must be competent to organise and train a staff of assistants, and he must keep in close touch with and enlist the co-operation of European scholars, and at the same time be capable of checking and revising their work and of helping them with his advice, comments and notes; in short, exercising complete editorial control over the work of European collaborators. It will not be possible, I fear, to find an Indian scholar, qualified to do all this.[72]

Marshall's support for a non-Indian to fill the top post in the scholarship of Indian epigraphy also illuminates his strong views for maintaining the past excellence of the Survey's epigraphy department.[73] Considering the paucity of jobs in Sanskrit within European and American universities at the close of the nineteenth century, we would anticipate that an employment within the seemingly robust Archaeological Survey might have appeared as a highly attractive career option for many western Sanskritists and Persianists. However, the resignation from the Survey by Hultzsch (1904), Konow (1906) and Vogel (1913) to take up teaching posts in universities at Halle, Christiania and Leiden, respectively, reveals the ambivalence among them in pursuing a life-long career within the institution. A letter to Konow from David Brainerd Spooner (1879–1925) proves the point.

Spooner was the only non-British westerner to have created his career within the Survey. He was an American with a doctorate in Sanskrit from Berlin, and had joined the Survey as superintendent officer of the Frontier Circle in 1905. Although the re-organisation of the Archaeological Survey as a permanent institution in 1906 stipulated that the 'new European officers

---

[72] D.O. letter from Marshall to Secretary, Education, 1 May 1914, Simla, *Proceedings of Education Department, A&E*, No. 894, pp. 433–35.

[73] With reference to Leonard Woolley's critical assessments of the Archaeological Survey of India in 1939 Aurel Stein held the view, which he conveyed privately to 'the Baron', namely Fred Henry Andrews, that 'complete "Indianisation"' as now practically achieved, must mean a setback just as it can be foreseen in more important directions. History will judge whether it was unavoidable and of benefit for India as whole. For those who have to care for the future and are limited by the promises and actions of the past it is an exceedingly difficult problem. What a burden it must be for those responsible during this time of hard struggle'. Letter to The Baron, 13 February 1940, from the Archaeological Bungalow, Taxila, Stein MSS 61, Stein Collections.

whom it will be necessary to recruit should, if possible, be natural born British subjects', Spooner's appointment was waived with the understanding that 'objections to the employment of foreigners do not apply with full force to the appointment of Americans'.[74] He remained in the employ of the Survey until his untimely death. However, after a very successful excavation season at Shahji-ki-dheri in 1908–9, he had written to Konow bemoaning:

> I have a very well grounded fear that by remaining indefinitely I imperil my position as a Sanskritist. I had almost no Sanskrit to do since I came out and there is no denying the sad fact that when one is not advancing in a language one is surely going back! I do not want to lose all my Sanskrit, and it seems to me it would be wise to accept a Sanskrit post at Home if one were available, or when becomes so.[75]

Spooner's lament provokes a thought towards the celebration of Curzon by Indian archaeologists for keeping the new Survey philologist-free. For it shows that those who were committed to the philological scholarship may not have necessarily desired a permanent career within the Organisation.

The Birch Bark Manuscripts: Philological Discoveries and Archaeological Undertakings

Despite the transparently differential utility value which was endowed by the colonial government upon the scholarship of Indian archaeology and

---

[74] 'Re-organisation of the Archaeology Department', No. 18, *Proceedings of Revenue and Agriculture, A&E*, 1905.

[75] Letter from Spooner to Konow from Peshawar, dated 20 October 1909, MS Folio 4201: eske 1 (Nr 21), National Library of Norway. Spooner continued:

> As I wrote to Lanman, I accepted this post somewhat in the spirit of a Fellowship hoping it would furnish opportunity for widening my knowledge and gaining experience of a kind as valuable as it is rare among Indianists in Europe. These hopes have been in no way disappointed. But it is evident and will be especially to you that the educational value of my appointment must in the nature of things decrease from year to year as I become familiar with material. This does not mean to imply that I am in any danger of <u>loosing it all!</u> But it does imply that I question the wisdom of continuing in the post indefinitely when I feel that by doing so I am endangering my Sanskrit and my hope of ultimately getting a Sanskrit post at home.

philology at the beginning of the twentieth century, the connected histories of the two forms of historical enquiries leave some of the strongest traces from this period. The discoveries of numerous birch-bark manuscripts from the 1880s led to new archaeological searches for 'ancient written antiquities' within Central Asia, and the decipherments and explorations established the rich and relatively unknown histories of the cultural connections between the ancient worlds of India, China, Iran and Classical Greece during the first millennium.

In 1881, fragments of a birch-back manuscript were dug up from a 'ruined enclosure' at Bakshali (North West Frontier, Yusufzai District, Pakistan). They were subsequently read by Hoernle as an arithmetical treatise in the Sharada script and Gatha dialect. The leaves had been sent to Hoernle in 'great confusion' and 'mutilated form', and his successful reading by the mid-1880s established his reputation as the foremost authority of archaic Indian scripts.[76] This reputation grew with Hoernle's subsequent successes at deciphering the so-called 'Bower' manuscript, which was found in 1889 by treasure hunters who had rifled a stupa at Ming-oi near Kucha (Kashgaria). The manuscript was collected by Hamilton Bower who brought it to Calcutta in 1890. Hoernle was given the manuscript to decipher in 1891, and he announced this to 'date from the second half of the fifth century (say about 475 AD)', and the 'result' he declared 'will probably be startling to most readers', because 'there exists a pretty general tendency to discredit any claim to great age on the part of any Indian manuscript'.[77] Hoernle was of the opinion that precise knowledge of the manuscript would initiate the 'whole modern movement of the archaeological exploration of Eastern Turkistan'.[78] His first publications on the manuscript in 1891 inspired the Russian Archaeological Society to set off an immediate exploration for similar treasures in Kashgar and other areas of Central Asia. In 1893, Hoernle was given another ancient birch-bark manuscript, which had come into the possession of Revd Weber of the Moravian Mission at Leh.[79] The knowledge of the Bower and the Weber manuscripts, as they came to called, and of the Russian successes led Hoernle to request the Government of India to instruct its political

---

[76] Hoernle (1887, pp. 3–4).

[77] Hoernle (1891, p. 93). The manuscript is a medical manuscript in the late Brahmi script. See also Hoernle (1892).

[78] Quoted by Sten Konow in his review of Hoernle's translation. See Konow (1914, p. 179).

[79] Hoernle (1893).

Illustration 1.1
Pillar near Badal, Dinajpur (Bangladesh). Engraved plate from drawing by
Charles Wilkins, circa 1770s, *Asiatick Researches* (Vol. I).
Courtesy: Cambridge University Library.

Illustration 1.2
Sculptures at Elephanta. Drawing by Capt Baker (1712), *Archaeologia* (Vol. 7).
Courtesy: Cambridge University Library.

Illustration 2.1
Assyrian relief at Nimrud. Engraved plate from drawing by George Scharf Jr,
1846–47. Layard directed the inscription across the artefact to be removed in the
reproduction because he saw that to interfere with the 'forms of the figure'.
The Monuments of Nineveh, plate 5.
Courtesy: Cambridge University Library.

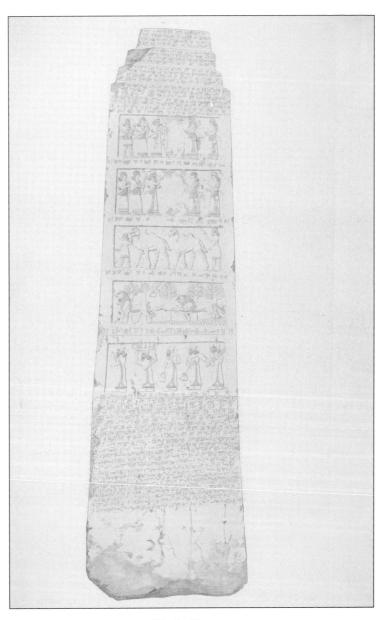

Illustration 2.2
The 'Black Obelisk' at Nimrud, 'First Side'. Engraved plate from drawing by
George Scharf Jr, 1846–47, *The Monuments of Nineveh*, plate 53.
Courtesy: Cambridge University Library.

Illustration 2.3
Display of Assyrian collections, CSVMS, Mumbai, Photograph, 2013.
Courtesy: CSMVS.

Illustration 2.4
'Restoration of the palaces of the western side of the platform at Nimroud'.
Lithograph in colour from drawing by Baynes, supervised by James Fergusson,
circa 1850, *A Second Series of The Monuments of Nineveh*, plate 1.
Courtesy: Cambridge University Library.

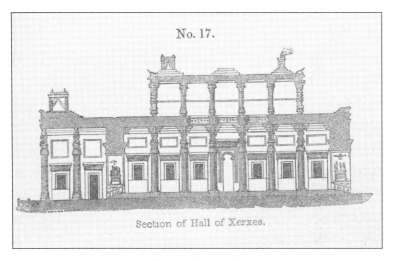

Illustration 2.5(a)
Hypostyle Hall of Xerxes, Persepolis. Drawing by James Fergusson,
The Palaces of Nineveh and Persepolis Restored, plate 17.
Courtesy: Cambridge University Library.

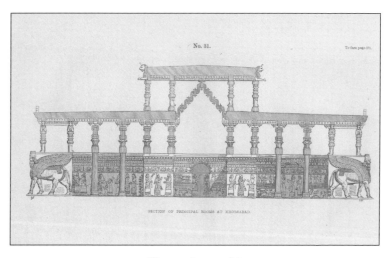

Illustration 2.5(b)
Palace at Khorsabad near Mosul. Drawing by James Fergusson,
The Palaces of Nineveh and Persepolis Restored, plate 31.
Courtesy: Cambridge University Library.

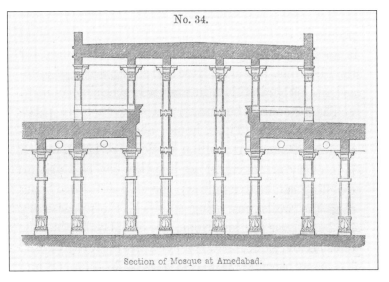

Illustration 2.5(c)
Jami Masjid, Ahmedabad. Drawing by James Fergusson,
The Palaces of Nineveh and Persepolis Restored, plate 34.
Courtesy: Cambridge University Library.

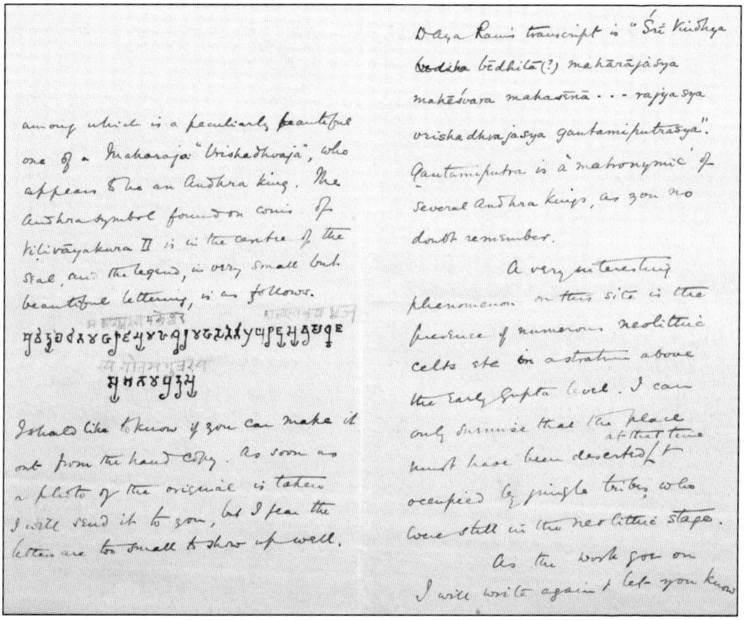

Illustration 3.1
Letter from John Marshall to Sten Konow,
13 January 1910, from Camp Bhita, Allahabad District.
Courtesy: National Library of Norway.

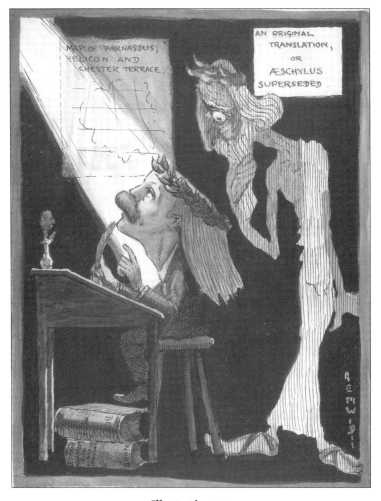

Illustration 3.2
'Cartoon'. Drawing by R.E.M. Wheeler, 1911, Box 452, British Academy Archives.
Courtesy: Carol Pettman and her Sister.

Illustration 4.1
Display of prehistoric pottery from Baluchistan, Annexe Gallery, Central Asian
Antiquities Museum, New Delhi. Photograph, 1934–37, ASI, Neg. No. 359.
Courtesy: Archaeological Survey of India.

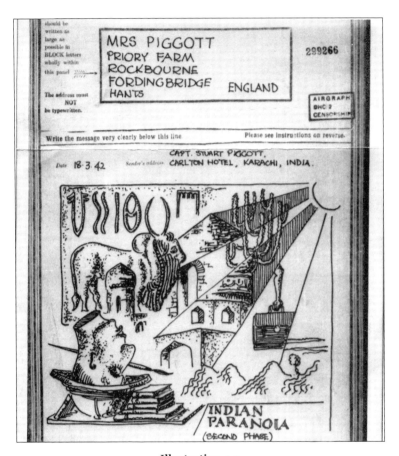

Illustration 4.2
Drawing by Stuart Piggott, showing his head with hat upside down,
March 1942, India.
Courtesy: Institute of Archaeology, Oxford.

Illustration 5.1
Text panel and Cemetery H Jar, National Museum,
New Delhi, Photograph 2013.
Courtesy: Author.

Illustration 5.2
Prayer for skeletons at VS site, Mohenjodaro.
Photograph, 1925–26, ASI, Neg. No. 183/97.
Courtesy: Archaeological Survey of India.

agents in Central Asia to collect similar artefacts. 'Between 1893 and 1900', as Ursula Sims-Williams has recorded in her research of the Hoernle Collection at the British Library (London):

> 23 consignments of antiquities were forwarded to him in Calcutta by the British representatives in Kashgar and Kashmir: George Macartney, Stuart Godfrey and Adelbert Talbot. The resulting 'British Collection' included manuscripts in Sanskrit (seven substantial Buddhist manuscripts), Khotanese (parts of six Buddhist manuscripts and 69 documents), Tocharian (17 leaves of a Tocharian medical manuscript), Uigur (24 documents), Persian (four documents) and Chinese (12 documents), in addition to what proved to be forged manuscripts and blockprints (45) in unrecognisable scripts.[80]

Stein exposed the remarkable forgeries during his first archaeological expeditions in Central Asia in 1900–1, whose plans he had embarked upon in 1898 when the third birch-bark manuscript after Bakshali and 'Bower', namely the Prakrit Dhammapada was found in a cave in Khotan in 1897. The quick and favourable reply from the colonial government to Stein's detailed proposal, as Sims-Williams has stated, was to a considerable extent due to Hoernle's influence.[81]

The 'triad of memorable explorations' within Central Asia that followed the finds of the birch-bark manuscripts represents the forceful agency of nationalism in directing government investments in transnational archaeological projects. Thus, we notice that George Grierson, who shaped and headed the Linguistic Survey of India (1898–1928), recalled the expeditions apart from the British ones by Stein as 'those for the Russians by Klementz, for the Germans by Grünwedel and Von Le Coq, for the Japanese by Otani, and for the French by Pelliot'.[82] Therefore, in emphasising the need for a British archaeological expedition to Central Asia in 1898, Stein prudently reminded the colonial government that Khotan was in the 'British sphere of influence', and since a Russian commission was going to Turfan and the Swedish explorer Sven Hedin was contemplating a second visit to the area, he hoped that the British government too would send an expedition to the region and take credit for the discoveries.[83]

---

[80] Sims-Williams (2012, p. 1).

[81] Ibid., p. 4; on the forgery see Sims-Williams, 2007 (updated 2012).

[82] Grierson (1919, p. 117).

[83] Sims-Williams (2012, p. 3); Sven Anders Hedin (1865–1952), was a Swedish geographer and explorer who led four expeditions to Central Asia: 1893–97, 1899–1902, 1905–08 and

Stein's proposal to the Secretary of State for India for a second expedition, which he undertook between 1906 and 1908, was forwarded by his supporters, including Curzon as: 'it would be for many reasons inadvisable of us to withdraw at this juncture from a field in which the first serious attempts at archaeological investigation was carried out under our auspices'.[84] Stein, as is well known, garnered the anxieties of the British Empire for sustaining his own intellectual pursuits, and hence he urged the British government to secure its patrimony by emphasising that:

> Chinese Turkestan has indeed, proved an archaeological treasure house of the ancient civilisations ... [and]... I may assert that this treasure house is not *inexhaustible*. If systematic efforts are now continued for a series of years it will be possible to secure for India what Monsieur Senart, in the letter of which I enclose a copy, justly styles '*un patrimoine de l'Inde*'. Otherwise most, if not all, of the remains which the sands of Eastern Turkestan have so far preserved, will within a generation find their ways into Russian and German collectors or else be destroyed by 'treasure seeking' natives in the attempt to satisfy the curiosity of the amateur collector.[85]

However, the British patrimony, which Stein alluded to, manifested as the heritage of Ancient India due to Stein's own Central Asian expedition in the year 1900–01. In his 'personal narrative' of the expedition, *Sand-buried Ruins of Khotan* (1904), Stein had recorded that the 'Bower' manuscripts 'plainly showed that, together with Buddhism, the study of the classical language of India also found a home in that distant land beyond Himalaya'.[86] Searching for similar manuscripts Stein had reached the 'remote Central Asia settlement' of Niya in 1901 where he excavated textual records 'inscribed on wooden tablets in an Indian language and writing [that is, Khotanese] and issued by officials with strangely un-Indian titles, whose seals carry us to the classical world far away in the West'.[87] The discoveries made by Stein in Niya, Miran,

1927–35. Stein undertook four extraordinary Central Asian expeditions: 1900–01, 1906–08, 1913–16 and 1930.

[84] 'Proposed Deputation for M.A. Stein for Archaeological Research in Eastern Turkestan', *Proceedings of Revenue and Agriculture Department, A&E,* No. 11, Jan 1905, File No. 4, S. No. 1, pp. 13–15.

[85] 'Extracts from a letter from Dr M.A. Stein, Inspector General of Education and Archaeological Surveyor, NWFP and Baluchistan, 24 June 1905', *Proceedings of Home Department, A&E,* No. 14, 1906, pp. 2–4.

[86] Stein (1904, p. xv).

[87] Ibid., p. xvii.

Dandan Uilig and other ancient places, including Tun Huang, garnered public attention in Europe of the archaeological scholarship of India, which was significantly novel. As Stein subsequently explained, 'archaeological research in the great fields of India and China' had not received much public 'sympathy and interest' as they had lain 'beyond the stimulating influence of the Bible associations'. Hence, the European public had 'so far little opportunity of learning to appreciate the great historical problems' that were involved in the researches.[88]

Stein's two explorations within Central Asia created the understanding of the immense potentials of the Ancient Indian history. This was conveyed at the time in the following remark of Konow, who in reviewing Hoernle's translation of the 'Bower manuscript', in 1914, had stated:

> We are now able to see, much more clearly than was formerly the case, what a predominant role Indian Civilisation played in Asia at a very early period, and to trace the various elements that contributed to the history of Central and Eastern Asia during long centuries. And from the finds of Turkestan unexpected light has already been thrown on many questions concerning Indian archaeology itself, Indian art, Indian literature, and Indian history.[89]

We could ask whether the new historical evidence of the cultural connections between the ancient worlds in Asia during the first millennium which Stein's first explorations in Chinese Turkmenistan during 1900–01 established, directed the urgency to excavate Ancient Gandhara, and the dynastic histories of the Indo-Greeks, Indo-Scythians, Kushans and Hunas, which were undertaken by the Archaeological Survey of India within the first two decades of the twentieth century. This question leads to a more important question, which is whether Marshall's aims of excavating at Taxila which he expressed in 1902, shortly after his arrival to India had any bearings upon the magnificent finds of Stein in the 'Chinese Turkmenistan'.

The archaeological scholarship of Taxila, and of the political dynasties of the early 'foreign' rulers of India, such as the Bactrian-Greeks and Kushans was most certainly influenced by the discoveries of the scholarship in epigraphy and numismatics. In this respect, we can trace a lineage of the connected histories of archaeological enquiries and philological research by

---

[88] Stein (1904, p. xii). For a short but comprehensive summary of Stein's discoveries, see Rust and Cushing (no date).

[89] Konow (1914, p. 179).

following the track of the 'advancements' within the study of Kharoshthi that followed the finds of the birch-bark manuscripts. The script had been deciphered by James Prinsep in the 1830s, but the thrust towards the philological scholarship of Kharoshthi followed the discoveries of the birch barks. The scholarship was more or less launched in 1895 after Bühler demonstrated the possible evolution of the script from Aramaic. Stein's finds at Niya fuelled the growing philological research, which proved to be of immense value for the archaeological enquiries at Taxila.[90]

Marshall's Taxila and Konow's Kharoshthi: A Note

Although there is no direct evidence to relate Marshall's plans of excavating Taxila with Stein's spectacular discoveries during his first Central Asian explorations, the impetus to look for evidence and seek connections is guided by the knowledge that even in 1902, Marshall, who was then a novice to Indian archaeology, would have known that the ruins of Taxila promised rich archaeological yields because of its unique historical geography.

Taxila, or rather the archaeological site of Shah Dheri, had been identified as an Indo-Greek city with a strong Buddhist cultural history by Alexander Cunningham during his field visits in 1863–64, 1872–73 and 1878–79,[91] and Marshall possibly planned his excavations of the ancient ruins at the site during his maiden excavations with Vogel at Charsada (February–April, 1903). They had travelled together in the Frontier Provinces in November 1902, and their plans of excavating at Charsada, which they made at the time, were definitely predicated upon their understanding that the site might have been the former Pushkalavati, the 'capital' of the kingdom of Gandhara, which had been inhabited by Greeks, Scythians, Parthians and Kushanas during the first century.[92]

---

[90] Bühler (1898). On the importance of Stein's finds, see Luder (1906, p. 291).

[91] See, however, footnote 2 in Spooner, (1912, p. 39). Spooner had shown that during his second visit Cunningham had correctly identified the mound at Shahji-ki-dheri with the stupa built by Kanishka (ibid.).

[92] Cunningham (1871b, pp. 89–90); Marshall and Vogel (1904). See ibid., p. 142, for the histories of explorations and explorations at the site following Cunningham's. It might be

An article on 'Buddhist Gold Jewellery', which Marshall wrote the same year in which he and Vogel excavated at Charsada, documents, cogently, his expectations of rich yields from the ruins of similar stupa sites throughout the North West Frontier Provinces. In describing the ornaments—some found from the village at Trodher in Yusufzai District and some collected from antique sellers in Rawalpindi who claimed that the objects came from Taxila—Marshall compared their designs with the gold casket at Dih Bimran (near Jalalabad, Afghanistan) that had been found by Charles Masson during his excavations of the stupa in 1833–34. Marshall historicised the linkages between the pieces of jewellery, gold casket and 'analogous ornaments of the pre-Christian era from Asia Minor' through a review of the possible affinities in designs, and concluded that the stylistic similarities:

> point to their being the outcome of that widely diffused cosmopolitan art of Western Asia, which was chiefly developed from the fusion of Hellenic and Oriental influences in the fourth and third centuries BC, and which gradually permeated eastward and was assimilated at a later date into the Buddhist art of Northern India.[93]

The understanding that the ancient cosmopolitan city of Taxila would provide spectacular finds would not have failed Marshall's notice.

Therefore, the fact that Marshall sought the permission of the Punjab government to excavate at Taxila in 1902–03 acquires significance, although he had to wait 10 years for the acceptance of his request. As he recalled, this was because of the anxieties of the government for hosting excavations so close to the 'unruly frontier', in the anticipation that any disturbance to the 'ancient mounds might easily lead to trouble'.[94] On the eve of his large-scale excavations in 1913, Marshall sketched the historical geography of Taxila as positioned 'on the great trade route which used to connect Hindustan with Central and West Asia'.[95] Thus, although he may not have foreseen

---

worth noting that Vogel's appointment within the Indian archaeology department was due to Stein's input. He had met Stein in Ambala in 1900, and the latter had brought his 'capacities to the attention of the Panjab government', which had led to Vogel's appointment in 1901 as Archaeological Surveyor of the Northern Circle within the Public Works Division of Punjab. See Theuns-de Boer (2008, p. 13).

[93] Marshall (1904c, p. 194).

[94] Marshall (1951, p. xv).

[95] Marshall (1916, p. 1). For a concise history of the historical knowledge of Taxila, and the archaeological discoveries at the site before Cunningham's explorations, see Errington (2007).

in 1902 the historical connections between Taxila and the ancient cities in Central Asia that Stein had excavated a year before, his knowledge of the historical geography of Taxila would have been a strong factor in his plans to undertake excavations at the site.

In his sumptuous volume on the excavations, *Taxila: An Illustrated Account* (1951), Marshall provided a short retrospective note of the strong attraction he had felt for the ruins and the surrounding landscape during his first view in 1902, and stated that they had reminded him then of the Greek countryside and evoked memories of the happy days spent in Greek archaeology (1899–1901), before he had joined the Survey.[96] However, neither the emotional pull for the site, nor his anticipation of Taxila's Greek histories detract from the possibility that Marshall may have also conceived of the excavations in the hopes of spectacular finds which could embellish, illuminate or perhaps even outshine, Stein's discoveries. His great expectations from Taxila shine through a letter to Konow, which he wrote in 1909 after he had visited the ruins. The occasion of the visit was his visit to Spooner's excavations at Shahji-ki-Dheri, and after describing the finds of the reliquaries and 'Kanishka casket' from the stupa that had been excavated by Spooner and his workforce, Marshall concluded with the exclamation:

> Next autumn I am going to start on Taxila! What riches we shall get there! I dream of them nightly since I revisited the site this spring.[97]

Apart from allowing us to speculate upon the possibilities that Marshall may have competed with Stein for accruing similar, if not greater, spectacular successes in his archaeological explorations, the history of the archaeological scholarship of Taxila also documents the value, which he and other archaeologists saw in the complimentary histories of the scholarship of philology and archaeology. The excavations produced the largest collection of Kharoshthi inscriptions until then known, and in regarding the finds, Konow, by then the expert of the script had noted that 'there can be little doubt that its place of origin was Gandhara, perhaps more specifically Taxila'.[98] Marshall made extensive uses of the inscriptional evidence for deciphering the cultural

---

[96] See Marshall (1951, p. xv).

[97] Letter from Marshall to Konow, dated 29/04/09 from Simla, Mss folio 4201: eske 1 (nr 21), National Library of Norway. Of Marshall's visit to Shahji-ki-dheri, see Spooner (1912, p. 48).

[98] Konow (1929, p. xiv).

histories of the Parthian city of Sirkap at Taxila, which he had excavated at length, and lauding Konow on the publication of his magnum opus, *Kharoshthi Inscriptions: With Exception of Those of Asoka* (1929), he wrote, possibly in 1936, that:

> I am publishing a new edition of my 'Taxila Guide'. I do hope you realize what a tremendous admiration I have for your volume and what an immense help it has been to me in my work in Taxila. Few people perhaps understand as I do the amount of labour and scholarship that you have put into it.[99]

In a subsequent letter to Konow, Marshall engaged in a long discussion regarding the historical viability of a 'Parthian Era', which is quoted below at some length. He wrote:

> You say that Lüders has shown that the Mathura inscription of annus 299 is dated in the 'Parthian Era.' What is meant by the 'Parthian Era?' On their coinage the Parthians invariably used the Seleucid era starting in 312 B.C., and the Macedonian months. Rapson once suggested (Num. Chron. 1893, p. 212) that the Parthians had a native era starting in 249–8 B.C., but his only evidence was a single coin and his suggestion was not accepted by numismatists. Rapson also suggested that the era (Cam Hist of India, pg. 570) used in the Patika copper plate was a Parthian era which commemorated the incorporation of Sistan into the Parthian Empire, but here again Tarn (The Greeks in Bactria and India, pp. 494–502) has shown that the era there used was much more probably a Saka era dating from c. 155. I agree with Tarn and have adopted this date, c. 155 BC, as the initial date of the era used in the Hashtnagar, Loriya Tangai and other records. It fits in very well with the political and artistic history. At Mathura, I suggest that a Saka era is much more likely to have been in use than a Parthian. There is not a shred of evidence that the Surens of East Iran, either Vonones in the 1st century B.C., or Gondophernes and his successors in the 1st century AD ever got as far as Mathura. On the other hand, all the Satraps and Great Satraps of Mathura were Saka, not Parthian. I should be grateful if you could let me know to which 'Parthian era' Lüders refers, and give me any other details you can about the Mathura inscription of the year 299. Now that I have finished my Taxila book, I have sent back all the books I had borrowed from the India Office and other libraries, and have very few books of my own.[100]

---

[99] Letter from Marshall to Konow, 15 June (no year, but probably dating to the publication of the 3rd edition of Marshall's *Guide to Taxila*, 1936), from 36 Gloucester Terrace, W. 2 Paddington, London, Mss Folio 4201, National Library of Norway.

[100] Letter from Marshall to Konow, dated 11 November 1945, from Avondale, Surrey, Ibid.

The quotation above allows a good view of Marshall's critical engagement with inscriptional data, and of his deep knowledge of the scholarship of epigraphy.[101] His personal letters to colleagues who were scholars of Sanskrit in the Survey, notably Konow and Vogel, are strewn with similar debates regarding eras and chronology, and many carry examples of inscriptional legends in his handwriting for proving a point (Illustration 3.1).[102] In searching for examples of Marshall's skills in copying and transcribing inscriptions, we are shown that Spooner had thanked Marshall for making 'admirable impressions' of those on 'Kanishka's casket'.[103] Following Marshall's non-official correspondence, we are thus able to see the investments of the philologists and archaeologists into the methodologies of each other's subjects. Such examples are inevitably non-representative within the archives of the Archaeological Survey whose contents are specific to the administration of archaeology. The examples, therefore, draw our attention to the value of thinking through creations of the archival sources in writing the histories of scholarship and disciplinary practices.

Different Perspectives from Different Archives

Historians of South Asian archaeology have increasingly begun to publish the feats of their discoveries of archives,[104] and in doing so they add to the understanding of finding facts 'out there'. The celebration of archival

[101] See particularly footnotes between pages 38 and 73 in Marshall (1951).

[102] Letter from Marshall to Konow from Camp Bhita, near Jasra, Allahabad Dist, dated 13 October 1910, Mss fol 4201: eske 1 (nr 21), Ibid. Marshall had described the legend on the coin of Vilivayakura II, as being in the centre of the seal, very small but beautiful. He had provided a detailed account of his excavations and finds to Konow and in his dry humour had stated that:

> Bhita must go back to the very remote antiquity, and you may guess that I am eagerly looking forward to the possibility of finding some antiquities or buildings on the same level. A single inscription of 600 or 700 B.C. (if not earlier) would be invaluable.

[103] Spooner (1914, p. 135).

[104] For a recent example see Lahiri (2011), on her discovery of three diaries of Alexander Cunningham in the collections of the Central Library of the Archaeological Survey of India in New Delhi.

discoveries, however, overlooks the reasons for the neglect of the same archives, which had once been specifically created. In this respect, the exhibitions of the discoveries of the 'lost' archives of the recent past preclude the understanding that histories of archaeologies often reside within the acts of archiving and within the histories of the creations and neglect of archives.

'The archival power', as Laura Anne Stoler would remind the users of colonial archives, 'was no more monolithic than the growing practices that it enabled and on which it was based'.[105] The prescriptions of engaging with 'archiving-as-process rather than archives-as-things' which she has magnificently built upon for illuminating the disquiet, uncertainties and anxieties of the 'formulae of the officialese',[106] encourage a search for the manner in which an archive, to quote Certeau, 'redistributes things, redefines elements of knowledge, inaugurates the place for a new beginning [...] that will make an entirely different history possible'.[107] The promise of histories to be made, which collections and archives convey through their own life histories, encourage a note of the ways in which epistemic practices are developed and worked through genres of documentation.

The archives that were created through the administration of 'Archaeology and Epigraphy' were specifically established in duplicate, one for the India Office, at London, and one to be retained in India. Their locales shifted between 1881 and 1921 within the repositories of the departments of home, revenue and agriculture, and education, health and lands. With the creation of the Archaeological Survey of India, the documents representing the administration of archaeological work through the D.G.A.'s office (that is, Director General of Archaeology) came to reside in the Survey's head quarters, first at Simla and subsequently after 1946 at New Delhi.[108]

---

[105] Stoler (2009, p. 51).

[106] Ibid., p. 2.

[107] Certeau (1988, pp. 73–74).

[108] A brief history: The Department of Archaeology (or rather the office of the D.G.A.) moved between Simla and Delhi along with other central offices of Government of India until 1939, when it was permanently located along with other offices in Delhi. But in 1942, as wartime measure, it was found expedient to shift the office to Simla. It was moved to New Delhi in 1946 on the recommendation of the Accommodation Advisory Committee, as in actual working this department was tied to the Department of Education, which had shifted to the city, and also because the D.G.A. was directly responsible for the preservation and conservation of the monuments of Delhi. But the excavation branch of the archaeology department remained in Simla, and was brought to New Delhi only in 1949.

After independence, this 'central' collection of the colonial Survey was designated for re-housing within the precincts of the National Archives.

The creation of the National Archive in New Delhi as a repository of the non-current records of permanent value has a history of colonial 'origins' in the 'Imperial Record Department', which was established in Calcutta in 1891.[109] The new Archive re-shaped the old colonial archives, which it absorbed through new systems of cataloguing, classification and storing. Pending the move, the D.G.A.'s archives of the colonial Survey was officially curated from 1953 by the Monuments Section of the Archaeological Survey of India, as it held reference value for the new projects of conservation and restoration. However, as technologies of restoration 'advanced' and changed, and conservation projects began to accumulate their own histories in independent India, the archive was left to gather dust within the Survey's housekeeping schemes.

The above resume of the physical neglect of a particular archive provides one context within which discoveries of forgotten archives are celebrated. The different contents of different archives attune us to the changes within the representations of archaeology and archaeological work through time. In contrast to the 'officialese' archives of the colonial Archaeological Survey of the twentieth century, to borrow Stoler's term, the bulk of which was curated within India, the personal archives of the officers who worked for the Survey inform of the great rift between the older generation who served Marshall and the new generation, which was largely trained during the directorship of Mortimer Wheeler. The rift bears upon the perception of intelligible archaeological work, and informs us of the changes in excavation methods and the novel focus upon prehistory, which Mortimer Wheeler flamboyantly declared as having brought into the archaeology of India.[110] Wheeler's incessant criticism of Marshall is well known. However, the ferocity with which Marshall's former colleagues in the Survey dismissed his attacks is not known, and can be gauged only through the perusal of personal correspondence. The letters create a regard of the fallacy of abiding by Wheeler's portraiture of

[109] For a summary of the history of the National Archives of India, see http://nationalarchives.nic.in/

[110] On this, see points 20 and 37 on 'prehistory' and 'needs of Indian Prehistory' respectively, in 'the measures of re-organisation', which Wheeler declared he had undertaken in his *Director General's Report on the development of the Department, 1944–48*, pp. 1–16, pp. 7–8. File E/1/11, Wheeler archives.

Marshall as a dictatorial figure, which the latter had claimed was conveyed to him as a 'beech tree under which nothing grew'.[111]

Of the examples, a letter written in 1949 by Vogel to Harold Hargreaves, who was Marshall's immediate successor as director general of the Survey (1928–31), shows that Wheeler had raised objections to Marshall's inferences of Taxila long before the definitive volumes of the excavations were published. He would have done so by gleaning information of the excavations from the Survey's annual reports, and Marshall's *Guide to Taxila* (1936). The ferocity of Vogel's remonstration illustrates the depth of support for Marshall by many of his former colleagues, who were also his personal friends. Vogel stated that:

> Wheeler, as far as I can see, has not made any [important discoveries] despite his superior methods of excavations. His articles in 'Ancient India' (a periodical which fortunately has been discontinued) are illustrated by a series of plates showing numerable earthenware pots and potsherd, the interest of which I fail to see. But I am not a prehistorian. It is unfortunate that he has trained dozens of Indians in this kind of research.[112]

Days after the publication of the excavation volumes, in 1951, Wheeler tried to entice the editor of the *Journal of the Royal Asiatic Society of Great Britain and Ireland* into seeking a short article from Marshall regarding the latter's method of dating Sirkap, which he hoped could be 'published together' with his own critical views of Marshall's 'facts' within the same volume. Marshall withdrew from the combat despite having written a draft, stating that he was 'too old and too ill to engage in controversy'.[113] Hargreaves conveyed Wheeler's intentions of confronting Marshall to R.B. Whitehead, the eminent scholar of the history of the 'Indo-Greeks' whose contributions to the history of Taxila, Marshall had highly valued while also disagreeing with him on

---

[111] Wheeler (1955, p. 182). Wheeler had stated that 'a friend and admirer' of Marshall's had made the remark, but that he took it seriously is quite clear from his continuing statement:

> Marshall was of a temperament, which hinders the confidential delegation of responsibility, and hinders therefore the adequate training of subordinates to assume responsibility. It may be that something in the air of Edwardian India, some germ surviving from the India of the Moghuls, had entered early into Marshall's system. (ibid.)

[112] Letter from Vogel to Hargreaves, dated 4 July 1949, from Oegstgeest. Box 1, Envelope 137–43, Whitehead Papers.

[113] Letter from Mrs N. Davis, Secretary, Royal Asiatic Society, London, to Wheeler, dated 11 February 1951. Box 454, *Misc Correspondence up to December 1951*, Wheeler Papers.

many issues. He stated that Wheeler's criticism of Marshall's inferences of dates, and of excavation methods reflected 'jealousy yellow', and that in 1932 when he had visited Wheeler's excavations at St Albans, he had 'formed a very high opinion of this work'. However, he commented astutely, Wheeler was 'no historian when it comes to India and his "Five Thousand years of Pakistan" was ridiculous in title and full of errors. Marshall's work will be remembered in India when Wheeler is forgotten'.[114]

The letters above of Vogel and Hargreaves add to the visibility of the distinctions in the contents of the departmental archives of Archaeology and Epigraphy and the personal archives of those who had worked for the Survey. The former informs us of the political evaluations of the utility value of archaeology and philology, which precipitated the feeling of being 'left out' among the Sanskritists. The latter documents the equal valuations of the philological and archaeological explorations of India during the early twentieth century by all scholars of Indology. A disregard of the differences in information from the archives allows the understanding that archaeology scored over philology in the history-making of Ancient India, practically and intellectually. A regard of the differences allows us to engage with issues of methodology, as this bears upon the manner in which we choose to historicise the scholarship of archaeology and archaeological practices.

After the Indian independence, Indian epigraphists have often reflected upon the neglect of the Archaeological Survey of India towards its Department of Epigraphy. The noted epigraphist Dinesh Chandra Sircar (1907–84), who was government epigraphist of the Survey (1949–61), was of the opinion that the study of epigraphy and numismatics would have thrived in India had the colonial government created a separate department outside the organisation.[115] Sircar may have echoed the sentiments, which Hultzsch had expressed in 1902. However, he also saw the languishing of the scholarship in his own times due to increasing government investments into 'prehistoric antiquities'.[116] With respect to the waning of interest within the scholarship of epigraphy in the field archaeology of the 1960s, Sircar had indeed touched the right pulse. And if we care to map the strengths of the

---

[114] Letter from Hargreaves to Whitehead, 24 April 1953, Whitehead Papers, Box 1, Envelope 116–17.

[115] Sircar (1965, p. 11, footnote).

[116] Ibid.

thriving departments of archaeology within the Indian universities in the post-colonial times, such as in Poona (at Deccan College) we are shown that the fashion for prehistoric archaeology took away resources from the nurture of the scholarship of historical archaeology.

Although the epigraphy branch of the Survey was re-organised during Wheeler's tenure,[117] the uses of inscriptions and texts for establishing archaeological inferences languished visibly with his leadership of Indian archaeology. Thus, we note his unconditional emulation of the colonial historiography within the archaeological narrative of the 'Roman' town of Arikamedu, which he excavated in 1945. The emulation appears in the excavation report, where the 'Prakrit graffito' that were found inscribed on ceramics are shown but left unattended, and the sherds with early Tamil graffiti are mentioned in a cursory manner. The latter were dated to the third and second centuries BCE on 'theoretical' grounds, and in 'contradistinction to the dating of the Arikamedu sherds' with Italian graffiti that were ascertained as 'objective and secure'.[118] The report marginalised the 'indigenous' texts, and we note that Wheeler referred to the Tamil epic *Silappadikaram* only for pursuing the references of the 'yavanas' therein, for deriving inferences regarding the presence of Romans in Arikamedu during the first century. The Epic, however, conveys a rich description of the ancient port of Kaveripattinam, or Puhar, which Wheeler could have sourced, had he chosen, for extending his understanding of the ancient port which he had excavated.[119]

Although Wheeler neglected the Indian texts in his archaeological scholarship of India, he pursued the Roman archaeology of Britain by drawing upon the textual traditions of the Classical world. For, after all he was educated as a scholar of Classics, and Illustration 3.2 is a graphic representation of his educational background in his own hand. Therefore, it becomes meaningful to regard the following question which students sitting for the Diploma in

---

[117] The two separate posts of government epigraphist and superintendent of Epigraphy which had overlapping responsibilities were merged into one, and the branch came to be headed by a government epigraphist. A new post of a Muslim epigraphist was established, and an assistant librarian was appointed to catalogue and maintain the records of the branch. See point 19, *Director General's Report on the Development of the Department, 1944–48*, File E/1/11, Wheeler Archives.

[118] Wheeler *et al.* (1946, pp. 52, 109). N.P. Chakravarti, who succeeded Wheeler as DGASI deciphered most of the 'early Tamil' inscriptions, see ibid., pp. 109–14.

[119] Ibid., pp. 19, 21. See also Wheeler (1976, pp. 56–57).

Prehistoric Archaeology and Comparative Technology at University College London were required to answer. The students were asked that:

> The archaeologist may find the tub but altogether miss Diogenes. He may answer with botanical precision Browning's question "What porridge had John Keats?" Without a passing recognition of the author of Endymion?' (R.E.M. Wheeler). Pursuing this train of thought discuss the limitations of archaeological evidence.[120]

In their answer, the examinees would have been required to illustrate the limitations of archaeological evidence and of the inherently partial nature of the archaeological record. We may correctly conjecture that they had written about the heuristic value of texts and inscriptions for the archaeological scholarship for putting—as one would say colloquially—'flesh upon the bones'. The importance, which archaeologists, including Wheeler, endowed to texts as sources, creates the reasons for engaging with the methodological implications of the connected histories of philology and archaeology. For it is only by noting the histories that we are prevented from historicising archaeology as a list of excavations, explorations and other field- and laboratory-based projects, which nurture the understanding that archaeological evidence can exist as facts upon the ground.

---

[120] Question No. 8, Part II in Prehistoric Archaeology and Comparative Technology, II, Diploma and Certificates in Anthropology, 15 June 1954, Wheeler Archives.

4

Fashioning the Unknown: Gordon Childe's Imprints upon the Indus Civilisation

Until the excavations at Harappa and Mohenjodaro (Pakistan), in 1921 and 1923 respectively, the Bronze Age, which in Europe was known to have 'intervened between the Neolithic and Early Iron periods', was regarded as untraceable in India, and the bronze artefacts that had been found within the megalithics of southern India, especially from the 'Tinnevelly urns', were all judged as 'imported'. The 'Indian tradition' was considered younger than the ancient civilisations of Egypt and Mesopotamia despite the understanding that human beings had lived in India from the time 'when hippopotamus and other strange beasts of which no memory remains dwelt in Indian forests and waters'.[1] The 'cities' of the third millennium BCE, therefore, created a rare opportunity for John Marshall and his officers in the Archaeological Survey to engage directly with the emerging scholarship of prehistory within Britain for establishing archaeological evidence of the newly discovered 'Indian' Bronze Age.

At this time, and for over the next two decades until the early 1950s, the Australian born pre-historian of Britain and Europe, Vere Gordon Childe (1892–1957) virtually shaped the archaeological study of prehistory in much of the western world. The nascent scholarship of the 'prehistoric civilisation' of India, which the excavations at Harappa and Mohenjodaro launched, was therefore greatly influenced by the scholarship of Childe, and in this respect we note that Marshall began his chapter on the 'Age and Authors of

[1] Smith (1941, pp. 1, 4).

the Indus Civilisation' in the lavish volumes of *Mohenjodaro and the Indus Civilization* (1931), which he also edited, with the statement that 'anyone familiar with the prehistoric archaeology of western Asia will at once perceive its close resemblance both to what professor Childe has called the "Second Prediluvian Culture" of Elam and Mesopotamia and proto-historic culture of Sumer'.[2] Marshall's numerous references to Childe in other chapters, such as on 'the country, climate and rivers' and 'extent of the Indus Civilization', show quite prominently that he drew into Childe's accounts of the West Asian Bronze Age for unravelling and historicising the unknown. Yet, despite the references, the archaeological histories of the Indus Civilisation that have been written since the 1970s have largely managed to obliterate Childe's intellectual influences. The Chapter reviews Childe's imprints within the early scholarship of the Civilisation for drawing attention to some of the ways in which the archaeological scholarship establishes evidence of an unknown past.

Within the histories of the archaeology of South Asia, Childe is mostly recalled for his supposed intellectual influence upon Mortimer Wheeler with respect to the latter's theories regarding the origins and decline of the Indus Civilisation. Childe's theories of culture diffusion are perceived to have shaped Wheeler's classic theory of 'stimulus-diffusion', through which the latter had claimed that 'the idea of civilization came to the Indus from the Euphrates and Tigris, and gave the Harappans [i.e. inhabitants of the Indus Civilization] their initial direction or informed their purpose'.[3] Childe's ideas regarding the 'Aryan' destruction of the Indus Civilisation influenced Wheeler to establish theories regarding the decline of the phenomenon along these lines. However, the theory of culture diffusion was not a Childean invention. It had a long history from the nineteenth century, and Childe and other archaeologists who were active in the mid-twentieth century adapted the theories in their own scholarship of prehistory. The theory of 'Aryan invasion' of the Indian subcontinent, which was developed in the nineteenth century, lent to easy assimilation within the prevalent diffusionary theories, and its uses by Childe and Wheeler for seeking the decline of the Indus Civilisation is, therefore, not surprising. Wheeler's interpretations of the 'rise and fall' of the Indus

---

[2] Marshall (1931, p. 102). Marshall's first reference to Childe in the book is in a footnote with respect to climate changes in Baluchistan and Sind following the last glacial which provided regions with 'relatively bountiful rainfall more or less evenly distributed throughout the year' (Smith [1941, pp. 1, 4]).

[3] Wheeler (1953, p. 95).

Civilisation were, thus, to a large extent, reflections of the contemporary academic scholarship of cultural histories.

The distinctions between the early and mature scholarship of the Indus Civilisation has often been defined through the following four paradigmatic changes, namely: (a) concepts of sudden and late origins, (b) long periods of static cultural unity, (c) sudden and uniform collapse and (d) the 'Indo-Aryan invasion'.[4] Well until the 1980s, archaeologists have also viewed the early scholarship of the phenomenon through the theories of Wheeler and his peer Stuart Piggott, who was in India between 1942 and 1945 for war service in the Royal Air Force. Hence, archaeologists have also unproblematically accepted the truisms of a paradigm shift within the scholarship of the Indus Civilisation during the Marshall and Wheeler 'eras'. The Chapter interrogates the claims of paradigmatic shifts and demonstrates the need for intellectual histories that attend to the nuances of the historiography.

A Small History of the Notions of Valid Evidence: Neolithic Jericho

In recalling Childe's scholarship of prehistory, we are shown the myriad ways in which ideologies have infiltrated the archaeological research of archaic civilisations in the past and dictated the considerations of valid evidence. A novelty of Childe's scholarship, which had been succinctly historicised by Andrew Sherratt, was to create a growing body of factual material for contextualising the long-standing debates about trajectories of social evolution.[5] Childe, thus, attributed discrete artefactual profiles to the theories of social evolutionary stages of savage, primitive, barbaric and civilised, which he also adapted for the archaeological study of prehistory. In this, he envisaged the promise of the archaeological scholarship in eroding the ideational meanings of the social stages. He therefore asserted, albeit erroneously, that 'by providing a history of technological progress, archaeology sheds light on the most important aspects of human development, while by failing to preserve a detailed record of prehistoric religious beliefs, the archaeological record

---

[4] Dyson (1993 [1982], p. 571).
[5] Sherratt (1989, p. 152).

merely casts into oblivion the memories of human folly'.[6] Nevertheless, Childe strongly objected to the evidence of a town for neolithic Jericho (or rather pre-pottery neolithic levels in the mound of Tell es-Sultan, West Bank, Palestine), as this failed to match his expectations of the material contents of the barbaric society of the Neolithic. The following summary of the academic debate in the 1950s regarding the possibilities of the existence of towns during the Neolithic highlights the reasons for reflecting upon the ways in which evidentiary terrains are construed through the archaeological scholarship.

Jericho was excavated between 1952 and 1956 by Kathleen Kenyon, who had described the pre-pottery Neolithic horizon as a town and had dated it provisionally to the eighth millennium BCE. Kenyon's description, which was supported by her teacher Mortimer Wheeler, was to a considerable extent based upon the finds of a spectacular 'wall', which she suggested in her Marett Memorial Lecture at Exeter College, Oxford, on 5 May 1956, bespoke of a 'town wall', and hence of the 'civilization of Neolithic Jericho'. Aware that the descriptions would 'come as a shock to purists', Kenyon nevertheless maintained that the wall was a 'massive affair with great stones brought from the mountains', and that it was 'undoubtedly a community undertaking'. Through this fact, she asserted that 'here clearly we have a *civitas*, therefore by derivation it is not inaccurate to talk of a civilization'.[7]

The inference that there could be a town during the Neolithic provoked a charged debate regarding the expected contents of a prehistoric civilisation and the environments within which the latter could emerge. Childe admonished Kenyon in her use of the words 'civilization', 'city', 'town' [...] in reference to Neolithic Jericho' as he felt that this 'in no wise enhances the transcendent significance of the site. It just deprives prehistorians of convenient terms for giving expression to economic and sociological distinctions that can be recognized in the gross material data provided by dirt archaeology.[8]

Childe was not merely quibbling over terminologies. Having by then established the theoretical foundations for historicising the evolution of food-producing neolithic economy into agriculture-based urban societies of the Bronze Age he simply found it 'tempting to profit by the unique advantage

---

[6] Childe (1956, p. 172).
[7] Kenyon (1956, p. 187).
[8] Childe (1957, p. 36).

of the English language and call settlements such as Jericho [and also Troy, Thermi, and Phylakopi] more complex than villages yet not deserving the title of 'city' or 'towns'.[9]

Wheeler, however, supported Kenyon and added to the rationale of her inferences by establishing a new theory, the 'Oasis Theory of Civilization', to which Leonard Woolley, the excavator of Ur (1922–34), objected. Mindful of future possibilities in the slippage of Ancient Mesopotamia's premier status as the foremost pristine archaic civilisation, Woolley, the pioneering excavator, remarked that the world's earliest civilisations 'using the word in its accepted sense—started in the valleys of the Euphrates, the Nile, the Indus and the Huang Ho', and although 'they benefited by the arts and crafts developed elsewhere by "preliterate" or "barbarous" cultures', the failure to distinguish them from those cultures would erase 'all historical perspective'.[10] In his reply, Wheeler judiciously reiterated that his intentions were not to undermine the reputation of Mesopotamia as the premier civilisation of the ancient world, and to assuage his opponent changed the terminology of his 'Oasis Theory of Civilization' to that of 'Oasis Theory of Urbanization'. He, however, maintained that civilisations could rise within an oasis environment, and following Kenyon's inferences stated that the pre-pottery neolithic Jericho had provided 'an astonishingly early phase of urbanisation'.[11]

The academic milieu in archaeology at that time considered the emergence of urbanism and attainments of a civilised society as coeval. Hence, to most archaeologists, a town of very high antiquity within the Neolithic, with self-sufficient food-producing economy built by a non-literate society in a desert environment, albeit near an oasis, appeared as a myth. In a long article following the Woolley–Wheeler confrontation, Robert Braidwood, who was then excavating at a site near Jericho, at Jarmo (in Iraq), refuted the dating, the status of a town and, inevitably, the usage of the word civilisation for pre-pottery Neolithic Jericho. Braidwood argued for a much younger 'incipient town' in a 'somewhat marginal region' of the 'Fertile Crescent' to which Kenyon responded that 'an incipient town of 5000 BC would still be a remarkable development'.[12] At the conclusion of her four-year

---

[9] Childe (1957, p. 38).
[10] Woolley (1956, p. 225).
[11] Wheeler (1956), 'Sir Mortimer Wheeler replies:' (Ibid.).
[12] Braidwood (1957, p. 80); Kenyon (1957, p. 84).

excavations, Kenyon authoritatively asserted that of all areas within the Near East where a movement towards a settled way of life had taken place, Jericho had indeed provided the earliest and most complete picture, which was available until then.[13]

Childe's ire against Kenyon's evidence and Woolley's non-acceptance of Wheeler's theory inform us of the fashioning of archaeological knowledge, in which notions of valid evidence validate the descriptions that are attributed to the excavated and explored phenomena. The negotiations regarding the possibilities of a Neolithic town of Jericho, thus, occasion a reminder of the contingent nature of the 'hard facts' that are collected, and/or excavated, from the archaeological field. They also illuminate the manner in which ideologies often permeate the knowledge claims of the archaeological scholarship.

Childe in India

Throughout his academic life as an archaeologist, Childe searched for the 'cradle' of the technologies of civilisation. The search led him to explore the prehistory of the Indo-Iranian borderlands, Iran, Iraq and southern Turkey from the late 1920s, and keep abreast of the excavations of the Bronze Age sites in Mesopotamia and the Indus Civilisation, which were initiated in the early years of the 1920s. In 1928, he published a seminal book on this prehistory, *The Most Ancient East*.[14] However, by the early 1930s, the new wealth of data regarding the prehistoric societies of West Asia, Baluchistan and the Indus Valley prompted him to re-write the above book. In his wish to see this new material before undertaking the task, Childe made his maiden journey to the Orient in 1933, and visited Iraq and India.

Childe was educated in Classics in the universities of Sydney and Oxford, and the education in Latin brought him to the scholarship of the Sanskrit language. There were speculations after his death that the reason he did not perform as well in his *Tripos* at Oxford as was expected of him was because 'he had devoted so much time to the study of Sanskrit that he had neglected

---

[13] Kenyon (1958).
[14] Childe (1928).

Latin and the Greek texts, which he should have been studying'.[15] As the first Abercromby Professor of Archaeology at the University of Edinburgh (1927–46), Childe would have known Arthur Berriedale Keith (1879–1944), the Regius Professor of Sanskrit and Comparative Philology and lecturer of Constitutional History of the British Empire (1914–44) as a colleague, and his biographer has noted that 'he had much in common with Keith'.[16] Keith was the premier reviewer of *Mohenjodaro and the Indus Civilization*, and he had astutely predicted the pernicious legacy of the excavations by concluding his review with the statement that they gave reasons 'to search for the beginnings of our civilisation in a more remote period than has hitherto been dreamt of'.[17] Keith had celebrated the presence of a Bronze Age civilisation in the Indus valley euphemistically as the 'Ancient Mesopotamia of India', and we may infer with considerable certainty that his knowledge of the prehistory of the Iranian plateau, which he revealed in the review, and which he thought 'make[s] it possible for enterprising minds to believe that here was the original home of the inventors and pioneers of modern civilization' bespoke of his knowledge of Childe's scholarship.[18]

On his visit to India, Childe was shown the reserve collections of the Archaeological Survey in the Museum of Central Asian Antiquities in New Delhi. They included the new discoveries of the 'prehistoric' artefacts from Baluchistan, from sites such as Nal and Shahi Tump, Rana Ghundai, Periano Ghundai and Sur Jungal that had been made by Harold Hargreaves and Aurel Stein in 1924–25 and 1927–28, respectively, and from sites in Sind, including Amri which was excavated by Nani Gopal Majumdar in 1929–30 (Illustration 4.1). Childe was also taken to Mohenjodaro and Harappa, and although he found the 'ruins exciting and worth the trouble', he found 'India detestable' and 'beastly hot'. He noted that the country was 'overpopulated' with all the 'defects of small isolated communities', and that the 'sahibs' in

---

[15] Letter to Glyn Daniel by I.F. Jones, dated 21 February 1972, from 36 Euroka Street, New South Wales, Australia. Jones was a former student of Marlborough Grammar School when Childe had taught Latin at the school for a brief period. His letter to Daniel was in response to the latter's enquiries regarding Childe's career in Australia. Jones mentioned that he could not vouch for the story as he 'got it third hand'. Box B/4/4, Wheeler Archives.

[16] Green (1981, p. 61).

[17] Keith (1931, p. 1002).

[18] Ibid., p. 1000. The theory was not Childe's alone. It was considered widely by contemporary historians and orientalists.

'their narrow self-contained community with their golf courses and evening dress every night' gave no encouragement to the Indians to take responsibilities. Hence, he declared that 'when the Indians did get responsible positions, they were "either too helpless, and generally corrupt"'.[19] Childe's discomfort of India during the first visit contrasts sharply with the enthusiasm of his visit to Iraq. Although information regarding Childe's itinerary appears scanty at present, it is quite likely that he may have had met Marshall during this visit.

Childe visited India a second and last time in 1957, when he was invited to attend the Indian Science Congress which was held at Agra. He was on his way to Australia then, having left England permanently. During this visit, he presented a series of lectures at the Department of Anthropology at Calcutta University 'and elsewhere'. His discussions 'on some controversial problems and interpretive concepts in Prehistory' were noted within India at the time as leading to 'a fruitful understanding of certain problems facing Indian prehistorians'.[20]

In the new edition of the *Most Ancient East*, which was published as *New Light on the Most Ancient East* (1934), Childe virtually quoted Marshall from the latter's chapters in the *Mohenjodaro* for illuminating the cultural aspects of this 'Indian civilisation', including religion and manner of disposing the dead. He also received Marshall's characterisations of the Indus Civilisation as showing cultural uniformity, and abided by the opinions of Ernest Mackay, who had directed excavations at Mohenjodaro between 1927 and 1931, that the people of the city were peaceful, and had no 'enemies of more consequence than occasional raiding parties from the mountains of Baluchistan'.[21] Childe embellished Mackay's opinions through the statement that the Civilisation represented a 'democratic bourgeoisie economy as in Crete, in contrast to the obviously centralised theocracies and monarchies' of Egypt and Mesopotamia.[22] Childe's emulation of Marshall's and Mackay's inferences is one example among many of the errors of etching paradigm changes between the scholarship of Marshall and his 'men' and the 'young Turks' of prehistory of the 1930s, notably Childe himself, Piggott and Wheeler.

---

[19] Letter from Childe to Mary Alice Evatt, wife of the Australian labour politician, H.V. Evatt, dated 1933, and quoted in Green (1981, p. 93).

[20] For a brief mention of the visit, see Sen and Ghosh (1996).

[21] Childe (1934, p. 207). See also Marshall (1931, p. 91) and Mackay (1938, p. 442).

[22] Childe (1934, p. 207).

Childe in Marshall's *Mohenjodaro*

Despite the differences in their age, Marshall and Childe shared an educational background in Classical Archaeology, which during their studentship was informed through a long-standing debate regarding the origins of the Bronze Age Mycenaean Civilisation (ca. 1600 BCE to 1100 BCE). Mycenae, near Athens, had been excavated by Heinrich Schliemann in 1874 and 1876, and the debate evolved around two contrary propositions, namely (a) that the Civilisation was native to Europe, and (b) that its origins were in Asia as it appeared to some as a pale reflection of the Oriental culture. The French archaeologist of Greek Civilisation Salmon Reinach (1858–1932) propounded the former, and his contemporary, the Swedish archaeologist Oscar Montelius (1843–1921), who had refined the concept of seriation through his study of Egyptian hieroglyphs, inevitably supported the latter through the theory of *ex orientale lux*.[23] The debate raged during the last two decades of the nineteenth century, and initiated the search for cultural connections between Europe and Asia that predated the period of the Mycenaean Civilisation. It was critically reviewed at the beginning of the twentieth-century, by two Classicists at Oxford of considerable repute, Arthur Evans (1851–1941) and John Myers (1869–1954). Evans believed that the Aegean Civilisation, or rather the entire Bronze Age in Greece, including the Mycenaean Civilisation, owed something to both Europe and Asia. Myers was more Asia oriented in his approach. He mapped the spread of civilisation in the ancient world from Egypt and Mesopotamia to eastern Mediterranean, Italy and north Europe in his influential book *The Dawn of History* (1911). Both, however, judged the theories of Reinach and Montelius as being mutual, and gave primacy to the cause of trade and ethnic contact in the spread of civilisation.[24] Their views were highly influential when Marshall and Childe were students of Classical Archaeology.

Marshall studied the Classical *tripos* in Cambridge (1895–1900), and participated in the archaeological excavations in Greece during and after his graduation, which included those at Knossos that were led by Evans. He kept abreast of the archaeological scholarship of the Classical world throughout

---

[23] The theory of *ex oriente lux* entailed the view that all major inventions in prehistory had occurred in Egypt, from where they diffused, spread by the 'children of the Sun'.

[24] For details, see Daniel (1975, pp. 180–81).

his life, and his views regarding the religion of the Indus Civilisation in *Mohenjodaro* provide a glimpse of the subtle manner in which he used and disputed Myers's and Evans's inferences of the statuettes from the Minoan, Mycenaean and Babylonian civilisations for describing the terracotta statues, which he and his officers had found during excavations at Harappa and Mohenjodaro.[25] Childe was taught by Myers at Oxford, and his academic search for the 'rise of the West in prehistory', which he pursued in his seminal monograph *The Dawn of European Civilization* (1925), was inspired through the latter's scholarship. He accommodated the theories of both Myers and Evans in the book through the premise that 'the Occident was indebted to the Orient for the rudiments of the arts and crafts that initiated man's emancipation from bondage to his environment and for the foundations of those spiritual ties that co-ordinate human endeavours'.[26]

By the time the volumes of *Mohenjodaro and the Indus Civilization* were published, *The Dawn* had gained wide recognition as a classic. By then Childe's three other consecutive books, namely *The Aryans: A Study of Indo-European Origins* (1926), *The Most Ancient East* (1928) and *The Danube in Prehistory* (1929), had also been received within the academic world of archaeology and ancient history with great enthusiasm. We can only postulate, although with considerable certainty, that Marshall had read *The Dawn*. Marshall's education and his formidable knowledge of the archaeology of the Orient would have aroused his curiosity towards Childe's novel method of classifying archaeological cultures and his new theories of technological diffusion, which the latter had sketched, for explaining the rise of Neolithic communities and Bronze Age civilisations within the Levant, Anatolia and Crete.[27] That Marshall had read Childe's three other books is quite clear from his chapters in *Mohenjodaro*.

Childe had pioneered the heuristic value of the trait-list constructs of archaeological cultures in *The Dawn*, through which he also established a method that allowed archaeologists to see social evolution in material terms.[28] He declared that an archaeological culture represented a complex

[25] See Marshall (1931, p. 50), footnotes 4–6.

[26] Childe (1925, p. xiii).

[27] Marshall had excavated in Crete (1899–1901), and hence it is not farfetched to suggest that he would have read the chapters on 'Orient and Crete', 'Anatolia and the Royal Road to the Aegean' and 'Maritime Civilization in the Cyclades'. He drew many analogies between Minoan Crete and Harappa and Mohenjodaro in his publications and official correspondence.

[28] See Piggott (1958, p. 79).

of associated traits regarding the ways of life of a particular community, or a group of people, which provided a 'normative view' of the 'trait-lists' of each.[29] His approach was retrospectively misrepresented through errors of simplification, particularly by the North American archaeologists of the 1960s and the 1970s. Therefore Trigger, who had summarised Childe's contribution as providing 'archaeologists with a model of how they might deal with archaeological data elsewhere' had felt the need to make the point that although North American archaeologists, such as Lewis Binford (1931–2011) and Jeremy Sabloff dismissed Childe as 'yet another early twentieth-century archaeologist who viewed cultures as collections of homogenously shared, and hence, diagnostically equivalent traits', Childe had clearly distinguished the traits that he considered were ethnic indicators, and those he deemed were technological markers.[30] The distinct indices of ethnic and technical traits, which Childe had established, are important to bear in mind when examining his intellectual influences upon the early scholarship of the Indus Civilisation.

Childe argued that hand-made pottery and burial customs represented ethnic traits, as they tended to remain relatively unchanged over time among particular groups and could provide evidence of group identity. In contrast, he stated, new and more efficient tools and weapons, including the potter's wheel, were significant indices of the functional traits of technology as they were likely to have diffused from one place to another more quickly. He firmly believed that the evidence of both types of traits was important for the historical analyses of culture change, as the ethnically persistent traits allowed archaeologists to establish distinctions of social groups in prehistory, and the technical traits allowed them to gauge the relationships between the various cultures. Trigger had noted that although Childe made distinctions between ethnic and technical traits on the basis of common sense, 'he was one of the first archaeologists to introduce explicitly functional considerations into the study of archaeological data'.[31] As is shown in Chapter 5, in formulating the methods of New Archaeology to cast aside Childe's approach to culture

---

[29] The view was best described by Childe in *The Danube in Prehistory* in the statement: 'we find certain types of remains—pots, implements, burial rites and house forms—constantly recurring together. Such a complex of associated traits we shall term a "cultural group", or just a 'culture'. We assume that such a complex is the material expression of what today would be called a 'people', see Childe (1929, pp. v–vi); also Johnson (2010, p. 17).

[30] Trigger (1980, p. 53; 1994, p. 12).

[31] Trigger (1994).

and culture change which they declared was simply erroneous, his North American critics emulated his functionalist trait lists for fashioning material evidence of ethnicity in prehistory.

Childe had intellectually ventured into *The Most Ancient East* for locating the homelands of the primary technologies. He firmly believed that local appropriations and adaptations of technologies had been instrumental in instantiating local processes of cultural developments and progress, and that culture change involved technological diffusion through movements of people and instances of their contact through trade. He developed this understanding through the theory of the 'unity of the Oriental world at the end of the fourth millennium', which he stated 'can be summed up in the blessed word "trade"'. He was of the view that trade 'intercourse' between 'autonomous communities' was 'unmistakably linked by cultural traits [that did not] arise independently'. Thus, Childe's normative theory of culture accommodated the diversity of cultural expressions, as in local adaptations and transformations of technologies, and also bespoke of cultural unity among the various technological 'ages', such as within the civilisations of the Bronze Age. His theory of cultural diversity and unity was functionalist in inspiration, and the ways in which he used this for historicising culture change from the savage to civilisational stages of mankind is best illustrated in his claim that the 'Egyptian, Babylonian and Indian civilizations, for all their common basis and regular intercourse, each possess a ripe and distinct individuality by 3000 BC'.[32]

In *Mohenjodaro*, Marshall followed Childe's guideline of seeking evidence of unity and diversity in prehistory by placing the Indus Civilisation within the remit of a 'Chalcolithic Age' that 'extended across the broad Afrasian belt' to as 'far west as Thessaly and Southern Italy, and as far East ... as the Chinese provinces of Honan and Chih-Li'. Marshall historicised the civilisation 'as an integral part of the whole', and emphasised that its 'unity' to the Chalcolithic Age had 'to be stressed, because it has been the fashion to emphasize the diversity of this civilization, while ignoring its essential homogeneity'.[33] Marshall dwelt upon Childe's technologically significant traits for situating the Indus Civilisation within the Bronze Age, and delved into the similarities in artefact types between civilisations of Elam, Sumer, Babylonia and Indus,

[32] Childe (1928, p. 221).
[33] Marshall (1931, pp. 93–94).

through which he also established a profile of their relative chronologies for substantiating his argument that a 'wholly isolated and independent growth' would engender misunderstandings of the history of the emergence of the Indus Civilisation.[34] In following Childe, Marshall also distinguished the 'local and national complexion' of the Indus Civilisation, which he pursued through the arts, styles of painted pottery, ceramic forms, architectural features and writing systems.[35] Marshall's statement that the authors of the Indus Civilisation were 'born, perhaps, rather of the soil itself and of the rivers than of the varied breeds of men which they sustained'[36] illustrates his emulation of Childe's views regarding the 'ripe and distinct individuality' of the Bronze Age civilisations of the fourth millennium in the Orient.

Although Marshall did not engage with Childe's ethnically significant traits in his descriptions of the nature of the Indus Civilisation, in concluding the technologically significant trait list for the Civilisation he remarked:

> some [traits] may have originated among the Indus people, but many must have been derived from elsewhere, borrowed, may be from other regions, or in some cases inherited from earlier ages, when the races of Afrasia were perhaps less heterogeneous.[37]

Marshall refused to speculate upon the 'origins' of the Indus Civilisation on the premise that the data he had at his disposal was meagre. So he did not venture into Childe's pursuit of culture diffusion, which greatly influenced Wheeler and Piggott. Instead, Marshall intuitively drew upon the 'cruder stone implements from the Rohri hills', and other Neolithic sites in Sind and Kirthar Hills, which had been known from the 1860s, for presenting the possibilities of the antecedents of the Indus Civilisation.[38]

Marshall's disregard of Childe's constructs of the ethnically significant traits through which the latter established his theories of culture diffusion is best seen in the short archaeological history of the Indo-Sumerian Civilisation.

---

[34] Marshall (1931, p. 94). Among the list of 'associated traits' which Marshall attributed to the 'culture' excavated at Harappa and Mohenjodaro, were domestication, cultivation, irrigation, organisation of societies in cities, spinning and weaving, navigation by river, metallurgy (or the working in gold, silver, copper and tin), use of the potter's wheel, fashioning of ornaments, and recording of speech by writing (ibid., p. 95).

[35] Marshall (1931, p. 95).

[36] Ibid., p. 105.

[37] Ibid.

[38] Ibid., p. 93.

Although this history has very little bearing upon the subsequent research of the Indus Civilisation, it enriches our understanding of the historiography.

Marshall's 'Indo-Sumerian' Hypothesis and Childe's Views

The Indus Civilisation was archaeologically exposed in the shadow of a powerful hypothesis that the Ancient Sumerians were ethnically of the same stock as the Ancient 'Dravidian' people. The hypothesis was proposed by the Egyptologist Henry Hall who, in his book *The Ancient History of the Near East* (1913), claimed that the Sumerians had migrated into Mesopotamia from the East, possibly India, at some 'prehistoric' date.[39] Hence, the excavations at Harappa and Mohenjodaro, which were undertaken throughout the 1920s, raised expectations of finding material proof of Hall's hypothesis. Marshall examined and partially adopted Hall's thesis in his initial hypothesis regarding the nature of the 'prehistoric' civilisation of the Bronze Age cities in Harappa and Mohenjodaro. In his second article on the excavations in *The Illustrated London News* (1926), he inferred that the cities might represent an Indo-Sumerian Civilisation. However, he also highlighted the conjectural nature of his theory, which involved envisaging the inhabitants of Sumer and Indus valley in prehistory as 'Dravidians', and stated that 'should this [i.e. the theory] prove to be correct it may be expected that this prehistoric culture which is now being brought to light in the West of India will be found to have extended over a much larger part of the peninsula'.[40] Childe sourced Marshall's theory in his history of *The Aryans* (1926). He drew attention to the similarities of artefact types between the Sumerian and Indus civilisations which Marshall had brought to notice, but contrary to the latter's reticence, he affirmed unequivocally that the common cultural elements meant that they were both peopled by the 'Dravidian' race.[41]

The Aryans was published at a time when Marshall had foreseen the implausibility of forging Indo-Sumerian cultural connections during the third millennium BCE. The large scale excavations at Mohenjodaro in

[39] Hall (1913, pp. 172–74).
[40] Marshall (1926, p. 398).
[41] See Childe (1926, p. 35).

1925–26, which he personally directed, had assured Marshall of the disparity of the artefact assemblages between the Sumerian and 'Indus' cities, which he stated were 'more numerous and striking than the points of similarity'.[42] Thus, in his last account of the Indus Civilisation in *The Illustrated London News* (1928), Marshall declared that if there had been 'linguistic or racial connections' between the two, it must have been at an age 'much anterior' to the Chalcolithic period which had been exposed through the excavations.[43] In *Mohenjodaro*, Marshall therefore also made a point of dismissing Childe's claim in *The Aryans* that the Indus and Sumerian civilisations were authored by the Dravidians. For, Marshall was convinced by then that 'any attempt to equate the Sumerian with Ancient Dravidians is complicated at the outset by the difficulty of defining either the Sumerian or the Dravidian type'.[44]

Yet, the change in Marshall's views did not persuade Childe to reject Hall's hypothesis of the Dravidian and Sumerian connections. He used the hypothesis to claim evidence of Indo-Sumerian racial connections in *The Most Ancient East*, which appeared nine months after Marshall's last article in *The Illustrated London News*. In a footnote of the chapter on Indus Civilisation (Chapter IX), he also made it amply clear that he had in fact read Marshall's article.[45] However, Childe overlooked the evidence from the excavations at Mohenjodaro, of the many dissimilarities between the artefactual repertoire between this site and those found during excavations at Ur, Kish, Susa and other sites of the third-millennium Mesopotamia, and asserted that 'it is fantastic to suggest that the wheel and carts had been independently invented in both lands'. Instead, he dwelt upon the common elements of stylistic traits between the assemblages at Harappa, Mohenjodaro and the aforementioned Mesopotamian sites, to ask the question 'if so had the Sumerians themselves come from the Indus or at least from some region within its immediate sphere of influence?' To detract criticisms from his convictions and assertions of Indo-Sumerian connections, he explicitly asserted in a rhetorical manner: 'Does not some ethnic kinship perhaps underlie these [namely Indian and

---

[42] Marshall (1926, p. 398).

[43] Marshall (1928, p. 80).

[44] Marshall (1931, pp. 107, 110).

[45] See footnote 2, Childe (1928, p. 244). The next footnote reveals that Childe had also read Marshall's article on the Indus Civilization in the *Annual Report of the Archaeological Survey of India for the Year 1923–24* (in the section on 'Exploration and Research') which had been published in 1926.

Mesopotamian] commercial ties?'[46] In the new edition of the book, namely *New Light on the Most Ancient East*, for which he had visited India and Iraq to gather data, he declared that 'however, organised politically, the Indus civilization was built upon the same primary inventions and discoveries as the Nilotic and the Mesopotamian. Its authors may even have included men of the same racial types'.[47]

Childe's pursuit of Hall's hypothesis was based upon his presumption that if it could be proved true, then this would reveal the geographical 'cradle' of the invention of the wheel. Yet, his overlook of Marshall's rejection of the Indo-Sumerian theory reveals rather clearly the manner in which he presented his own judgements as evidence. The conscious overlook provokes a recall of Childe's disregard of Kenyon's inferences regarding the possibilities of a Neolithic town at Jericho. In both the cases, the excavator's evidence contradicted his own expectations of what that evidence ought to have been. The disregard occasions a critical reflection of the ways in which evidentiary values are ascribed, reminding us that our notions of valid evidence is usually contingent upon what we think things should look like.

Paradigm Change or a Change in Focus of Enquiry

In *New Light on the Most Ancient East*, Childe had asserted that:

> The delicate and, as we now see, enduring adaptation to the Indian environment represented in the Indus civilization, can only have been created and spread over a vast area after a long period of incubation on the spot. Yet, this civilization, though contrasted to the Egyptian and Sumerian as specifically Indian, rests upon the same fundamental ideas, discoveries, and inventions as they. The agreements are indeed mostly quite general and abstract—city life, cultivation of cereal, domestication of cattle and sheep, metallurgy, a textile industry, manufacture of bricks and pots, drilling of hard stone for beads, an affection for lapis lazuli, a knowledge of fayence. But even so they can hardly be regarded as independent inventions accumulated in similar environments. [...] the Harappa civilization is not the result of a mere transplantation or

---

[46] Childe (1928, pp. 211–12).
[47] Childe (1934, pp. 207–08).

imitation of the Early Dynastic Sumerian. Both are based on the same fundamental discoveries and inventions, but these have plainly undergone a long divergent development in the two areas since the latest common elements reached Mesopotamia in Uruk times.[48]

The statement above sums up one of Childe's inferences of a common home for the primary technological inventions, from where developments within human cultural life had supposedly diffused into different areas in different manner and had taken different forms. Marshall had drawn upon Childe's sketch of the elements of unity and individuality in all 'Bronze Age cultures', which Wheeler too drew upon. However, in contrast to Marshall, Wheeler also absorbed Childe's theory of diffusion to explain the rise of the Indus Civilisation. Thus, Wheeler saw the 'points of resemblance' between the Indus and Mesopotamian civilisations as more than an aspect of cultural sameness, or unity, but as representing 'inherent cousinship of a social phase' in which the 'common generalities', he wrote, were 'the product of stray seeds readily fertilized in similar historical and geographical setting', and 'the particularities' represented the 'abundant and significant local variation'.[49] Of the 'particularities', which he listed as art, glyptic forms, seals and 'possibly language', Wheeler affirmed that their 'integrity stands unchallenged', and they present 'a notable absence of borrowing' from West Asia.[50] In his choice of the particular cultural elements, Wheeler, we note, echoed Marshall's sketch of the national character of the Indus Civilisation.

In Wheeler's views, which can at best be retrospectively described as contradictory, the borrowed 'idea' was representative of the shape of the cities, their uniform material contents, and their governance. Yet, the Indus Civilisation, he declared, was developed in isolation and was a product of its unique geography. It was authored by indigenous people and represented local cultural expressions. The characterisation of an isolated and centralised military theocracy for the Indus Civilisation, which Wheeler developed alongside all the above features, was subsequently emulated by Piggott, who studied the prehistory of Baluchistan.[51] The description of a stagnant and conservative civilisation, which Wheeler and Piggott endowed upon

---

[48] Childe (1934, p. 223).
[49] Wheeler (1968, p. 136).
[50] Ibid.
[51] Piggott (1950, p. 152–3).

the remains at Harappa and Mohenjodaro, has been received within the historiography as a paradigmatic shift.[52] Yet, in many ways the delineation of paradigm change is an imposition upon the historiography, as it obfuscates the differences between the views of Wheeler and Piggott, and the similarities of their views with Marshall.

Paradigm shifts in the Kuhnian sense implies that an older system of explanation for a certain phenomenon is replaced by a newer system that makes better sense not merely of the previous one, but because it has a greater predictive value. The shift entails new traditions of thinking, which engender 'new narrative of origins, a new way of reading, understanding and coming to terms with the past'.[53] Thus, a change in paradigm implicates histories of origins, and it is in this respect that we should be evaluating whether there was indeed a paradigmatic change within the historiography of the Indus Civilisation.

As has been stated earlier, Marshall and Wheeler emulated Childe's approach to the cultural histories of the ancient civilisations by building upon the notions of unity and individuality. So did Piggott. All the three also thought alike in vesting the origins of the cities in Harappa and Mohenjodaro to the productivity of the local riverine environment and trade contacts with West Asia, and perceived the civilisation as exhibiting a 'complete uniformity of culture'.[54] They, however, differed in their perceptions of the manner in which the cities had grown. Marshall was convinced that the complex city life with buildings and excellent art and crafts could have only 'resulted from long centuries of previous endeavour', and Piggott following the logic of the excavation profile of nine building phases at Mohenjodaro and six at Harappa stated quite clearly that 'the Harappa culture is known only in its mature form.... An origin outside India is inherently improbable, but where and in what form this origin was is quite unknown'.[55] Wheeler differed from both in his assertions that whatever the actual form, the people of Harappa and Mohenjodaro received the idea of civilisation from

[52] See, for example, Possehl (1999, 134–35).

[53] Prickett (2009, p. 17).

[54] Marshall (1931, p. 91); Piggott (1950, pp. 138–39); Wheeler (1953, p. 2). See also Possehl (2002, p. 19), who noted the prominent features of the 'Marshall paradigm' within the 'Wheeler–Piggott interpretation' in terms of analogy with Sumer and Egypt, contextualising the Civilisation within a bigger historical setting, and similar inferences on environmental conditions, craft production and science.

[55] Marshall (1931, p. 103); Piggott (1950, p. 140).

Mesopotamia, where towns and cities existed during the latter half of the fourth millennium BCE.[56]

Wheeler had indeed proposed a new narrative of origins of the cities by grasping the theory of 'stimulus diffusion' from Mesopotamia. He was certain, albeit erroneously and without evidence, that the 'ill sorted industries and cultures' of the Baluchi Hills were unlikely to throw any light upon the origins of the Indus Civilisation, as they had no primary or organic relationship with its culture.[57] Hence, he declared that the ideational stimuli of a civilisation arrived into India 'across southern Afghanistan [...] through Chaman and Quetta and alternatively down the Bolan Pass'.[58] Yet, to denote a paradigm change within the scholarship of the Indus Civilisation, we would need to ask ourselves exactly what kinds of evidence did Marshall and Wheeler look for in historicising the phenomenon of civilisational origins.

Both, as is well known, had affirmed that the population of Harappa and Mohenjodaro was indigenous. Marshall had, however, attributed the reasons for finding an urban Bronze Age civilisation in the Indus Valley to geographical conditions, and Wheeler had sought external origins for the civilisational ideology that he deemed was planted into a topography that was fertile for reception. Therefore, in conceptualising a paradigmatic change between the approaches of Marshall and Wheeler, we submit to a theoretical slippage between their notions of civilisational origins and of their understanding of the authorship of a civilisation because both saw the Indus Civilisation as indigenous in its origins in the dictionary meaning of the term. The question we could ask instead is why have archaeologists felt the need to locate a paradigm change within the early scholarship of the Indus Civilisation. In digressing into aspects of Wheeler's archaeological scholarship of India, we are shown a clue.

The 'Wheeler–Piggott Paradigm'

Wheeler had attributed Harappa and Mohenjodaro to 'citadel mounds' well before he excavated the sites in 1946 and 1950, respectively. In fact, by

---

[56] Wheeler (1968, p. 135).
[57] Ibid., p. 9.
[58] Ibid., pp. 23–24.

1945, he had postulated the militaristic and imperialist nature of the Indus Civilisation through 'observation' alone. Piggott had noted this act in *Some Ancient Cities of India* (1945) and remarked that:

> Dr. Wheeler, has in recent examination of the sites come to a conclusion which I share, and recognized in the great Stupa Mound of Mohenjodaro, on a platform of brick twenty feet high, and in the AB mound at Harappa with its traces of a defensive wall and probably bastion turrets, the citadels of a ruler, be he emperor or priest-king.[59]

In a footnote following the above remark, Piggott stated that Wheeler had mentioned this 'extremely important observation' to him in a conversation in 1944, but had not yet published the information. In seeking logic for Wheeler's inferences, Piggott subsequently emphasised that 'to a British archaeologist the inevitable parallel is the Roman Empire supervening upon the prehistoric Iron Age barbarian settlements of his own country'.[60]

After his excavations in Harappa in 1946, Wheeler proclaimed that 'whatever the source of their authority—and a dominant religious element may fairly be assumed—the lords of Harappa administered their city in a fashion not remote from the priest kings or governors of Sumer and Akkad'.[61] Piggott abided by Wheeler's descriptions and presented the Indus Civilisation as a centralised empire with possibly two kingdoms and a stagnant uniformity, and the latter he suggested represented the 'innate conservatism' of the Indian tradition.[62] This understanding was no doubt different from Marshall's and Mackay's. However, archaeologists usually speak of a 'Wheeler–Piggott' paradigm, which brings with it the understanding that Piggott and Wheeler

---

[59] Piggott (1945, p. 15).

[60] Piggott (1950, p. 133).

[61] Wheeler (1947a, p. 76). He described the Mesopotamian cities as 'massively fortified [...] stronghold of undivided religious and secular authority'. 'In essence', he said, 'the picture is one of rigid and highly evolved bureaucratic machine, capable of organising and distributing surplus wealth and of defending it, but little conducive to the political liberty of the individual' (ibid).

[62] Piggott (1950, p. 140). Following Piggott and Wheeler, Childe shed his earlier emulation of Mackay's descriptions of the cities through standardised brick sizes and drainage systems, and recalled Harappa and Mohenjodaro as 'dominated by an artificial citadel, girt with a massive rampart of kiln-baked bricks, containing presumably a palace and immediately overlooking an enormous granary and the barracks of artisans' (cf Childe, 1950, p. 12).

thought alike with respect to the nature of the Indus Civilisation. [63] Yet, unlike Wheeler, Piggott was of the opinion that 'the combination of elaborate social and economic organization over a huge empire with an isolation, which rendered many of its technological processes astonishingly primitive makes one think not so much of contemporary Sumer and Egypt, but rather of the Central American pre-Columbian civilizations'.[64]

The 'Wheeler–Piggott paradigm' attracts a review, as it is construed and conceptualised in many ways. In recent years, the occurrence of a paradigm change is perceived in the endowments of Wheeler and Piggott of 'militaristic imperialism' upon the nature of the Indus Civilisation, and is construed as being 'colored' by their training in Classical Archaeology and their experiences in World War II.[65] Even if we ignore the logic of connecting the scholarship in Classics with the militaristic nature of the Indus Civilisation, the notion that Wheeler and Piggott had both attributed militaristic features upon the phenomenon because of their own services in the military masks the misgivings of Piggott towards Wheeler's adulation of the army, as well as of the insignificance he saw in the uses of military service for the conduct of archaeological fieldwork.

Piggott's Views of Wheeler

Piggott had shared his war service in India with the aspiring archaeologists Glyn Daniel and T.G.E. Powell, but he undertook his apprenticeship of Indian archaeology alone. In a letter to Cyril Fox, his mentor and the director of National Museums of Wales (1926–48), he had lamented that 'I jointly rule the destinies of our curious craft [i.e., archaeology] and mystery of this theatre of war with Glyn Daniel, who I fear lost his soul while gaining the whole world of a successful RAF career, and thinks and talks of nothing

---

[63] For example, Possehl (1999, p. 134–36), who stated that although Piggott too attributed a theocratic nature to the Indus Civilisation based on contemporary understanding of the Mesopotamian Civilisation, he was more subtle in his 'treatment of the Sumerian matter' (p. 135).

[64] Piggott (1950, p. 139).

[65] Wright (2010, p. 12).

else'.[66] Piggott was also wary of Wheeler's adulation of the military, and an example is an ode 'To R.E.M.W.' which he composed in November 1944 while dining with Wheeler and members of the R.A.F. in Delhi. The poem, which is quoted below, and which he posted to his wife Cecily Margaret, better known as Peggy, was accompanied with a note that stated that 'the incident and the appalling statement' were said in connection with Gus Bradford. Piggott wrote:

Last night we dined
I held the colleague's mask before my hate
Though self-love keeps you blind.
You purred and patronized and tossed a crust
to this or other lucky one–
Oh, you were great,
so fiercely gracious with your rasping tongue
honeyed to sickliness. And then the snarl.
And twist of lips as you thump
down the searing phrase–
'the young men should go forward to be killed.
I did not build my façade yesterday. I did not speak
knowing that vengeance was not mine to wreck,
but rather felt a little wonder
at a man who with a word
makes so sure when he dies
(and you not now so young)
that judgement should not be deferred
but he straightaway must stand
and see his sentence in the puzzled eyes
and strained pale faces of those murdered boys.[67]

---

[66] Letter from Lt Col Piggott to Fox, at Rhibwana, near Cardiff, dated 14 March 1943, from RAF HQ New Delhi, WO5/5/6, MAA. Fox had joined the National Museum of Wales as Keeper in 1922.

[67] Letter from Piggott, addressed from Section 17 HQ, BAESEA, RAF India, to 'Mrs Piggott, Priory Farm, Rockbourne, Fordingbridge, Hants', dated 4 November 1944, Box SP/35/35, Piggott Archives.

The poignancy of the 'ode' resides in the note that Piggott sent with it, enquiring from his wife whether she had any news of Michael Wheeler (Mortimer Wheeler's only child), since 'unreliable sources say that [he] is killed'.

Piggott's critical stance towards Wheeler's appetite for war and the military can be seen in many of his letters and notes to colleagues. An example is a letter that he wrote to Fox ten years later after he composed the above 'ode'. The letter conveys Piggott's assessment of Wheeler's autobiography *Still Digging* (1955), and he stated that he found Wheeler's statement that the latter would have been a fretful and restless man without the wars 'most revealing'. Piggott emphasised that 'here one sees an unhappy demon-pursued man. [...] He has had to drive at full speed all the time to prevent himself thinking.' Piggott confessed to Fox that he found the book 'dull', 'disappointing and sad', with 'only a picture of an undignified scramble from job to job; each sucked (fairly) dry and chucked aside as a better opportunity for smash and grab presents itself'.[68]

Such notes are avowedly personal, but they provide a view of the uneasy relationship which Piggott shared with Wheeler, and which was aptly illustrated by Roger Mercer, secretary of Royal Commission on the Ancient and Historical Monuments of Scotland (1990–2004), in his obituary for Piggott. Mercer was Piggott's close friend and a colleague at Edinburgh University; he noted that on becoming the director general of the Archaeological Survey in 1944, Wheeler had sought Piggott's release from the 'women's work of air photographic service' so that the latter could be seconded to the Survey. But, wrote Mercer, 'fortunately the army vetoed the idea—as Piggott and Wheeler would have, almost certainly, composed a volatile cocktail, the excellent qualities of both being polar expressions of the same dedication'.[69] Piggott's stay in India overlapped for less than a year with Wheeler's, and by the time Wheeler excavated at Harappa in 1946, Piggott held the Abercromby Chair in Prehistory in Edinburgh, having succeeded Childe to the post.[70]

---

[68] Letter from Piggott to Fox at Rhibwana, from 7 Gloucester Place, Edinburgh, dated 19 January 1955, WO5/5/6, MAA.

[69] Mercer (1998, p. 429).

[70] In a letter to Wheeler, Piggott had enquired: 'I'm delighted to hear of your gateway—is it in the Citadel, or have you found town walls as well?' Dated 30 December 1946, from the Department of Prehistoric Archaeology, University of Edinburgh, Box 453, Wheeler Papers.

Unlike Wheeler's archaeological career in India, and subsequently in Pakistan, which he and his peers recorded as bringing innovations within field methods and in the planning and administration of archaeology, Piggott recorded his career in Indian archaeology to Fox as 'nothing more than making the best of a bad job' while longing to 'return to England and its archaeology'. He stated that he loathed 'the country and the climate and the breach with English civilization it entails' and felt 'like one of those Dark Ages Irish monks who made homesick notes in the margins of the Ms at St Gall'.[71] In this respect, Piggott's visual rendition of the 'Indian Paranoia', which is the Illustration 4.2, is a literal transcription of his personal sentiments. Yet, Wheeler had tried to entice Piggott back into the Indian subcontinent following his preliminary survey and excavations at Mohenjodaro in 1950. Wheeler had hoped that Piggott and he could undertake a joint excavation at the site, and castigating the excavations that had been undertaken by Marshall and Mackay as 'an astonishing monument of utter incompetence, sugared on with specious "science"', he had proposed that:

> Now, Stuart, the more I see of Mohenjodaro the more convinced I am that, before you do anything else, we must put in 2 sessions' work there, chiefly citadel, which could be a priceless gem. By 'we' I don't mean Pakistan, which hasn't an anna. But couldn't we put a reasonable all-British show together and do the job? We'd be welcome and would get 50% of the loot. I'll guarantee already first class results. We'd want a total of £5000. Couldn't you and I do it together? The two of us would rewrite the Indus Valley. Think it over. It's a chance, and the time is <u>now</u>.[72]

---

[71] Letter from Piggott to Fox at Rhibwana, from Air Headquarters New Delhi, 14 March 1943, WO5/5/5, MAA.

[72] Letter from Wheeler to Piggott, undated, Box 36, Piggott Archives. The letter conveys contemporary conditions:

> Very little archaeology is possible here at present. The only solid work being attempted is a <u>comprehensive</u> plan of Mohenjodaro. You know, whole areas of excavation there have never been planned at all! And the existing plans are of course to all sorts of scale, and unrelated to one another.... Anyway, now I have got some help from the Survey of Pakistan and <u>may</u> get something done. I went down there for one day last week-32 and 1/2 hours in lungful trains and 12 hours on the site. Spend a small surveying school there, measured a building, prepared a conservation scheme (the place is tumbling down), and shot 4 partridges. It was a pleasant interlude from interminable office work and intrigues here.

Although the letter can easily be read as an expression of Wheeler's 'colonialist' views, it conveys much more forcefully his opportunism, of which Piggott had spoken to Fox in his letters. Despite the plans, Wheeler did not excavate at Mohenjodaro beyond one season in 1950, and his letter to Piggott (above) allows us also to remember that the latter had written about the Indus Civilisation without undertaking any excavations, be they at Mohenjodaro or Harappa.

Returning to constructs of paradigms, we may be right in assuming that Wheeler had certainly hoped at creating a view of a major paradigm change within the historiography through his castigations of the excavations of Marshall and Mackay as the 'very parody of scientific method'.[73] He had proclaimed that the adoption of the method mentioned earlier would ensure that 'as a *civilization*, the Mohenjodaro complex would not have existed for us, and it is as a civilization, not as a mere local culture that Mohenjodaro looms over the prehistory of Asia'.[74] Yet, Wheeler's theory of an isolated prehistoric civilisation in the Indus Valley, which he visualised as an offspring of opportunity and genius and whose ideational gene he traced within the Mesopotamian Civilisation, remains a description of a local culture that rose and fell without much impact on the soil that had received it. His ruminations regarding the civilisational legacy of the 'metaphysics that endured' was based upon his sourcing of Marshall's writings on aspects of religion, trade, crafts and other technologies of the Indus Civilisation, through which the latter had made a pioneering effort in *Mohenjodaro* for historicising a Bronze Age civilisation.[75] In registering a paradigm change within the historiography of the Indus Civilisation through Wheeler's contributions, we thus endorse the view, which Wheeler would have hoped subsequent generations of South Asian archaeologists would promote.

[73] Wheeler (1947b, pp. 144–45).

[74] Ibid., pp. 143–44. In a subsequent address to the Council for British Archaeology, Wheeler, however, conceded that although the excavators 'may be said to have *shown*' and not *delivered* the Indus Civilisation to the world, at least they did that. He continued: 'it was all very scandalous, but we have to admit that they, like Schliemann, added a chapter to the history of civilization, where we, the grandchildren of Pitt Rivers might have added a paragraph to a catalogue of cultures.' See Wheeler (1966, p. 105).

[75] Wheeler (1968, p. 137).

Histories Beyond Paradigms:
Piggott and Baluchistan

By disengaging with locations of paradigm changes within the archaeological histories of the Indus Civilisation, we are able to see the important contributions of Piggott to the archaeology of South Asia. Similar to the contributions of Childe to the scholarship, not field surveys, of the prehistory of the Indian subcontinent those of Piggott also remain marginalised, although both undertook pioneering research.

In his archaeological search for the invention of the potter's wheel in West Asia, Childe had endeavoured to map a chronological and cultural sequence of the prehistory of Iran in 1942. He had expressed the view that the areas to the East may yield further evidence of technological diffusion.[76] Piggott, who came to India the same year, committed his research quite explicitly to test the above theory, and explored for 'the Indian evidence for dating the Iranian prehistoric sequence'.[77] He made efforts to classify and order the archaeological cultures of the Near East, and his field surveys in the district of Quetta in 1944, where he was stationed, were specifically aimed at seeking 'a new culture which ought to be very early and link up the south Persian Buff wares with Anau II'.[78] Although Piggott did not aim his research towards the scholarship of Indian archaeology, the comparative and analytical methodologies he developed during his study of the prehistory of Baluchistan, and of the copper hoards in the Gangetic valley provided methodological and theoretical orientations to the archaeological research of prehistory within Pakistan and India, which the discovery of the Indus Civilisation demanded.

---

[76] Childe (1942, pp. 353–58).

[77] Quote from Piggott, in his letter to Fox, dated 14 March 1943, from RAF HQ New Delhi, WO5/5/5, MAA.

[78] Letter from Piggott to Fox, dated 26 February 1944, WO5/5/5, MAA. Subsequently, in *Prehistoric India*, Piggott recorded: 'Already in 1933 Professor Gordon Childe had made a penetrating synthesis of the North-west Indian material in its relation to the other cultures of the most ancient East; ten years later the accidents of war brought me to New Delhi and enabled me to start on a revision of Childe's basic work in the light of the accumulated new knowledge of the intervening decade, and this has been continued since the war by Donald McCown of the Oriental Institute of Chicago' (1950, p. 19). See also 'Chronological Table I' which is at the end of the chapter on 'Communities in Western India' in Piggott (1950, p. 65).

At a time when physical dating techniques had not been invented, comparisons of artefacts from stratified contexts, especially ceramic forms and their painted styles, allowed the means of fixing relative chronologies. Childe had established methods of classifying trait lists for undertaking sophisticated comparisons of vast quantities and ranges of artefact types from a vast geography in *The Dawn*, and in his maiden book, *The Progress of Early Man* (1935) Piggott emulated Childe's systematic and careful classificatory methods. The epistemic value of typologies, which Childe demonstrated through his methodologies, is rather well exemplified in a series of correspondence, which dates back to 1940. The correspondence is between Max Mallowan (1904–78), by then one of the leading archaeologists of Mesopotamia and Assyria, and Basil Gray (1904–89), historian of Islamic art and curator of Oriental antiquities at the British Museum. Their letters exist in the archives of Piggott in his handwritten copies, which suggest their academic importance to him. The correspondence relates to the pottery from Rana Ghundai (Baluchistan) from excavations at the site in 1940 by Major Martin, who donated them to the British Museum.

Gray had written to Mallowan with photographs of the individual ceramic 'types' that he said had been found within the stratified deposits, hoping to convince the latter that the excavations had been undertaken in a systematic manner. He wished Mallowan to subscribe to his theory, which he based upon the fact that the sherds had been found within stratified contexts, and that the 'mound [of Rana Ghundai] had an Iranian rather than Indian affiliation throughout its early history... [which] no doubt will prove to be true of all the north Baluchistan tells'.[79] Instead, Mallowan analysed the samples in detail with references to the pottery that had been collected by Aurel Stein during his excavations at Rana Ghundai, in 1927, of which he knew through Piggott, and through his own vast knowledge of ceramic types from Jemdet Nasr, Tell Halaf, Chagar Bazar, Arpachiyah and Al Ubaid.[80] He established a historical chronology of culture diffusion of Mesopotamia

---

[79] Letter from Gray to Mallowan, dated 2 July 1940, addressed from the British Museum, SP/Box 36, Piggott Archives.

[80] See Stein (1929). Stein's enthusiasm in exploring Baluchistan was triggered by the discoveries at Harappa and Mohenjodaro. However, it is worth noting that Stein had undertaken his first archaeological field survey in 1898 in the Persian Baluchistan (near Ketas) in search of Alexander's route. See Stein (1898).

through Syria and Iran to north Baluchistan through the references, and wrote back to Gray with the conclusion that

> the polychrome school continued to flourish in the backward highlands of Baluchistan and in the Indus Valley long after it was dead in the West. My theory is that the ancient trade of painted pottery was disturbed and finally destroyed by metallurgists of the early third millennium BC, and that the guild migrated Eastwards beyond the reach of the new mechanics. All this is probably heretical and requires proof. If someone conducted a scientific excavation on a mound like Sur Jungal or Periano Ghundai, where there are strong connections both with India and Iran, we should be well on the way to solving the problem.[81]

Mallowan's remark informs us of the research potentials of the Archaeological Survey's Reserve Collections at the Central Asian Antiquities Museum, which Childe had seen, and to which Piggott had paid a 'fleeting visit' in April 1942, when he had also visited Mohenjodaro.[82] This collection contained the sherds of Rana Ghundai, to which Mallowan had made references, and also contained almost all the other kinds of 'prehistoric shreds' that had been collected within India during the early twentieth century. In developing his scholarship of the prehistory of Baluchistan, Piggott was largely informed through the contents of this collection, and we note that Stein had specifically registered 'satisfaction' at the intentions of Piggott's study, in his reply to the latter's preliminary enquiries of his surveys in Baluchistan in 1927–28.[83]

---

[81] Letter from Mallowan to Gray, dated 29 June 1940, from Max Greenway House, Churston Ferrers, South Devon, Piggott Archives.

[82] In a letter to Fox at Rhibwana, dated 4 April 1942 from R.A.F. Calcutta, Piggott had mentioned, 'by devious means I even managed to visit Mohenjodaro and another Indus culture site while waiting for instructions at Karachi, and have made a fleeting visit to the Central Asian Museum at New Delhi, WO5/5/5, MAA.

[83] Stein had stated:

> It is a satisfaction to me that the ceramic materials collected by me on my archaeological tours in the N.W. Frontier and in British Baluchistan, and kept by the Archaeological Department at New Delhi have attracted your attention. I am sure the systematic examination of them and comparison with prehistoric pottery from the Indus Valley, Siestan, etc., by an expert student might still yield useful results. [...] My endeavours in the field have always had to be confined to breaking new ground for future detailed investment.

> Letter from Stein to 'Captain Piggott', from 'Camp, c/o Postmaster, Srinagar, Kashmir', and dated 25 June 1942. Box SP/36, Piggott Archives.

The possibilities of drawing Baluchistan into the history of the antecedents of the Indus Civilisation had been foreseen by Stein, and Marshall's discussions of 'the extent of the Indus Civilisation' in *Mohenjodaro* provides an overview of the manner in which ceramic types from various sites were compared in an effort to map the prehistory of the region.[84] In following Childe's hopes of finding cultural connections between Iran and the Indus Valley that could inform of the homeland of the wheel, and also metallurgy, Piggott devised 'the chronology of prehistoric north-west India'. He employed Childe's methodology of '"zoning" cultures beyond [the] primary centres' of urbanisation, and envisaged that the Neolithic cultures of North India, including central India and Kashmir, 'were more likely to be the result of folk movement from the west than independent invention', and suggested that to 'understand the subsequent prehistory of India' one 'must book beyond its present frontier to the other lands of West Asia'.[85] Yet, after sketching the background to the 'Cities and Towns of Sind and the Punjab', he remarked that although it is 'unlikely that [the Indus Civilisation] springs from any separate ultimate origin [...] somewhere behind it lie the peasant cultures of the type of Mehi and Rana Ghundai'.[86] Thus, despite his proclivity of ascertaining a West Asian heritage for the Neolithic and Bronze ages in northern South Asia, Piggott too like Stein and Marshall foresaw the possibility of placing the prehistory of Baluchistan within the history of the evolution of the Indus Civilisation.

Therefore, Piggott's equivocation regarding the contributions of Baluchistan to the Indus Civilisation ought to be distinguished from Wheeler's opinion. For unlike Piggott's ambivalence, even in the third edition of *The Indus Civilization* (1968) and well after large-scale excavations had been undertaken at Amri (1959–62) and a non-pottery Neolithic horizon found at Kili Gul Mohammad (Quetta, 1950–51), Wheeler persisted in his beliefs that none of the Baluchi hill sites 'show any clear primary and organic relationship with the Indus Valley culture, which remains obstinately a creation of its own lowland environment', and that 'much playing with potsherds and culture-spreads may help a little to define the opportunity but cannot explain the genius'.[87] The differences in the ways in which Wheeler

---

[84] Marshall (1931, pp. 96–101).
[85] Piggott (1946, p. 9).
[86] Piggott (1950, pp. 40, 141).
[87] Wheeler (1968, pp. 9, 25).

and Piggott thought about the 'archaeology of India' are also representative in the ambivalent reception by Wheeler of Piggott's recommendations regarding the archaeological enquiries he could initiate as the new director general of the Archaeological Survey.

Piggott's Directions and Wheeler's Actions: Dabar Kot and Bala Hisar

Piggott was in India when he heard the news of Wheeler's appointment. He had welcomed the choice of Wheeler as 'ideal', since he was of the opinion that 'only by a ruthless scrapping of old ideas and instilling of new can anything be done' to improve Indian archaeology.[88] He was certain that Wheeler would be capable of the task, and in his congratulatory letter to the latter, wrote that he had been 'going round proclaiming the advent of the Golden Age in terms that make the Ninth Eclogue a modest understatement'.[89] In the letter, Piggott also communicated to Wheeler some of his impressions of the 'present state of Indian official archaeology' and the 'future work' that could be undertaken for expanding the scholarship. By then Piggott had had nearly two-year experience of Indian archaeology and, as he himself stated, this involved:

> working in the Central Asian Antiquities Museum on exhibited and reserve collections, frequent conversations with various members of the Staff of the Survey, visits to excavated sites and to one excavation in progress [at Ahichhatra, near Ramnagar, Uttar Pradesh], and a limited amount of fieldwork [at Quetta].

As a result of working on Indian protohistory and prehistory, he, therefore, wished to put forth his views regarding 'the new and specific subjects', which Wheeler could undertake.[90]

---

[88] Letter from Piggott to Fox, dated 26 February 1944, from HQ Air Command, South East Asia, WO5/5/5, MAA. He wrote that the appointment was received by 'apprehension by some and delight by a few' and asked Fox if he knew 'who was responsible for advising so well' (ibid).

[89] Letter marked 'Confidential' by Piggott to Wheeler, dated 9 December 1943, addressed from headquarters, South East Asia Air Command, Box 453, Wheeler Papers.

[90] Ibid.

In his long letter to Wheeler, Piggott also described the malaise of Indian archaeology, which he stated was to a large extent due to the poor intellectual calibre of the Indian and British officials of the Archaeological Survey.

The correspondence mentioned earlier is part of a discrete collection of informal and confidential letters which Wheeler received at his appointment from 'old India hands', which no doubt included eminent scholars of Indology and archaeology, such as John Marshall, Kenneth de Burgh Codrington, and F.J. Richards. The letters are eclectic in content, and provide diverse informa-tion on diverse topics, such as the details of influential colonial officers who could be approached for steering the affairs of the Survey, where to go fishing, buy wool stocking, and whom to appoint as bearers and domestic servants.[91] Some are from scholars who had never been to India, but who researched on aspects of Indian prehistory through collections that had been brought back to Britain. An example is a correspondence from Miles Burkitt (1890–1971), the first lecturer of prehistory at Cambridge, in the Museum of Archaeology and Ethnology, who was preparing chronologies of the 'Indian stone tools' from the Museum's recently acquired collection through the Yale–Cambridge Expedition of 1935. Burkitt had compiled for Wheeler a useful bibliographic reference of the nascent scholarship of Indian prehistory.[92]

In his letter to Wheeler, Piggott listed six potential areas of archaeological enquiries, namely (a) antecedents of the Indus culture, (b) 'The Aryans', (c) contacts with the Roman West, (d) 'Iron Age' sites in South Asia, (e) general Field Work, and (f) 'Air Photography'.[93] Wheeler followed Piggott's direc-tions, but in ways that were quite different from the actions which Piggott had recommended.

Through his research on 'Dating the Hissar sequence', which was published in *Antiquity* (1943), Piggott came to regard the archaeological mounds at Dabar Kot as a possible venue of the formative phases of the

---

[91] See Box 453, Wheeler Papers. A few examples of the personal advise to Wheeler within the letters: (a) 'On the "aesthetic side" Dr Stella Kramrisch (a Hungarian Jewess) knows her subject and is an indefatigable worker. Unfortunately she writes in a fantastic jargon (popular now among high brow aesthetes) which is unintelligible to ordinary reader' F.J. Richards to Wheeler, 27 December 1943; (b) 'if you ever want furs, foxes or caracul, write to Aurangzeb Khan, c/o Shahzada Mhd. Yusuf, Lloyd's Bank, Lahore, or tell Peshawari to dig him out in Peshawar', K. de B. Codrington to Wheeler, 2 February 1944; (c) 'Are you taking a mosquito net with you? You will need one wherever you go', Marshall to Wheeler, 7 February 1944.

[92] 'Notes from Burkitt', Typescript, Box 453, Wheeler Papers.

[93] Letter from Piggott to Wheeler, 9 November 1943, Box 453, Wheeler Papers.

Indus Civilisation. The research had given him opportunities for establishing scholarly networks with archaeologists of West Asia, for example Seton Lloyd, who was an archaeological advisor to the Directorate of Antiquities of Iraq at Baghdad (1939–49), and who empathised with Piggott's views and asserted that 'mounds like Dabar Kot [...] do most seriously needs attention, and one can only hope for more co-ordination and official support for archaeology in those parts after the War'.[94] Thus, with respect to tracing the 'antecedents of the Indus Culture', Piggott wrote to Wheeler:

> Eventually, Stein's explorations and hole digging will have to be supplemented by proper excavations on one or more Baluchistan 'tells'. Dabar-Kot which is 93 ft high, with a Harappa occupation on top is an obvious target, and what remains of Rana Ghundai should give more precision to the Hissar I relationships. In the south, Mehi seems the most likely site—here correlations with Early Dynastic Sumer are possible.[95]

Although Wheeler took cognizance of Piggott's emphasis for probing into the antecedents of the Indus Civilisation, the archaeological plans that he formally mapped and executed towards this end did not include Piggott's advice of extending the remit of Stein's explorations of Baluchistan. Instead, following his own theory of stimulus diffusion of the ideology of civilisation, Wheeler concentrated on seeking the route of cultural diffusion from Iran into India via Afghanistan, and sought for opportunities to excavate at Bala Hisar at Charsadda (Pakistan). Of the four-year excavation programme Wheeler retrospectively recorded that Bala Hisar had 'occupied the final position of honour on my list'.[96] The site, as mentioned in Chapter 3, was Marshall's very first excavation in India, in January–March 1903, and three decades later, in 1939, during his review tour of Indian archaeology Leonard Woolley noted it to be

> an extensive ruin-field embracing three large mounds. A good deal of nonsense has been written about it on the assumption that it was itself a stupa and monastery whereas it is a normal stratified site. Excavations in 1902–3 produced a great deal of Gandhara sculpture now in the Peshawar Museum; this seems to have been found at a depth of about 20 ft. below the mound's summit. As it

[94] Letter from Seton Lloyd, Directorate General of Antiquities, Iraq Government, to Piggott, dated November 1944, Box SP/ 36, Piggott Archives.

[95] Letter from Piggott to Wheeler, 9 November 1943, Box 453, Wheeler Papers.

[96] Wheeler (1976, p. 18).

is about 40 ft. high (at a guess) above the plain, which must itself have risen, there is a possibility of earlier remains. But the top layers are very late, almost modern, and excavation would be very costly in consequence. It is a site which could be tackled only by a well-financed long term expedition anxious for Gandhara work; it should not be undertaken by the Dept. [i.e. the Survey].[97]

In planning excavations at Bala Hisar in 1947 through the Archaeological Survey, Wheeler flouted Woolley's injunctions. However, as Wheeler noted, although 'work was due to begin there in the latter part of 1947, in August of that year momentous political events intervened'.[98] Wheeler eventually excavated Bala Hisar in 1958 (November–December) through the Department of Archaeology of Pakistan.

Although Wheeler did not include excavations at Dabar Kot within his archaeological plans as the Survey's director general, he showed commitments to Piggott's recommendations subsequently. In a visit to Pakistan in 1966 on a UNESCO mission for the preservation of Mohenjodaro, he helped the department draft a 'Five-year Programme of Excavation'. By then, the granting of permission to foreign archaeological expeditions had become a national issue within Pakistan, hence, Wheeler drafted the proposal as a national scheme which the 'department could both devise and control', and through which it could use 'all possible resources, whether Pakistani or foreign, within the framework of its own planning'. To achieve substantive archaeological results through systematic excavations, he suggested that the department take up the problems 'which surround the borderland cultures preceding and following the Indus Civilization', by examining the 'outstanding key site in the problem, namely Dabar Kot'.[99] Despite his recommendations to the Government of Pakistan, and his emphasis on the importance of Dabar Kot in the last edition of *The Indus Civilization*, the site awaits a formal study through excavations.[100]

[97] 'Sir Leonard Woolley's Notes', typescript with annotations in Wheeler's hand, File E/1/3 Wheeler Archives.

[98] Wheeler (1962, p. xi). For details of subsequent excavations at Charsadda, see Magee *et al.* (2005, p. 715–18).

[99] 'Five-Year Programme of Excavation', Pakistan Department of Archaeology. Typed draft of two pages with corrections in Wheeler's hand. Box F/1/7, Wheeler Archives.

[100] See, for example, Wheeler (1968, p. 62), where he stated that the 'potentiality' of the site

lies largely in the fact that the Harappan occupation seems to occur *near the top* of this tall mound, so that a careful excavation of it in depth may be expected to reveal

Wheeler also flouted Piggott's second advice, of a field survey along the river Ghaggar for tracing 'the Aryans' archaeologically. Piggott would have seen the reasons for researching the 'problem' due to his careful study of the copper hoards from the Gangetic plains in 1943. He had explained to Wheeler that:

> I am personally entertaining faint suspicions that some extraordinary finger-tipped and encrusted wares from the Ghaggar and from, e.g., Kaudani (where John Reid Dick picked up a lot of stuff last year) may date from 'Vedic' times. There seems a possibility of such wares in Iran being contemporary with the 'Luristan Bronzes' and so 1400–1200 BC.[101]

Wheeler dwelt upon the 'Aryan problem', and famously sought evidence for the invading 'Aryans' through his excavations at Mohenjodaro in 1950. However, he did not pursue explorations along the river Ghaggar, whose importance was also foreseen by Marshall, albeit for exploring the extent of the Indus Civilisation.[102] He excavated at Harappa instead.

Yet, in bidding farewell to the 'old Archaeological Survey' at the independence of India and Pakistan, Wheeler emphasised the importance of surveying the 'Ganges valley', and stated that although from 'time immemorial' the region has been a 'fountain of legend and history', the archaeological knowledge of this valley is limited to scraps and hints. He also suggested to his former Indian colleagues in the Archaeological Survey of India that now since the Survey had become 'freer than before' through the 'removal of the north-western provinces in which the greater part of the Department's exploratory

> the antecedents of the Indus Civilisation to an extent perhaps unparalleled elsewhere. Such a certainty may be regarded as compensation for the remoteness of the site and the consequent difficulties which will confront the excavator.

[101] Letter from Piggott to Wheeler, 9 November 1943, Box 453, BA archives.

[102] See Marshall (1931, p. 96). He had drawn attention to the need for archaeological explorations in the valleys of the Yamuna, Ganga, Narbada and Tapti for knowledge of 'prehistoric cultures' to determine whether its 'peoples possessed cities and houses and all the amenities of life' as found in Sind and Punjab, and had noted:

> There is nothing in the Vedic or later literature or in the diffusion of the pre-Aryan races or languages, so far as they are known to us to suggest that the pre-Aryan people of the Punjab and Sind are markedly different in culture from those of the Jumna and Gangetic basins further east, and it may also be added that a people accustomed to carry on trade and commerce as far afield as the Indus people were, *prima facie* likely to have made their influence felt far beyond the limits of the Indus Valley.

work' had been done in the past, it could turn to the systematic exploration of this region, and 'results of outstanding value could be predicted'.[103]

Wheeler's choice of the site of Bala Hisar for excavations demonstrates his hopes of finding the route of the 'Aryan' invasion into India. Such a discovery, he thought would contribute to the lifting of the 'Dark Age', which he, and Piggott, saw as looming over Indian history for over two thousand years, from the end of the Indus Civilisation at ca. 1900 BCE to the beginning of the Mauryan Empire at ca. 321 BCE. On his appointment to head the Archaeological Survey, he therefore specifically planned his archaeological mission in India for recovering evidence for illuminating this 'Age', and hoped at locating at least one archaeological site with deposits of the Indus Civilisation followed by those from the 'early historical' period.[104] But being sensitive to the reasoning that a single site with occupational deposition from 'Harappan' to 'early historical period' may not be easily located, Wheeler, to use his student B.B. Lal's words, thought of tackling the problem differently. He declared the importance of knowing first what the 'early historical' looked like in archaeological terms and suggested that the first task was to assess and stratify the various cultures of the early historical period through an assured ceramic sequence.[105]

Despite Wheeler's neglect, Baluchistan was explored throughout the 1940s by amateur British archaeologists, such as Colonel D.H. Gordon and Brigadier E.J. Ross, and subsequently through collaborative projects between archaeologists in British, American and French universities and the newly

---

[103] 'Message from the Director General', *Staff Memorandum No. 9*, dated 1947, Archaeological Survey of India (August, New Delhi), File E/1/11, Wheeler Archives.

[104] In his first 'Staff Memorandum' of May 1944, Wheeler had emphasised:

At present time, one historical problem stands out beyond all others. The two thousand years which elapsed between the period of the Indus Valley civilisation of the third millennium BC may fairly be described as the great formative period of Indian civilisation. It was the period of the Vedas and of the "Aryan migrations", and, without some archaeological knowledge of it, we are unable adequately to reconstruct and appreciate the orderly growth of subsequent Indian civilization. At present the whole period is, archaeologically, a complete blank. The blank can be filled by systematic fieldwork, and it is my intention, in so far as means are available at the present time, to undertake the initial stages of that work. (*Staff Memorandum No. 1, Message from Dr R.E. Mortimer Wheeler, Director General of Archaeology, to the staff of the Archaeological Survey of India*, File L22 DGA (36), Survey Archives)

[105] Lal (1949, p. 37).

formed departments of archaeology of the Federal State and universities of Pakistan. The promise of 'Prehistoric Baluchistan' for the scholarship of the Indus Civilisation was substantively exposed through excavations at Mehrgarh (Sibi district, Pakistan 1974 –85), and the nearby Nausharo (1986 –93) and Pirak (1968–74), which were initiated by French archaeologists, in their aims at complimenting and extending the scope of the 'French' excavations at Amri, that had been excavated between 1959 and 1962 by Jean-Marie Casal. The finds at Mehrgarh demonstrated that the Indus Civilisation could be connected to 'an economic and cultural substrate going back at least to the seventh millennium without a clear break'.[106]

The Neolithic horizon at Mehrgarh, often colloquially expressed as one of the 'first villages' of South Asia, compares in date to that of Neolithic Jericho, and patterns of plant uses and faunal economies at the site provide inalienable evidence of local domestication processes. The new evidence from Baluchistan no doubt vindicates the enquiries of Childe into the prehistory of the region. But it also firmly dismisses Childe's reasons for formulating the enquiry. Besides, systematic field surveys within Baluchistan and the Greater Indus–Hakra–Ghaggar valleys now promises information regarding local histories of the exploitation of plants and animals during the Holocene. Recent excavations at Rakhigarhi, which has entailed the 'discovery' of two more mounds with archaeological assemblage of the 'Harappan material' at the site (2013–14), and the numerous finds of Harappan sites that have been made in the state of Haryana (India) within the twenty-first century, such as Kunal, Bhirrana, Farmana, Girawad and Mitathal (the last, however, was also excavated in the 1980s), now prompts Indian archaeologists to declare that the 'beginning of the Harappan Civilisation' may have taken place in 'the Ghaggar basin in Haryana'.[107] Such declarations can be ignored as disingenuous as they trivialise the problem of historicising origins for an archaeological construct that occupies more than 100,000 sq. km. The reasons for the errors of historicising civilisational origins is explained in Chapter 5, and to sum them up briefly, we could say that they equate with the fallacy for searching the origins of the Indian Civilisation. Yet, we need to concede that the location of a fifth-millennium settlement at Rakhigrahi, which has also shown a 'mature urban' period in the subsequent levels reveals

---

[106] Jarrige (1995, p. 86).
[107] Cf. 'Rakhigarhi: The Biggest Harappan Site', *The Hindu*, 27 March 2014.

the possibilities of finding many more similar sites of deep antiquity within the Indian share of the Indus Civilisation. The earliest occupational horizons at Rakhigarhi can indeed be juxtaposed with Mehrgarh, for burying Childe's history of civilisational diffusion to the Indus Valley during the third millennium BCE.

Relevance of Childe in Indian Archaeology

So why recall Childe's contribution to the archaeological histories of the Indus Civilisation? The logic of the question would strike readers despite the sketch above of the various ways in which Childe had influenced the evidence and understanding of the Indus Civilisation during the formative years of research. Additionally, the virtual obliteration of Childe from the histories of the Indus Civilisation since the 1970s has not made any significant impact upon the advances in the scholarship of the phenomenon. Yet, in ignoring Childe, archaeologists of the Indus Civilisation and South Asia disregard the ethics of responsible research, which he represented. And this creates the importance of drawing upon Childe's contributions for enhancing the twenty-first-century scholarship of South Asian archaeology.

The evidential errors in Childe's various, and changing, theories of inventions and migrations were highlighted with the launch of the C-14 dating technique in 1949, which demonstrated that the archaeological cultures which Childe had deemed the product of external influences were older than their putative parent cultures. By the 1960s excavations and explorations within the Old and New Worlds also provided enough evidence for questioning Childe's views regarding the originary 'cradles' of primary technological inventions, and his criteria for the Neolithic and Urban 'revolutions'.[108] The 'New Archaeology' which emerged from North America during this decade, emphasised the need for exploring cultural processes, perceived cultures as systems, and through theoretical approaches of functionalism and adaptations eschewed the logic of Childe's normative culture histories.[109] In the search for the relevance of archaeology, the premier New Archaeologist,

[108] Regarding the 'revolutions', see Childe (1950).
[109] For a critical summary of Childe's culture history approach, see Thomas (2004, pp. 112–13) and Figure 2.3 in Johnson (2010, p. 19).

Lewis Binford called for a rejection of the historical particularism of Childe's approach, and affiliated the subject specifically with anthropology to 'explicate and explain the total range of physical and cultural similarities and differences characteristic of the entire spatial–temporal span of man's existence'.[110] The theoretical rupture which Binford hoped to establish from the Childean views has been recalled in an evocative manner by a former member of the 'Binfordian' group, Kent Flannery, who has stated that

> I don't know whether I could see my version of processual archaeology in anything that Childe wrote. It is possible that if I searched for it, I might find parallels in his work; but what we were all looking at were people doing ecological studies, who were trying to show that seemingly insignificant behavioural changes can have enormous long-term consequences, and that you can't always identify cause and effect by seeing them close together in time and space. In the case of some long-term and very important systemic changes, the cause may lie so far back in time, or so far away in space, that simple correlation of that type would not discover their actual relationship.[111]

Flannery is one of the remarkably few North American New Archaeologists to have reflected upon the heuristic value of Childe's scholarship. He also ranks among the pioneers in the archaeological scholarship of the New World, wherein Childe's theories of culture diffusion and patterns of migrations proved to be of no value, and Childe's theoretical schemes of 'revolutions' failed to fit the 'Nuclear American' data. Yet, Flannery has concluded decisively, and with justification that 'what matters is that Childe had a vision of evolution at a time when other archaeologists had only chronological charts'.[112]

During the 1970s, and echoing their contemporaries, the New Archaeologists of North America, the Processualist Archaeologists of Britain, who could be recognised as a group by then, were equally critical of Childe. However, even before the formal emergence of this group, the British prehistorian Grahame Clark had posed a challenge to Childe's approach to the

---

[110] Binford (1962, p. 217). For summary of the 'New' and 'Processual' archaeology, see Johnson (2010, pp. 15–44); for detailed bibliography, see also Smith (2004, pp. 34–42).

[111] Flannery (1994, p. 119).

[112] Ibid., p. 110; Childe has also been recalled by social anthropologists in recent years, prominently by Jack Goody and Marilyn Strathern. The latter finds his idea of civilization, with loosely integrated uniformities of behaviour and expectations over large area, capable of evoking complimentary and reciprocal engagements from archaeologists and anthropologists. See Strathern (2010, p. 176).

study of prehistory through his own research of *The Mesolithic Settlement of Northern Europe* (1936). Clark's subsequent scholarship of *Prehistoric Europe: the Economic Basis* (1952), argues John Coles, 'was a pioneering approach to the concept of ecosystems, the widest possible view of societies tied to, and coping with, environmental change, economic variability, the building of social networks and addressing the concerns of everyday survival and prosperity'.[113] Subsequently, David Clarke, the premier Processualist of Britain, challenged the non-explicit and intuitive nature of the Childean approach to typologies, cultures and assemblages through his seminal scholarship of *Analytical Archaeology* (1968).[114]

Yet, unlike their North American peers many 'young Turks' of Processual and Post-Processual Archaeology within Britain made subsequent discursive moves, by the close of the twentieth century, for negotiating the inadequacies of Childe's theories of culture change. Their efforts at reinterpreting Childe's views were informed by explorations of alternative models of evolution, such as the epigenetic model, which was developed by Jonathan Friedman and Michael Rowlands in the 1980s. They undertook a careful and critical review of the cultural ecological approach which was theorised during the 1940s by the North American social anthropologist Julian Steward, and which the New Archaeologists who were Childe's strongest critiques had unreservedly embraced. Friedman and Rowlands declared that while Childe's excessive diffusionism was rightly criticised, his theories regarding the emergence of social hierarchies and 'secular urban centres on the periphery of major centres of Near Eastern Civilization' remained valuable because they informed of the socially determined productive relations. By drawing upon the sophisticated interrelationships between social and technological features within Childe's theories, the British critiques of New Archaeology demonstrated that unlike him Steward had only occasional insights into the processes of structural transformations. Their research has shown that the mechanical materialism of Steward's theory reduces cultural evolutionary stages to a series of super-structural 'boxes', which are simply linked by 'time's technological arrow'.[115]

It is noteworthy that Friedman and Rowlands had used the epigenetic model for critiquing the culture–ecological approaches towards social evolution, in which developmental relationships were perceived through 'eras'.

---

[113] Coles (2010, p. 8).
[114] Clarke (1968).
[115] Friedman and Rowlands (1978, pp. 202, 271–72).

For, this approach, as we shall see in Chapter 5, is being increasingly used at present by North American archaeologists of the Indus Civilisation for devising schema of periodisation. Also, despite the blatant determinisms of culture ecology, which has been raised as a theoretical issue for the last twenty years by many archaeologists, the value of Steward's ecologically determinant theories to the archaeological scholarship of the Indus Civilisation is being increasingly exhibited by the North American archaeologists of South Asia, who add that unfortunately the available data lends little support to many of his ideas.[116]

As Childe became an inconsequential figure within the growing scholarship of the New and Processualist archaeologies of the 1970s, even the few British archaeologists of South Asia of the early post-colonial years, who did not follow the above schools, began to erase his intellectual presence from the historiography of the Indus Civilisation. Thus, Bridget Allchin and Raymond Allchin evoked Childe only with references to Wheeler, as the latter's supporter who abided by his views that the 'invading Aryans' had destroyed Harappa and Mohenjodaro, and for substantiating their own view that the Indus Civilisation was 'thoroughly individual and technically the peer of the rest'.[117] Inevitably, Childe's diffusionist perspectives were overtly, and erroneously, simplified by the North American archaeologist Jim Shaffer, who studied the prehistory of Baluchistan in the 1970s, as 'locating the origin of an idea' and 'then ascribing its presence in other areas as a result of the processes of secondary diffusion, migrations/invasions and occasionally trade'.[118] Archaeologists of South Asia are now providing reasons for rejecting the normative and processualist culture history approach of Childe's, and also of his North American critics. Yet, this critical literature also misinforms in declaring that Wheeler was the 'first systematic propagator' of the culture–history approach within South Asian archaeology.[119]

Childe's scholarship of the Orient in prehistory would no doubt seem irrelevant to all twenty-first-century archaeologists of South Asia, as his theories are known to have been riddled with factual errors, and he is known to

---

[116] For support of Steward's approach for the Indus Civilization, see Wright (2010, p. 14).

[117] Allchin and Allchin (1982, pp. 225, 350).

[118] Shaffer (1978, p. 100).

[119] Johansen (2003, p. 197). For a perception of the culture history approach by the New and Prosessualist archaeologists, see Binford (1968, pp. 267–75), and contributions in Renfrew (1973).

have blatantly disregarded the prehistoric topography of Asia that was being discovered through archaeology from the late-1920s through excavations in China and South East Asia. Also, Childe's assumption that the Oriental civilisations remained culturally stagnant after their remarkable efflorescence in prehistory belongs to the discarded historiography of Oriental Despotism. We can conjecture with considerable certainty that Childe would have echoed the sentiment of Piggott that 'the pattern and standard of material culture within India set by the second millennium BC has not radically changed to this day'.[120] Yet, Childe's scholarship defies trivialisation as being Orientalist, to borrow the Saidian cliché.

Unlike his contemporaries, and because of his political leanings towards Marxist ideologies, Childe, as Michael Rowlands has demonstrated in a commemorative volume, 'laboured against the idea that cultural progress could be measured by the achievements of a single people'. Hence, for Childe, 'Egypt was the horror story of what happens when moribund social relations isolate a people from external contact—"Four centuries after the Iron Age had opened in Greece, we find the Egyptian Smith still using the clumsy tools of the Bronze Age"'.[121] By highlighting the force of local adaptation processes in histories of culture change Childe moved away intellectually from the pan-diffusionist racial theories which permeated the academic milieu of his times, and which historicised an 'active dynamic centre acting upon a socially passive periphery'.[122] Such views had gained wide currency in the Britain of the 1920s, due to the propagations by the anatomist Grafton Elliot Smith (1871–1937), and the anthropologist William Perry (1868–1949). Childe counteracted them intellectually through, to quote Rowlands, the focus 'upon routes instead of roots' for exploring evidence of cultural identities in prehistory.[123] Through the emphasis he consciously engaged with the ethical dimensions of the archaeological scholarship in developing humanistic concerns within the contemporary world, and created consciousness of the implications of archaeological knowledge.[124]

---

[120] Piggott (1945, p. 2).
[121] Rowlands (1994, p. 48), quoting from Childe (1944, p. 23).
[122] Rowlands (1994, p. 49). This theory did much to discredit the moderate diffusionism of Childe's and others', who looked for evidence of independent invention in the archaeological record.
[123] Ibid.
[124] Ibid.

This understanding of the value of Childe's scholarship bears no relationship to the fact that he wrote *The Aryans*.

Without any blatant theorising, Childe implicitly anchored his scholarship within the realms of the real, by establishing philosophical spaces for considerations of the material consequences of archaeological knowledge. In contrast, the New and Processualist archaeologies that overthrew the Childean culture-history assumed objectivity and scientific rigour as their representational form, which as Laurajane Smith has aptly remarked 'cannot incorporate self reflexivity even if it wanted to'. This is because 'privileging empirical knowledge leaves little room for analysing the experiences of archaeological and non-archaeological participants in debates over material culture'.[125] Childe's sensitivity of the social responsibilities of the archaeological scholarship poses as a sharp contrast to the 'stand back' attitude of the later generations of archaeologists. In the context of South Asian archaeology, archaeologists have often sought to disengage with the manipulations of archaeological knowledge for political purposes by projecting as ludicrous the act of censuring interpretations that are, or can be proven, wrong.[126] Therefore, the ethics of Childe's diffusionary theories bear consideration within the growing scholarship of the Indus Civilisation, which through an unabashed mapping of a questionable South Asian civilisational tradition continues to facilitate essentialisms within the archaeological representations of culture constructs.

The positivist archaeological research environment of South Asia either acknowledges that a nationalist archaeology is a viable protest against the colonial historiography, or else abstains from critical engagement by invoking concerns of logical plausibility and testability. To this milieu the considerations of the consequences of archaeological knowledge makes little sense. Professional archaeologists may find it virtuous to remain apolitical by forwarding the, erroneous, logic that they interpret the archaeological record as it partially exists in nature. However, considering that the archaeological scholarship draws visibility and power through its public profile, the implications of responsible scholarship demands intelligent engagements with

---

[125] Smith (2004, p. 43).
[126] See specifically Lamberg-Karlovsky (2008, p. xxii), where he poses the question and leaves it unanswered, with the conclusion that it reflects the 'sad reality of modernism' in which there is 'a rapid rise in the industry of rewriting history to serve a present agenda'.

realms outside the academia over issues of knowledge creations through field research. As we may note from the many non-academic Hindu histories of the Indus Civilisation in the public domain, which draw their facts from the archaeological histories of the phenomenon, the archaeological discipline contributes substantively to the ideologies of cultural politics in the real world. This contribution creates the relevance of emulating the ethics of Childe's scholarship even though his diffusionary theories have long been proved invalid.

5

Civilisation, Heritage and the Archaeological Scholarship

In refuting explanations of culture change based upon diffusionary theories, such as Childe's, archaeologists of the Indus Civilisation promote the cause of indigenous origins. However, they insufficiently address the manner in which perceptions of territorial and cultural boundaries are sought through fieldwork alone. They are important to note as they bear upon the manner in which material evidence of the foreign and indigenous is established. The Chapter attends to the neglect while also reviewing the archaeological creations of cultural facts about the Indus Civilisation, including its supposed tangible heritage to the Indian Civilisation.

The numerous 'pre-', 'early', 'mature' 'late' and 'post-' Harappan sites (between ca. 3200 BCE and 800 BCE) in southern Afghanistan, Baluchistan, Sind, Cholistan, Gujarat, eastern Uttar Pradesh, Haryana, Punjab, Rajasthan and parts of the Deccan, which have Neolithic and Chalcolithic cultural assemblages, and which predate the Painted Grey Ware (PGW) iron-age sites of the western Ganga Plain have changed the historiography of the 'rise' and 'fall' of the Indus Civilisation. The evidence of food-producing communities in Baluchistan from Mehrgarh from the seventh millennium and from Kili Gul Mohammad and Rana Ghundai from the sixth millennium, coupled with the absence of any evidence of large waves of human 'invasions' into South Asia during the first millennium BCE now allows the understanding that (a) the Indus Civilisation has a long and indigenous history of developments within the geography of northern South Asia and (b) the decline of the urban elements does not constitute the vanishing of a civilisation, but represents the changing forms of the societies of the Bronze or Chalcolithic Age within South Asia. Moreover, the archaeological finds of a continuous settlement history from the Bronze Age to the beginning of the early Historic Period (ca. 600 BCE) within northern South Asia now illuminates the previously unknown 'dark age' between the Indus and the so-called Gangetic civilisations.

The above evidence is increasingly producing chauvinistic histories of cultural legacies and heritage. This is because the evidence nurtures a singular focus upon the theme of cultural continuity, which encourages archaeologists of South Asia to seek material residues of an essence or 'ethos' of an Ancient South Asian civilisational tradition, and allows those who sponsor for a nationalist archaeology of India to Indianise the Indus Civilisation. A blatant example of the latter is the increasing attributions of 'Hindu' characteristics upon the artefacts and artefact styles, such as the following descriptive label of a burial jar of the Cemetery H archaeological culture at Harappa, which is on prominent display at the National Museum in New Delhi (Illustration 5.1). The label records:

> According to Hindu beliefs, after death man in the form of Sukshma Sarira or Atma, i.e. spirit body, goes to stay in Svarga, or the world of fathers, which is in the skies. Midway he has to cross the terrible river Vaitarni. This he crosses and proceeds ahead with the help of cattle, like a cow, bull and goat which are sacrificed and given as gift to a priest. He then reaches the gates of the court of Yama, the Lord of Death, where the guards, two ferocious dogs, attack the party. After the final judgment at the Court and undergoing the sentences, if any, the spirit body reaches the Abode of the Bliss, which is a radiating solar world with beautiful stars, birds, fish, and flower for final rest.

The above text is followed by a short paragraph describing the object as 'some 4000 years old' and 'unique in the ancient world for having an elaborate painting depicting a scene which recalls the Hindu beliefs as embodied in the Vedic and Epic literature as narrated above'. The object label accrues pedagogical authority as it is authored by the National Museum of India.

The example provides a fair idea of the manner in which the nationalist Indian scholarship places its claims upon the Indus Civilisation. It also prompts us to note that although the Indus Civilisation has now been feted as 'pure bred' of the South Asian soil for more than two decades, scholars continue to quibble about questions of nativity. In particular, Indian archaeologists now increasingly reject the 'Baluchi story' of their western colleagues who excavated the Harappan sites of Pakistan, according to which the roots of the civilisation's incipient technologies can be traced through the history of domestication at Mehrgarh. Instead, they put forth an alternative 'origin story' focused upon evidence gathered within India, which highlights the origins of rice and millet domestication in the 'Indus-Hakra-Ghaggar alluvium', and of the 'innovations in metal technologies within the Aravalli hills during the 4th to mid-3rd millennium BCE'.[1] Their assertions have provoked the surprising counter-claim that possible evidence for the indigenous growth of Taxila, Charsada and Peshawar (Pakistan) into important commercial cities by ca. 600 BCE calls into question the 'time honoured models', describing the derivation of 'Indian culture' from 'a Gangetic homeland'.[2] This is a surprising claim because although the region of Magadha in the Gangetic valley was the heartland of the classical kingdoms of Ancient India, it has never been regarded as the 'homeland' of the 'Indian culture'. In all models since the nineteenth century, the 'homeland' has remained the Sapta Sindhu, believed to be in and around the area of Punjab, which is in Pakistan today, and where the early Vedic hymns were supposedly composed. The assertions, which are nationalist in intent, and the counter assertions may appear childish, but they clearly demonstrate the performative uses to which evidence of the indigenous is put within the scholarship of South Asian archaeology. They also create sensitivity of the conflicts within a scholarship that demands traversing the geographical and cultural boundaries of modern nation states, and add to reasons for exploring the kinds of legacies that are established through the archaeological scholarship of archaic civilisations.

The archaeological searches for the material representations of the cultural legacy of the Indus Civilisation misleadingly convey heritage as immutable. The searches, therefore, also nurture expectations of finding the relics of legacies and heritage through innovative research methodologies.[3] This chapter interrogates this heritage-making enterprise, and reviews the functionalist models of cultural tradition that have been employed by North American archaeologists since the late 1970s in their study of the Indus Civilisation. The theoretical and analytical value of the above construct is supported through the belief that this is the most useful analytical tool for

[1] Chakrabarti (2006, p. 134).
[2] Kenoyer (2006a, p. 46).
[3] For a critique, see Smith and Waterton (2009, p. 42 ff).

ordering and periodising the vast amount of data, which has been gathered with respect to the life history of the Indus Civilisation and of some of the other nearby clusters of neolithic and chalcolithic cultures for over 90 years.[4] The construct, however, allows the mutation of conflicting historiographical traditions within the archaeological histories. The Chapter explores the mutations and sows seeds of caution towards all forms of valorisation of civilisational ethos within disciplinary archaeology. By engaging with the manner in which civilisational heritage is often created through the archaeological scholarship, it also aims at critiquing the increasing archaeological investments into the productions of tangible 'heritage industries'.[5]

In analysing the histories, theories and methodologies of 'deciphering' the Indus Civilisation, I am guided by the consciousness that many factual errors exist within the available data that has been amassed of the phenomenon until now, and that they can be only rectified through careful fieldwork. For instance, one prominent error is the inexact and misleading citations of the locations, numbers and compositions of sites within the available site lists in the Ghaggar river basin. This is being amended at present through new explorations.[6] Another is more theoretical in nature, but it bears upon our understanding of the functions of the architectural features. This involves the transposition of insinuations as descriptions of buildings, of which a classic example is the architectural remains at Harappa that was conjectured as the 'state granary' by Mortimer Wheeler, and is now considered to represent a venue for treating and dying textiles.[7] The identification of a 'Bailey' and 'Castle' at the site of Dholavira, which was excavated between 1989 and 2003, also illustrates the need for considering what the descriptions often mean. In this particular case, the definition seems to obscure instead of revealing the nature of the architectural topographies.[8] The attributions add to reasons for a self-reflexive scholarship of the Indus Civilisation, which as the Chapter demonstrates demands awareness of the versatility of historiographical interventions.

---

[4] For example, Shaffer and Lichtenstein (2005); Kenoyer (2006b); Wright (2010, pp. 84–85).

[5] For examples, see also Guha (2014).

[6] See for example, Singh *et al.* (2011).

[7] For re-definitions of the 'granary' at Harappa, see Fentress (1984); Meadow and Kenoyer (2008); Possehl (2002, pp. 103–04).

[8] Bisht (1991).

Claims for an Indian Patrimony

The Indian scholarship of Ancient India during the late nineteenth century aimed at establishing a chronologically coherent political history of the 'earliest times'. The scholars attempted to meet the aims by sourcing the known Sanskrit corpus and in their efforts they clearly contradicted the British histories of Ancient India, such as those written by Mounstuart Elphinstone (1841), James Talboys Wheeler (between 1867 and 1881), John Clark Marshman (1875) and Meadows Taylor (1870), which unanimously declared that 'the early portions of Hindoo chronology [were] undefinable', and that 'India [had] no authentic historical records before the era of Mahomedans'.[9] Thus, the Indian administrator-scholar Romesh Chunder Dutt began his history of Ancient India of the 'Vedic and Epic Ages' (1889) with injunctions to his readers to take cognisance of the 'irony of fate that the past should be considered a blank in a country where ancient sages have handed down traditions and elaborate compositions through thousands of years'.[10] Dutt asserted:

> Other nations claim an equal or even a higher antiquity than the Hindus. [...] But there is a difference between the records of the Hindus and records of other nations. The hieroglyphic records of the ancient Egyptians yield little information beyond the names of kings and pyramid builders, and accounts of dynasties and wars. The cuneiform inscriptions of Assyria and Babylon tell us much the same story. And even the ancient Chinese records shed little light on the gradual progress of human culture and civilisation.
>
> Ancient Hindu works are of a different character. If they are defective in some respect, as they undoubtedly are, they are defective as account of the advancement of civilisation, of the progress of the human mind, such as we shall seek for in vain among the records of any other equally ancient nation. The literature of each period is a perfect picture—a photograph, if we may so call it—of the Hindu civilisation of that period. And the works of successive periods form a complete history of ancient Hindu civilisation for three thousand years, so full, so clear, that he who runs may read.[11]

Dutt's endorsement that the 'ancient Hindu works' provided a 'perfect picture' of the period of their creation was contrary to the colonial histories

[9] Taylor (1870, p. 39); Marshman (1875, p. 1).
[10] Dutt (1889, pp. xi, 1).
[11] Ibid., p. 1.

of Ancient India. The endorsement illustrates the value which many Indians gave to the ancient Sanskrit texts as keepers of historical information. In attributing the value, they knew that they were contradicting the contemporary historiography. By the early twentieth century, those who taught and studied Ancient India began to consciously explore the early Indian literary traditions for establishing dynastic histories of the period before the kingdom of Magadha, and hence before the period that had been historicised by the 'western' historians of India. Thus, in his *Political History of Ancient India* (1923), Hemchandra Raychaudhuri announced that the novelty of his book lay in the sketch he had provided of the political dynasties from 'Parikshit to Bimbisara'. Raychaudhuri rightly claimed that because this history could only be grasped by sourcing the Sanskrit texts, it was therefore missing from Vincent Smith's widely acclaimed textbook of Indian history, *Early History of India from 600 BC to the Muhammadan Conquest* (1907), whose revised edition had been recently published (1919).[12] Inevitably, then the Indian scholars, who had been more critical than their British and European peers of the vastly divergent chronologies that had been historicised for the age of the *Rig Veda*, hoped that the archaeological discoveries at Harappa and Mohenjodaro would allow a more precise dating of the Vedic corpus. So, although the two 'cities' were excavated as decidedly 'non-Vedic', the Vedas crept into the academic research of the Indus Civilisation from the start as potential and relational source material.

The Indus Civilisation was discovered during the period of the Khilafat Movement (1919–24) when there was an increasing resistance within India to the British rule. The Indians immediately feted the discovery as a national treasure and the Indian media, for example, *The Amrita Bazar Patrika*, reported the discovery as 'monumental evidence' of the fact that the 'Indian civilisation' was 'as ancient as any in Asia'. The newspaper urged the colonial government to liberally finance the systematic excavations of the sites, emphasised that they were of 'national', not 'provincial', importance, and suggested that the Archaeological Survey of India 'reserve their best energy and funds' for the purpose, and leave 'off [excavations at] Taxila, Sarnath, Nalanda and so forth for the time being'. Berating the Survey for failing to protect the site of Harappa through the Ancient Monuments Act (1904), and for not making the archaeological discovery of the Indus Civilisation

---

[12] Raychaudhuri (1996 [1923], p. 2).

decades earlier, the report scathingly asked: 'What were these high paid officers doing for more than half a century? Were they sleeping and snoring till they suddenly woke to find themselves made famous by the Assyriologists and Egyptologists?'[13]

The sense of national ownership, which the discoveries generated among educated Indians, is also well represented in the questioning, which Marshall was subjected to at the Council of States in New Delhi in January 1925. Khan Ebrahim Haroon Jaffer, an Indian member of the Imperial Council, had asked Marshall whether it was true that the Indian press had been refused photographs, while *The Illustrated London News* in which Marshall had published the maiden article (1924), had been granted access.[14] In contrast to the garrulous nationalisation of the Indus Civilisation by the Indian media, the upcoming Indian scholarship of Ancient India, however, staked patrimonial claims of the archaeological phenomenon in more subtle ways.

As excavations proceeded at Harappa and Mohenjodaro from 1924, Indian Indologists began combing the Vedic corpus for evidence of knowledge of the civilisation and its authors among the Vedic hymns. The pioneering study was undertaken by Ramaprasad Chanda (1873–1942), superintendent of the Archaeology section at the Indian Museum in Calcutta, who hoped to find 'the co-ordination of the data of Archaeology with literary evidence' and who concluded that 'the much maligned Panis' could have been possible representatives of the 'earlier commercial civilisation'. Chanda, thus, brought to scholarly attention the 'inferior material culture of the arya speaking

---

[13] 'A Word to the Archaeological Department', *Amrita Bazar Patrika*, 1 January 1925. The opening paragraph began as:

Archaeological excavations in Sind and the Punjab have become a universal topic of discussion with the intelligentsia in India. Formerly the archaeologists and historians asserted that the civilization of India did not go much beyond 1200 B.C., but now these explorations have furnished us with monumental evidence which shows that it is as ancient as any in Asia. What Indian is there who will not feel proud that the civilization of his country thus reaches up to the hoary age of the third of the fourth millennium B.C.? He must therefore fully sympathise with the Archaeological Department that is now carrying on a vigorous campaign in the Press to win popular help and support for further excavations in the Indus Valley which at present seems limitless. We therefore stoutly maintain that the systematic excavation of these sites is not simply of provincial but of national importance and we strongly urge the Government of India to spare no money until this object is fully realized.

[14] For details of the case, and on sense of ownership by Indians, see Guha (2010, pp. 165–66).

invaders', which inspired Indian historians to reappraise the contributions of the 'Aryans' to the history of the 'Hindu culture'.[15] Thus, R.C. Majumdar (1888–1980), who was regarded as the premier 'ancient Indian historian' of northern India by the mid 1950s, highlighted the richness of the 'Sindhu (Indus) Valley Civilisation' for emphasising that:

> There is a general belief that all the best elements in Hindu religion and culture are derived from the Aryans, and whatever is lowly, degrading, or superstitious in it represents the primitive non-Aryan element mixed up with it. This view is certainly wrong, and we must admit that the Aryan religion, thoughts, and beliefs have been profoundly modified by those of the Proto Australoids and Dravidians with whom they came into contact in India. Though the extent of their influence is not yet fully known, there is no doubt that they underlie the whole texture of Hindu culture and civilization and their contribution to it is by no means either mean or negligible.[16]

Following the historical consensus of the time, Majumdar perceived the authors of the Indus Civilisation as Dravidians, who had arrived into the Indian subcontinent during the remote past.[17] Hence, his erosion of the impact of the 'Aryans' within the make-up of the Hindu culture cannot be perceived today as his efforts to dismiss the 'foreign' influences upon an indigenous 'Sindhu Civilisation'. For, like all his peers who studied Ancient India, Majumdar too accepted the theory that the Dravidians had come as 'foreigners' to the Indian soil. However, he ignored to contextualise the Indus Civilisation with the other archaeological cultures of the Bronze Age through which Marshall, Mackay, Piggott and Wheeler had derived evidence of the chronology, economy, religion and material contents. Therefore, although

---

[15] Chanda (1926, p. 5). See also Chanda (1929), where he suggested that 'on the eve of the Aryan immigration, the Indus Valley was in possession of a civilized and warlike people. The Aryans, mainly represented by the Rishi clans, came to seek their fortune in small numbers', which would 'warrant' the inference that we might be able to recognise 'the Bharatas, Purus Yadus, Turvasas, Anus, Druhyus and the other celebrated in the Rig Veda—the representatives of the ruling class of the indigenous chalcolithic population' (p. 25). Chanda sought to establish the link between the Indus and Vedic civilisations by analysing some of the stone statuettes from Mohenjodaro, in which he read features from the Vedic, Jaina and Buddhist religious iconography.

[16] Majumdar (1952, pp. 18–19).

[17] As the previous chapter informs us, the theory of the migrating 'Dravidians' had shaped Hall's thesis, which he had formulated 20 years before Majumdar's history, and through which he had historicised the linkages between the Sumer and India in prehistory.

Majumdar echoed Marshall's inferences of the ostensible legacy of the religion of the Indus Civilisation to the Hindu religion, he also systematically obliterated from his synthesis Marshall's views regarding the possible similarities among the religions of the Bronze Age civilisations of Indus, Mesopotamian and pre-dynastic Egypt. The obliteration allows us to anticipate the methods through which many Indian archaeologists have established the cultural legacy of the Indus Civilisation.

An 'Indian' Historiography through Dismissals of Foreign Accounts

The Indus Civilisation has been formally claimed as the *Sindhu–Saraswati Sabhyata* or 'Indus-Saraswati Civilisation' by Indian archaeologists only from the 1990s.[18] However, from the time of Indian independence, a few Indian archaeologists made a move towards the dismissal of the 'western' accounts of the phenomenon. Thus, Kedar Nath Sastri, who had participated in the excavations at Harappa that were supervised by Madho Sarup Vats (1926–34) and Wheeler (1946), and who had excavated Cemetery H in 1928 and Cemetery R37 in the late 1930s and early 1940s, extended the date of the Indus Civilisation to the fourth millennium BCE. Sastri postulated that the Civilisation was partly contemporary with 'Vedic times', and knowing full well the extent to which his 'new' interpretations differed widely from the accepted dates of the Bronze Age cities at Harappa and Mohenjodaro and of the *Rig Veda*, he asserted in his monograph, *New Light on the Indus Civilization* (1954) that 'we must not accept anything and everything cooked and offered to us by foreigners. We should have independent views and the capacity to test others' views on the touchstone of independent evidence.'[19]

Sastri's 'independent thinking' was applauded by the historian R.K. Mookherji, who wrote the 'forward' for his book and who emphasised that what lent weight to 'Mr Sastri's views and conclusions is his special

---

[18] For example, Gupta (1995); Lal (2000); Chakrabarti and Saini (2009); Lal (2014). For a critical and detailed history of the empirical transformation of the Ghaggar Hakra into the Saraswati of the *nadi-stuti* hymn in the *Rig Veda*, see Chadda (2011).

[19] Sastri (1957, p. 5).

knowledge of the cultural and Sanskritic background in the light of which alone a proper interpretation of prehistory has to be approached'.[20] The remark arrests our attention since the uniqueness, which it gifted to Sastri's inferences would have held little meaning within the contemporary scholarship of Indian prehistory of the 1950s, which distanced itself quite specifically from the text-based fieldwork of the earlier centuries, and with those of historical archaeology. Mookherji, instead, expressed the nationalist aspirations that geared the study of Ancient India during independence, to which Majumdar's history also belonged and which aimed towards an ostensibly non-biased historical narrative of the long ancestry of the Hindu Civilisation. The anti-colonialist nationalist historiography that prevailed in the 1950s also launched the archaeological scholarship of the Indian Epic traditions.

The field surveys for historical truths within the Epics were initiated by B.B. Lal through excavations at Hastinapura, which he undertook between 1951 and 1953. Lal, who subsequently became the director general of the Archaeological Survey of India (1968–72), aimed at gathering field evidence of the events described in the *Mahabharata*, and his objectives and methods were followed by H.D. Sankalia, professor of archaeology at Deccan College, Pune (1939–73), who during the 1960s initiated a similar archaeological search for the events of the *Ramayana*. The explorations were premised upon the rationality of obtaining material truths about a literary and mythological universe,[21] and Sankalia expressed the reasons for the undertaking through the remark that 'one has to recognize that this [namely India] is an ancient land, where traditions have survived in a distorted form, and therefore the traditional accounts do contain a grain of truth which we must endeavour to discover by long and continuous sieving'.[22]

Considering that the historical scholarship of Ancient India since the eighteenth century has entailed the corroboration of incomparable sources, namely, literary traditions and assemblages of artefacts, the 'Archaeology of the Epic Traditions' by Lal, Sankalia and their followers was not a novel methodology. However, their fieldwork marked a new venture into public archaeology, as it was specifically aimed at creating national interest in the

---

[20] Mookherji (1957).
[21] For a summary of the projects, see Lal (1981); Sankalia (1973). For a comprehensive critique, see Chattopadhyaya (1975–76).
[22] Sankalia (1975–76, p. 85).

archaeology of India. At the time Sankalia had summed up the objectives quite honestly and explicitly through the statement that when material traces of Rama and Krishna cannot be seen through archaeological undertakings, 'people, including scholars, think that we—archaeologists—are wasting our time and nation's money'.[23]

The projects were launched during the period when another ambitious research project of establishing a critical edition of the *Mahabharata*, which had been undertaken for over half a century from 1919 until 1966, was being brought to a successful close. Unlike this philological project, which built upon the strengths of international collaborations, the archaeological projects were decidedly conceived as Indian ventures for creating an Indian narrative of the history of Ancient India. Many contemporary Indian archaeologists and ancient Indian historians had openly expressed their criticism of this 'Epic Archaeology' at the time. Thus, M.C. Joshi had berated the theories propounded by the 'reputed archaeologists' as 'laboured ones', and emphasised that they had 'twisted the traditional accounts or invented their own legends to suit their interpretations'. In questioning the legitimacy of the aims of the projects Joshi had rhetorically asked 'when the excavations [by Sankalia] at Maheshwar (ancient Mahismati) could not unfold the mystery of the great Haihaya monarch Kartavirya Sahasrarjuna, a contemporary of Parasurama and Ravana, how digging at Ayodhya will solve the problems of Ramayana' [sic].[24] The question demands a recall in today's nationalist milieu of India, where myths, epics, legends and traditions are all being exposed through the archaeologists' spades.

Embedded within the archaeological explorations of the epics in the 1950s was an anti-western stance, which followed the anti-foreign cultural politics of the closing years of the British rule. Thus, for example, in 1946 even Wheeler, the director general of the Archaeological Survey, had considered it prudent not to request the Government of India for a research permit for his American friend and colleague, the prehistorian Hallam Movius because, as he explained to the latter, 'things are at the moment a bit touchy here in all matters relating to foreign intervention'.[25] Although blatant

---

[23] Sankalia (1975–76, p. 46).

[24] Joshi (1975–76, p. 102). He was quite clear that the 'Indian tradition, Vedic or Puranic, is not likely to help much in the interpretation of archaeological data' (ibid.).

[25] D.O. letter, from Wheeler to Hallam L. Movius Jr. at Harvard, Cambridge, dated 25 July 1946, from New Delhi. File 33/51/47, Survey Archives.

anti-foreign expressions within academic publications, such as those of Sastri's, were an exception in the early years of independence, it is possible to note a tendency among Indian archaeologists for twisting tales to prove a point, which had caught Joshi's attention. Outside the efforts of interpreting and re-interpreting the ancient texts for gleaning truths about traditions, such expressions constituted subtle misrepresentations of the views of the western peers and predecessors. A classic example is the manner in which Wheeler's theory of the 'Aryan destruction of the Indus Civilisation' was disseminated by a few Indian archaeologists to students of the new School of Archaeology that was established by the Archaeological Survey of India in 1959.

Wheeler's 'Aryan Invasion' and Its Knowledge Creation

Wheeler was one of the external examiners (1961–65) of the diploma course that was offered by the aforementioned school, whose establishment was aimed at creating a professional cadre of trained field archaeologists. After reading some of the answer scripts on Indian proto-history, he wrote an indignant letter, in 1962, to his former star pupil B.B. Lal who was teaching the course, to complain that:

> Several candidates assert that I regard the cemetery H people at Harappa as the Aryan destroyers of the Indus Civilisation. This of course is utter rubbish and has never been said by me. If you will be kind enough to look at my 'Indus Civilization' (1960), pp. 55–56, you will see that I draw special attention to the hiatus between the Harappan civilisation and Cemetery H and I have said the same thing elsewhere.
>
> Then again, I am supposed to have said that the Indus Civilization was destroyed by the Aryans, without referring either to: a) the very tentative character of my suggestion, b) the fact that in any case the only manifest occurrence of violence is at Mohenjodaro, and c) in any case such violence was merely one of a number of causes, which included above all economic decline.
>
> It would appear that these views, which are both tentative and accumulative, are transmitted to your students with an excess of emphasis. There is no doubt about violent scenes at Mohenjodaro and Dales's new evidence, as demonstrated by him to me on the ground, is consistent. Dales has of course one new idea—namely, intensive flooding as the result of geomorphic

changes—and is inclined to regard this idea as a substitute for all older ones. In point of fact there is no doubt some element of truth in all the theories, old and new, but they must be kept in proportion.[26]

Within less than two months, Wheeler reiterated his irritation, this time to S.R. Rao. Felicitating Rao for his publication of the preliminary report of his excavations at Lothal (1955–60) in the journal of the Lalit Kala Akademi, Wheeler chose to remind him that not only was his attribution to him of the correlation between the Cemetery H people with the 'Aryans' wrong, but so also was his bibliographic references for the misinformation. By quoting from his own excavations at Harappa, which he reported in *Ancient India* (1947), and by recalling Childe's remarks in the *New Light on the Most Ancient East,* Wheeler also made it clear to Rao that the equation between 'Cemetery H people and the Aryans' was not his idea, but Childe's. He concluded the letter with the statement that can certainly be questioned in retrospect, that 'right from the outset I had no support for Gordon Childe's view. This is no doubt a small point, but since it constantly crops up in the products of the Delhi School, it is obviously a fairly widespread misattribution!'[27]

Wheeler's letters to Lal and Rao inform us of the effective strategy that was adopted by many Indian archaeologists, and which persists even to this day, of eroding the nuances from theories that are targeted for attack.[28] There is no doubt that Wheeler perceived the 'Aryan invasion' as one of the major causes of the decline of the Indus Civilisation. In fact, he presented many graphic descriptions of the 'event' in his popular narratives of the destruction of Mohenjodaro.[29] However, he had speculated upon the cause of the decline by maintaining that the excavations of 1946 had shown a hiatus in stratigraphy between the bearers of the Cemetery H culture and destroyers of the old Harappa. In his report of the excavations, he had therefore quite explicitly stated:

The intrusive culture, as represented by its pottery, has in origin nothing to do with the Harappa culture [...] its analogues have not yet been

[26] Letter from Wheeler to Lal, 28 May 1962, E/2/9, Wheeler Archives.

[27] Letter from Wheeler to Rao, 9 July 1965, E/2/9/, Wheeler Archives.

[28] For an example of Lal's erosion of the nuances in Mackay's statements regarding the possible finds of a terra-cotta horse like animal at Mohenjodaro, see Guha (2007, p. 343).

[29] For example, Wheeler, (1950, p. 30). The description is quoted from a longer passage in Wheeler (1947c).

identified, and it appears in fact as abruptly as did its Harappan predecessors. The suggestion has been made very hesitatingly [here Wheeler quoted Childe 1934, p. 223] that the Cemetery H intruders "may belong to the Aryan invaders", the conventional date for whose incursion into India is the fifteenth century B.C. And here the risk which Indian archaeology is always ready to run in the search for a literary context lies once more across our path.

However, Wheeler continued:

> Nor am I altogether disinclined to face the risk [...] on circumstantial evidence Indra stands accused [...] nevertheless even Indra's hostile citadels may be represented, not by Harappan sites, but by others yet unknown to us. If so, we have to assume that, in short interval which can, at the most, have intervened between the end of Harappa and the first Aryan invasions, an unidentified but formidable civilization arose in the same region and presented an extensive fortified front to the invaders. The assumption is not an easy one, and seems to involve a wilful rejection of the massive fortifications with which the Harappans are now known to have girt themselves. Digging, more digging, will ultimately solve the problem.[30]

As the above quotation demonstrates, although Wheeler had shown no hesitancy in building upon the presumption that the 'Aryans' may have destroyed the Harappans, he presented a nuanced view of the possibilities of equating the Cemetery H 'culture' with the 'Aryans' by quoting Childe and by carefully marking the clearly visible hiatus in stratigraphy between the 'late-Harappan' and Cemetery H depositional horizons. Amalananda Ghosh, Wheeler's former colleague, who subsequently became the director general of the Archaeological Survey (1953–68), best explained the problem of Wheeler's narrative as representing a mismatch between cause and evidence. In a letter to Wheeler in 1953, on receipt of the latter's book *The Indus Civilization*, Ghosh reminded him that:

> I find that very rightly you have now given up the theory of the authors of the Cemetery H Culture being identical with the Aryans. This theory has, I regret to note, been very much misunderstood, and I have heard it said that the 1946 excavations at Harappa have proved that the decadent Harappans were ousted by the Aryans. Your pithy statement about Indra standing accused has not always been understood. However, I note that you still hold that the Aryans destroyed the Harappan Culture. That may have been very easily so,

---

[30] Wheeler (1947a, pp. 81–83).

but as you have not utilised the evidence of the painted grey ware I do not see what archaeological justification there is for this view. If neither Cemetery H nor Jhukar is Aryan, and if we leave aside evidence of the painted grey ware, we are faced with a situation which appears to me anomalous, that though the Aryans destroyed the Harappan culture they did not leave any vestige of traces on the Harappa sites.[31]

In his characteristic articulate manner, Ghosh pinpointed the reasons for contesting Wheeler's theory, namely, in its inability of commanding proof, to which Wheeler replied that 'I am inclined very much to agree with you that we should cut the word "Aryans" out of our archaeological discussions for a considerable time to come—that is, until the new pottery evidence has been fully sorted out stratigraphically.'[32] A comparison of Ghosh's note to Wheeler and the latter's to Lal, demonstrates two very different ways in which archaeologists of independent India trained by Wheeler approached the theoretical 'errors' of their former chief. We would be justified in conjecturing that in 1962 when Wheeler had written to Lal complaining about the misrepresentations of his views, he was greatly apprehensive of the enduring value of his theory of the 'Aryan' destruction of the Indus Civilisation, which was being debated at the time, and which was empirically laid to rest within less than two years by George Dales who made a clear case for 'the mythical massacre at Mohenjodaro' (1964). Dales demonstrated that the skeletons, which had been conjectured by Wheeler as evidence of the 'Aryan' massacre of the inhabitants of the city, did not belong to a single period and presented the cause of the decline of the urban features at Mohenjodaro to changes in the environment and ecology of the Indus Valley at the close of the third millennium BCE.[33]

Therefore, in 1965 and possibly in the certainty of knowledge of the assured fall of his theory, Wheeler suggested to D.D. Kosambi, whose scholarship he held in high esteem, that the latter could rectify his views regarding 'the culture of Cemetery H' in the successive edition of his highly admired book,

---

[31] Letter from A. Ghosh to Wheeler, dated 15 April 1954, Box 460, Wheeler Papers, also as D.O. No. 8310 in Survey Archives.

[32] Letter from Wheeler to Ghosh, 28 May 1954, Wheeler Papers. The reference to the new pottery here is of the Painted Grey Ware, which Lal had found at Hastinapura, and which he had associated culturally with the 'early Aryans', and dated to c. 1200 BCE.

[33] Dales (1964). See also Dales (1966).

The Culture and Civilization of Ancient India in Historical Outline (1965). This letter to Kosambi was on receipt of the above book, and Wheeler emphasised that the Cemetery H was 'of very local occurrence and certainly cannot represent the Aryan invaders in any extended sense. Moreover, it is clear that an appreciable interval lapsed between the end of Harappa and the arrival of the Cemetery H people'. In an effort to redeem himself, he added, that 'this is clear in the report of the 1946 excavations', at Harappa.[34] We may add the supposition that even though Wheeler supported the theory of the 'invading Aryans' in the last edition of *The Indus Civilization* (1968), he did so knowing full well that its shelf-life was over. If we can prove this, then Wheeler's letter to Lal would appear poignantly misjudged in retrospective. Because to substantiate his own theories about the indigenous 'Vedic Harappans', Lal has with persistence exhibited the 'unwarranted' manner in which his former 'chief' had represented 'his newly found data' of the 'Aryan invasion' at Harappa.[35] The subsequent aggressive assaults on Wheeler's bad judgements follow Lal in conveying nationalist agendas, and in taking cognisance of the assaults we are encouraged to follow the example of Ghosh in noting the nuances within the views we might consider flawed and contestable.

The Indus Civilisation in India

The Indian archaeological surveys of the Indus Civilisation from the 1950s through which a young nation attempted to recuperate its loss of history is rather well known. The partition of British India had left the country bereft of the Civilisation, and following Aurel Stein's explorations of the dried-up beds of the rivers Hakra and Ghaggar in 1942–43, Ghosh undertook a pioneering survey of the river Ghaggar on the Indian side of the Indo-Pakistan border ten years later in 1951–52.[36] Emulating Stein's terminology, Ghosh

---

[34] Letter from Wheeler to Kosambi thanking him for his book, which Wheeler wished he had written, dated 3 August 1965, Box E/2/9, Wheeler Archives.

[35] For example, Lal (2005, p. 52).

[36] The explorations comprised the region, which was east of the Indo-Pakistan border between Hanumangarh and Suratgarh, which Ghosh called the Saraswati valley, and about 22 kilometres east of the river Bhadra, in the Drishadvati valley. For details, see Ghosh (1952, 1953).

referred to the river as forming the Saraswati valley, and its tributaries, the Bhadra and Chautang, as forming the Drishadwati valley, and successfully traced a new 'Sothi' occupational horizon which he rightly perceived as belonging to the 'pre-urban' phase of the Indus Civilisation (ca. 3000 BCE–2600 BCE). Similar in time to Ghosh's findings of the 'Sothi' phase was the location of the site of Kot Diji (in Khairpur District, Sind) in 1955 by Fazal Ahmed Khan, then director of the Department of Archaeology of the Federal Government of Pakistan, who formally excavated at the site in 1955 and 1957. Khan echoed Ghosh's inference and classified the 'fortified' settlement as pre-urban and pre-Harappan, and representative of inhabitants who were 'fore-runners' of the Indus Civilisation.[37]

Ghosh was able to report more than 25 'mature Harappan' settlements through a season's fieldwork, of which many were of considerable size, such as Chak 86, and he hoped that they would be excavated at a later date. Apart from Ghosh's surveys, other officers of the Archaeological Survey made significant finds of the Indus Civilisation within India during the 1950s. For example, the excavations at Ropar (Punjab) between 1952 and 1955, which were undertaken by Y.D. Sharma, yielded the first evidence of 'mature Harappan' deposits in a stratified context below the PGW levels, and those by him in 1959 at Alamgirpur (Uttar Pradesh) also promised a similar sequence. By the end of the 1950s, India had also acquired a Harappan 'port' with a 'docking basin' through Rao's excavations at Lothal (Gujarat), and at the close of the next decade, explorations in Haryana, Uttar Pradesh, Rajasthan and Gujarat undertaken by the Archaeological Survey and archaeology departments of Indian universities further furnished the young nation with an impressive list of Bronze Age 'towns' and 'cities', such as Banawali Surkotada, Dholavira, Mithatal and Rakhigarhi, which promised comparability in size and contents with those at Mohenjodaro and Harappa. The decade also brought to light the supposedly earliest ploughed field of South Asia from the 'pre-urban' levels of Kalibangan (excavated between 1961 and 1969).[38] Therefore, during the next decade, in the 1970s, the increasing

---

[37] Khan (1965, pp. 30, 45).

[38] Of the chronology of Kalibangan B.K. Thapar, who was one of the two lead archaeologists, wrote:

> The significant part of the evidence, however, relates to the discovery of a non-Harappan settlement immediately underlying the occupational levels of the Harappan citadel (KLB-1). Kalibangan thus became the fourth site, after Amri, Harappa and Kot Diji,

number of settlements that could be associated with the Indus Civilisation led to hopes among Indian archaeologists of finding evidence of the cultural precedent of the urban phase within the borders of north India. However, by then excavations at Kili Gul Mohammad (1950–51), Kot Diji (1955–57), Amri (1959–62), Nindowari (1962–65), Mundigak, and Gumla (1971) and Damb Sadaat (Pakistan and southern Afghanistan) by British, French, North American and Pakistani archaeologists had also created similar hopes among Pakistani archaeologists of obtaining evidence of an evolutionary history of the Bronze Age within the territories of their new nation. Additionally, the prominent Pakistani archaeologist of the Indus Civilisation, Rafique Mughal, began to insist for a change of terminology from 'pre-Harappan' to 'early-Harappan' for the Sothi and Kot Diji 'cultures' as he was convinced this would illustrate the histories of indigenous evolutionary developments of the Bronze Age within the Indus Valley.[39]

In contrast to Indian archaeology's investments in the searches for a historical profile for the Indian civilisational heritage through the Indus Civilisation, the new Islamic Republic of Pakistan absolved national stakes in a Civilisation that represented a pre-Islamic past. Yet, significant to the historiography is Mughal's remark in 1973 that 'lately, Indian and some western archaeologists have been insisting on a change of name, and favour the term "Harappa Culture" instead of the "Indus Civilization" as the former follows the site name where the civilisation was first discovered.'[40] The Indian insistence of the use of the terminology 'Harappan Civilisation' was not novel within the history of the scholarship. Way back in 1935, Ernest Mackay had instructed the use of the term, which represented the first site where the Civilisation was first detected, and Childe and Piggott had both emulated Mackay's views.[41] Mughal considered the Indian assertions as a mere quibble, and was of the opinion that the terminology of the 'Indus Valley Civilisation', which was popularised by Wheeler as quite adequate.

---

all in Pakistan, where the existence of preceding cultures below that of the Harappan has been recognized.

In 1971, as Thapar reported, excavations in Pakistan 'added yet another site of this class at Gumla in the Gomal Valley'. See Thapar (1975, p. 19).

[39] For a detailed and analytical account of the explorations and excavations of the Indus Civilisation that were undertaken until the beginning of the 1980s, see Thapar (1984, pp. 1–10).

[40] Mughal (1973, p. 2).

[41] See, for example, the note by Childe (1937, p. 351).

He rightly stated that the 'spread of Harappan culture beyond the main Indus Valley should not astonish for, likewise, cultural traits of the Mesopotamian Civilisation are found in Khuzistan in south-western Iran in Saudi Arabia and along the Arabian coast of the Persian Gulf'.[42]

Mughal's attention to the debate during the early 1970s demonstrates that the Indian claims upon the Indus Civilisation had touched a raw nerve amongst the involved Pakistani archaeologists. Therefore, although the Indus Civilisation may not have contributed to the heritage-making policies of the young Republic of Pakistan, the archaeological endeavours towards its exposure and scholarship within the country, albeit through international collaborations, precipitated strong sentiments towards its ownership among the Pakistani archaeologists.

Tensions within the 'Western' Scholarship

The early post-colonial archaeology of the Indus Civilisation presents the intellectual shift away from the dominant force of the British archaeological scholarship of South Asia to an emerging North American one. This shift has left a rich collection of official correspondence, which offers an insight into the spectacular conflicts between the British old guard, some of whom, such as Mortimer Wheeler, continued to serve as diplomats of Indian archaeology and the young 'non-native' entrants into the field. The numerous examples of professional clashes between the British and American camps demonstrate the fallacy of reducing the power politics of the post-colonial archaeological scholarship in South Asia to a simple dichotomy of foreign versus native.

Prior to 1947, David Spooner and Ernest Mackay were the only two North American employees of the Archaeological Survey of India (1906–21 and 1927–31 respectively).[43] Although few North Americans, such as

---

[42] Mughal (1973, p. 2). Mughal defended his choice of terminology by emphasising that 'an overwhelming' number of Harappan sites were to be found west of the Ganges-Yamuna doab, and that the Rann of Kutch was formed by and lay in the Indus deltaic region. For conflicts in terminology, see also Possehl (1984) and Konishi (1984).

[43] Mackay subsequently excavated at Chanhu-daro in 1934–35, but not as an employee of the Survey. For details of American interests in excavating sites related to the Indus Civilisation, fundraising for the project and applications to the Archaeological Survey for licence, see Possehl (1999, pp. 95–98).

Donald McCown, explored northern India in the years leading to the end of the raj,[44] a distinct historiographical tradition of the American scholarship of the Indus archaeology began to crystallise from the 1950s, when graduate students of North American universities began to seek a professional career in South Asian archaeology. This was also the decade when the Indian government firmly protected the academic interests of the Indian Archaeological Surveys and of those of the nascent departments of archaeology within the Indian universities. The government, therefore, curtailed permits to western archaeologists to undertake field surveys in India. In contrast, Pakistan, which had lost the Survey, judiciously elicited Mortimer Wheeler's help as the advisor of Archaeology (1949–50), and on his recommendations embarked upon international collaborations with British, European and North American universities as a means of training a new cadre of archaeologists. Yet, permissions were often denied, or possibilities of their issues jeopardised, often due to perceptions by the Pakistan government of the 'brash' behaviour of the western archaeologists towards their Pakistani colleagues.[45] The archives that relate to Wheeler's career as the secretary of the British Academy (1949–68) allow many glimpses of the fraught histories of professional relationships amongst the western archaeologists, which arose from the competitions for securing permissions from the federal government of Pakistan for undertaking field research. A series of correspondence from May to October 1953, between Wheeler and Hugh Hencken, and Ernest Hooton at Harvard regarding the candidature of Walter Fairservis Jr. for a PhD, allows a perspective of the kinds of tensions, which prevailed within

---

[44] On details regarding McCown's explorations in Baluchistan, see Possehl (1999, pp. 137–38).

[45] An example is the local perception in Pakistan of George Dales's attitude towards F.A. Khan and Pakistani staff, which was reported by Robert Raikes to Wheeler, in a letter marked 'strictly confidential', which dated from 1965 (no date or month) File F/1/10, Wheeler Archives. Raikes wrote that 'on all sides the story is the same: that this is not a question of a government policy of exclusion of foreigners; nor a question of anti-americanism etc, etc.' He reported that the Pakistani archaeologists were of the opinion that 'either University of Pennsylvania should send a different director or that they should lay off work for a year and only resume in 1966/67. The two alternatives come to the same thing in practice, as a refusal to give permit for the coming season would mean that Dales would have to transfer his activities elsewhere' (ibid.). In this letter, Raikes also stated that the Pakistan government had refused permits to Beatrice de Cardi, Walter Fairservis and F.R. Allchin that year (ibid.). De Cardi, we know from Fairservis's letter to Wheeler, see footnote 46, was refused a permit in 1951.

a scholarship that required treading upon the intellectual, methodological and geographical terrains of others.[46]

During 1950–51, Fairservis had undertaken a rewarding season of field survey within the districts of Kandahar (south Afghanistan) and Quetta-Pishin (Pakistan), and had excavated the pre-pottery, food producing, Neolithic horizon at Kili Gul Mohammad (Quetta). He subsequently submitted a thesis that related to the above research, on the prehistory of Baluchistan, for consideration for a PhD at the Department of Anthropology at Harvard. Following the submission, he was asked by the Faculty in 1953 to formally respond to rumours of professional misconduct, as his field methods had provoked the Pakistan government to consider withdrawing permissions for field explorations to all western archaeologists. Hence, the faculty was forced into making an official enquiry into the matter. With an inkling that the members might have contacted Wheeler for information—since the latter had recommended Fairservis to the Pakistan government—but with no official knowledge that a formal request had been made to this end, Fairservis wrote to Wheeler to clear his name, and show why 'the blame' rested not on him 'but on the varied circumstances involved in these international relations'. He asserted that 'from the inception of research', he and 'others' had 'been under one form of attack or another from supposedly distinguished men in the discipline' and believed that the 'trouble [lay] in the non-objectivity which leads to jealousies and childishness to which the field is unfortunately subject, no matter what the nationality'.[47] Thus, although 'nationalism', as

[46] Letters from Wheeler to Hencken, 14 May 1953, Hooton to Wheeler, 6 October 1953, and Wheeler to Hooton, 14 October 1953, Box 459, Wheeler Papers. Hencken was then curator of European archaeology at the Peabody Museum (1945–72) and Hooton was professor of physical anthropology at Harvard (1930–54). Two substantial charges against Fairservis were: (a) that his excavation methods, which involved seriation techniques were faulty. Leslie Alcock, then British attaché in Pakistan, who had participated in Fairservis's excavations at Quetta conveyed his misgivings to Wheeler, and Piggott and Dales also shared similar misgivings, and (b) that Fairservis had shown considerable lack of judgement, scholarly and professional, in publishing in the *Collier's Weekly* a co-authored article, which was populist in tone, titled 'Christmas in Kabul' (1951, December). Apart from Wheeler, many of his American colleagues, including Louis Dupree, also thought this was in poor taste.

[47] Fairservis to Wheeler dated 4 September 1953, Wheeler Papers. On receiving a reply to this letter from Wheeler, Fairservis wrote at length to him absolving responsibilities from the two charges mentioned in the above footnote (letter dated: 17 September 1953). However, Wheeler, who had helped Fairservis obtain his initial permit of fieldwork from the government of Pakistan remained unconvinced, and maintained that he would be 'sorry to see him with a high Harvard degree after his name' (Wheeler to Ernest Hooton, 14 October 1953), Box 459, Wheeler Papers.

D.H. Gordon subsequently wrote to Wheeler in 1959 'affected [native] ideas' regarding the unfairness of 'western colleagues',[48] the 'distinguished men' of Indian archaeology continued to direct patronage of scholarly merit, which precipitated unwarranted rivalries among the young entrants within the field.

The North American Historiography of a 'Sub-continental' Civilisation

One of the striking aspects of the early North American scholarship of the Indus Civilisation was the move towards receiving the phenomenon as decidedly sub-continental. This move needs to be noted because of the growing emphasis by many Indian archaeologists to present the sub-continental ethos of the Civilisation as a novelty of their own scholarship.[49] Initiated by Fairservis through his article on 'The Origin, Character and Decline of an Early Civilization' in the *American Museum Novitates* (1967),[50] the move represented new directions within the scholarship of archaeology within North America, where anthropological theories began to be sourced quite transparently from the late 1940s for establishing the theoretical parameters for the archaeological scholarship of culture. The direction was summed up famously by the premier archaeologist of Mesoamerica, Gordon Willey and his younger colleague and co-worker Philip Phillips through the declaration that 'American Archaeology is Anthropology or nothing'.[51]

The New Archaeologists of the 1960s therefore saw culture through the definition proposed by the anthropologist Leslie White, as 'man's extra-somatic means of adaption', and lodged their methodological approaches for deriving specific historical explanations of culture change through theories of 'cultural ecology', that had been proposed by another anthropologist,

---

[48] Letter from D.H. Gordon to Wheeler, dated 2 September 1959, which informs of Indian and Pakistani archaeologists challenging the lower chronologies that western archaeologists often assigned, Box 458, Wheeler Papers.

[49] On this, see Chakrabarti (2006, p. 211), who has stated that 'at the grass-roots level, the Harappan scenario is something we closely recognize among the traditional villages of the subcontinent today'.

[50] Fairservis (1967).

[51] Willey and Phillips (1958, p. 2); see also Binford (1962).

Julian Steward.[52] Fairservis may have followed the New Archaeologists in using contemporary anthropological studies of India for his archaeological scholarship, although his methods were remarkably different from the overtly functionalist systems-based theoretical approaches and the attendant methods, which they followed. Fairservis may have also emulated the New Archaeologists in his aims of mapping a particularistic history of cultural evolution but unlike their research methods, he built upon the prevalent theories of diffusion to explain culture change. He postulated that the presence of an aceramic Neolithic habitation at Kili Gul Mohammad cannot be 'divorced from the obvious line of cultural development within Baluchistan and Afghanistan' since the 'urban situation in the Indus River valley was a logical development from an advanced village farming in an optimum situation'.[53] In this, he rejected the Childean diffusionary approach, but he followed the theories of cultural diffusion that were then prevalent in North America, predominantly those of Robert H Dyson Jr, the leading North American archaeologist of Iran at that time, who had propagated the diffusion of culture from the early dynastic Sumer into Iran during the third millennium BCE. Fairservis extended Dyson's thesis of the 'developmental motive from Iran' further east, for explaining the rise of 'sedentary village life' in the Indo-Iranian Borderlands, and concluded that the impetus for culture diffusion triggered changes from regionalisation in the Indo-Iranian borderlands to urbanisation within the Indus valley.[54]

In rejecting Childe, Fairservis no doubt rejected the characterising of the Indus Civilisation by Piggott and Wheeler. However, he also differed from Marshall in his inferences. He evoked an 'essential style' for the Indus, or the Harappan Civilisation, as he called it, on the lines of the 'Great Tradition of the Indian Civilisation'. The theories of great and little Indian traditions were being proposed at the time by North American social anthropologists of India, such as Robert Redfield and Raymond Firth, and Fairservis used them to summarise the processes of urbanisation in the Indus valley through another thesis, that of 'the cultural role of cities', which had been propounded by Redfield and Milton Singer.[55] Thus, he searched for the social

---

[52] Binford (1962, p. 218); White (1959); Steward (1955).

[53] Fairservis (1967, pp. 15, 19).

[54] Ibid., pp. 9–10.

[55] See Redfield and Singer (1952), for their descriptions of ancient cities, its orthogenetic aspect, and primary and secondary urbanisations. It is most likely that Fairservis had participated

and cultural impact of the stages of primary and secondary urbanisation in the 'character and history' of the Indus Civilisation, and maintained that 'it was a civilisation with cities, but not politically at least a state. Thus, it was neither Sumerian-like nor Egyptian-like but stands forth unique in its civilised character.'[56] By mining into the works of two other social anthropologists of India, Oscar Lewis and Mckim Marriott, he pronounced that the 'Harappan communities' had its local orientations, 'its "little" style, while at the same time participating in the "great" style of tradition in which it had an established role'.[57] Through the theories of the 'great' Sanskritic and 'little' folk traditions of India, Fairservis affirmed that the 'real riddle of the Harappan Civilisation's origin is the *raison d'etre* for its Indianness', which he characterised as being 'essentially village ethos'.[58]

The above characterisation was no doubt informed through the vast number of 'village-like' archaeological sites, which Fairservis had listed and encountered during his surveys in southern Afghanistan and Baluchistan in 1950–51, 1959 and 1964. However, his ascription also demonstrates his assumptions about the Indian Civilisation, and what this ought to look like in terms of archaeological evidence, which was informed through the anthropological constitution of the Indian civilisational tradition as comprising the 'little' traditions of the village-like India. The characterisation bespoke of the emulations of the British colonial historiography by the post-war anthropological scholarship of India in North America, and the borrowings are transparently visible in the manner in which the uniqueness of India's civilisational traditions was sourced through its village-orientated and caste-based society. The all-consuming force of this supposedly timeless, hence, conservative, tradition had been well described by Stuart Piggott as being far greater than the 'ambitions of an individual ruler' and 'the secular instability of a court'.[59] Fairservis enhanced the ancestral heritage of this force through his inferences of the nature of the Indus Civilisation as: 'here [was a] society whose traditions were so strong as to support without apparent question the

---

in the symposium, which was organised by Redfield and Raymond Firth on 'The Cultural Pattern of Indian Civilization' in Chicago in 1955.

[56] Fairservis (1967, p. 43).

[57] Fairservis (1971, p. 302); For his use of the anthropologists' theories, see Fairservis (1967, pp. 43–45; 1971, p. 295, footnote 41).

[58] Fairservis (1971, pp. 239, 299).

[59] Piggott (1950, pp. 150–51).

almost exact repetition of the familiar both in every day activities as well as in the creation of new settlements'.

Similar to his British predecessors of Indus studies, Fairservis perceived 'each Harappan site an emulation of the next one', but he invested the uniformity to the social fact that 'everyone had his place in the settlement'. Through this logic, he challenged Wheeler's and Piggott's characterisations of the military autocracy of Mohenjodaro and Harappa, and stated that the uniformity was an 'expression of a society to which the traditions lend their moral basis, their mystique, which sets forth the dharma in such a fashion that change is a disharmony and counter to the nature of the society'.[60] According to Fairservis, the adherence to *dharma* had caused minimal changes to the Indian society, and this belief led him to speculate upon the grand legacy of the Indus Civilisation as 'probably the great gap between this ancient civilisation and medieval India that we are prone to emphasise does not exist'.[61] He dwelt upon this speculation for establishing his thesis *The Roots of Ancient India* (1971), and declared that:

> The story of prehistoric India, which stretches back to a time so remote that it conforms to a Hindu Kalpa of untold generations reaching to a primordial world, nonetheless repeats again and again the pattern which was not to change until the East India Company ships moved up the Hooghly.[62]

The above statement provokes a recall of the nineteenth-century British views of India's unchanging history, which was expressed even by Meadows Taylor, who unlike his contemporaries, had recorded a changing 'Hindoo society' in his history of India (1870). In presenting the reasons for writing the book, Taylor had declared:

> The historical events of the ancient classic nations of Greece and Rome still possess a charm which time has not diminished; but the condition of their people has become altogether changed. It is not so, however, with India; and it is strange to us now to see Hindoos, who hold the same Pagan faith and follow the same customs as their forefathers who fought with Alexander the Great on the banks of the Indus, submitting themselves to a Christian nation

[60] Fairservis (1971, p. 301).
[61] Fairservis (1967, p. 44).
[62] Fairservis (1971, p. 381).

so far distant from them as ours, and vying with ourselves in loyalty to our gracious queen.[63]

Fairservis's understanding that the civilisational traditions of India could be recognisable throughout its *longue durée* from ancient to modern times has subsequently been given a sophisticated theoretical spin through the various models of the archaeological construct of a Cultural Tradition.

Cultural Tradition in the Early Indus Scholarship: A Short History

The functionalist construct of Cultural Tradition was brought into the South Asian archaeology by Jim Shaffer during his study of *Prehistoric Baluchistan* (1978), and was 'worked' through the Systems Theory. When Shaffer borrowed the construct, it had been established by the New Archaeologists as an archaeological theory, and Shaffer used it initially for gauging developments within Baluchistan as an 'essentially *indigenous* phenomena' that had to be sought 'within an internal cultural and chronological framework'.[64] He, thus, dismissed the theoretical orientations towards diffusionism of Fairservis and all others before him. Yet, despite the abject dismissal, Shaffer too like all his predecessors committed to the historicity of an essentialist South Asian civilisational tradition. For, the construct is premised upon the existence of a recognisable essential core over vast chronologies and geographies.

Contemporary to Shaffer's use, the notion of tradition was also employed by Gregory Possehl and Louis Flam in the 1970s for accommodating continuities between the 'mature' and 'late' urban phases of the Indus Civilisation, and for sketching an archaeological narrative 'that created suspicion' of the theories of 'cataclysmic decline'. In his use, Possehl followed the lead of his teacher Fairservis and by reviewing the 'late Harappan' sites (ca. 1700–1300 BCE) in Sind, Punjab and Gujarat suggested that the continuities in the cultural tradition 'can be hypothesised to have played at least some role in

---

[63] Taylor (1870, pp. vii–viii).
[64] Shaffer(1978, p. 111).

determining the character of what we now identify as Indian Civilisation'.[65] Possehl too, like Fairservis, conceded that the decline of the state system did not destroy 'a much larger cultural tradition', which continued until the beginnings of the iron technology. However, he explicitly pointed out that his usage of tradition represented 'cultural affiliation'.[66]

Considering that the archaeological constructs of Cultural Tradition, which were established from the 1960s were inspired from the contemporary anthropological models, it is perhaps helpful to point out that the documentation of the unselfconscious continuance of this phenomenon came largely from the anthropological scholarship of primitive societies. The construct bore no relationship with the traditions of interpretation that were being analysed by philosophers and literary theorists at the time, who were interested in questions of hermeneutics, and of whom Hans Georg Gadamer had emphasised, quite notably, that the 'essence of tradition is to exist in the medium of language'.[67] The archaeological scholarship of Cultural Tradition, as the definition of Possehl informs us, simply saw tradition in the continuities of stylistic elements within the artefactual repertoire. The functionalist theories through which the construct was made applicable for recording cultures gestated for over a decade during the 1980s, and were then pursued anew from the close of the twentieth century for periodising the archaeological cultures of northern South Asia.

'Cultural Tradition'
The Archaeological Model

Before critiquing the epistemic and utility values of the construct of Cultural Tradition for the scholarship of the Indus Civilisation, it is useful to draw into some of the histories of the construct, as they remain remarkably ignored. The genealogy of the functionalist construct of Cultural Tradition can be traced quite specifically to the 1940s as an analytical tool. It was established primarily by Gordon Willey and Philip Phillips for documenting culture change and continuity within the 'prehistoric' settlement patterns of the

---

[65] Possehl (1977, p. 254).
[66] Ibid., p. 243.
[67] Quoted in Phillips (2004, p. 18).

Viru Valley (Peru).[68] Willey and Phillips had presented the construct as a method for undertaking 'historical integration', which they emphasised, was the 'primary and descriptive level of archaeological task'. They had declared that *'an archaeological tradition is a (primarily) temporal continuity represented by persistent configurations in single technologies or other systems of related forms'.*[69] Tradition, they said, gave 'depth' in contrast to 'horizon' that gave 'breadth' to 'the genetic structure of cultural historical relationships on a broad geographical scale'. The authors were of the opinion that maintaining distinctions between the two features and searching for 'oscillations' between them in the archaeological residues from prehistoric sites was necessary for mapping the 'social transmittal' of complex civilisations.[70]

Through the model, whose merits they declared was overarching in its applicability, they strived to establish the 'baseline for American prehistory' and fashioned a methodology for classifying the continuities and changes within the processes of evolution from hunting-gathering to agricultural economies in the New World. In this, they employed two existing units, namely 'phases' and 'stages', which were being used by contemporary archaeologists, but which they also established as analytical categories by changing their representations from sequential to non-sequential and non-deterministic. Thus, they stated that although the general development of the societies in the New World is 'historical as well as developmental' the individual stages 'can have no correspondent historical reality or unity'. Many cultures might, therefore, pass through several 'stages', but the latter did not represent any evolutionary law that demanded all cultures to pass through a particular trajectory of developmental sequence.[71] In this, their model was an elegant expression of the multi-lineal evolutionary perspective of culture change, which had been designed by Steward as the 'culture ecology' approach, and which was quite specifically different from the Childean approach to culture history.

Binford re-fashioned the construct in his uses to emphasise that tradition in archaeological terms was 'a demonstrable continuity through time in the formal properties of locally manufactured craft items'. The archaeological

---

[68] See, for details, Willey and Phillips (1958). On Willey's scholarship of settlement archaeology, see Preucel (1999); on refuting Willey's pioneering status in devising methods of archaeological settlement pattern analysis, see Lamberg-Karlovsky (2008, p. xxii, footnote).

[69] Willey and Phillips (1958, pp. 37–38; original emphasis).

[70] Ibid., p. 38.

[71] Ibid., pp. 39–40.

construct of culture tradition, according to him, referred 'either [to] a single cluster of artifactual materials, such as ceramics, or to several classes of artefacts of a single socio-cultural system which exhibit continuity through time'.[72] Binford also emphasised that the latent 'continuity' of Culture Tradition is to be perceived 'in secondary [not primary] functional variability only' and construed a 'sphere of tradition' that rooted 'style' as one among three variables of cultural processes, the two others being 'interaction sphere' (based upon inter-societal relations) and 'adaptive sphere' (based upon common means of coping with the physical environment).[73]

As Binford's construction of the 'spheres' might inform us, the archaeological construct of Tradition, which he re-fashioned was based upon the stylistic features of artefact assemblages, which he considered could be classified into types, and mapped across geographies and over time for gleaning culture spread, culture continuity and culture change. Inevitably, a singular style became translatable as archaeological evidence of a singular cultural identity, and in this respect, the functionalist model of Cultural Tradition substantiated all existing, not only the Childean, culture history approaches by embellishing the 'homologous, as opposed to analogues' similarities.[74] Therefore, Binford's definition of archaeological tradition was also quite similar to Childe's list of culture traits, as this too served the classification of archaeological cultures through diagnostic or indexical markers.

Shaffer used aspects of the Binfordian construct to study the prehistory of Baluchistan, and present the flaws in the scholarship of Childe and Piggott, who had pioneered the archaeological scholarship of the subject. His move to use the construct for engaging with an aspect of South Asian archaeology creates a reason for recalling the rampant use of the term 'tradition' within the scholarship of Indian and American archaeology at the time. 'The long tradition of India', as Amalananda Ghosh had remarked in 1975, was not a matter of debate among Indian archaeologists who considered this a 'well-established' fact. However, Willey had specifically chosen to explore tradition as a marker of style in his archaeological scholarship of Mesoamerica because of the rampant use of the word within the histories

[72] Binford (1965, p. 208).

[73] Ibid.

[74] Webster (2008, p. 14). Webster provides a careful critique of the culture history approach, and interrogates the related theories that were first documented by James Ford in 1954 in *American Anthropologist*, in the article 'On the concept of types' (Vol. 56, pp. 42–53).

of South American civilisations.[75] Not wishing to war with his esteemed colleagues, Ghosh had recommended the delinking of 'the use of archaeological terms from national prestige',[76] and in using the construct of Cultural Tradition in the expectation that this would facilitate a scientific archaeological study, Shaffer unknowingly complied with Ghosh's request.

Shaffer's Cultural Tradition

During his maiden research of the prehistory of Baluchistan, Shaffer devised clusters of Cultural Tradition of the Zhob, Quetta, Nal, Bampur, Kulli and Indus Plain. As the terminology demonstrates, he had identified the clusters through classifications of artefact traits, mainly of the types of painting on ceramics, and in this, as he himself admitted, he had imposed the 'stylistic sphere' of tradition, which Binford had defined, upon his data.[77] However, by the early 1990s, he incrementally extended the construct from representations of small and discrete regional clusters based upon classifications of specific artefactual features, to historicising three large regional clusters, namely the Cultural Tradition of the Indus Valley, Helmand and Baluchistan from their origins until the 1st millennium BCE.[78] In this subsequent coverage, he followed Willey's and Phillips's subsequent attempts for securing a baseline of a universal prehistory for a larger geography. In their case, it was from the Viru Valley to the entire Mesoamerica, in Shaffer's case it was from Baluchistan to the entire northern South Asia.

The next re-fashioning was quite specifically dictated by the assured knowledge in the 1990s of the myth of the 'Aryan invasion' into South Asia. In presenting the model of an 'Indo-Gangetic Cultural Tradition' in 1995, Shaffer and co-author Dianne Lichtenstein emphasised quite specifically the utility of the overarching nature of the construct for presenting the continuous cultural history of northern South Asia, which had not been historically disrupted by invasions from the West. They stated that an overarching archaeological construct of Cultural Tradition over the entire northern South Asia allows a clearer view of the 'synchronically and diachronically' adaptive

---

[75] Ghosh (1975, p. 125); Willey and Phillips (1958, p. 34). See also Willey (1953).
[76] Ghosh (1975, p. 125).
[77] On this, see Shaffer (1978, p. 121).
[78] Shaffer (1992, see specifically pp. 426–28).

patterns of the ecological changes within the greater Indus-Hakra-Ghaggar and western Gangetic plains, and tidies the myriad 'divisions' and 'stages' of the prevalent periodisation schemes, which, they emphasised, have all been ill representative of the evidence of indigenous cultural continuity.[79] In a further revision of the model a decade later, in 2005, they extended the chronological representation of the Indo-Gangetic Cultural Tradition 'to the present', and emphasised that:

> It is currently possible to discern cultural continuities linking specific prehistoric social entities in South Asia into one cultural tradition. This is *not* to propose social isolation *nor* deny any outside cultural influence. Outside influence did affect South Asian cultural development in later, especially historic periods, but an identifiable cultural tradition has continued, an Indo-Gangetic Cultural Tradition linking social entities over a time period from the development of food production in the seventh millennium BC to the present. [...] Within the chronology of the archaeological data for South Asia describing cultural continuity, however, a significant *indigenous discontinuity* occurs, but it is one correlated to significant geological and environmental changes in the prehistoric period. This indigenous discontinuity was a regional population shift from the Indus Valley area to locations in the east, that is Gangetic Valley, and to the southeast, that is Gujarat and beyond.[80]

Considering that historical blanks do not exist in space and time but only in our knowledge of the past, the above assertions of a continuous cultural history for South Asia from the beginnings of the Holocene cannot be disputed. Neither is the apparent contradiction within the assertion—namely of a continuous Cultural Tradition which embodies instances of discontinuities—unexplainable given the wish of the authors to dismantle the erroneous theory of the 'Aryan invasion' that had been imposed upon the histories of Ancient India since the nineteenth century. By focusing on continuity Shaffer and Lichtenstein dismiss the 'invasion' theory and by including discontinuity, they aim at accommodating the changing histories of settlement patterns that are associated with the Indus Civilisation and the 'post-Harappan' settlements within Punjab, Eastern Uttar Pradesh, Haryana and Gujarat.

However, the conceptualisation of a unique and identifiable cultural tradition from the seventh millennium BCE until today nurtures essentialism in the very fact that it is envisaged as an archaeological construct. The model is

---

[79] Shaffer and Lichtenstein (1995, p. 141).
[80] Shaffer and Lichtenstein (2005, p. 93).

premised upon the presumption that Cultural Tradition can be archaeologically studied, which nurtures the understanding that this entity is materially recognisable because its core features have remained unchanged. Shaffer and Lichtenstein perceive the core features to be the 'economic and cultural focus on cattle' and agriculture.[81] To suggest that cattle- and agriculture-based subsistence economy defines the South Asian cultural tradition might appear facile. But more importantly, the choice glaringly overlooks all other subsistence activities that have prevailed within South Asia's prehistory and history. In devising a uniquely cattle-based Cultural Tradition, which has ostensibly continued over vast swathes of time and over vast territories, the authors have, no doubt, also aimed at dismissing the prominence that had been given in the past to the 'pastoral nomadic economy of the invading Aryans'. However, the choice fails to inform us what the 'indigenous discontinuities' would be.

The assertions of 'indigenous discontinuity' creates the need for considering the heuristic value of the term indigenous for mapping the cultural histories of a vast topography that includes today's north-western and northern South Asia. In trying to acquire knowledge of what might have been indigenous of the cultures of societies that had existed more than 4,000 years ago, we are forced to regard the limitations of the archaeological scholarship in sourcing past perceptions of territories and cultural geographies. For, evidence of such boundaries and identities cannot be sufficiently 'extracted' through the analyses of settlement patterns and artefact assemblages alone, and with respect to the Indus Civilisation the problem of sourcing is compounded by the following facts, namely that (a) the 'uniformity' reported of the urban phase of the civilisation (ca. 2600 BCE–1900 BCE) is ephemeral due to the immense variations of individual 'towns' and 'cities', and their contents and (b) the shifting geography of city/town formations through time poses a challenge for the possibilities of finding representative markers.

The above evidence makes us acutely aware of the epistemic constraints of the typological method, which archaeology largely follows because of its specific subject focus upon material residue. Additionally, the historical scholarship of pre-colonial India demonstrates that cultural and territorial

---

[81] Shaffer and Lichtenstein (1995, p. 143). The authors quote Willey and Philips and state that 'a cultural tradition refers to persistent configurations of basic technologies and cultural systems within the context of temporal and geographical continuity' (p. 141). See also Shaffer and Lichtenstein (2005), where they root continuity on 'economic focus on cattle together with agricultural production' (p. 75).

identities do not conflate. Thus, careful historians of Ancient and Early Medieval India have illustrated the non-equivalence of physical and cultural geographies even with respect to the references of 'desha' within the Sanskrit texts and inscriptions of the eighth- to the fourteenth-centuries. While searching for perceptions of Muslim communities in the above literature, B.D. Chattopadhyaya has noted that even they were not regarded as 'others' by the Hindus because 'the notion of territorial outsider in a political sense [was] not compatible with the early cosmological/geographical concept'.[82] Hence, exploring the Indus Civilisation as indigenous to South Asia becomes a vacuous academic exercise as this neglects the pertinent question, namely, how did the various inhabitants of the Civilisation distinguish their cultural territories, and what notions of the indigenous did they foster with respect to their own cultural affiliations?

The problems of presenting archaeological evidence of past perceptions of territories and identities through artefacts alone encourage us to take stock of the manner in which the regional has been established within the long archaeological scholarship of the Indus Civilisation. And we realise that apart from creating a sensitivity of the problems of trait-list classifications, this scholarship has yet to establish any viable method that might allow us to explore, or indeed engage with, the shifting perceptions of boundaries and cultural affiliations during the Bronze Age. The uses of the construct of Cultural Tradition as a schema of periodisation, therefore, takes us to the heart of the epistemic limitations of an archaeological culture.

Cultural Tradition as a Schema of Periodisation

In contrast to the single Cultural Tradition, which has been fashioned by Shaffer and Lichtenstein and which they constitute as representative of the archaeological and historical realities of northern South Asia from the seventh millennium BCE until to-date, J.M. Kenoyer, the principal excavator of

---

[82] Chattopadhyaya (1998, p. 90). Chattopadhyaya has substantially added to his earlier examples of blatant misrepresentations of historical territories in his lectures on 'The Concept of Bharatavarsha and its historical implications' and 'Of Others and Otherness: Early Indian Perceptions', which he presented for the Radhakrishnan Memorial Lecture Series at All Souls College, Oxford, in May 2012.

Harappa in recent years and a pioneering scholar of the archaeology of craft specialisation in South Asia, has used the model in a remarkably different manner for devising schema of periodisation. Kenoyer has conceptualised many discrete clusters of archaeologically identifiable Cultural Tradition for a vast geography, which he has classified as the Bactro-Margiana, Indo-Gangetic, Ganga-Vindhyan, Malwa-Rajasthan and Deccan, and indeed, the Indus Tradition, each with varying 'eras' and 'phases', and so with varying trajectories of developments from prehistory until the 'early historical' period (ca. 300 BCE).[83] The scheme, to some extent, shares Shaffer's creation in the 1990s, of the three different cultural traditions for northern South Asia, and seeks the utility of the model quite specifically in its overarching applicability. Kenoyer too, like Shaffer, believes that this specific feature allows a theoretical perspective of the long-term histories of cultural adaptations and culture changes in a specific geographical area. Moreover, he has specifically located the utility value of the model in its suitability for the 'nature of archaeological data and dating techniques' and has stated that this allows 'focus on the major activities of societies at particular periods'. Thus, for Kenoyer, the 'reference therefore is not just to a chronological bracket but also to how a society was organised and why it was so'.[84] Yet, the reasons why societies changed, are not revealed through the application, and the only knowledge of cultural changes which we may derive, and which we would inevitably be able to source irrespective of the application of any model/s, are those due to changes of environmental conditions.

In exploring the possibilities of the uses of the construct of Cultural Tradition, Kenoyer too, like Shaffer and Lichtenstein, has drawn upon the 'cultural links' between the Indus Tradition and 'regional cultures' of 'the Gangetic and Deccan regions', albeit by applying the model in a very different manner.[85] In describing the Indo-Gangetic tradition through the understanding that it reflects 'the major human adaptations that eventually encompass the larger geographic region extending over the Ganga–Yamuna river valleys as well as the greater Indus river valley and much of Peninsular India', he has proposed that:

> Although this Tradition has significant links to the earlier Indus Tradition, it represents a dramatically different trajectory and builds on the regional cultures

---

[83] Kenoyer (2006b), also Kenoyer (1991).
[84] Kenoyer (2006b, p. 50).
[85] Ibid., p. 59.

that were established in Western India, the Gangetic and Deccan regions. The Indo-Gangetic Tradition is directly correlated with the emergence of Early Historic states and urban centres during the period from 600 to 300 BC. Initially centred in the Ganga-Yamuna river valley and parts of the northern Indus Valley, this tradition spreads out gradually and over many centuries to the entire sub-continent and includes Afghanistan and Central Asia. It also eventually incorporates areas of Nepal, the Brahmaputra river valley (modern Assam and Bangladesh) and the eastern regions of northern Assam including parts of modern Burma.[86]

Thus, we note that, unlike Shaffer and Lichtenstein, Kenoyer has attended quite specifically to the historic fact of discontinuity,[87] which, to quote Rita Wright sums up: 'the basic character of the [Indus] civilization [...] its planned cities, technical virtuosity, systems of weights, seals and sealings, narrative imagery and Indus script, all [...] came to an end in the Post urban period'. As Wright has cautioned correctly, one simply has to await 'the results of continued investigations of the PGW that [may] clarify its connections to the early historic and provide for vestiges of an Indus presence'.[88]

The archaeological construct of a functionalist, adaptive and overarching Culture Tradition may be useful as a sophisticated classificatory scheme, yet it needs to be regarded and used only as a method for establishing categories, and for classifying. The construct has shown to have very little explanation value, and its application becomes transparently problematic in epistemological terms. Because the usage, quite similar to the construct of archaeological culture, often slips from things to people. We see the slippage when we follow the classifications, whereby the grouping of sites and their contents through the classifications of crafts and the patterns of their production, lead to inferences of kin-related activities, and to inferences of kin-based social groups in a settlement. The slippage is subtle but apparent, and the implications have been rather clearly pointed out—although they remain remarkably ignored—in the statement that 'the extrapolation of social structures or a common uniting tradition' from the 'material evidence' is 'problematic'.[89] In this respect, one of the authors of the above statement, Jaya Menon, has

---

[86] Kenoyer (2006b).
[87] For example, Kenoyer (2005, pp. 23–24).
[88] Wright (2010, p. 326).
[89] Menon and Varma (2005, p. 44).

also explained in depth and with specific references to histories of firing and polishing techniques, the flaws in Kenoyer's mapping of continuity in the technological traditions of bead making.[90]

Cultural Traditions and Questions of Cultural Identity

Considering that the New Archaeologists specifically targeted the slippage between technology and cultural identity within Childe's normative views of culture, it becomes pertinent to note Binford's remark that 'historical continuity and social phylogeny are particularly amenable to analysis through the study of stylistic attributes'.[91] In following Binford, Shaffer and Lichtenstein had sketched the applicability of cultural tradition within the wider domain of the greater Indus region through the conviction that:

> A cultural tradition is [...] composed of one or more patterned sets of archaeological assemblages, such as the Kot Diji, Amri or Harappan cultural complexes [...] These patterned sets are designated here as ethnic groups. [...] The definition of such boundaries may involve diverse cultural factors, but in an archaeological context such salient cultural traits are material cultural symbols such as distinctive ceramic styles, used to indicate membership in cooperative social units, organized to facilitate access to source production and reproduction.[92]

Because material things constitute archaeological enquiry, the use of style as a marker of identity has inevitably inundated the scholarship of technology and craft specialisation of the Indus Civilisation. Thus, specialists of the field, prominently Kenoyer *et al.*, have long contended that the production processes of lapidary, stoneware bangle manufacture, lithic industry, steatite based crafts, brick making, shell working etc., is likely to provide evidence of ethnic identities.[93] The changing fashions of theoretical archaeology

---

[90] Menon (2006, pp. 259–63).
[91] Binford (1965, pp. 207–08).
[92] Shaffer and Lichtenstein (1989, p. 119).
[93] An early example of relating craft specialisation to ethnic identities is Bhan *et al.* (1994).

have progressively eliminated the inferences of ethnic identities from the archaeological literature. However, inferences of kin-based craft specialists continue to foster theories regarding the possibilities of tracing such and other kinds of identities within the Indus Civilisation. The strong plea for envisioning a caste-based society within the Indus Civilisation, which was made by the eminent North American archaeologist of West Asia, C.C. Lamberg-Karlovsky in the closing year of the twentieth century is recalled here to add to the emphasis of the importance of seeing the ways in which conflicting traditions of historiography permeate the archaeological literature.[94]

Lamberg-Karlovsky had substantiated the logic of his plea by documenting the possibilities of acquiring evidence of ritual purity and pollution through the 'facts' of: (a) water management, which he derived from the presence of wells and drainage systems in the Indus cities and the Great Bath at Mohenjodaro; (b) kin-based, hence caste-based society, which he saw in the uniformity within the style of the unicorn motif on seals and (c) a lineage society, which he gleaned from the presence of 'classic Harappan' sites, such as Shortugai, within 'alien' cultural landscapes.

He, therefore, concluded that the 'enigma' of the Indus Civilisation, namely a vast geographical span of extraordinary uniformity in material culture but without highly centralised socio-political entity was probably 'characterised by an exceptional social organization, one that has deep and distinctive roots in South Asia: the caste system'.[95] Although similar inferences had circulated as speculations for decades—we are reminded of S.C. Malik's theories regarding the possible presence of caste system in the Indus Civilisation, in 1965—Lamberg Karlovsky's search was specifically geared towards formulations of new methodologies for extracting evidence of the ideas embedded within the material remains. The problem of such research enquiries, which Lamberg-Karlovsky has subsequently acknowledged elsewhere with specific references to ethnicity is, that it is difficult to ascertain the cultural markers from archaeological assemblages.[96]

The complex histories of the modern social phenomenon of caste cannot be mapped as histories of evolution, because as many historians of pre-colonial

---

[94] Lamberg-Karlovsky (1999).
[95] Ibid., p. 93.
[96] Lamberg-Karlovsky (2005, p. 169).

India have quite convincingly shown caste resists origin stories.[97] Yet, the fascination of deriving material inferences of caste in prehistory continues, and many biologists and geneticists have begun to enquire into questions of bio-ancestory in the hope of finding a resolution. A detailed study by the sociologist Ann Morning, which cautions us of the 'return of the biological race within the social sciences' provides the most incisive reasons for con-sciously disengaging with the enquiries into the genetic make of population groups for configuring cultural aspects. Morning has observed that 'close readings of the arguments linking genes, race, ethnicity, admixture and migration should be undertaken not just to guard against simplistic assump-tions about our ability to analyse biological data in a bias-free manner, but also simply to ascertain whether they have new knowledge to contribute.' She illustrates the reasons for questioning the genetic data 'about "natural", objective population in the human species',[98] in relation to the pursuit of 'objective science', and she states:

> Since our inferences about biological groupings are informed by our cultural beliefs about human difference, it is impossible to gauge how close or how far our racial classifications are to any independent reality of clusters, classes or clines. [...] As sophisticated as contemporary genetic analyses may seem, we must not forget that geneticists are not in the driver's seat when it comes to developing ideas about race. As was true of the cutting-edge sciences of past-like taxonomy, craniometry, anthropometry and serology—which were called into corroborate the biological 'realities' of race, when it comes to race genetics is for all its bells and whistles simply another handmaiden recruited to bolster an Eighteenth-century worldview: the notion there 'really' are black and white people, yellow and red people, independent of cultural biases or proclivities we may have. [...] The sociology of scientific knowledge has repeatedly demonstrated that our beliefs and ways of seeing the world [...] shape what we 'discover' there, even when we think we are simply taking objective measurements and conducting impartial analyses. [...] In this academic environment, where biologists ostensibly have stronger 'scientific' credentials because of their supposed superior competence and adherence to scientific principles and virtues, it is no surprise that social scientists may feel that their expertise is of lesser value and they themselves are less qualified to intervene. [...] Misgivings about the place of the social sciences in debates about the nature of race, however, are completely unfounded. Instead, disciplines

---

[97] For example, see Thapar (2001).
[98] Morning (2014, p. 1683).

like anthropology, sociology and history are especially well placed to critically assess the racialization of new biostatistical constructs'.[99]

Although prescient archaeologists who consider the possibilities of sourcing knowledge of the 'origins of caste in South Asia' dismiss the search for an ancient 'caste system' through the mapping of gene pool, they suggest that 'scholars from all disciplines need to develop a greater theoretical and methodological appreciation of the complex social, economic, political and cultural trajectories that have led to what is today referred to as the "caste system"'. They propose interdisciplinary research orientations into the archaeological enquiries of the ancestry of caste in India, and emphasise that:

> Rather than shying away from the investigations of caste in the light of these complexities, or caste's political implications, scholars need to work together to create and maintain an informed discussion about the origins of caste, its role in the structuring of biological diversity, and its place in South Asian society.[100]

The historical certainty that caste, or rather its seminal feature, namely *jati* affiliations, has remained an inherently changing social phenomenon should be sufficient to demonstrate the errors of the searches for representations of caste through gene pools. However, considering that even the supposedly 'fixed' aspect of this 'system', which is the *varna* affiliations, require gauging inferences of colour-based distinctions, the logic of finding evidence of caste within the archaeological assemblages even through interdisciplinary research methods becomes difficult to follow. The scholarship of archaeological artefacts, including architectural topography, brings home the understanding that through them we can only infer examples of social, political and economic hierarchies, and identities of inequalities which relate to occupational and economic specialisations. To impose the inference of caste upon the above examples—by noticing occupational specialisation—illustrates the imposition of an expectation of the social mores of Ancient India.

Despite the dismissal of the Childean measures of ethnic trait lists, the New and Processual archaeologies brought in many more ways of inferring

---

[99] Morning (2014, pp. 1679–82).

[100] Boivin (2007, p. 357). Boivin presents the interpretive contents of the genetic analysis to show why natural sciences cannot be considered objective, and states: 'it is very clear that many of the studies actually start out with some assumptions that are clearly problematic, if not in some cases completely untenable' (ibid., p. 352). For a detailed literature of the genetic studies of the tribes and castes of India, see the Bibliography of this book.

ethnic and other non-materially traceable identities through their models and constructs, such as through 'spheres of interaction' and 'culture tradition'. The problems in the methods have been quite well explained subsequently by many archaeologists themselves. For example, in her study of the 'archaeology of ethnicity', Sian Jones has shown quite clearly that 'the "balanced", "objective" and "reliable" interpretations' of past identities 'can only be made on precisely the same principles of interpretation that underlie the "unbalanced" and "distorted" representations of [...] nationalist archaeologist.'[101] Thus, we note that the inferences of Lamberg-Karlovsky with respect to the possible provenance of the caste system in the Indus Civilisation find an echo within an avowedly 'nationalist' history of Indian archaeology which declares that 'the Harappan society was organised along the line of castes', through the fact that:

> even if one gives up thinking of higher caste groups [...] it is difficult to believe that the system of regularly cleaning the waste in a settlement like Mohenjodaro [...] could be modelled on anything but the system which was followed in many places in India till recently.[102]

This remarkable overlap of the processualist and nationalist theories demonstrates that new theoretical turns do not necessarily bring with them the promise of new evidence. Thus, the notion of an age-old caste-based society in India, which Piggott, following the colonial historiography of India's unchanging traditions had described as 'conservative' and Fairservis, following the anthropological literature of his times submitted as representing the 'adherence to dharma', continues to re-emerge within the supposedly more scientifically robust archaeologies of Cultural Traditions.

The methodologies of deriving inferences of social identities within the Indus Civilisation, be they of ethnicity or caste, would elicit the caution of the twenty-first century social anthropologists, who demonstrate that people 'can't be put into a box anymore'. The new anthropological scholarship of India and Africa considers these geographical areas as 'obvious examples' of societies of long-standing superdiversity not only of the 'late modern'.

---

[101] Jones (1997, p. 12). The quote is Jones's assessment of the claims of Kohl and Testskhladze. They consider legitimate the rights of the Georgians to territories on the basis of the presence of Christian monuments, but denounce the logic of searching for ethnic and linguistic identities from material remains.

[102] Chakrabarti (2006, p. 211).

The historical fact of this superdiversity—understood as 'diversification of diversity'[103]—should lead us to dismiss the archaeological evidence of a caste-based social structure within the artefacts and layouts of the Indus cities.

Texts, Tradition and the Indus Civilisation

Unfortunately, the archaeological searches in the twenty-first century for a continuous history of South Asia shows a renewed vigour in sourcing vastly disparate Sanskrit and Pali texts, both in intent and chronology, such as the Vedas, *Asthadhyayi, Arthashastra*, Epics, *Manusmriti* and *Milindapanha*, for understanding the political formations and cultural ideologies of the Indus Civilisation.[104] This new combing of the literary corpus of Ancient India is remarkably different from the perusal of the Vedic corpus in the early-twentieth-century for gleaning knowledge of the authors of the Indus Civilisation. Chanda, we may recall, had searched the texts for the authors. The new searches comb the texts for ascertaining archaeological evidence of the polities and societies of the Bronze Age. Thus, for example, in describing the urban phase of the Civilisation as representative of non-monarchical city states, Kenoyer has suggested that:

> the literary evidence from the Early Historical period brings a new perspective to mute archaeological patterns of the Harappan phase. There is no need to look outside the subcontinent to find analogies when we have such strong cultural and historical continuities in the actual region of study.

He has concluded that 'similar approaches have been the norm in Mesoamerica for generations, but only recently has it been possible to begin making the connections in the Indian subcontinent'.[105]

The literary traditions of Ancient India is now also unhesitatingly used for ostensibly eschewing the 'positivistic and economically deterministic' theories through which the Indus Civilisation has been studied in the past,

---

[103] Jørgensen and Juffermans (2011).

[104] For a critique, see Menon and Varma (2005, pp. 44–45). For a view of the diverse textual corpus that are now drawn upon for configuring the ancient South Asian Civilisational tradition, see Eltsov (2008).

[105] Kenoyer (1997, p. 63).

and for establishing an archaeological scholarship that ostensibly promotes focus upon histories of ideas. Thus, the texts and the excavated material are sourced for 'ideas of the ancient city civilization—[ostensibly] the two key concepts in the archaeology of complex societies and ancient history'.[106] Of the many other presumptions that are read into the artifacts of the Indus and Gangetic civilisations through the reading of texts is also the understanding that 'the very fact that authorities both in the Harappan and Ganges Civilisation expressed their ethos in similar material symbols—various forms of fortification, circumvallation—indicates that the forms of authorities in these two civilisations may have been similar as well', and that the 'deep structure' of the South Asian Civilisation was fashioned from the Neolithic period and can be defined through 'five traits, namely agricultural economy, an orally transmitted code of conduct, an orally transmitted sacred knowledge, an idiosyncratic sociocultural system and a set of ritual and sacrificial practices'.[107] In establishing histories of 'deep structure', the above research echoes the focus of cultural continuity within the applications of the archaeological construct of Cultural Tradition.

While reworking their own variants of Cultural Tradition during the 1990s, Shaffer and Kenoyer had both taken care to emphasise the possibilities of an ethnically diverse and culturally plural historical landscape within northern South Asia from prehistory till-date.[108] The new anti-processualist, ideology-orientated, text-based archaeological research of the Indus and Gangetic civilisations also seeks to be similarly politically correct in its intellectual orientations. Hence, it constitutes the grand civilisational tradition of South Asia as multi-ethnic, multi-lingual and religiously diverse. Nonetheless, this new literature overlooks the blatant essentialisms embedded in the idea of a unique South Asian Civilisational ethos. After all, few academic archaeologists would care to propose the archaeological history of a unique, age-old civilisational ethos for Western Europe, North America, Britain, France, Unites States or any other regional or national domains of the Western world.

This usage has little bearing on the phenomenon that was sketched and explained in detail by Marcel Mauss, and subsequently by Pierre Bourdieu.

---

[106] Eltsov (2008, p. 1).

[107] Ibid., pp. 165, 185. See however, Shrimali, K.M. 2014, pp. 244–45, for an appreciation of the 'extremely nuanced proposition' (ibid., p. 244).

[108] For examples of 'cultural mosaic', see Shaffer and Lichtenstein (2005, pp. 83–84).

Conceding that 'power, plurality and human agency are all a part of how traditions come about', tradition is being re-conceptualised as an analytical category outside its earlier functionalist form in two different ways. On the one hand, archaeologists of the Americas, such as Timothy Pauketat, empha-sise the importance of engaging with tradition for formulating enquiries regarding 'how do people throughout history become separate *peoples* with seemingly different identities, ways of doing and thinking, and specific tech-nologies to cope with the outside world?'[109] Classical archaeologists, on the other hand, such as Robin Osborne, poise the utilitarian value of tradition against that of *habitus*, and emphasise that in contrast to the latter, which is inherited and acquired by habituation, 'tradition allows a more robust engagement with the inherent forces of human agency'.[110] Their views are radically different from the manner in which Shaffer and Lichtenstein have incorporated the concept of *habitus*. For, the latter do so for demonstrating the efficacy of the functionalist model of Cultural Tradition in revealing the adaptive responses of culture to ecological changes.[111] This usage has little bearing with the phenomenon that has been amply explained by Marcel Mauss, and subsequently by Pierre Bourdieu.

The values which Pauketat, Osborne and their colleagues attribute to tradition are premised upon the feasibility of establishing different meth-odologies for exploring the practices of past communities towards their self-definition. In providing theoretical thrust towards exploring tradition they aim at securing possible methodologies through which archaeological evidence of agency can be sourced. It is also worth noticing that classical archaeologists and prehistorians both see the value of engaging intellectu-ally with the historicising method, since this illustrates the new professional closeness amongst archaeologists who have consciously sought to distinguish their theoretical orientations as different, and divergent, from each other throughout the latter half of the twentieth century.

The functionalist and processualist archaeology of the 1960s and 1970s, as we know from Chapter 4, came to ill repute by the late 1980s when many archaeologists, especially within Europe and Britain, came to recognise that the inherent positivism of the processualist approach encouraged an abject disregard for human agency, and hence also for the basic responsibilities of

---

[109] Pauketat (2001, p. 3; original emphasis).

[110] Osborne (2008, p. 288).

[111] See Shaffer and Lichtenstein (1995, pp. 141–42).

archaeological scholarship. The thrust for mapping a civilisational tradition for South Asia through the archaeology of the Indus Civilisation forces a recall of the intellectual dismissal of this school, and homes in on the importance of interrogating the manner in which ideological notions of legacies and heritage are given immutable forms through the archaeological scholarship. In this respect, the photograph from Mohenjodaro taken during the largest excavation of the site to-date, in 1925–26 (Illustration 5.2), succinctly represents the rich potentials of enquiries into the encounters with the past within the archaeological field that often leads to material creations of legacies and heritage.

Given that western archaeologists often criticise their non-western counterparts for failing to adopt new theoretical approaches, the continued dominance of the processualist school of thought in the archaeology of the Indus Civilisation is somewhat surprising. For, this demonstrates the theoretical poverty of even the western studies of South Asian archaeology. In this respect too, the archaeological construct of a 'Great South Asian Tradition' through the modern scholarship of the Indus Civilisation forces us to interrogate the intellectual obligations of today's postcolonial archaeology.

A Vision for Archaeology: Partition, Nationalism and the 'Indian' Pasts

The Atranjikhera site was located by R.C. Gaur, Nurul Hasan's young colleague who handles most of the fieldwork. He did it after walking over almost the whole of Etah district and scraping away at every likely mound. Permission to dig was granted by the Dept. of Archaeology because it was expected that nothing of any importance was likely to turn up. Now that so much has emerged, difficulties are being made about publication, field grants etc. on the ground that the Muslim University people ought really to do nothing more than medieval archaeology. Nurul Hasan, having been brought up in the good old nawabzada tradition, doesn't speak for himself in the committee meetings, and no one else speaks for him.
(D.D. Kosambi to Mortimer Wheeler, 30 April 1965)[1]

The above excerpt from Kosambi's letter to Wheeler conveys two major aspects of the nascent practices of the Indian scholarship of the archaeology of India that followed the Indian independence, namely (a) the undisputed authority which the Archaeological Survey of India wielded in staking claims upon the explorations, excavations, conservation and displays of the 'important' sites; and (b) the dictates of religion that guided the archaeological curation of the ownership of national patrimony. They illustrate the legacy of the British administration of the 'monumental heritage' of India upon the secular policies of the Indian government with respect to rights of ownership of the nationalised historical landscape. The colonial inheritance continues within the methods of classifying monuments, whereby the 'dead' and 'heritage-endowed' relics are regarded as Hindu, Muslim, Jewish, Buddhist, Christian and such, and the possible histories of their worship by other communities remain buried within their architectural forms. A case

---

[1] File E/2/9, Wheeler Archives. The letter, addressed by Kosambi from P.O. Deccan Gymkhana, Poona, is marked by Wheeler as 'seen on 4 May 1965'.

study could be the archaeological curation of the Dhamek stupa at Sarnath within independent India, which is commemorated and preserved for tourists and Buddhists alike as a historical stupa, but whose worship by the Hindu communities even as late as the nineteenth century remains consistently ignored within the descriptive labels that are placed by the Archaeological Survey for visitor information.[2] The omission perpetuates despite the efforts of the Survey in recent years to make such labels error-free.

Additionally, the British often contradicted their own administrative measures in the curation of the 'spoils' from excavations. Thus, the government granted permission to Buddhists living outside India to excavate Indian sites, provided they did not carry away the antiquities. Yet, at the same time, it also donated the reliquaries that were collected by the Archaeological Survey during the excavations of ancient stupas within India to prominent Buddhist communities in Japan, China, Thailand, Sri Lanka and elsewhere.[3] Moreover, in establishing policies regarding the governance of monuments, the colonial government routinely pitted one religious community against the other. An example is the charge which the political agent of Bhopal tried to bring against the 'Mahomedan population' of the princely state for intending to neglect the caretaking of Sanchi 'topes' with a view to install, unsuccessfully, a Buddhist caretaker.[4] The growing communal tensions within British India throughout the 1930s contributed to the logic of the religion-orientated curatorial practices of the colonial Survey. The practices entrenched the Indian

[2] See, for example, Ewen (1886, p. 50). In his 'handbook' of Benaras, Ewen had noted that 'the Hindus worship the Dhamek. On the north side will be seen pure gold rubbed on as offering by a Raja, besides numerous patches of gold leaf affixed by Bengalis who were desirous of imitating him.'

[3] For example: In 1902 Count Kozui Otani, a Japanese Buddhist was allowed to excavate at Gridrhakuta (near Rajgir) with the stipulations that the antiquities were to become the property of the Government of India, and monthly reports and site plans were to be sent to the director general of the Survey (*Proceedings of Home Department, A&E*, Nos. 55–56, December 1909). Yet, the contents of the crystal reliquaries at Shah-ji-ki-dheri, found during the excavations undertaken by the ASI in 1909 were distributed to the Buddhist communities outside India, but not given to the Muslim owners of the land who had demanded a share on the grounds that since the excavations had 'made the land uncultivable and unculturable, the government had to make good the price.' 'Petition from Sayed Amir Badshah and Sayed Ahmed Shah', *Proceedings of Home Department, A&E*, No. 15, December 1909, pp. 273–75, p. 274.

[4] Quote from a letter of Lt Col W.W. Baker to Secretary Govt. of India, Foreign Department, *Proceedings of the Home Department, A&E*, 9 October 1906, No. 1250–s–; Also *Proceedings of the Home Department, A&E* 13 November 1905, No. 180-C and 17 November 1905, No. 123.

psyche and have left numerous traces quite specifically within the early years of independence in India. Thus, we note that in 1969, the commissioner for Scheduled Caste and Tribes, Nirmal Kumar Bose, saw nothing untoward in bringing before the Archaeological Survey his objection to the worship inside the Nagarjuna Cave by a local Muslim peer. Bose deemed this to be a 'wrong use of a Buddhist cave',[5] and the administrative and academic milieu to which he belonged would have expected the 'Muslim University', in Aligarh to explore and study the history of the 'Muslim Medieval India' without deeming such expectations contrary to India's secular credentials.

The correspondence between Kosambi and Wheeler, which date between 1964 and 1966 and which includes the letter quoted above, inform us of another feature that had also begun to crystallise as a post-colonial feature of South Asian archaeology, namely the apprehension of the western scholars of South Asian archaeology towards the dates which their South Asian colleagues and the new scientific laboratories of the region provided, especially if they appeared as being too 'early'. An example is from the archaeological site of Atranjikhera, which was excavated in 1964 for the first season. The excavations indicated the possibilities of a deeper antiquity of the Iron Age than that which was known until then from the Indian subcontinent and provided evidence of continuous occupation from, to quote the excavator R.C. Gaur, 'the earliest phase of the proto-historic period (second millennium BC) of the Doab to Akbar's time'.[6] Of the iron samples that were sent for C14 dating to the new radiocarbon laboratory, which was established in 1961 at the Tata Institute of Fundamental Research (TIFR, Bombay), one was given the date of 1025±110 BCE. The date sparked disbelief from the British archaeologists regarding the chronology of the 'advent of iron' into the Indian subcontinent. The ambivalence towards the date was buttressed by

---

[5] The complaint raised enquiries into the history of the cave, and highlighted the paucity of knowledge. Investigations revealed that the cave had been mentioned in a 'nineteenth-century article on the Antiquarian remains in Bihar', which had stated that its interior was not worshipped, and the Archaeological Survey concluded that the brick ruins in front of the cave may have been a site of worship in the past. File dated and titled 10 August 1968 (no other information), Survey Archives. Bose was Director General of Anthropological Survey of India between 1959 and 1964. For a subsequent archaeological history of the 'rock-cut caves, Buddhist and Muslim ruins' in the Nagarjuni Hills near Gaya, see Patil (1963, pp. 294–99). Bose's reference may have been 'the Gopi or Milk-maid's Cave' (see ibid., pp. 294–95), which was surveyed by Francis Hamilton Buchanan in the year 1812–13.

[6] Gaur (1983, p. xiii).

the fact that the samples that had been sent to the British Museum came back with very late dates (ca. 470–90 BCE). Kosambi, who had shown hesitations to accept the veracity of the dates given by TIFR, was approached by Nurul Hasan, then head of the Department of Ancient Indian History Culture and Archaeology at Aligarh Muslim University to help with sourcing the reasons for the discrepancy. He requested Wheeler, who had openly expressed his misgivings regarding the correctness of the dates from TIFR, to enquire into the dating procedures at the British Museum, and stated:

> When Gordon Childe and R.D. Barnett paid me the compliment over ten years ago of asking for suggestions for the then new radiocarbon unit, I took to the BM [British Museum] the most competent local statistician whom I knew: Prof G.A. Barnard of the Imperial College, South Kensington. The reason was that the Geiger counts have to be interpreted by delicate statistical methods, not just by the usual rule of thumb formulae. Could you ask Barnard to check the calculations once again, from the primary BM records? Assuming of course that the right samples were taken.[7]

It is worth nothing that Nurul Hasan had asked Kosambi, and not any senior archaeologist, to sort the problems of the dates. As a careful historian himself, Hasan greatly admired Kosambi's critical attention to the methods of dating, which was a unique and striking feature of his historical scholarship of Ancient India in his own times, and which no doubt bespoke of his professional training as a mathematician.[8] By the mid 1960s, as his letters to Wheeler also illustrate, Kosambi had influential connections within the international academic world, among different sciences, and Hasan would

---

[7] Letter from Kosambi to Wheeler, 1 August 1966, File E/2/9, Wheeler Archives. Through his excavations at Hastinapura (1951–2) B.B. Lal had suggested that the 'Painted Grey Ware Culture', which he had found at the site, could be dated to ca. 1100–800 BCE. He identified the 'Culture' with the 'Aryans', who were perceived as having brought 'iron' into India. However, since the accepted dates for the earliest uses of iron in South Asia at the time was ±500 BCE, which came from Marshall's excavations at Taxila, Lal's dates were fiercely disputed by D.H. Gordon. The samples of Painted Grey Ware that were sent for dates to the Tata Institute of Fundamental Research also substantiated Gordon's views of the origins of the 'iron age' in India in around ca. 700–400 BCE. The new dates for the iron samples from Atranjikhera therefore sparked a fierce row. For an overview of the ferocity of the debate, see the questions following the introduction by N.R. Banerjee to *The Iron Age in India* in Misra and Mate (1964, pp. 199–211).

[8] On the importance of dating in Kosambi's historical methods, see Chattopadhyaya (2002, p. xx).

have approached him knowing that he was regarded by this world as 'one of the most powerful Indian intellects'.[9]

Kosambi's respect abroad accompanied the increasing overlook of his views at home regarding the nature of many archaeological sites, and he too nurtured a 'healthy disrespect' towards the views of the Indian archaeological scholarship.[10] His letters to Wheeler express his distaste of the religion-tinged descriptions of historical landscapes, which many Indian archaeologists were then establishing, and of the professional conflicts between the archaeologists and historians which had implications for the manner in which the Indian government distributed grants-in-aid for research in archaeology and history.[11] The contents might provoke us to dismissively retort what, if anything has changed within the domain of Indian archaeology since then, although they also highlight the importance of engaging with a vision for the scholarship of archaeology in South Asia. Therefore, I begin this concluding chapter with a recall of the 'nation-serving archaeology' that was developed within India following independence, as this allows me to establish the historical context for some of the possibilities.

Partition and Nationalism

The communal politics that led to the Partition in 1947 has left different kinds of traces within the archives of the colonial Survey. A vast bulk of the official correspondence and clippings of newspaper reports that were appended to departmental files, and which date between 1930 and 1947, relate to grievances in matters of personnel and appointments, and those from 1934 onwards engage quite specifically with the violations of the communal ratio that was fixed in that year for filling vacancies within the government offices. A persistent news item of the decade of 1934–44 is the remarkable absence of senior Muslim officers in the Survey. For example, on 15 July 1938

---

[9] Letter from Peter G. Hewlitt, Head of British Council, Bombay, to Wheeler, dated 9 March 1960. Kosambi was invited to the UK during the year, and Hewlitt hoped that Wheeler would make the time to meet him as he felt sure that he would 'like him personally and professionally', File E/2/9, Wheeler Archives.

[10] In the letter as mentioned in Note no. 9, ibid.

[11] The letters are archived in File E/2/9, ibid.

The Star of India, which was published from Calcutta, pointed out that the British policy of Indianising the offices of the Central Government has been 'construed to mean "Hinduisation" by the countrymen', and the following week the Lahore-based *Eastern Times* re-published the story for its readers to 'reveal' that 'all officers in the Archaeological Department right from the Director General down to the Office Superintendent and then in the Department of Education, Health and Lands, which is the controlling Department of Archaeology, [...] are all Hindus'.[12] A year-and-a-half later, while reporting a charge that had been brought by (Sir) Ziauddin of the Muslim League against the Archaeological Survey for recruiting a Hindu epigraphist to the post of Deputy Director General, *The Star of India* documented that in sharp contrast to the four Hindus who had held permanent positions as archaeological superintendents since the establishment of the organisation in 1902, no Muslim had ever been recruited to the position even temporarily.[13] Muslim officers and staff continued to feel marginalised within the Archaeological Survey of independent India, and the various archival references well into the late 1960s provide a glimpse of the religious-based communitarian identities of the organisation's workforce.

With respect to the documents that date from the year of Partition, the archives of the 'Old Survey', as Wheeler would subsequently call the organisation he served, inevitably illuminate the heavy losses of staff, personal tragedies and professional travails of the employees. Additionally, they create a strong reminder of the physical dismemberment of the institution itself through the re-distribution of all its contents. The meticulous inventories of camp furniture, stores, field and laboratory equipments and collections that were itemised for division between India and Pakistan included objects as diverse as typewriters, almirahs, field cameras, printing boxes, magnifying glasses

---

[12] *The Star of India*, 'Indianisation', 15 July 1938; *Eastern Times*, 'Indianisation or Hinduisation?' 22 July 1938.

[13] *The Star of India*, 'Muslims in Archaeology Department: Sir Ziauddin's plea for proper consideration', 7 December 1939. In opposing the decision of the Survey, Ziauddin had pointed out that even Mohmmad Sanah Ullah, the reputed, Archaeological Chemist, who had joined the Survey in 1914 was not considered for the post of deputy DG as he was a technical officer, and the department's policy was not to appoint such officers as DG and DDG as they had no experience in excavation and conservation work. Thus, he challenged the offer to a Hindu epigraphist who too was a 'technical officer', and documented communal bias in the fact that 'there are Muslim officers in the administrative line senior enough to be entitled to the post'.

and collections of antiquities, photographs and administrative documents.[14] The procedures for partitioning the contents make depressive reading and demand critical histories. A cursory sifting of the related documents also allows a view of the concerted efforts that were made by the members of the steering committees of the Partition Council in 1947, for using the situation to establish the material identity of their respective nations.

Thus, with a view towards building a national collection, India sought a share of the archaeological collections of the Peshawar Museum (recorded as containing 90 per cent of the finest Gandhara specimen), site museums of Taxila, Harappa and Mohenjodaro, the museum in the Lahore Fort ('superb' collection of Indian arms and armour of the seventeenth to the nineteenth century), Lahore Central Museum (antiquities from Mohenjodaro and Harappa that had been placed there in 1945), and Victoria Museum, Karachi (discrete collection of Harappan objects). In terms of the re-distribution of cultural properties, the India–Pakistan shares were fixed according to 'territorial basis', and were therefore constituted in terms of the ratio of 70:25, or 70:30, or 60:40. Yet, when the negotiations for the distributions were ultimately undertaken upon the 'educational needs' of the two countries, for the 'acceptance of the *status quo*' it was considered 'necessary to transfer to India additional antiquities' from Pakistan 'over and above her present share'.[15]

One of the first steps taken by India for establishing a visible profile of the nation-serving archaeology was the curation of a 'nationally important' collection in 1948 in New Delhi at the Government House with the objects that came back to the partitioned subcontinent from the India exhibition at the Royal Academy, London.[16] Other strategies that followed included: (a) efforts towards the exposure of the Indus Civilisation in India, which is noted in Chapter 5; (b) sending Indian expertise to archaeological missions abroad, of which early expeditions were to Afghanistan (1956), Nepal (1961–62) and Egypt (1962–63); (c) plans towards establishing a national landscape of historical monuments, which has subsequently aided the Indian

[14] For example, 'Partition of India: Assets and liabilities', File 33/31–63/47, Survey Archives.

[15] 'A Note on Partition of the Antiquities in the Museums Branch', dated 29 July 1947 and signed by V.S. Agrawala, then superintendent Museums Branch, ASI, *Partition–Division of Museums and Archives*, File 33/62/47, pp. 1–3, p. 1 Survey Archives. On the partitioning of the collections from Mohenjodaro, see the entries for necklaces and girdles found within the 'hoards' in Kenoyer 1997. Additionally, for the refugee occupation and destructions of monuments that attended the partition, see Lahiri (2013).

[16] On this see, Guha-Thakurta (2004, Chapter 6).

representations of the monuments and habitats for World Heritage status (since 1983); and (d) commemorating the 'hoary' histories of ancient sites through on-site exhibitions and new site museums, which has also allowed the Indian nation to forget some of the more 'modern' histories of the historical topography.[17] Additionally, the academic presentations of a unified Indian archaeology by the Archaeological Survey, and through research projects that were undertaken by the new departments of archaeology within the field surveys of India by Indian universities, inform us of the manner in which the archaeological scholarship was developed and nurtured for three decades after independence, for presenting a national cultural history of India. The following few leads provide a glimpse of the histories that connect the academic scholarship of archaeology and the cultural politics of the new nationalism.

Partition had entailed the loss of the long antiquity of the 'Indian Civilisation' not only through the loss of the Indus Civilisation, but also through the loss of the 'Soan Culture' that had shown the possibilities of the presence of humans in India from the Pleistocene times, before 10,000 years ago. This acheulean or the old stone-age, archaeological culture had been noted in the Soan river valley of Kashmir by geologist Helmut De Terra of Carnegie Institute (Yale University), archaeologist Thomas Paterson at the Museum of Archaeology and Ethnography (University of Cambridge), and the French Jesuit priest, Teilhard de Chardin, who was trained as a geologist and palaeontologist, during their explorations in the Siwalik Hills, Salt Range, Soan Valley and Potwar Plateau in the early 1930s (between 1931 and 1935).[18] The Indian 'loss'—as the area came under Pakistan—established the ontological value of prehistory for the young Indian nation, and we note that immediately after 1947 Indian archaeologists began to classify the 'Megalithic sites' of south India as 'national monuments'.[19] Thus, the

---

[17] One example is from Kurukshetra where the modern spectacular diorama and other such popular exhibitions prominently present the association of the site with the Great Battle in the *Mahabharata*. They have obliterated the association of the site with the rule of Harshavardhana of Thaneswar during the seventh century. I am grateful to Tapti Roy for allowing me to quote from her field research of Kurukshetra in 2010–12.

[18] For details, see De Terra and Paterson (1939). The geologist D.N. Wadia had alerted of the palaeolithic finds in the Salt Range in 1928. For a summary of explorations leading to those of De Terra, Paterson and Teilhard, see Dani (1966, p. 72).

[19] The officer for prehistory in the Archaeological Survey, V.D. Krishnamurti had reported in a letter to Wheeler, dated 10 November 1948, that he was giving popular talks to school teachers in Tamil for awakening public feeling with respect to the megaliths as 'national treasure

circumspect director general of the Archaeological Survey of independent India, Niranjan Chakravarti (1948–50), felt obliged to mention in one of the first government publications on *Archaeology in India* (1949) that:

> it is hoped that in course of time, by methodological eastward and westward extensions of our explorations we should be able to supply the missing link between the Indus Valley civilization and the civilization of the so-called historical times. It is also to be hoped that one day we may even be able to prove the theory already put forward by some eminent scientists that India was one of the cradles of human civilization.[20]

A striking aspect of the post-independence Indian historiography is the immediacy with which the earlier histories of a physically sheltered India, surrounded by its mountains and oceans, were shed. Instead, 'India's position on the cultural map of Asia' came to be vigorously historicised as 'the hub of a wheel with spokes radiating towards Iran and Afghanistan [...] Central Asia, Tibet and China [...] Burma, Siam, Indo-China and Indonesia [...] and Ceylon', in which the ancient routes into the subcontinent were perceived as contributing 'not so much in the formation of Indian civilisation as in the reverse direction, as channels for the diffusion of Buddhism and Buddhist art from India to Central Asia and to China' and of the 'Hindu' religion and culture into Southeast Asia.[21] The archaeological explorations for prehistory enhanced the possibilities of finding a deep antiquity of the trans-Asiatic contributions of the 'Indian culture', which could add to the histories above of 'Greater India'.[22]

In 1950, H.D. Sankalia presented a proposal for the archaeological explorations of the Narmada Valley to the Archaeological Survey quite specifically for rectifying the historical loss of 'Sind and Punjab where the earliest traces of city-civilizations were unearthed'.[23] In asking for support, he drew upon new 'facts' that had been established by his home institution,

---

to be safeguarded by one and all'. 'Prehistoric Work in the Southern Circle from October 1946 to March 1947', File 33/66/48, Document No. 13, Survey Archives.

[20] Chakravarti (1950, p. 14).

[21] Agrawala (1950, p. 197).

[22] Ibid.

[23] Proposal from H.D. Sankalia to N.P. Chakravarti, 29 June 1950, 'In Search of India's Past Cultures: A Scheme of Archaeological Investigations on the Narmada', *Explorations in Narmada Valley*, File No. 19/25/1950, pp. 1–3, Survey Archives.

Deccan College, which revealed that 'early man' had walked upon the banks of Sabarmati, Mahi and Orsang 'more than 2,50,000 years ago'. On the basis of the finds, he suggested that 'a proper idea of the development and evolution of Indian culture' be undertaken through the archaeological explorations of the 'oldest geological' terrain in India. The uses of scientific methods for investigating truisms about the ethos of the Indian tradition, which Sankalia subsequently perfected, and which Sheena Panja has succinctly exposed through her scholarship of the historiography, is well documented in this proposal, which was also Sankalia's first formal archaeological proposal to the government of India. Sankalia began the document by emphasising the importance of Narmada as the 'holiest river of the Indian tradition', which he stated was regarded by some Puranas as 'even more sanctifying than the Ganges', and ended the proposal with the declaration that from all points of view, 'Puranically, geologically and archaeologically (as indicated by surface features), the Narmada valley seems to be an area, where one may seek for the origins of man, his subsequent development through semi-historical times when he became civilised, to the historical period'.[24] The lavish support of the Indian government for the archaeology of 'prehistoric India' throughout the 1950s, which also inspired private contributions towards the aims, can be amply illustrated through Sankalia's own academic career as a pre-historian, which he also established during the same decade.

The 'academic archaeology' of India that was developed from the 1950s also nurtured the cultural politics of regionalism of the new Indian nation.[25] By instructing PhD students to undertake field surveys of their home states, the new university departments of archaeology rapidly 'filled' up the archaeological profile of the new Indian states. The lead in this 'method' was specifically taken up by the Department of Archaeology at Deccan College under Sankalia's command, who himself had been asked to explore the historical landscapes of his home state, Gujarat, by his teachers K. de B. Codrington and F.J. Richards during his doctoral study in London in the 1930s. Following his return to India, he was encouraged to survey the prehistory of the above state by the director general of the Survey, K.N. Dikshit (1937–44), and not of Sind which had been his choice of terrain, for he had hoped to continue

---

[24] Ibid., p. 2. For the scientific scholarship of the archaeology of tradition and belief, which Sankalia perpetuated, see Panja (2002, specifically p. 17) (DOI: 10.1177/025764300201800101).

[25] On this, see Panja (ibid., pp. 5–6).

the explorations of the region, which had been initiated by Nani Gopal Majumdar in 1929.[26] The field 'method' that Sankalia had learnt during his studies in London, and which he prominently perpetuated, was premised upon the benefits of local knowledge, whereby the natives of the states by virtue of their knowledge of the language/s and local terrain were considered the natural interlocutor of the archaeological, and historical topography. The method followed the logic of the recruitment of natives within the field surveys of India by British and European explorers since the eighteenth century, and such uses of 'colonial' field techniques for obtaining knowledge of a nation is one among the many overlapping aspects of the 'colonialist' and 'nationalist' histories of South Asian archaeology. By the early 1960s, Sankalia was able to report that the 'students and staff' of Deccan College

> have so far systematically covered parts of Andhra, Karnataka, Maharashtra, Gujarat, Malwa, Central India, Southern Rajputana and Orissa. Of late, offi-cers of the Department of Archaeology have also been reporting discoveries in some of the areas besides those in the former Central Provinces. [...] The result of these investigations is that the Palaeolithic map of India is being rapidly filled up. One may say, without being contradicted, that the Early Stone Age man roamed at will along the small and large river valleys almost everywhere in India, expect in Assam, Kerala, Sind, Western Rajasthan and probably the Central Gangetic Valley.[27]

Sankalia's monograph, *Prehistory and Proto-history in India and Pakistan* (1962–63), provides a comprehensive view of the rapidness with which the new geography of India, from Kashmir to Tamil Nadu and Bengal to Gujarat, was given a prehistoric ancestry. In this respect, the 'chalcolithic cultures' that were discovered within 'the Gangetic Valley, Rajasthan, Central India, Saurashtra and the Deccan' during the 1950s also allowed professional archaeologists the possibilities of deliberating upon the 'question of the indigenous origin or the diffusion of civilization into India'.[28] Yet, this nation-serving archaeology was able to show remarkable restraints in embellishing an obscurant nationalism. Thus, senior officers of the Survey, such as Chakravarti, and premier Indian archaeologists, such as Sankalia, felt the need to reiterate that although 'the subcontinent is divided today the

---

[26] See Sankalia (1978, p. 40).
[27] Sankalia (1962, pp. 35–36).
[28] Sankalia (1962–63, p. iii).

fact remains that its civilization has been one throughout ages',[29] and that 'one's pride' in the antiquity of one's country can be 'as in Nazi Germany [...] grievously misused'.[30] Their statements provoke us to reflect upon the present-day tug-of-war, which is played by the nationalist archaeologists of India and western archaeologists of Pakistan, by veering towards an India-leaning or Pakistan-leaning topography for locating the 'origins' of all the 'essentials' of a civilisation, beginning with the domestication of staple crops and knowledge of the technologies of metallurgy.[31]

As the preceding chapters have amply demonstrated, the celebration of a nationalist archaeology builds upon many aspects of the historiography that sustained the 'colonial archaeology' of India. The British had highlighted the merits of their archaeological scholarship of India for developing a history of the cultural benefits of their imperialism, and in a manner quite akin to the methods they had adopted, the nationalist archaeologists of India today build upon the value of the archaeological scholarship for shaping a narrative of the historical achievements of a nation. As mentioned in the Introduction Chapter, the latter do so by informing us of the promise of the archaeological scholarship in showing evidence of the reconciliations of the changing ethnic, linguistic and other differences within India throughout history.[32] Such endowments of utility values upon the archaeological scholarship, namely, of presenting a past that enshrines contemporary hopes, ought to home in on the overlaps in methods between the 'colonialist' and 'nationalist' enterprises.

Without doubt, the twenty-first century demands for a nationalist archaeology of India articulate the fears of the impositions of neo-colonialism, which attend to the economic and cultural politics of the new globalisation. Yet, assertions such as 'tensions between the First and the Third World archaeologists would only dissolve if the former concede that it is essentially the business of the Third World archaeologists to seek specific paths of their own in their own countries' ought to be noted with disbelief and dismay.[33] For they enshrine the validity of the authoritarian closure of rights to participate and debate in cultural domains that are not one's own. Such

---

[29] Chakravarti (1950, p. 15).

[30] Sankalia (1964, p. 259).

[31] See Chapter 5. One may note this dispute even with respect to the earlier periods of Indian prehistory. For an example, see Chakrabarti (2006, pp. 477–79).

[32] See also Chakrabarti (2003, p. 279).

[33] Chakrabarti (2012, p. 130).

assertions simply lend to racism 'on the grounds', to quote the social anthropologist Michael Herzfeld 'of preserving authenticity, indigenity, and local heritage'.[34] Considering that dissent and plurality in the nationalist discourse is suppressed with 'bromides about "unity and diversity" and the like', it is indeed remarkable that the nationalist archaeologists of post-colonial South Asia rarely bother to interrogate the model of a nation state which they so ardently defend, as this was a creation of the imperialist West.[35]

Additionally, the reticence of the 'western' archaeologists of South Asia to speak against the creations of archaeological evidence for nationalist histories, which is being fostered quite specifically by members of their own profession, is also confounding. It is tempting to juxtapose the hesitance with another western view that has been harboured by those who attempt to bring clarity within the debates regarding the history of the 'origins' of the Indo-Aryan. They suggest that the intellectual dismissal of the Hindu nationalist histories of the origins of the phenomenon within the Indian subcontinent 'would be equally allowing ideological beliefs to manipulate historical interpretations'.[36] We may dismiss such sentiments of political correctness as expressions of naïvity. But more importantly, we need to interrogate the positivist world views which such statements build upon, and which fail to see the historical ties between objectivity, empirical fundamentalism, and national and imperial politics. In our encounters with the archives of the Archaeology Survey, we are shown many examples of the way in which a positivist and conservative archaeological scholarship enhances the aims of imperialist politics. The following instance creates a regard of the marginalisation of the archaeology of gender within the scholarship of South Asian archaeology, and shows pitfalls of the positivist scholarship nurtured by nationalist archaeologists.

Authority and Positivism

The male-dominated archaeological scholarship of the India of the early-twentieth-century remained disengaged from the emerging presence of

---

[34] Herzfeld (2009, p. 231). See also Herzfeld (2012, p. 54).

[35] The need for the archaeological scholarship to engage with the critique of the western models of nation states has also been raised by Sen (2002).

[36] Bryant (2005, p. 499).

women archaeologists within the Asian fields from the late 1910s. The prominent British examples were Gertrude Bell (1868–1926), who established the British School at Iraq and wielded considerable influence upon the British administration of Iraq, Dorothy Garrod (1892–1968) who excavated the 'Natufian culture' at Mount Carmel, Palestine, and who subsequently became the first woman professor, and remains the only woman Disney professor of Archaeology at the University of Cambridge, and Dorothea Bate (1878–1951), the palaeontologist, who worked with Garrod in Mount Carmel and subsequently went to China with Percy Lowe to study fossil ostrich and pioneer the field of archaeozoology. With respect to the British archaeology of India, the only known woman participant in fieldwork was Wheeler's wife, Margaret (Kim), who was with Wheeler during his first field school at Taxila (1944), and at his excavations at Harappa (1946), where she instructed on draftsmanship. Although if we recall a photograph of Wheeler and her with archaeology students at Chandravalli in 1947, we also see a female student sitting beside her who remains curiously unknown.[37] Notwithstanding the possibility of stray examples, professional women archaeologists of South Asia, whether British or Indian, remain unknown from the colonial period—or rather from the last decade of the colonial period—and in this respect the DGA's archive informs us that appointments as Class I officers in the Survey were specifically declared closed to women in 1941. The 'ineligibility', we are told, was legislated 'due to considerations of administrative work' that included a 'considerable number of touring and fieldwork', which was deemed unsuitable for women because of the 'circumstances in India'. Thus, women, the director general of the Survey proclaimed, could be 'curators, custodians, assistant curators [...] gallery assistants in museums or epigraphic assistants in Epigraphical Branch of the department', but not field explorers. The latter, no doubt, was regarded within the profession as mandatory for a 'proper' archaeologist.

The sexist injunctions cannot be impugned as an example of the colonial policy of cultural relativism. For the Survey, which deemed that 'the risk of having a lady student for training in fieldwork outweighed the advantages',

---

[37] For the photograph, see Guha (2003, p. 48, Plate 3). M.N. Deshpande to whom I had shown the photograph had not been able to name her. Wheeler's first wife Tessa was an accomplished archaeologist in her own right, whose field methods, draftsmanship and scholarship contributed substantively to Wheeler's reputation as a seminal British archaeologist. See Carr (2012).

and found it difficult to say 'when there will be such favourable conditions in this country when ladies can be trained for an archaeological career' was headed by K.N. Dikshit and not a British director general, and was mainly manned by Indians in all senior posts.[38] The censorship appears blatantly ironical considering the strong participation of Indian women during the same period in the independence movement and, thus, literally in the field, which also entailed facing long and arduous marches and violent protests. Yet, despite the discouraging letter from the director general of the Survey, the convenor of the sub-committee of education for the Delhi Provincial Council of Women maintained that she would include archaeology in her pamphlet 'on "professions for women in India" as it may give a "line" to someone', and substantiate her organisation's effort 'to enlarge the scope for women in all kinds of work, with a view to getting them away from the attitude that teaching is the only career, which results in many sad misfits'.[39]

The participation, or not, of women in archaeology has little relevance to the epistemic value of the archaeology of gender, which was developed quite specifically within Britain and North America in the early 1980s. However, the archival encounter creates a reminder of the 'gendered archaeology' that continued to thrive within India during the same period, which many women students of Indian archaeology discovered often unwittingly.[40] In raising the question of why feminist archaeology did not develop within South Asia during the 1980s—co-incidentally the only time when the Archaeological Survey was headed by a woman, namely, Debala Mitra (1975–83)—we are shown the effects of the deep-rooted positivist scholarship, which, as the demands for a nationalist archaeology shows, continues unabated within the archaeological scholarship of India.[41]

[38] Letter from DG ASI, K.N. Dikshit, addressed from New Delhi, to Mrs M. Wood Robinson in Simla, dated 1 August 1941. File 'Delhi Provincial Women's Council—Request for Supply of Information on Archaeology', No. 31/8/41, Survey Archives.

[39] Letter from Robinson to Dikshit, 28 August 1941, Ibid.

[40] Examples could be from my own studies in archaeology at Deccan College between 1983 and 1989.

[41] The reference here to the Survey's leadership is of the period when archaeologists headed the organisation. Since the late 1990s the Survey has seen a few women directors general, who are all civil servants. The growing enquiries within the archaeological scholarship into representations of women, has largely involved searching for data of the activities that were undertaken by women. They do not represent the archaeological scholarship of gender, which questions the methods of data creations. For an example of the positivist orientations of the Indian scholarship, see Ray (2004b).

The 'archaeology of gender', as we now know, has deconstructed positivist objectivity by foregrounding the element of prior knowledge, which archaeologists have habitually brought into their inferences throughout the greater part of the twentieth century. The scholarship has sought to erase the exclusions and representations of inequality from the practices of archaeology, and in this endeavour has also addressed the problems of presentism within the discipline.[42] The non-development of feminist archaeology within South Asia is a stark reminder that a methodologically positivist scholarship systematically fails to confront the various kinds of biases, intellectual and practical, within the modes of analyses it seeks to develop.[43] Therefore, the South Asian archaeological scholarship also averts from engaging with the connected histories of philosophical positivism and intellectual authoritarianism, which are quite well mapped by historians of the eighteenth- and nineteenth-century Europe.[44]

Discipline Making and Exclusions

In returning to the archives of the Archaeological Survey of India, we note the establishment of the Central Advisory Board for Archaeology in 1945 as a significant move of the 'Old Survey' towards the future administration of Indian archaeology. The Board, however, was established as a reconciliatory measure to appease some of the recommendations for Indian archaeology that had been made by Leonard Woolley in 1939. Woolley, as is quite well known, had rather harshly assessed the practices of the Survey, and had also instructed the Institution to make closer contacts with Indian universities.[45]

---

[42] See Conkey and Spector (1984).

[43] Archaeologists may argue that the women archaeologists of South Asia have failed to bring up the topic, although this would simply add to the stereotypical mores which the subject, feminist archaeology, emphatically rejected. There exists, however, a professional body that dates from 2009, and which represents The International Association of Women Archaeologists working in South Asia.

[44] For example, Sutton (1983).

[45] Woolley's report was unduly offensive in tone and ill-informed on many aspects, and had to be withdrawn very soon after its partial circulation as a 'confidential' document. Wheeler, however, found the report 'a sincere and single-minded appreciation of the situation by an entirely detached observer, and in experience […] accurate in all essentials. In his 'reforms' and 're-adjustments', as the Survey's director general, he declared that he 'had not always followed its

The draft proposal for establishing an Advisory Board, which was drawn in August 1944, was therefore aimed to show that the 'Survey would benefit from contact, criticism and discussion, and the universities, collateral departments in the states, and the general public through their societies would benefit by closer collaboration with it, and so gain an opportunity of appreciating its work and of influencing its policies.'[46] The advisory committee that subsequently met to discuss the functions of the Board consisted of 'representatives of universities, learned societies, the Government and Indian states'. They deemed that the purpose of the Board was 'reviewing and advising the Central Government on the needs of archaeology in India, current and future', and 'to act as an intermediary between the archaeological services, the world of learning and administration, and in some small degree the wider public'.[47] Thus, the hope in the late 1940s was that the Survey would draw 'upon enlightened public opinion', and 'lose something of the remoteness and impersonality' of 'an exclusive government department'.[48] Yet, the immediate criticism, which the institution attracted from the erstwhile physical anthropologist Biraja Shankar Guha for not including any anthropologists among the committee members, informs us of the exclusive methods of discipline creations. Guha, who rightly saw the exclusion of the physical anthropologists as undermining the research of 'prehistoric archaeology' complained:

> During the last 20 years [initiated through excavations at Mohenjodaro] the Anthropological Section of the Zoological Survey of India, Col. Sewell and I, not only reported on the human and animal remains but spent months in the sites in excavating and later on restoring and taking care of bones. While our contributions were duly published in the standard works of the department and full advantage was taken of our assistance and collaborations we were left outside the holy precincts of the counsel![49]

---

leads', but where his 'course had differed it has generally differed along parallel lines'. 'Director General's Report on the Development of the Department 1944–48, Archaeological Survey of India', File E/1/11, Wheeler Archives.

[46] See 'Constitution of an Advisory Board of Archaeology in India', File 28/12/44, Survey Archives.

[47] Ghosh (1953, p. 44).

[48] 'Constitution of an Advisory Board of Archaeology in India', File 28/12/44, Survey Archives.

[49] Letter from B.S. Guha, Zoological Survey of India, to Wheeler at Camp Taxila, dated 6 February 1945, from Kaiser Castle, Benaras Cantonment, 'Advisory Board of Archaeology', File No. 28/1/44 Survey Archives.

Guha had addressed his grievance to Wheeler, then director general of the Survey, who assured him that he would bear the omission in mind, and who also reminded him that even geologists and geographers had been neglected from this first advisory committee, and they too had reasons to seek close associations with the Survey. The reasons for the neglect, Wheeler assured Guha, were because the first priority of the Board was to 'make as many contacts as possible with the public life in India'. For, as Wheeler said, no one feared that the co-operation between archaeologists and professional scientists would suffer in the future, although he and the Government of India were very much aware that the 'co-operation between archaeology and the public has not yet begun'.[50] We note that in enhancing the public profile of the Survey and its archaeological work the committee saw no reasons for questioning the distancing of the contributory subjects that had shaped the creations of archaeological knowledge. This act of promoting the Survey's archaeological work by neglecting to also accommodate the participation of the other disciplines illustrates the endeavour to enhance archaeology's unique disciplinary profile.

The twenty-first-century Survey continues to build its public profile in a similar manner, which provides reasons for recalling Guha's ire. In exhibiting its national value and efforts towards the preservation of India's tangible and intangible heritage, the Survey often sidelines the contributions of other disciplines. The feeling of marginalisation that is frequently expressed by conservation architects at present who work with the Survey, and who feel that they are kept way from major decision-making policies on many aspects of the archaeological preservation of the Indian heritage, creates a resonance of the discord between the architects and indologists within the Survey that was headed by John Marshall.[51] Thus, the practices of the colonial Survey keep filtering into the practices of the national Archaeological Survey of India in curiously tangential ways.

The correspondence between Guha and Wheeler prominently documents the importance of the physical and natural sciences in the creations of archaeological knowledge. And in noting the imprints of the experimental sciences within the archaeological scholarship, we also notice the exclusion of the introspective social sciences, such as history and social anthropology,

---

[50] Letter from Wheeler to Guha, 11 February 1945, from Taxila, ibid.

[51] The expressions of resentment are informally conveyed, including to me at a conference on Heritage and Archaeology in New Delhi (IIC) in December 2013.

within the methods of establishing archaeological evidence. Therefore, in trying to establish methods for accommodating and sourcing the many different claims upon the past, archaeologists—not of South Asia however—now make considerable efforts towards bridging this historic divide.[52] They unpick at the ontological differences between their creations of the archaeological record and the creations by anthropologists of ethnographic records,[53] and the latter bring the cultural practices of archaeology 'into the range of ethnographic gaze'.[54] The growing intellectual exchange between archaeologists and social anthropologists attends to the truism of 'ephemeral evidence', which is worth noting as the negotiations and concerns towards the epistemology of evidence are conspicuously absent within the practices and scholarship of South Asian archaeology. Instead, those who aim at fostering an 'archaeology of the grass roots' for India remain disengaged with new theoretical orientations within social anthropology, for specifically exploring the notions of 'grass roots' as an object of study. It is perhaps circumspect to emphasise here that the intellectual negotiations between archaeologists and anthropologists in the world of mutual scholarship are not about the borrowing of techniques for enhancing knowledge of the specific uses of artefacts that are found during fieldwork, and neither for the undertaking of 'ethnoarchaeology'. Such borrowings, which bespoke of the positivist archaeology of the New Archaeologists, continue unabated within South Asian archaeology to date.

Plurality and Inclusion

The scholarship of archaeology in South Asia remains quite fixated upon making discoveries in the field. Yet, curiously, it shows a remarkable neglect towards the methodologies for eliciting 'multivocality' and undertaking 'public archaeology', both of which have been brought into prominence by archaeologists elsewhere through their field experiences.[55] The neglect has

---

[52] For example, chapters in Okamura and Matsuda (2011).
[53] McFayden (2010, pp. 49–50); Lucas (2010, p. 36).
[54] Edgeworth (2010, p. 64).
[55] The notion of multivocality has been given a theoretical framework through the practices at the excavations at Catal Huyuk (Turkey), and the impetus for public archaeology in the

no bearing upon the increasing public involvement in the archaeological projects within the region, of which there are many examples from India.[56] Rather, my references of the disengagement is to the perceptible absence of empirically grounded case studies of the kinds of conflicts that we may anticipate in the creations of archaeological policies that aim towards accommodating the various perceptions and claims of cultural heritage.

A basic methodological attention towards plurality would demand: (a) negotiating the fault lines of nationalist and statist constructs of secular and sectarian cultural representations, (b) anticipating that different communitarian groups seek different material representations of the past for 'fixing' historical truths about their unique identities in the present, and (c) the ability to confront the conflicts of 'multivocality' with intelligence. In this respect, a group of archaeologists in Bangladesh have presented a robust critique of some of the homogenising practices of heritage archaeology, which in the aspirations towards the preservation and curation of a modern secular public culture erases the histories and realities of communal and class conflicts, and ideological dissent.[57]

With respect to the methods for representing the plural pasts through the archaeological scholarship of India, perhaps the relevant question to ask is the extent to which the curatorial authority of the Archaeological Survey of India should be eroded. For, the merits of the Survey's authorial voice is quite evident with respect to some of the enlightened measures the Organisation has historically adopted, such as the provisions of the Antiquities Act (1947), The Ancient Monuments and Archaeological Sites and Remains Act of 1958 and The Ancient Monuments and Archaeological Sites and Remains Rules of 1959. Considering that archaeological activities within India are governed by the amended versions of the above,[58] the Survey's power also remains quite unaffected despite the decline of its moral credentials in protecting the past following its participation in the demolition of the Babri Masjid in 1992. The policing powers, which the Survey accrues through permissions for excavations and controlling the movements of antiquities

---

UK initially grew from the campaigns of the 'Viking Dublin' during the late 1970s–80s. Two early references for the two practices are Hodder (1997) and Schadla-Hall (1999), respectively.

[56] For example, Selvakumar (2006) (DOI: 10.1080/14736480600939256); Hole (2013).

[57] Sen *et al.* (2006).

[58] Namely, the Ancient Monuments and Archaeological Sites and Remains Act (Amendment and Validation) of 2010. All archaeological activities within India are controlled by this act, and for its authoritarian reach, see Panja (2002, p. 4); Varma (2010, p. 4).

from *in situ* conditions are much needed, and the academic support of the Survey's policies no doubt would include the understanding that the gap between 'compelling historical representation and entertainment is steadily narrowing as heritage has become increasingly tied to substantive investment and economic concerns'.[59] However, the different demands of the different claims to the past, which are of national, regional, ethnic, religious and many other kinds, create the urgency for a careful scrutiny by professional archaeologists of the administrative measures and practices of heritage, that are adopted by the Survey.

The aims towards establishing methods for a pluralist archaeology that can build upon the understanding that evidence is never absolute, does not entail regaling in 'fads' or 'hyper-relativism', which concerned Trigger. The demanding nature of the aims have been aptly summed up by Alison Wylie in her emphasis that:

> the endorsement of epistemic pluralism [...] requires several additional premises: for example, that strict incommensurability holds between competing claims about the cultural past; that the principles invoked to justify these claims are self-warranting [...] that the content of specific historical/archaeological claims, including evidential claims is determined (wholly and comprehensively) by context-specific interests.[60]

Thus, in attending to the possibilities of sourcing the pasts through archaeological practices, which are also capable of expressing multivocality, we engage with the empirical strengths of archaeology *while* attending to the many notions of valid evidence. Inevitably, the negotiations would demand that the decisions to excavate, conserve or/and commemorate ancient sites and buildings are undertaken through consensus with the inhabitants of the terrain, and therefore also, the dismissal of the unequal intellectual transactions of the ethno-archaeological practices, which are premised upon 'fact collections' from 'informants'. Aditionally, the attention to plurality requires methods of acquiring through the archaeological data we glean, the changing histories of the local understanding of historical terrains,[61] which could

[59] Silberman (2008, p. 141).
[60] Wylie (2008, p. 203).
[61] An example would be the argument developed by Kathleen Morrison for the archaeological representations and evaluations of landscapes by noting relationships within the life histories of the features and structures that are built at different times, but which sit side by side. See Morrison (2009).

inform us of the shifts and transformations in the ways in which evidence is constituted through time. Thus, we need to address methodological issues for establishing archaeological representations of the many meanings and consumptions of a specific phenomenon at a certain point of time and also over a considerable period. A promising attempt would be to map the changing notions of cultural heritage in a specific place over time, and in this respect, the vast literary corpus of pre-colonial India, which informs us of changing historical consciousness within and between societies, may allow us to conceptualise new methodologies of field enquiries for configuring the changing epistemologies of evidence.

In concluding this book, I would emphasise that our evaluations of historiographies and histories of archaeologies add to the possibilities of the linkages between texts and field enquiries in souring material evidence of a changing society. They enhance our awareness of the many ways in which we refashion the past, and in this they add to the reasons for engaging with the constructs of archaeological knowledge and evidence as artefacts of history.

Bibliography

Abraham, S.A., Gullapalli, P., Raczek, T.P. and Rizvi, U. 2013. 'Connections and Complexity: New Approaches to the Archaeology of South Asia', in S.A. Abraham, P. Gullapalli, T.P. Raczek and U. Rizvi (Eds), *Connections and Complexity: New Approaches to the Archaeology of South Asia*, pp. 15–36. Walnut Creel California: Left Coast Press.

Agrawala, V.S. 1950. 'Greater India', *Archaeology in India*, pp. 197–208. Bureau of Education, India, Publication No. 66; Delhi: Bureau of Education (Ministry of Education, Govt. of India).

Alam, M. 2003. 'The Culture and Politics of Persian in Precolonial Hindustan', in S. Pollock (Ed.), *Literary Cultures in History: Reconstructions From South Asia*, pp. 131–98. Berkley: University of California Press.

———. 2004. *The Languages of Political Islam in India, c. 1200–1800*. New Delhi: Permanent Black.

Ali, D. 2000. 'Royal Eulogy as World History; Rethinking Copper-Plate Inscriptions in Cola India', in R. Inden, J. Walters and D. Ali (Eds), *Querying the Medieval: Texts and the History of Practices in South Asia*, pp. 165–229. Oxford: Oxford University Press.

Allbut, J. 1835. *Elements of Useful Knowledge in Geography, Astronomy and Other Sciences; Compiled for Young Persons*, 15th edition (much enlarged and improved). London: Jackson and Walford.

Allchin, B. and Allchin, F.R. 1982. *The Rise of Civilization in India and Pakistan*. Cambridge: Cambridge University Press.

Anquetil, L.P., Rollin, C., Prinsep, J. and Pearson, J.D. 1830. *An Epitome of Ancient History Containing a Concise Account of the Egyptians, Assyrians, Persians, Grecians and Romans; Prachin Itihasa Samuchhai*. Calcutta: Calcutta Book Society Press.

Appiah, K.A. 2006. *Cosmopolitanism: Ethics in a World of Strangers*. New York: W.W. Norton.

Asher, C.B. and Talbot, C. 2006. *India Before Europe*. Cambridge: Cambridge University Press.

Atalay, S. 2006. 'Indigenous Archaeology as Decolonizing Practice', *The American Indian Quarterly*, 30(3–4): 280–310.

Badger, G.P. 1847. 'The Mound of Nimrood', Correspondence Section, *The Bombay Times and Journal of Commerce*, 24 February 1847, p. 151.

Bhan, K.K., Vidale, M. and Kenoyer, J.M. 1994. 'Harappan Technology: Theoretical and Methodological Issues', *Man and Environment*, 19(1–2): 141–57.

Bhandarkar, D.R. 1981. 'Allahabad Stone Pillar Inscription of Samudragupta', in B. Chhabra and G.S. Gai (Eds), *Corpus Inscriptionum Indicarum*, pp. 203–19, Vol. (Inscriptions of the Gupta Kings', revised by Bhandarkar). New Delhi: Archaeological Survey of India.

Bhandarkar, R.G. 1887. *Report of the Search for Sanskrit MSS in the Bombay Presidency 1882–83*, Bombay: Bombay Govt. Central Press.

———. 1889. 'My Visit to the Vienna Congress', *Journal of the Bombay Branch of the Royal Asiatic Society*, 17(1887–89), Part I, No. 46: 72–96.

Binford, L.R. 1962. 'Archaeology as Anthropology', *American Antiquity*, 28: 217–25.

———. 1965. 'Archaeological Systematics and the Study of Culture Process', *American Antiquity*, 31 (2), Part I: 203–10.

———. 1968. 'Some Comments on Historical Versus Processsual Archaeology', *Southwestern Journal of Archaeology*, 24(3): 267–75.

Bird, J. 1844. 'Hamaiyaric Inscriptions, From Aden and Saba, Translated in English; with Observations on the Establishment of Christian faith in Arabia', *Journal of the Bombay Branch of the Royal Asiatic Society*, 8 (October): 30–39.

Birdwood, G. 1859. 'The Annual Report of the Bombay Government Central Museum for the Year Ending 30th April 1859', *The Bombay Times and Journal of Commerce*, 25 June 1859, p. 406.

———. 1864. *Report on the Government Central Museum and on the Agricultural and Horticultural Society of Western India for 1863*, Bombay.

Bisht, R.S. 1991. 'Dholavira: New Horizons of the Indus Civilization', *Puratattva*, 20: 71–82.

Boer, W. Den. 1968. 'Graeco-Roman Historiography in Its Relation to Biblical and Modern Thinking', *History and Theory*, 7(1): 60–75.

Bohrer, F.N. 2003. *Orientalism and Visual Culture: Imagining Mesopotamia in Nineteenth-Century Europe*. Cambridge: Cambridge University Press.

Boivin, N.2007. 'Anthropological, Historical, Archaeological and Genetic Perspectives on the Origins of Caste in South Asia', in M.D. Petraglia and B. Allchin (Eds), *The Evolution and History of Human Populations in South Asia: Interdisciplinary Studies in Archaeology, Biological Anthropology, Linguistics and Genetics*, pp. 341–61. The Netherlands: Springer.

Braidwood, R.J. 1957. 'Jericho and its Setting in Near Eastern History', *Antiquity*, 31(122): 73–80.

Briggs, C.S. 2011. 'Some Notable British Excavations Before 1900', in J. Schofield, J. Carman and P. Belford (Eds), *Archaeological Practice in Great Britain*, pp. 12–24. New York/ Dordrecht/Heidelberg/London: Springer.

Brusius, M. 2012. 'Misfit Objects: Layard's Excavations in Ancient Mesopotamia and the Biblical Imagination in Mid-Nineteenth Century Britain', *Journal of Literature and Science*, 5: 38–52.

Bryant, E.F. 2005. 'Concluding Remarks', in E.F. Bryant and L.L. Patton (Eds), *The Indo-Aryan Controversy: Evidence and Inference in Indian History*, pp. 468–506. London/New York: Routledge.

Bühler, G. 1877. 'Detailed Report of a Tour in Search of Sanskrit MSS Made in Kasmir, Rajputana and Central India', *Journal of the Bombay Branch of the Royal Asiatic Society*, Extra Number.

———. 1888. 'Pandit Bhagvanlal Indraji', *The Indian Antiquary*, 17, October: 292–7.

———. 1892.'Asoka's Twelfth Rock-Edict According to the Shahbazgarhi Version', *Epigraphia Indica*, 1: 16–19.

———. 1894. 'Specimens of Jaina Sculptures from Mathura', *Epigraphia Indica* (New Imperial Series), 14(2): 311–23.

———. 1895. 'Some Notes on Past and Future Archaeological Explorations in India', *Journal of the Royal Asiatic Society of Great Britain and Ireland*, 649–60.

Bühler, G. 1898. 'On the Origin of the Indian Brahma Alphabet', *Indian Studies*, Vol. 3, 2nd edition. Strassburg.

Burgess, J. [Anon]. 1872. 'Prefatory', *The Indian Antiquary: A Journal of Oriental Research*, 1, January 5: 1–2.

Burgess, J. [Anon]. 1905. 'Sketch of Archaeological Research in India During Half a Century', *Journal of the Bombay Branch of the Royal Asiatic Society*, Extra Number: 131–48

Campbell, L. 2006. 'Why Sir William Jones Got it All Wrong, or Jones' Role in how to Establish Language Families', *Anuario del Seminario de Filología Vasca*, 40: 245–64.

Carr, L.C. 2012. *Tessa Verney Wheeler: Women and Archaeology Before World War Two.* Oxford: Oxford University Press.

Carter, H.J. 1852. 'Memoir on the Geology of the South East Coast of Arabia,' *Journal of the Bombay Branch of the Royal Asiatic Society,* 4(15), (January): 21–96.

Certeau, M. de, 1988 [1975]. *L'Écriture de l'histoire* (Trans. T, Conley, *The Writing of History*). New York: Columbia University Press.

Chadda, A. 2011. 'Conjuring a River, Imagining Civilization: Saraswati, Archaeology and Science in India', *Contributions to Indian Sociology*, 45(1): 55–83.

Chakrabarti, D.K. 1981. 'Indian Archaeology: The First Phase, 1784–1861', in G. Daniel (Ed.), *Towards a History of Archaeology*, pp. 169–185. London: Thames and Hudson.

———. 1988. *A History of Indian Archaeology From the Beginning to 1947.* New Delhi: Munshiram Manoharlal.

———. 1997. *Colonial Indology: Sociopolitics of the Ancient Indian Past.* New Delhi: Munshiram Manoharlal.

———. 2003. *Archaeology in the Third World: A History of Indian Archaeology Since 1947.* New Delhi: D.K. Printworld.

———. 2006. *The Oxford Companion to Indian Archaeology: The Archaeological Foundations of Ancient India, Stone Age to AD 13 Century.* New Delhi: Oxford University Press.

———. 2009. *India an Archaeological History: Palaeololithic Beginnings to Early Historic Foundations*, 2nd edition. New Delhi: Oxford University Press.

———. 2012. 'Archaeology and Politics in the Third World, With Special Reference to India', in R. Skeates, C. McDavid and J. Carman (Eds), *The Oxford Handbook to Public Archaeology*, pp. 116–32. Oxford: Oxford University Press.

Chakrabarti, D.K. and Saini, S. 2009. *The Problem of Saraswati River and Notes on the Archaeological Geography of Haryana and Indian Punjab.* New Delhi: Aryan Books International

Chakravarti, N.P. 1950. 'The Story of Indian Archaeology', *Archaeology in India*, pp. 1–15. Bureau of Education, India, Publication No. 66; Delhi: Manager of Publications.

Chambers, R. 1798. 'A Discourse Delivered at a Meeting of the Asiatick Society on the 18th of January', *Asiatick Researches*, 6: 1–5.

Chambers, W. 1788. 'Some Account of the Sculptures and Ruins at Mavalipuram, a Place a Few Miles North of Sadras, and Known to Seamen by the Name of the Seven Pagodas', *Asiatick Researches*, 1: 145–70.

Chanda, R.P. 1926. 'The Indus Valley in the Vedic Period', *Memoirs of the Archaeological Survey of India*, Vol. 31: Calcutta: Government of India Press.

———. 1929. 'Survival of the Prehistoric Civilization of the Indus Valley', *Memoirs of the Archaeological Survey of India*, Vol. 41. Calcutta: Govt. of India Press.

Chatterjee, K. 2009. *The Cultures of History in Early Modern India: Persianization and Mughal Culture in Bengal.* New Delhi: Oxford University Press.

Chattopadhyaya, B.D. 1975–76. 'Indian Archaeology and the Epic Traditions', *Puratattva*, 8: 67–72.

———. 1998. *Representing the Other? Sanskrit Sources and the Muslims.* Delhi: Manohar.

Chattopadhyaya, B.D. 2002. 'Introduction', in D.D. Kosambi, *Combined Methods in Indology and Other Writings* (complied, edited and introduced by Chattopadhyaya), pp. xiii–xxxvii. New Delhi: Oxford University Press.

———. 2003. 'Cultural Plurality, Contending Memories and Concerns of Comparative History: Historiography and Pedagogy in Contemporary India', in B.D. Chattopadhyaya (Ed.), *Studying Early India: Archaeology, Texts and Historical Issues*, pp. 263–77. New Delhi: Permanent Black.

Chen, K. 2010. *Asia as Method: Toward Deimperialization*. Durham: Duke University Press.

Childe, V.G. 1925. *The Dawn of European Civilization*. London/New York: Kegan Paul, Trench, Trubner& Co.

———. 1926. *The Aryans: New Light on Indo-European Origin*. London/New York: Kegan Paul, Trench, Trubner& Co./Alfred A. Knopf.

———. 1928. *The Most Ancient East: Oriental Prelude to European Prehistory*. London: Kegan Paul, Trench, Trubner& Co.

———. 1929. *The Danube in Prehistory*. Oxford: Clarendon Press.

———. 1934. *New Light on the Most Ancient East: The Oriental Prelude to European Prehistory*. London: Kegan Paul, Trench, Trubner& Co.

———. 1937. 'The Indus Civilization', *Antiquity*, 11(43): 351.

———. 1942. 'Ceramic Art in Early Iran, *Antiquity*, 16(64): 353–8.

———. 1944. 'Archaeological Ages as Technological Stages', *Journal of the Royal Anthropological Institute*, 77: 7–24.

———. 1950. 'The Urban Revolution', *Town Planning Review*, 21: 3–17.

———. 1956. *Piecing Together the Past*. London: Routledge and Kegan Paul.

———. 1957. 'Civilization, Cities and Towns', *Antiquity*, 31(121): 36–38.

Clarke, D.L. 1968. *Analytical Archaeology*. London: Methuen.

———. 1973. 'Archaeology: The Loss of Innocence', *Antiquity*, 47(185): 6–18.

Coles, J. 2010. 'Grahame Clark–A Personal Perspective', in A. Marciniak and J. Coles (Eds), *Grahame Clark and His Legacy*, pp. 3–27. Cambridge: Cambridge Scholars Publishing.

Conkey, M.W. and Spector, J.D. 1984. 'Archaeology and the Study of Gender', in M. Shiffer (Ed.), *Advances in Archaeological Method and Theory*, Vol. 7, pp. 1–38. New York/London: Academic Press.

Conley, T. 1988. 'Translator's Introduction: For a Literary Historiography', *The Writing of History* [English translation of Certau, M., de, 1975, *L'Écriture de l'histoire*], pp. vii–xxiv. New York: Columbia University Press.

Cox, W. (Ed.). 2013. 'Kalhana's Rajatarangini and Its Inheritors', Special Issue of *The Indian Economic and Social History Review*, No. 50 (2), April.

Cunningham, A. (under the pseudonym 'Archaeologist'). 1848a. 'A Few Remarks on the Bearing of Archaeological Study and Its Application', *Benaras Magazine*, December, pp. 91–102.

———. 1848b. 'Proposed Archaeological Investigation', *Journal of the Royal Asiatic Society of Bengal*, 17: 535–6.

———. 1854. *The Bhilsa Topes, or, Buddhist Monuments of Central India: Comprising a Brief Historical Sketch of the Rise, Progress, and Decline of Buddhism; With an Account of the Opening and Examination of the Various Groups of Topes around Bhilsa*: London: Smith Elder.

———. 1864. 'Report of the Proceedings of the Archaeological Surveyor to the Government for the Season of 1862–63 (Received 16 April 1864)', *Journal of the Royal Asiatic Society of Bengal*, Supplementary Number: 1–lxxxvii.

Cunningham, A. 1865. 'Report of the Proceedings of the Archaeological Surveyor to the Government for the Season of 1862–63 (Received 3 February 1865)', *Journal of the Royal Asiatic Society of Bengal*, 34, Part 4: 195–287.

———. 1871a. 'Introduction', *Four Reports Made During the Years 1862–63–64–65*, Vol. I, pp. i–xliii. Simla: Govt. Central Press.

———. 1871b. 'Section XXV. Banaras, Sarnath', *Four Reports Made During the Years 1862–63–64–65*, Vol. 1, pp. 103–30. Simla: Govt. Central Press.

Cuno, J. 2008. *Who Owns Antiquity? Museums and Battle Over Our Ancient Heritage*. Princeton: Princeton University Press.

Dales, G. 1964. 'The Mythical Massacre at Mohenjodaro', *Expedition*, 6(3): 36–43.

———. 1966. 'The Decline of the Harappans', *Scientific American*, 241(5): 92–100.

Dani, A.H. 1966. 'Prehistoric Pakistan', in D. Sen and A.K. Ghosh (Eds), *Studies in Prehistory: Robert Bruce Foote Memorial Volume*, pp. 71–75. Calcutta: Firma K.L. Mukhopadhyay.

Daniel, G. 1950. *A Hundred Years of Archaeology*. London: Gerald Duckworth.

———. 1975. *150 Years of Archaeology*. London: Gerald Duckworth.

Deshpande, M. 2001. 'Pandit and Professor', in A. Michaels (Ed.), *The Pandit: Traditional Scholarship in India*, pp. 119–54. New Delhi: Manohar.

De Terra, H. and Paterson, T.T. (Eds). 1939. *Studies On the Ice Age in India and Associated Human Cultures*. Washington D.C.: Carnegie Institution.

Dharamsey, V.K. 2004. 'Bhagvanlal Indraji and the Beginnings of Indian Archaeology, in H.P. Ray and C. Sinopoli (Eds), *Archaeology in Early South Asia*, pp. 80–97. New Delhi: Indian Council for Historical Research/Aryan Books International.

Dunkins, A.J. (Ed.). 1844. *Report of the Transactions and Excursions of the British Archaeological Association at their First Congress. Canterbury*, London: John Russell Smith.

Dutt, R.C. 1889. *A History of Civilization in Ancient India: Based on Sanscrit Literature, Vedic and Epic Ages*, Vol. 1. London: Trubner and Co, Calcutta: Thacker, Spink and Co.

Dutta, S. 2009. 'Artefacts and Antiquities in Bengal: Some perspectives Within an Emerging Non-Official Archaeological Sphere', in U. Singh and N. Lahiri (Eds), *Ancient India: New Research*, pp. 11–38. New Delhi, Oxford University Press.

Dyson, R.H. 1993. 'Paradigm Changes in the Study of the Indus Civilization', in G.L. Possehl (Ed.), *Harappan Civilization: A Recent Perspective* (Second Revised Edition), pp. 571–81. New Delhi/Calcutta/Bombay: American Institute of Advance Studies and Oxford IBH Publishing Co. Ltd [first edition 1982].

Edgeworth, M. 2010. 'On the Boundary: New Perspectives from Ethnography of Archaeology', in D. Garrow and T. Yarrow (Eds), *Archaeology and Anthropology: Understanding Similarity, Exploring Difference*, pp. 53–68. Oxford: Oxbow Books.

Eltsov, P. 2008. *From Harappa to Hastinapura: A study of the Earliest South Asian City and Civilization*. Boston/Leiden: Brill.

Errington, E. 2007. 'Exploring Gandhara', E. Errington and V.S. Curtis (Eds), *From Persepolis to the Punjab*, pp. 211–226. London: British Museum Press.

Errington, E. and Curtis, V.S. 2007. 'The Explorers and Collectors', in E. Errington and Curtis, V.S. (Eds), 2007, *From Persepolis to the Punjab: Exploring Ancient Iran, Afghanistan and Pakistan*, pp. 3–16. London: British Museum Press.

Evans, C. and Murray T. 2008. 'Introduction: Writing Histories of Archaeology', in C. Evans and T. Murray (Eds), *Histories of Archaeology*, pp. 1–12. Oxford: Oxford University Press.

Ewen, J. 1886. *Benares: A Handbook for Visitors*. Calcutta: Baptist Missionary Press.

Fagan, B.M. 2007. *Return to Babylon: Travelers, Archaeologists and Monuments in Mesopotamia*. Boulder: University of Colorado Press.

Fairservis, W.A. Jr. 1967. 'The Origin, Character and Decline of an Early Civilization', *American Museum Novitates*, 2302, October 20: 1–48.

———. 1971. *The Roots of Ancient India: The Archaeology of Early Indian Civilization.* London: Allen and Unwin.

Falk, H. 2006, *Asokan Sites and Artefacts: A Source-Book with Bibliography.* Mainzam Rhein: Verlag Philipp Von Zabern.

Fentress, M.A. 1984. 'The Indus "Granaries": Illusion, Imagination and Archaeological Reconstruction', in K.A.R. Kennedy and G.L. Possehl (Eds), *Studies in the Archaeology and Palaeoanthropology of South Asia*, pp. 89–97. New Delhi: Oxford and IBH Publishing.

Fergusson, J. 1846. 'On the Rock-Cut Temples of India', (Read 5 December 1843), *Journal of the Royal Asiatic Society of Great Britain and Ireland*, 8: 30–92.

———. 1847. *An Essay on the Ancient Topography of Jerusalem.* London: John Weale.

———. 1848. *Picturesque Illustration of Ancient Architecture in Hindoostan.* London: J. Hogarth.

———. 1849. *An Historical Enquiry into the Principles of Beauty in Art, More specifically with Reference to Architecture.* London: Longman, Brown, Green and Longmans.

———. 1851. *The Palaces of Nineveh and Persepolis Restored: An Essay on Ancient Assyrian and Persian Architecture.* London: John Murray.

———. 1880. 'Preface', in J. Fergusson and J. Burgess (Eds), *The Cave Temples of India*, pp. xiii–xx. London: W.H. Allen & Co.

———. 1884. *Archaeology in India with Especial Reference to the Works of Babu Rajendralala Mitra.* London: Trbüner and Co.

Flannery. K.V. 1994. 'Childe the Evolutionist', in D. Harris (Ed.), *The Archaeology of Gordon Childe: Contemporary Perspectives*, pp. 101–19. London: UCL Press.

Fleet. J.F. 1888. 'Junagadh Rock Inscription of Skandagupta—The years 136, 137 and 138', Inscriptions of the Early Gupta Kings and Their Successors, *Corpus Inscriptionum Indicarum*, Vol. 3. Calcutta: Supt. Govt. Printing

———. 1917. 'James Burgess, C.I.E, LL.D.', *The Indian Antiquary*, 46, January: 1–4.

Flood, F.B. 2003. 'Pillars, Palimpsests, and Princely Practices: Translating the past in Sultanate Delhi', *Res: Anthropology and Aesthetics*, 43(Spring): 95–116.

Foote, R.B. 1916. *The Foote Collection of Indian Prehistoric and Protohistoric Antiquities: Notes on their Ages and Distribution.* Madras: Madras Govt. Museum, Supt. Govt. Press.

Friedman, J. and Rowlands, M.J. 1978. 'Notes Towards an Epigenetic Model of the Evolution of "Civilisation"', in J. Friedman and M.J. Rowlands (Eds), *The Evolution of Social Systems*, pp. 201–76. London, Duckworth.

Fromherz, A.J. 2010. *Ibn Khaldun, Life and Times.* Edinburgh: Edinburgh University Press.

Gaur, R.C. 1983. *Excavations at Atranjikhera: Early Civilization of the Upper Ganga Basin.* Delhi/Centre of Advanced Study, Aligarh University: Motilal Banarsidas.

Ghosh, A. 1952. 'The Rajputana Desert–Its Archaeological Aspect', *Bulletin of National Institute of Sciences of India*, 1: 37–42.

———. 1953.'Exploration in Bikaner, India', Miscellanea, *Asiatica Occidentalis*, 18: 108–15.

———. 1953. 'Fifty Years of the Archaeological Survey of India', *Ancient India*, 9, Special Jubilee: 29–52.

———. 1975–76. 'At Random', *Purattatva*, 8: 123–5.

Goody, J. 2009. *Renaissances: The One or the Many.* Cambridge: Cambridge University Press.

Gough, R. (Anon.). 1770. 'Introduction: Containing an Historical Account of the Origin and Establishment of the Society of Antiquaries', *Archaeologia*, 1: i–xxxix.

Green, S. 1981. *Prehistorian: A Biography of V. Gordon Childe.* Bradford-on-Avon: Moonraker Press.

Grierson, G.A. 1919. 'August Frederick Rudolph Hoernle', *Journal of the Royal Asiatic Society of Great Britain and Ireland*, January: 114–24.

Guha, S. 2003. 'Mortimer Wheeler's Archaeology in South Asia and Its Photographic Presentation', *South Asian Studies*, 19(1): 43–55.

———. 2007. 'Book Review [*The Indo-Aryan Controversy: Evidence and Inference in Indian History*, E.F. Bryant and L.L. Patton (Eds)], *Journal of the Royal Asiatic Society of Great Britain and Ireland*, 17, Part 3: 340–43.

———. 2010. 'Photographs in Sir John Marshall's Archaeology', in S. Guha (Ed.), *The Marshall Albums: Photography and Archaeology*, pp. 137–77. Ahmedabad: Mapin and Alkazi Collection of Photography.

———. 2012. 'Material Truths and Religious Identities', in M.S. Dodson (Ed.), *Banaras: Urban Forms and Cultural Histories*, pp. 42–76. London/New York: Routledge.

———. 2014. South Asian Heritage and Archaeological Practices, in C. Sandis (Ed.), *Cultural Heritage Ethics: Between Theory and Practice*, pp. 103–16. Cambridge: Open Book Publishers.

Guha-Thakura, T. 2004. *Monuments, Objects, Histories: Institutions of Art in Colonial and Postcolonial India*. New York: Columbia University Press.

Gupta, N. 2000. 'From Architecture to Archaeology', in J. Malik (Ed.), *Perspectives of Mutual Encounters in South Asian History 1760–1860*, pp. 49–64. Leiden: Brill.

Gupta, S.P. 1995. *The 'Lost' Saraswati and the Indus Civilization*. Jodhpur: Kusumanjali Prakashan.

Hall, H.R. 1913. *The Ancient History of the Near East: From the Earliest Time to the Battle of Salamis*. London: Methuen & Co.

Haslam, M., Korisettar, R., Petraglia, M., Smith, T., Shipton, C. and Ditchfield, P. 2010. 'In Foote's Steps: The History, Significance and Recent Archaeological Investigation of the Billa Surgam Caves in Southern India', *South Asia Studies*, 26(1): 1–9.

Haug, M. 1878. 'History of the Researches Into the Sacred Writings and Religion of the Parsis: The European Researches', in M. Haug (Ed.), *Essays on the Sacred Language, Writings and Religion of the Parsis*, 2nd edition (edited by E.W. West), pp. 16–53. London: Trübner & Co.

Heringman, N. 2013. *Sciences of Antiquity: Romantic Antiquarianism, Natural History and Knowledge Work*. Oxford: Oxford University Press.

Herzfeld, M. 2009. *Evicted from Eternity: The Restructuring of Modern Rome*. Chicago: Chicago University Press.

———. 2012. 'Whose Right to Which Past? Archaeologists, Anthropologists, and the Ethics of Heritage in the Global Hierarchy of Value', D. Shankland (Ed.), *Archaeology and Anthropology: Past, Present and Future*, pp. 41–64. London/New York: Berg.

Hill, R. 2010. 'Gentlemen Did not Dig', *London Review of Books*, (Review of Jason Kelly's *The Society of Dilettanti: Archaeology and Identity in the British Enlightenment*), 32(12), 24 June: 25–27.

Hodder, I. 1997. 'Always Momentary, Fluid and Flexible: Towards a Self-Reflexive Excavation Methodology', *Antiquity*, 71: 691–700.

———. 2003. 'Sustainable Time Travel: Toward a Global Politics of the Past', in S. Kane (Ed.), *The Politics of Archaeology and Identity in a Global Context*, pp. 139–48. Boston, MA: Archaeological Institute of America.

Hodder, I. 2012. *Entangled: Archaeology of the Relationships Between Humans and Things*. Chicester: Wiley-Blackwell.

Hodges, W. 1793. *Travels in India, During the Years 1780, 1781, 1782 & 1783*. London: J. Edwards.

Hoernle, A.F.R. 1883. 'Correspondence and Miscellanea: Prof Bhandarkar and the Gatha Dialect', *The Indian Antiquary*, 12, July: 205–6.

———. 1884. 'Archaeology, History, Literature. Etc.', *Centenary Review of the Asiatic Society of Bengal From 1784 to 1883*, Part II, pp. 1–27. Calcutta: Thacker, Spink & Co.

———. 1887. *On the Bakhshali Manuscript*. Vienna: Alfred Holder.

———. 1891. 'On the Date of the Bower Manuscript', *Journal of the Asiatic Society of Bengal*, 60 (2), Part I: 79–96.

———. 1892. Date of the Bower Manuscript, *The Indian Antiquary*, 21 (February): 29–47.

———. 1893. The Weber Manuscript', *Journal of the Asiatic Society of Bengal*, 62(1–4, 1893), Part 1: 1–40.

———. 1904. 'Some Problems of Ancient Indian History: No. II, The Gurjara Empire', *Journal of the Royal Asiatic Society of Great Britain and Ireland*, 639–61.

Hole, B. 2013. 'A Many Cornered Thing: The Role of Heritage in Indian Nation Building', *Journal of Intervention and State Building*, 7(2): 196–222.

Hooks, B. 1995. 'An Aesthetic of Blackness: Strange and Oppositional', *Lenox Avenue: A Journal of Interarts Inquiry*, 1: 65–72.

Hultzch, E. 1925. 'The Girnar Rock', 'Texts and Translations', in 'Inscriptions of Asoka', *Corpus Inscriptionum Indicarum* (New Edition), Vol. I., pp. ix–x, pp. 1–27. Oxford: Clarendon Press, Printed for the Government of India.

Jacobi, H. 1898. 'A note on the facts of Bühler's career', *The Indian Antiquary*, 27: 367–8.

Jarrige, J.F. 1995. 'Introduction', in C. Jarrige, J.F. Jarrige, R.H. Meadow and G. Quivron (Eds), *Mehrgarh Field Reports 1974–1985 From Neolithic Times to the Indus Civilization*, pp. 51–103. Karachi: Government of Sind and French Ministry of Foreign Affairs.

Johansen, P.G. 2003. 'Recasting the Foundations: New Approaches to Regional Understanding of South Asian Archaeology and the Problem of Culture History', *Asian Perspectives*, 42(2) (Autumn): 192–206.

Johnson, M. 2010. *Archaeological Theory: An Introduction*, 2nd edition. Chichester: Wiley-Blackwell.

Jones, F. 1855. 'Topography of Nineveh, Illustrative of the Maps of the Chief Cities of Assyria; and the General Geography of the Country Intermediate Between the Tigris and the Upper Zab', *Journal of the Royal Asiatic Society of Great Britain and Ireland*, 14, Part II: 297–397.

Jones, S. 1997. *The Archaeology of Ethnicity: Constructing identities in the Past and Present*. London/New York: Routledge.

Jones, W. 1788a. 'The Third Anniversary Discourse' (delivered in the Asiatic Society, Calcutta, 24 February 1785), *Asiatick Researches,* 1: 415–35.

———. 1788b. 'A Discourse On the Institution of a Society for Inquiring into the History, Civil and Natural, The Antiquities, Arts, Sciences and Literature', *Asiatick Researches*, 1: ix–xvi.

———. 1798. 'The Tenth Anniversary Discourse, delivered 28 February 1793, On Asiatic History Civil and Natural', *Asiatick Researches*, 4: i–xx.

Jørgensen, J. N. and Juffermans, K. 2011 (November). 'Superdiversity'. http://hdl.handle. net/10993/6656 (accessed on 8 August 2010).

Joshi, M.C. 1975–6. 'Archaeology and Indian Tradition–Some Observations' *Puratattva*, 8: 98–102.

Karkaria, R.P. 1894. 'Assyrian Relics from Nimroud in the Possession of the B.B.R.A.S.', *Journal of the Bombay Branch of the Royal Asiatic Society*, 18: 97–108.

Karmon, D. 2011. 'Archaeology and the Anxiety of Loss: Effacing Preservation from the History of Renaissance Rome', *American Journal of Archaeology*, 115(2): 159–74.

Kaul, S. 2014. '"Seeing" the Past: Text and Questions of History in Rajatarangini', *History and Theory*, 53: 194–211.

Keith, A.B. 1931. 'The Ancient Mesopotamia of India: Town Planning 5000 Years Ago at Mohenjo-Daro', *The Illustrated London News*, 19 December, pp. 1000–4.

Kenoyer, J.M. 1991. The Indus Valley Tradition of Pakistan and West India, *Journal of World Prehistory*, 5(4): 331–85.

———. 1997. 'Early City States in South Asia: Comparing the Harappan Phase and Early Historic Period', in T.H. Charlton and D.L. Nichols (Eds), *The Archaeology of City States: Cross Cultural Approaches*, pp. 51–70. Washington, Smithsonian University press.

———. 2005. 'Culture Change During the Late Harappan Period at Harappa: New Insights on Vedic Aryan Issues', in E.F. Bryant and L.L. Patton (Eds), *The Indo–Aryan Controversy*, pp. 21–49. London/New York: Routledge.

———. 2006a. 'New Perspectives on the Mauryan and Kushana Periods', in P. Olivelle (Ed.), *Between the Empires: Society in India 300 BCE to 400 CE*, pp. 33–46. New York: Oxford University Press.

———. 2006b. Cultures and Societies of the Indus Tradition', in R. Thapar (Ed.), *India: Historical Beginnings and the Concept of the Aryan*, pp. 41–97. New Delhi: National Book Trust of India.

Kenyon, K.M. 1956. 'Jericho and Its Setting in Near Eastern History,' *Antiquity*, 30(120): 184–97.

———. 1957. 'Reply to Professor Braidwood', *Antiquity*, 31(122): 82–84.

———. 1958. 'Earliest Jericho', *Antiquity*, 33(129): 5–9.

Khan, F.A. 1965.'Excavations at KotDiji', *Pakistan Archaeology*, 2: 11–85.

Kielhorn, F. 1894.'Badal Pillar Inscription of the Time of Narayanapala', *Ephigraphia Indica*, 2: 160–67.

———. 1905–06. 'Junagadh Rock Inscription of Rudradaman; The Year 72', *Epigraphia Indica*, 8: 36–49.

Koch, E. 2004. 'The "Moghuleries" of the Millionenzimmer Schönbrunn Palace, Vienna', in R. Crill, S. Stronge and A. Topsfield (Eds), *Arts of Mughal India: Studies in Honour of Robert Skelton*, pp. 152–67. London/Ahmedabad: Victoria and Albert Museum and Mapin.

Konishi, M.A. 1984. 'Pre'-or 'Early' Harappan Culture: A Conceptual Battle', in B.B. Lal and S.P. Gupta (Eds), *Frontiers of the Indus Civilization: Sir Mortimer Wheeler Commemoration Volume*, pp. 37–42. New Delhi: Books and Books.

Konow, S. 1914. 'Review of The Bower Manuscript', *The Indian Antiquary*, 43, August: 179–81.

———. 1929. 'Kharsoshti Inscriptions: With Exception of Those of Asoka', *Corpus Inscriptionum Indicarum*, Vol. 2, Part I. Calcutta: Central Publication Branch.

Kosambi, D.D. 1965. *The Culture and Civilization of Ancient India in Historical Outline*. London: Routledge and Kegan Paul.

Lahiri, N. 2011. 'Alexander the Great', *Hindustan Times*, 11 August.

———. 2013. 'Partitioning the Past: India's Archaeological Heritage After Independence', in G. Scarre and R. Coningham (Eds), *Appropriating the Past: Philosophical Perspectives on the Practice of Archaeology*, pp. 295–311. Cambridge: Cambridge University Press.

Lal, B.B. 1949. 'Explorations and Excavations: The Prehistoric and Protohistoric Period', in H. Kabir (Ed.), *Archaeology in India*, pp. 17–50 (Bureau of Education, India, No. 66). Delhi: Manager of Publications.

———. 1981. 'The Two Indian Epics vis-à-vis Archaeology', *Antiquity*, 55: 27–34.

Lal, B.B. 2000. *The Saraswati Flows on: The Continuity of Indian Culture*. New Delhi: Aryan Books International.

———. 2005. 'Aryan Invasion of India', in E.F. Bryant and L.L. Patton (Eds), *The Indo-Aryan Controversy: Evidence and Inference in Indian History*, pp. 50–74. London/New York: Routledge.

Lal, M. 2014. 'The Saraswati River: Geographical Literature, Archaeology, Ancient Texts and Satellite Images', in D.K. Chakrabarti and M. Lal (Eds), *History of Ancient India, Vol. II: Protohistoric Foundations*, pp. 144–70. New Delhi: Vivekananda International Foundation/ Aryan Books International.

Lamberg-Karlovsky, C.C. 1999. 'The Indus Civilization: The Case for Caste Formation', *Journal of East Asian Archaeology*, 1: 87–113.

———. 2005. 'Archaeology and Language: The Case of the Bronze Age Indo-Iranians', in E.F. Bryant and L.L. Patton (Eds), *The Indo-Aryan Controversy; Evidence and Inference in Indian history*, pp. 142–178. London/New York: Routledge.

———. 2008. 'Forward', in P.A. Elstov, *From Harappa to Hastinapura*, pp. xvii–xxiv. Leiden: Brill.

Layard, A.H. 1849a. *Nineveh and Its Remains: With an Account of a Visit to the Chaldean Christians of Kurdistan, and the Yezdis, or Devil Worshippers; and an Enquiry Into the Manners and Arts of Ancient Assyrians*, Vol. I. London: John Murray.

———. 1849b. *Nineveh and Its Remains: With an Account of a Visit to the Chaldean Christians of Kurdistan, and the Yezdis, or Devil Worshippers; and an Enquiry Into the Manners and Arts of Ancient Assyrians*, Vol. II. London: John Murray.

———. 1849c. *The Monuments of Nineveh, From Drawings Made on the Spot* (Illustrated in 100 Plates). London: John Murray.

Layard, A.H. 1853. *A Second Series of the Monuments of Nineveh: Including Bas Reliefs from the Palace of Sennacherib and Bronzes From the Ruins of Nimroud, From Drawings Made on the Spot During a Second Expedition to Assyria* (71 Plates Executed Between 1849–52). London: John Murray.

Leumann, E. 1898. 'Buhler as a Collector of MSS', *The Indian Antiquary*, 27, December: 368–70.

Levine, P. 1986. *The Amateur and the Professional: Antiquarians, Historians and Archaeologists in Victorian England, 1838–1886*. Cambridge: Cambridge University Press.

Louis, R. Wm. 1999. 'Introduction', in R.W. Winks (Ed.), *Historiography: The Oxford History of the British Empire*, Vol. 5, pp. 1–42. Oxford: Oxford University Press [Reprint 2004].

Lucas, G. 2010. 'Triangulating Absence: Exploring the Fault–Lines Between Archaeology and Anthropology, in D. Garrow and T. Yarrow (Eds), *Archaeology and Anthropology: Understanding Similarity, Exploring Difference*, pp. 28–40. Oxford: Oxbow Books.

Luder, H. 1906. 'Kharosthi Records on Earthen Jars from Charsada', *Annual Report of the Archaeological Survey of India 1903–04*, pp. 289–91. Calcutta: Office of Suptd. Govt. Printing.

Macdonell, A.A. 1906. 'The Study of Sanskrit as an Imperial Question', in 'Miscellaneous Communications', *Journal of the Royal Asiatic Society* (New Series), 38(3), July: 673–89. Also published as 'The Study of Sanskrit as an Imperial Question'. In *Proceedings of the Home Department, A&E*, Nos. 13–14, December, 1906, 302–10.

Mackay, E. 1938. *Further Excavations at Mohenjodaro: Being an Official Account of Archaeological Excavations at Mohenjodaro Carried Out by the Government of India Between the Years 1927 and 1931*. Delhi: Manager of Publications.

Mackenzie, C. 1799. 'Account of the Pagoda at Perwuttum: Extract of a Journal By Captain Colin Mackenzie, Communicated by Major Kirkpatrick', *Asiatick Researches*, 5: 303–14.

Magee, P., Petrie, C., Knox, R., Khan, F. and Thomas, K. 2005. 'The Achaemenid Empire in South Asia and Recent Excavations in Akra in Northwest Pakistan', *American Journal of Archaeology*, 109: 711–41.

Majumdar, R.C. 1952. *Ancient India*. Delhi: Motilal Banarasidass.

Malafouris, L. and Renfrew, C. 2010. 'Introduction', in L. Malafouris and C. Renfrew (Eds), *The Cognitive Life of Things: Recasting the Boundaries of Mind*, pp. 1–12. Oxford: Oxbow Books.

Malet, C.W. 1799. 'To Sir John Shore, Bart' (letter dated 22 December 1794)', *Asiatic Researches*, 6: 382–87.

Malley, S. 2012. *From Archaeology to Spectacle in Victorian Britain: The Case of Assyria 1845–1854*. Farnham, Surrey: Ashgate Publishing Ltd.

Mantena, R.S. 2005. 'Vernacular Futures: Colonial Philology and the Idea of History in Nineteenth Century South India', *The Indian Economic and Social History Review*, 42(4): 513–34.

———. 2012. *The Origins of Modern Historiography in India: Antiquarianism and Philology, 1780–1880*. New York: Palgrave Macmillan.

Marchand, S. 2009. *German Orientalism in the Age of Empire: Religion, Race and Scholarship*. Cambridge: Cambridge University Press.

Markham, S.F. and Hargreaves, H. 1936. *The Museums of India*. London: The Museums Association.

Marshall, J.H. 1904a. 'Buddhist Gold Jewellery', in J.H. Marshall (Ed.). *Annual Reports of the Archaeological Survey of India 1902–03*, pp. 185–94. Calcutta: Superintendent Govt. Printing.

———. 1904b. 'Epigraphy', in J.H. Marshall (Ed.). *Annual Reports of the Archaeological Survey of India 1902–03*, pp. 225–31. Calcutta: Superintendent Govt. Printing.

———. 1904c. 'Introduction', in J.H. Marshall (Ed.). *Annual Reports of the Archaeological Survey of India 1902–03*, pp. 1–13. Calcutta: Superintendent Govt. Printing.

———. 1916. 'Excavations at Taxila', in J.H. Marshall (Ed.). *Annual Report of the Archaeological Survey of India 1912–13*, pp. 1–52. Calcutta: Supt. Govt. Printing.

———. 1926. 'Unveiling the Prehistoric Civilisation of India: Discoveries in Sind, the Punjab and Baluchistan—Cities Older than Abraham', *The Illustrated London News*, March 6, pp. 398–400.

———. 1928. A New Chapter in Archaeology: The Prehistoric Civilisation of India', *The Illustrated London News*, January 14, pp. 42–45, 78 and 80.

———. 1951. *Taxila: An Illustrated Account of Archaeological Excavations*. Cambridge: Cambridge University Press.

———. (Ed.). 1915. *Annual Report of the Archaeological Survey of India 1911–12*. Calcutta: Supt Govt. Printing.

———. (Ed.). 1931. *Mohenjodaro and the Indus Civilization*, Vol. 1. London: Arthur Probsthain.

Marshall, J.H. and Vogel, J. Ph. 1904. 'Excavations at Charsada in the Frontier Province', in J.H. Marshall (Ed.). *Annual Report of the Archaeological Survey of India 1902–03*, pp. 141–184. Calcutta: Govt. Central Press.

Marshman, J.C. 1875. *Abridgement of the History of India: From the Earliest Period to the Present Time*. Edinburgh/London: William Blackwood and Sons.

Mathur, S. 2007. *India by Design: Colonial History and Cultural Display*. Chicago: Chicago University Press.

McFayden, L. 2010. 'Spaces That Were Not Densely Occupied–Questioning Ephemeral', in D. Garrow and T. Yarrow (Eds), *Archaeology and Anthropology: Understanding Similarity, Exploring Difference*, pp. 40–53. Oxford: Oxbow Books.

McGetchin, D.T. 2009. *Indology, Indomania and Orientalism: Ancient India's Rebirth in Modern Germany*. Madison, Teaneck, Fairleigh: Dickinson University Press.

Meadow, R.H. and Kenoyer, J.M. 2008. 'Harappa Excavations 1998–1999: New Evidence for the Development and Manifestation of the Harappan Phenomenon', in E.M. Raven (Ed.), *South Asian Archaeology 1999*, pp. 85–109. Groningen: Egbert Forsten.

Menon, J. 2006. 'Technology and Tradition', in G. Sengupta, S. Roychoudhury and S. Som (Eds), *Past and Present: Ethnoarchaeology in India*, pp. 253–68. New Delhi: Pragati Publications in Collaboration with Centre For Archaeological Studies and Training, Eastern India.

Menon, J. and Varma, S. 2005. 'Defining Tradition: An Archaeological Perspective', in S. Saberwal and S. Varma (Eds), *Traditions in Motion: Religion and Society in History*, pp. 23–49. New Delhi: Oxford University Press.

Mercer, R. 1998. 'Stuart Piggott 1910–1996', *Proceedings of the British Academy*, No. 97, pp. 413–42.

Meskell, L. 2009a. 'Introduction: Cosmopolitan Heritage Ethics', in L. Meskell (Ed.), *Cosmopolitan Archaeologies*, pp. 1–27. Durham, North Carolina: Durham University Press.

———. (Ed.). 2009b. *Cosmopolitan Archaeologies*. Durham, North Carolina: Durham University Press

Misra, V.N. and Mate, M.S. (Eds). 1964. *Indian Prehistory: 1964*. Pune: Deccan College.

Mitra, R.L. 1885. 'History of the Society', *Centenary Review of the Asiatic Society of Bengal: From 1784 to 1883*, Vol. 1. Calcutta: Thacker, Spink and Co.

Mitter, P. 1977. *Much Maligned Monsters: History of European Reactions to Indian Art*. Oxford: Clarendon Press.

Mohl, J. 1850. *Letters of M. Botta on the Discoveries at Nineveh* [Translated from French by C.T.]. London: Brown, Green and Longmans.

Momigliano, A. 1950. 'Ancient History and the Antiquarian', *Journal of the Warburg and Courtauld Institutes*, 13: 285–315.

Mookherji, R.K. 1957. 'Forward', for K.N. Sastri, *New Light on the Indus Civilization*. Delhi: Atma Ram.

Morning, A. 2014. 'And You Thought We Had Moved Beyond All That: Biological Race Returns to the Social Sciences', *Ethnic and Racial Studies Review*, 37(10), September: 1676–86.

Morrison, K. 2009. *Daroji Valley: Landscape, History, Place and the Making of a Dryland Reservoir System*: New Delhi: Manohar.

Mughal, M.R. 1973. 'Present State of Research on the Indus Valley Civilization', in A.N. Khan (Ed.), *Proceedings of the International Symposium on Moenjodaro*, pp. 1–28. Karachi: National Book Foundation.

Mukharji, P.C. 1902. 'Report Made During the Progress of Excavations at Patna', Report No. 1, December 1896, *The Indian Antiquary*, 31: 437–41 and 495–8.

Murray, T. 2007. Rethinking Antiquarianism, *Bulletin of the History of Archaeology*, 17(2): 14–22.

Nair, S.P. 2007. 'Economic Logic Versus Enlightenment Rationality; Evolution of Museum–Zoo–Garden Complex and the Modern Indian city, 1843–1900', in S.J. Knell, S. Macleod and S. Watson (Eds), *Museums Revolution: How Museums Change and are Changed*, pp. 61–70. London/New York: Routledge.

Newton, C. 1851.'On the Study of Archaeology', *Archaeological Journal*, 8: 1–26.

Nicholas, G. 2010. 'Introduction', in G. Nicholas (Ed.), *Being and Becoming Indigenous Archaeologists*, pp. 9–18. Walnut Creek: Left Coast Press.

Oates, J. and Oates, D. 2001. *Nimrud: An Assyrian Imperial City Revealed*. London: British School of Archaeology in Iraq.

Oertel, F.O. 1908a. 'Excavations at Sarnath', in J.H. Marshall (Ed.). *Annual Report of the Archaeological Survey of India 1904–5*, pp. 59–104. Calcutta: Supdt Govt. Press.

———. 1908b. *Buddhist Ruins of Sarnath Near Benares*. Calcutta: Supt. Govt. Press.

Okamura, K. and Matsuda, A. (Eds). 2011, *New Perspectives in Global Public Archaeology*. New York: Springer.

Olsen, B., Shanks, M, Webmoor, T. and Witmore, C. 2012. *Archaeology: The Discipline of Things*. Berkeley/Los Angeles/London: University of California Press.

Osborne, R. 2008. 'Introduction: For Tradition as an Analytical Category', in R. Osborne (Ed.), 'Tradition', *World Archaeology*, Vol. 40(3): 281–94.

Paddayya, K. 2002. 'A Review of Theoretical Perspectives in Indian Archaeology', in S. Settar and R. Korisettar (Eds), *Archaeology and Historiography: History, Theory and Method*, Vol. 4 of the Series 'Indian Archaeology in Retrospect', pp. 117–58. Delhi: Indian History Council and Research/Manohar.

Panja, S. 2002. 'The "Third Space": The Creation of Archaeological Knowledge in Post-Independent India', *Studies in History*, 18, New Series, 1: 1–22.

Patil, D.R. 1963. *The Antiquarian Remains in Bihar*. Patna: K.P. Jayaswal Research Institute.

Pauketat, T.R. 2001. 'A New Tradition in Archaeology', in T.R. Pauketat (Ed.), *The Archaeology of Traditions*, pp. 1–16. Gainesville: Florida University Press.

Pels, P. and Salemink, O. 1999. 'Introduction: Locating Colonial Subjects of Anthropology', in Pels and Salemink (Eds), *Colonial Subjects: Essays on the Practical History of Anthropology*, pp. 1–52. Ann Arbor: University of Michigan.

Peterson, P. 1883. 'Detailed Report of Operations in Search of Sanskrit MSS in the Bombay Circle, August 1882–March 1883', *Journal of the Bombay Branch of the Royal Asiatic Society*, Extra Number.

———. 1899. *Reports 1–6 of operations in Search of Sanskrit Manuscripts in the Bombay Circle, 1882–1898*. Bombay: Bombay Govt. Central Press.

Phillips, M.S. 1996. 'Reconsiderations on History and Antiquarianism: Arnaldo Momigliano and the Historiography of Eighteenth-Century Britain', *Journal of the History of Ideas*, 57(2): 297–316.

Phillips. M.S. 2004. 'What is Tradition When it is not "Invented"? A Historiographical Introduction', in M.S. Phillips and G. Schochet (Eds), *Questions of Tradition*, pp. 3–32. Toronto: University of Toronto Press.

Piggott, J.R. 2004. *Palace of the People: The Crystal Palace at Sydenham 1854–1936*. London: C. Hurst & Co.

Piggott, S. 1945. *Some Ancient Cities of India*. London: Oxford University Press, India Branch.

———. 1946. 'The Chronology of Prehistoric North-West India', *Ancient India*, 1: 8–26.

———. 1950. *Prehistoric India*. Harmondsworth and Middlesex: Penguin.

———. 1958. 'The Dawn: An Epilogue', *Antiquity*, 32(126): 75–79.

———. 1989. *Ancient Britons and the Antiquarian Imagination*. London: Thames and Hudson.

Pinney, C. 2008.*The Coming of Photography in India*. London: British Library.

Plarr, V.G. 1899. *Men and Women of the Time: A Dictionary of Contemporaries*, 15th edition, London: George Routledge and Sons.

Possehl, G.L. 1977. 'The End of a State and Continuity of a Tradition: A Discussion of the Late Harappan', in R. Fox (Ed.), *Realm and Region in Traditional India*, pp. 235–54. New Delhi: Vikas Publishing.

———. 1984. 'Archaeological Terminology and the Harappan Civilization, in B.B. Lal and S.P. Gupta (Eds), *Frontiers of the Indus Civilization*, pp. 27–36. New Delhi: Books & Books.

———. 1999. *Indus Age: The Beginnings*. New Delhi/Calcutta: Oxford & IBH Publishing Co.

———. 2002. *The Indus Civilization: A Contemporary Perspective*. Walnut Creek/Lanham/ New York/Oxford: Alta Mira Press.

Prakash, G. 1999. *Another Reason: Science and the Imagination of Modern India*. Princeton: Princeton University Press.

Preston, W. 1775. 'Account of Opening One of the Largest Barrows on Sanford Moor, Westmoreland' in a Letter Dated Warcop Hall, Sept 5, 1766, to Bishop Lyttleton (Read at the Society of Antiquaries)', *Archaeologia*, 3: 273.

Preucel, R. 1999. 'Gordon Randolph Willey', in T. Murray (Ed.), *Encyclopaedia of Archaeology: The Great Archaeologists*, Vol. 2, pp. 701–12. Santa Barbara/Denver/Oxford: ABC-Clio.

Prickett, S. 2009. *Modernity and the Reinvention of Tradition: Backing into the Future*. Cambridge: Cambridge University Press.

Prinsep, J. 1835. 'Note on the Image of the Buddha Discovered by J. Stephenson', *Journal of the Asiatic Society of Bengal*, 39, March: 131–33.

Pyke, Capt. 1785. 'Account of a Curious Pagoda Near Bombay, Drawn Up by Captain Pyke, Who was Afterwards Governor of St. Helena. It is Dated From on Board the *Stringer East Indiaman* in Bombay Harbour 1712, and is Illustrated with Drawings. The Extract was Made From the Captain's Journal in Possession of the Honourable the East India Company, by Alexander Dalrymple, Esq. F.R. and A.S. and Communicated to the Society, Feb. 10 1780', *Archaeologia*, 7: 323–32.

Rawlinson, H.C. 1856. 'Researches and Discoveries in Assyria and Babylon (read in July 1855)', *Journal of the Bombay Branch of the Royal Asiatic Society*, 5(20): 478–91.

Raychaudhuri. H.C. 1996. *Political History of Ancient India From the Accession of Parikshit to the Extinction of the Gupta* (with a Commentary by B.N. Mukherjee), (first edition, 1923, Calcutta). Bombay/Calcutta/Madras: Oxford University Press.

Ray, H.P. 2004a. 'The History of Archaeology in India: Introduction', in C. Sinopoli and H.P. Ray (Eds), *Archaeology as History in Early South Asia*, pp. 12–33. New Delhi: Aryan Books International.

———. 2004b.'Gender and Archaeology', in C. Sinopoli and H.P. Ray (Eds), *Archaeology as History in Early South Asia*, pp. 464–80. New Delhi: Aryan Books International.

———. 2008. *Colonial Archaeology in South Asia: The Legacy of Mortimer Wheeler*. New Delhi: Oxford University Press.

Redfield, R. and Singer, M.B. 1952. 'The Cultural Role of Cities', *Economic Development and Cultural Change*, 3(1): 53–73.

Renfrew, A.C. (Ed.). 1973. *The Explanation of Cultural Change: Models in Prehistory*. London: Duckworth.

Renfrew, A.C. and Bahn, P. 1996. *Archaeology: Theories, Methods and Practice*. London: Thames and Hudson.

Rowlands, M. 1994. 'Childe and the Archaeology of Freedom', in D.R. Harris (Ed.), *The Archaeology of Gordon Childe: Contemporary Perspectives*, pp. 35–54. London: UCL Press.

Roy, S. 1953. 'Indian Archaeology From Jones to Marshall (1784–1902)', *Ancient India*, 9: 4–28.

Roy, S. 1961. *The Story of Indian Archaeology 1784–1947*. New Delhi: Archaeological Survey of India.

Russell, J.M. 1997. *From Nineveh to New York: The Strange Story of the Assyrian Reliefs in the Metropolitan Museum and the Hidden Masterpiece at Cranford School*. New Haven/London: Yale University Press in association with the Metropolitan Museum of Art.

Rust, W and Cushing, A. [no date].'The Buried Silk Road Cities of Khotan, *Athena Review*, 3(1).http://www.athenapub.com/9khotan1.htm(accessed on 23 March 2012).

Salama, M.R. 2011. *Islam, Orientalism and Intellectual History: Modernity and the Politics of Exclusion Since Ibn Khaldun*. London/New York: I.B. Taurus.

Sankalia, H.D. 1962. *Indian Archaeology Today*. London: Asia Publishing House.

———. 1962–3. *Prehistory and Proto-History in India and Pakistan*, (2nd edition, 1974, Poona: Deccan College Post Graduate and Research Institute Publications). Bombay: Bombay University.

———. 1964. 'Archaeology and Education', in V.N. Misra and M.S. Mate (Eds), *Indian Prehistory: 1964*, pp. 259–62. Pune: Deccan College.

———. 1973. *Ramayana: Myth of Reality*. New Delhi: Peoples Publishing House.

———. 1975–76. 'Prehistoric Colonization in India: Archaeological and Literary Evidence', *Puratattva*, 8: 72–86.

———. 1978. *Born for Archaeology: An Autobiography*. Delhi: B. R. Publishers.

Sastri, K.N. 1957. *New Light on the Indus Civilization*. Delhi: Atma Ram.

Schadla-Hall, T. 1999. 'Editorial: Public Archaeology', *European Journal of Archaeology*, 2(2): 147–58.

Schaffer, S. J. 2010. 'A Disciplined Eye', Tarner Lectures, *When the Stars Threw Down Their Spears*, Trinity College Cambridge, 3 March. Also available online at http://sms.cam. ac.uk/media/744393 (accessed on 14 July 2014).

Schlanger, N. and Nordbladh, J. 2008. 'General Introduction: Archaeology in the Light of Its Histories', in N. Schlanger and J. Nordbladh (Eds), *Archives, Ancestors, Practices: Archaeology in the Light of its History*, pp. 1–8. New York/Oxford: Berghahn Books.

Schnapp, A. 1996. *The Discovery of the Past: The Origins of Archaeology* [Orig. French, 1993, trans. by I. Kinnes and G. Varndell]. London: The British Museum Press.

———. 2002. 'Between Antiquarians and Archaeologists—Continuities and Ruptures', *Antiquity*, 76: 134–40.

———. 2013.'Towards a Universal History of Antiquarians', *Complutum*, 24(2): 13–20.

Selvakumar, V. 2006. Public Archaeology in India: Perspectives from Kerala, *India Review*, 5(3–4): 417–46.

Senart, E. 1898. 'An Appreciation of Bühler', *The Indian Antiquary*, 27, December: 364–7.

Sen, D. and Ghosh, A.K. 1996. 'Preface', in D. Sen and A.K. Ghosh (Eds), *Studies in Prehistory: Robert Bruce Foote Memorial Volume*. Calcutta: Firma K.L. Mukhopadhyay.

Sengupta, I. 2005. *From Salon to Discipline: State, University and Indology in Germany, 1821–1914*. Heidelberg: Beitärge Zur Sudasienforschung; Bd, ErgonVerlag.

Sengupta, S. and Gangopadhyay, K. (Eds). 2009. *Archaeology in India: Individuals, Ideas and Institutions*. New Delhi/Kolkata: Munshiram Manoharlal and Centre for Archaeological Studies and Training.

Sen, S. 2002. 'Community Boundary, Secularized Religion and Imagined Past in Bangladesh: Archaeology and Historiography of Unequal Encounter', *World Archaeology*, 34(2): 346–62.

Sen, S., Imran, M., Khan, A., Rahman, M., Kabir, N., Rahman, S., Sakeb, N., Islam, K.M. and Rahman, A. 2006. 'Can We Protect Our Past? Re-thinking the Dominating

Paradigm of Preservation and Conservation With Reference to the World Heritage Site of Somapura Mahavihara, Bangladesh', *Journal of Social Archaeology*, 6(1): 71–99.

Sewell, R. 1917. 'Dr James Burgess', *Journal of the Royal Asiatic Society of Great Britain and Ireland*, January: 195–99.

Shaffer, J.G. 1978. *Prehistoric Baluchistan With Excavation Report on Said Qala Tepe*. Delhi: B.R. Publishing Corp.

———. 1992. 'Indus Valley, Baluchistan, and the Helmand Drainage (Afghanistan)', in R.W. Ehrich (Ed.), *Chronologies in Old World Archaeology*, Vol. 2, pp. 425–46. Chicago: University of Chicago Press.

Shaffer, J.G. and Lichtenstein, D.A. 1989. 'Ethnicity and Change in the Indus Valley Cultural Tradition', in J.M. Kenoyer (Ed.), *Old Problems and New Perspectives in the Archaeology of South Asia*, pp. 117–126. Madison, Wisconsin: Department of Anthropology.

———. 1995. 'The Concepts of Cultural Tradition and Palaeoethnicity in South Asian Archaeology', in G. Erdosy (Ed.), *The Indo-Aryans of Ancient South Asia: Language, Material Culture, Ethnicity*, pp. 126–54. Berlin: Walter de Gruyter.

———. 2005. 'South Asian Archaeology and the Myth of Indo-Aryan Invasion', in E.F. Bryant and L.L. Patton (Eds), *The Indo-Aryan Controversy: Evidence and Inference in Indian History*, pp. 75–104. London/New York: Routledge.

Sherratt, A. 1989. 'Gordon Childe: Archaeology and Intellectual History', *Past and Present*, 125: 151–85.

Shrimali, K.M. 2014. 'Pali Literature and Urbanism', in D.N. Jha (Ed.), *The Complex Heritage of Ancient India: Essays in Memory of R.S. Sharma*, pp. 243–79. New Delhi: Manohar.

Silberman, N.A. 2008. 'Virtual Viewpoints: Multivocality in the Marketed Past?' in J. Habu, C. Fawcett and J.M. Matsunaga (Eds), *Evaluating Multiple Narratives: Beyond Nationalist, Colonialist, Imperialist Archaeologies*, pp. 138–143. New York: Springer.

Sims-Williams, U. 2007. 'Islam Akhun', *Indo-Iranica*. http://www.iranicaonline.org/articles/islam-akhun (accessed on 15 October 2011).

———. 2012. 'Rudolf Hoernle and Sir Aurel Stein', in H. Wang (Ed.), *Sir Aurel Stein, Colleagues and Collections*, pp. 1–6. London: British Museum.

Singh, R.N., Petrie, C.A., Pawar, V., Pandey, A.K. and Parikh, D. 2011. 'New Insights Into Settlement Along the Ghaggar and Its Hinterland: A Preliminary Report on the Ghaggar Hinterland Survey 2010', *Man and Environment*, 34(2): 88–106.

Singh, U. 2004. *The Discovery of Ancient India: Early Archaeologists and the Beginnings of Archaeology*. New Delhi: Permanent Black.

Sircar, D.C. 1965. *Indian Epigraphy*. New Delhi: Motilal Banarasidass.

Smith, C. and Wobst, H.M. 2005. 'Decolonizing Archaeological Theory and Practice', in C. Smith and H.M. Wobst (Eds), *Indigenous Archaeologies: Decolonizing Theory and Practice*, pp. 5–16. London/New York: Routledge.

Smith, C.R. 1883. 'The Canterbury Congress', *Retrospections, Social and Archaeological*, pp. 8–13. London: George Bell and Sons.

Smith, L. 2004. *Archaeological Theory and the Politics of Cultural Heritage*. London/New York: Routledge.

Smith, L. and Waterton, E. 2009. *Heritage Communities and Archaeology*. London: Duckworth.

Smith, V.A. 1924. *The Early History of India From 600 B.C. to the Muhammadan Conquest Including the Invasion of Alexander the Great*, 4th edition. Oxford: Clarendon Press.

———. 1941. [reprint of 1919]. *The Oxford History of India: From the Earliest Times to the End of 1911* (Second Edition Revised and Continued to 1921). Oxford: Clarendon Press.

Sørensen, M.L.S.S. and Carman, J. 2009. 'Introduction: Making the Means Transparent and Reflections', in M.L.S.S. Sørensen, and J. Carman (Eds), *Heritage Studies; Methods and Approaches*, pp. 3–10. London/New York: Routledge.

Spooner, D.B. 1912. 'Excavations at Shah-ji-ki-Dheri', in J.Ph. Vogel (Ed.). *Annual Report of the Archaeological Survey of India 1908–09*, pp. 38–59. Calcutta: Supt. Govt. Printing.

———. 1914. 'The Kanishka Casket Inscriptions', in J.Ph. Vogel (Ed.). *Annual Report of the Archaeological Survey of India 1909–10*, pp. 135–41. Calcutta: Supdt. Govt. Printing.

Stein, M.A. 1898. *Detailed Report of an Archaeological Tour With the Buner Field Force*. Lahore: Punjab Government Press.

———. 1900a. *Kalhana's Rajatarangini: A Chronicle of the Kings of Kashmir*, Vol. 1. Westminster: Archibald Constable and Company, Westminster.

———. 1900b. 'Preliminary Note on an Archaeological Tour on the Indus,' *Indian Antiquary*, 29, June: 145–6.

———. 1904. *Sand-Buried Ruins of Khotan: Personal Narrative of a Journey of Archaeological and Geographical Exploration in Chinese Turkestan*. London: Hurst and Blackett.

———. 1929. 'An Archaeological Tour in Waziristan and Northern Baluchistan', *Memoirs of the Archaeological Survey of India*, No. 37. Calcutta: Government of India Press.

Steward, J. 1955. *Theory of Culture Change*. Urbana: University of Illinois Press.

Stocking, G. 1982. *Race, Culture and Evolution: Essays in the History of Anthropology*. New York: Free Press.

Stoler, A.L. 2009. *Along the Archival Grain*. Princeton: Princeton University Press.

Strange, J. 1777. 'A Further Account of Some Remains of Roman and Other Antiquities in or Near the County of Brecknock in South Wales', *Archaeologia*, 4: 1–26.

Strathern, M. 2010. 'Commentary, Boundary Objects and Asymmetries', in D. Garrow and T. Yarrow (Eds), *Archaeology and Anthropology: Understanding Similarity, Exploring Difference*, pp. 179–184. Oxford: Oxbow Books.

Stukeley, W. 1776. *Itinerarium Curiosum: Or an Account of the Antiquities and Remarkable Curiosities in Nature or Art Observed in Travels Through Great Britain*. London: Messrs. Baker and Lee.

Subrahmanyam, S. 1997. 'Connected Histories: Notes Towards a Configuration of Early Modern Eurasia', *Modern Asian Studies*, 31(3): 735–62.

———. 2005. *From the Tagus to the Ganges: Explorations in Connected History*. New Delhi: Oxford University Press.

Sutton, M. 1983. *Nationalism, Positivism and Catholicism: The Politics of Charles Maurras and French Catholics, 1890–1914*. Cambridge: Cambridge University Press.

Sweet, R. 2004. *Antiquaries: The Discovery of the Past in Eighteenth-Century Britain*. New York/London: Hambeldon.

Tavakoli-Targhi, M. 2004. 'The Homeless Texts of Persianite Modernity', in R. Jahanbegloo (Ed.), *Iran: Between Tradition and Modernity*, pp. 129–61. Lanham: Lexington Books.

Taylor, P.M. 1851. 'Ancient Remains at the Village of Jiwarji Near Ferozabad on the Bhima (communicated by George Bust)', *Journal of the Bombay Branch of the Royal Asiatic Society*, 3(14), Part II: 179–93.

———. 1853. 'Notices of Cromlechs, Cairns and Other Ancient Scytho-Druidical Remains in the Principality of Sorapur', *Journal of the Bombay Branch of the Royal Asiatic Society*, 4(17): 380–429.

———. 1870. *A Student's Manual of the History of India: From the Earliest Period to the Present*. London: Longmans, Green and Co.

Taylor, P.M. 1920 [1878]. *The Story of My Life*, Edited by his daughter Alice Taylor with Preface by Henry Reeve (New Edition with Introduction and Notes). Oxford: Oxford University Press.

Telang, K.T. 1880. 'Babu Rajendralal Mitra, LL.D.', Proceedings of the Bombay Branch of the Royal Asiatic Society, January–December 1879, *Journal of the Bombay Branch of the Royal Asiatic Society*, 14: xix–liii

Thackston, W. 1999. *The Jahangirnama: Memoirs of Jahangir, Emperor of India* (Translated, Edited and Annotated). New York/Oxford: Smithsonian Institute in Association with Oxford University Press.

Thapar, B.K. 1975. 'Kalibangan: A Harappan Metropolis Beyond the Indus Valley', *Expedition* (Winter), 17(2): 19–32.

———. 1984. 'Six Decades of the Indus Studies', in B.B. Lal and S.P. Gupta (Eds). *Frontiers of the Indus Civilization*, pp. 1–26. New Delhi: Books and Books.

Thapar, R. 1961. *Asoka and Decline of the Mauryas*. Oxford: Oxford University Press (2nd Edition, 1973, New Delhi: Oxford University Press).

———. 1986.'Society and Historical Consciousness', in S. Bhattacharya and R. Thapar (Eds), *Situating Indian History for Sarvepalli Gopal*, pp. 353–83. New Delhi: Oxford University Press.

———. 1996. *Time as a Metaphor of History*. New Delhi: Oxford University Press.

———. 2001. 'The Rigveda: Encapsulating Social Change', in K.N Panikkar, T.J. Byres and U. Patnaik (Eds), *The Making of History: Essays Presented to Irfan Habib*, pp. 11–40. New Delhi: Tulika (reprinted).

———. 2013. *The Past Before Us: Historical Traditions of Early North India*. New Delhi: Permanent Black.

Thomas, J. 2004. *Archaeology and Modernity*. London/New York: Routledge.

Todd, J. 1920 [1829]. *Annals and Antiquities of Rajasthan or the Central and Western Rajput States of India*, Vol. 1 (Edited with an Introduction and notes by William Crooke). Toronto/Melbourne/Bombay: Oxford University Press.

Theuns-de Boer, G. 2008. *A Vision of Splendour: Indian Heritage in the Photographs of Jean-Philippe Vogel, 1901–13*. Ahmedabad/Leiden: Mapin in Association with Kern Institute.

Trigger, B.G. 1980. *Gordon Childe: Revolutions in Archaeology*. London: Thames and Hudson.

———. 1984. 'Alternative Archaeologies: Nationalist, Colonialist, Imperialist', *Man*, 19: 355–70.

———. 1994. 'Childe's Relevance to the 1990s', in D.R. Harris (Eds), *The Archaeology of V. Gordon Childe: Contemporary Perspectives*, pp. 9–34. London: UCL Press.

———. 2006. *A History of Archaeological Thought*. Cambridge: Cambridge University Press.

Varma, S. 2010. 'History of Archaeology: An Alternative View', (Review of G. Sengupta and K. Gangopadhyay (Eds.) 2009, *Archaeology in India: Individuals, Ideas, Institutions*), *The Book Review*, 34(5): 4–5.

Wagoner, P. 2003. 'Precolonial Intellectuals and the Production of Colonial Knowledge', *Society for Comparative Study of Society and History*, 45(4): 783–814.

Walhouse, M.J. 1878. 'Archaeological Notes: Trojan and Indian Prehistoric Pottery, and the Swastika Symbol, *The Indian Antiquary*, 7, July: 176–9.

Weber, A. 1880. 'Correspondence and Miscellanea;Prof. Weber and Babu Rajendralala Mitra', *The Indian Antiquary*, 8, 25 April: 226–9.

Webster, G.S. 2008. 'Culture History: A Culture-Historical Approach', in R.A. Bentley, H.D.G. Maschner and C. Chippindale (Eds), *Handbook of Archaeological Theories*, pp. 11–27. Lanham, Maryland: Alta Mira Press.

Wheeler, R.E.M. 1947a. Harappa 1946: The Defences and Cemetery R 37', *Ancient India*, 3: 58–130.

————. 1947b. 'The Recording of Archaeological Strata' Technical Section: 3, *Antiquity*, 3: 143–50.

————. 1947c. *Mohenjodaro*. Karachi: Govt. of Pakistan, Advertising, Films and publications.

————. 1950. *Five Thousand Years of Pakistan*. London: Royal India and Pakistan Society.

————. 1953. *The Indus Civilization* [Supplementary Volume, The Cambridge History of India]. Cambridge: Cambridge University Press.

————. 1955. *Still Digging: Interleaves from an Antiquary's Notebook*. London: Michael Joseph.

————. 1956. *Archaeology From the Earth*. London: Penguin.

————. 1962. *Charsada: A Metropolis of the North-West Frontier, Being a Report on the Excavations of 1958*. Oxford: Oxford University Press.

————. 1966. *Alms for Oblivion: An Antiquary's Scrapbook*. London: Weidenfeld and Nicolson

————. 1968. *The Indus Civilization*, 3rd edition. Cambridge: Cambridge University Press.

————. 1976. *My Archaeological Mission to India and Pakistan*. London: Thames and Hudson.

Wheeler, R.E.M, Ghosh, A. and Deva, K. 1946. 'Arikamedu: An Indo-Roman Trading Station on the East Coast of India', *Ancient India*, 2, July: 17–124.

White. L. 1959. *The Evolution of Culture*. New York: McGraw-Hill Book Co.

Wilkins, C. 1788. Inscription on a Pillar Near Buddal, Translated From the Sanskrit, *Asiatick Researches*, 1: 131–41.

Willey, G.R. 1953. Archaeological Theories and Interpretation: New World', in A.L. Kroeber (Ed.), *Anthropology Today*, pp. 361–85. Chicago: Chicago University Press.

Willey, G.R. and Phillips, P. 1958. *Method and Theory in American Archaeology*. Chicago: Chicago University Press.

Williams, J.G. 1982. *The Art of Gupta India; Empire and Province*. Princeton: Princeton University Press.

Wilson, H.H. 1825. 'Extracts From the Journal of a Native Traveller of a Route From Calcutta to Gaya in 1820, Translated From the Original', *Calcutta Annual Register 1822*. Calcutta: Government Gazette Press.

————. 1835. *A Manual of the Universal History and Chronology for the Use of Schools*. London: Whittaker and Co.

————. 1839. 'Account of Foe Kúe Ki, or Travels of FaHian in India, translated from the Chinese by M. Remusat' (read 9th March and 7th April 1838), *Journal of the Royal Asiatic Society of Great Britain and Ireland*, 5: 108–40.

————. 1858. 'Preface of the Editor', in J. Mill (Ed.), *The History of British India*, Vol. 1 (5th Edition with Notes and Continuation), pp. vii–xiv. London: Piper, Stephenson and Spence.

Wilson, J. 1850. 'Memoir on the Cave–Temples and Monasteries, and Other Ancient Buddhist, Brahmanical and Jaina Remains in Western India', *Journal of the Bombay Branch of the Royal Asiatic Society*, 3(13), Part II: 36–107.

————. 1853. 'Second Memoir on the Cave–Temples and Monasteries, and Other Ancient Buddhist, Brahmanical and Jaina Remains of Western India (presented in September 1852)', *Journal of the Bombay Branch of the Royal Asiatic Society*, 4(8): 340–79.

————. 1856. 'Review of the Present State of Oriental, Antiquarian, and Geographical Research Connected With the West of India and the Adjoining Countries,' *Journal of the Bombay Branch of the Royal Asiatic Society*, 18(20) (July): 497–520.

Winternitz, M. 1898. 'Georg Bühler, In Memoriam', *The Indian Antiquary*, 27, December: 337–49.

Woolley, L. 1956. 'First Towns?' *Antiquity*, 30(120): 224–5.

Wright, R.P. 2010. *The Ancient Indus: Urbanism, Economy and Society*. Cambridge: Cambridge University Press.

Wylie, A. 2008. 'The Integrity of Narratives: Deliberative Practice, Pluralism, and Multivocality', in J. Habu, C. Fawcett and J.M. Matsunaga (Eds), *Evaluating Multiple Narratives: Beyond Nationalist, Colonialist, Imperialist Archaeologies,* pp. 201–12. New York: Springer.

Yajnik, J.U. 1898. 'Memoir of the Late Pandit Bhagvanlal Indraji, L.L.D., Ph.D.', *Journal of the Bombay Branch of the Royal Asiatic Society*, 17: 18–46.

Archives

Fox Collection	MAA, Cambridge University
Konow Collection	National Library of Norway, Oslo
Piggott Archive	Institute of Archaeology, Oxford
Stein Collection	Bodleian Library, Oxford
Survey Archive	Archaeological Survey of India, New Delhi
Wheeler Archive	Special Collections, University College London
Wheeler Papers	Archives of the British Academy, London
Whitehead Papers	Fitzwilliam Museum, Cambridge University
Wilson Papers	European Manuscript Collections, British Library

News Journal

The Bombay Times and Journal of Commerce 1839–59
Sourced from: ProQuest Historical Newspapers Times of India (1838–2002).

Index

About the Author

Sudeshna Guha is an Associate Researcher at the Faculty of Asian and Middle Eastern Studies (FAMES) at the University of Cambridge and Tagore Research Scholar at the National Museum in New Delhi. She has curated photographic collections at Museum of Archaeology and Anthropology (Cambridge) for over a decade, and was Temporary University Lecturer of South Asian History at FAMES for four years. She researches on the cultural histories of archaeology and photography in South Asia, and continues to study aspects of state formation, polities and urbanisation in Early India, which had led her to study archaeology and the Indus Civilisation after graduating in history.

She has written extensively on issues related to the historiography and methodology of the archaeological scholarship of Ancient India, of which an example is her edited volume *The Marshall Albums: Photography and Archaeology* (Alkazi Collection of Photography and Mapin, 2010). The four essays below illustrate some of the reasons that have led to the present study: 'The Visual in Archaeology: Photographic Representations of Archaeological Practice in the Indian Subcontinent', *Antiquity* (2002); Negotiating Evidence: History, Archaeology and the Indus Civilisation', *Modern Asian Studies* (2005); 'Material Truths and Religious Identities: The Archaeological and Photographic Making of Banaras', in M. S. Dodson (Ed.), *Banaras: Urban History, Architecture, Identity* (2012) and 'Beyond Representation: Photographs in Archaeological Knowledge', in O. M. Abadia and C. Huth (Eds), 'Speaking Material: Sources for the History of Archaeology', *Complutum* (2013).

Currently, she is doing research on the practices of museums, archaeology and heritage-making within post-colonial South Asia.